MW01599046

National Identity

A volume in
Cross National Research
Richard R. Verdugo, *Series Editor*

National Identity

Theory and Research

edited by

Richard R. Verdugo

Universitat Autònoma de Barcelona

Andrew Milne

Sciences Po Toulouse

INFORMATION AGE PUBLISHING, INC.
Charlotte, NC • www.infoagepub.com

Library of Congress Cataloging-in-Publication Data

A CIP record for this book is available from the Library of Congress
http://www.loc.gov

ISBN: 978-1-68123-523-3 (Paperback)
       978-1-68123-524-0 (Hardcover)
       978-1-68123-525-7 (ebook)

Printed in the United States of America

CONTENTS

Introduction: National Identity: Theory and Practice 1
Richard R. Verdugo and Andrew Milne

PART I
THEORETICAL CONSIDERATIONS

1   Identities in Europe: Past and Present... 25
    Aladin Larguèche

2   The Crisis of Western Democracies and National Identity:
    Citizenship, Immigration, and Constitutional Patriotism 55
    Francis Luong

PART II
NATIONAL IDENTITY: CASE STUDIES

3   The Idiosyncrasies of Scottish National Identity 83
    Nathalie Duclos

4 Is a New Definition of Irish Identity Emerging in the Republic
  of Ireland in the 21st Century? 113
  Julien Guillaumond

5 Russian National Identity 147
  Oxana Karnaukhova and Richard R. Verdugo

6 The Impossible State: National Identities in Bosnia
  and Herzegovina 187
  Djordje Vukovic, Aleksandar Savanovic, and Aleksandar Vranjes

7 The Mental Wall: Identity in a United Germany 213
  Dana Martin and Richard R. Verdugo

8 National Identity in France: Immigration and the Validity
  of Civil Tests 245
  Andrew Milne

PART III

NATIONAL IDENTITY: THE IMMIGRANT EXPERIENCE

9 "How Can I Feel Belgian if Belgians Don't Accept Me?":
  Ethnic Boundary Perception and National Identity Among
  Turkish Belgians 273
  Klaartje Van Kerckem

10 British Muslims' Discourses of National Identity 311
   Saliha Anjum, Andrew McKinlay, and Chris McVittie

NATIONAL IDENTITY

Theory and Practice

Richard R. Verdugo and Andrew Milne

In 1958, 36 year old Thomas Kuhn accepted an invitation to spend a year at the Center for Advanced Studies in the Behavior Sciences. Within a short period of time, Kuhn discovered something fascinating that would eventually lead to the writing of his classic, *The Structure of Scientific Revolutions.* Kuhn was taken aback by the degree to which social scientists at the Center disagreed over fundamentals. In his words:

> I was struck by the number and extent of the overt disagreements between social scientists about the nature of legitimate scientific problems and methods. Both history and acquaintance made me doubt that practitioners of the natural sciences possess firmer or more permanent answers to such questions than their colleagues in social science. Yet, somehow, the practice of astronomy, physics, chemistry, or biology normally fails to evoke the controversies over fundamentals that today often seem endemic among, say, psychologists or sociologists.

It is not unusual, then, that the research surrounding national identity is also clouded in debate and disagreement. Indeed, national identity is

National Identity, pages 1–21
Copyright © 2016 by Information Age Publishing

1

such a slippery concept that some scholars have called for abandoning the concept entirely (Brubaker & Cooper 2000, p. 5). The complexities are the outcome of three significant issues. First, the definition itself is viewed from three angles. Second, there are competing forms of identity, such as social class, race/ethnicity, gender, and so on. Finally, there appears to be debate about differences between identity, nationalism, and patriotism.

It is, or should be, clear that as a concept, national identity is an "ideal type" to be used for analytic purposes; it would be a mistake to think of it otherwise. Max Weber viewed such concepts as *Gedankenbilder*, or thoughtful pictures. They are meant to help scholars make sense of a chaotic world, not to completely represent reality.

> We have in abstract economic theory an illustration of those synthetic constructs which have been designated as *"ideas"* of historical phenomena. . . . This conceptual pattern brings together certain relationships and events of historical life into a complex, which is conceived as an internally consistent system. Substantively, this construct in itself is like a *utopia* which has been arrived at by the analytical accentuation of certain elements of reality. Its relationship to the empirical data consists solely in the fact that where market-conditioned relationships of the type referred to by the abstract construct are discovered or suspected to exist in reality to some extent, we can make the *characteristic* features of this relationship pragmatically *clear* and *understandable* by reference to an *ideal-type*. This procedure can be indispensable for heuristic as well as expository purposes. The ideal typical concept will help to develop our skill in imputation in *research*: it is no "hypothesis" but it offers guidance to the construction of hypotheses. It is not a *description* of reality but it aims to give unambiguous means of expression to such a description. (Weber, 1949, p. 89)

Nevertheless, scholars do agree on a few points about national identity. Scholars tend to agree that national identity is a sense of "belonging" to a nation or state, something we will refer to as a geopolitical entity in order to avoid confusion. Moreover, many would agree that this sense of belonging is affected by many factors, including relational, normative, contextual, kinship, and historical factors. There are many elements within these two sets that affect national identity. Thus, we may represent national identity as a function of many subsets, and each subset having its own elements:

$$NI = \{\cdot\}$$

The definition to be used in this introductory chapter, is that national identity is a sense of belonging to a geopolitical entity.

In looking at the literature on national identity, and aside from definitional issues, a few analytical/theoretical problems exist. For example, one theoretical issue is whether national identity is fixed and based on blood or ancestry; if national identity is malleable, mutable, imagined, or invented for political reasons; or whether the concept should be dropped completely. Moreover, there are others who argue that epistemological work needs to be conducted prior to engaging in national identity empirical research (Checkel, 2006). The purpose of this introductory chapter is twofold. First, we introduce our views about national identity, based on our own assessment of the research, including the chapters in the present volume. Second, we summarize and place the findings from the chapters in this volume within the national identity literature.

BACKGROUND

Theories of National Identity

Definitions

National Identity should not be confused with two related concepts—*nationalism* and *patriotism*. *Nationalism* is a strong attachments to one's country and the sense that one's country, and that it is, is superior to all others. *Patriotism* is a strong devotion to one's country and one's behavior in support of its decisions and practices. *National identity* is a sense of belonging to and being a member of a geopolitical entity.

A *Nation* is a geopolitical construct where belonging is mainly driven by an Essentialist/Primordialist viewpoint. That is, belonging and being a member of a nation is based on blood, ethnicity, history, ancestry, common values, kinship, and language. In a nation, the focus of national organization is its people.

A *State* is a geopolitical construct where membership and belonging is based on shared civic values about citizenship. Membership is constructed and based on a constructivist/postmodern viewpoint of identification. The focus is a State's institutions and the values that legitimate its authority.

Nation-State is an imbrication of a Nation and a State. It is a system of political governance that derives its legitimacy from its people in governing and serving as a sovereign nation.

Dominant Views of National Identity: Essentialists, Constructivists, and Civic Theories

Three views dominate the national identity research. The earliest national identity theories were originally part of debates about ethnicity—Essentialist and Constructivist. In later years, a third national identity research has been added, though it has a long history in political thought—Civic identity. An extensive review of these theories is beyond the scope of our chapter, so we provide a brief summary. The categories are: Essentialist/Primordialist, Constructivist/Postmodernist, and Civic Citizenship.

Essentialist/primordialist. Essentialist scholars of national identity view national identity as fixed, based on ancestry, a common language, history, ethnicity,[1] and world views. Some noted scholars include Huntington (1997), Smith (1986; 1991), Geertz (1973), Van den Berghe (1981), Armstrong (1982), and Connor (1994).

Though Anthony D. Smith (1991) has generally been aligned with Essentialist views, his views are a middle-of-the-range theory[2] about national identity. Such a distinction is marked by his linking constructivism to essentialism—national identity is a hybrid of both "natural" continuity and conscious manipulation. Smith's position is interesting and, it seems to us, quite reasonable. In fact, what Smith seems to be arguing is that the Essentialist and Constructivist views lie on a scale as depicted below:

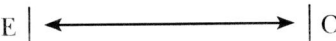

$$\text{E} \; \Big| \; \longleftrightarrow \; \Big| \, \text{C}$$

Identity involves both E (Essentialist) and C (Constructivist), and social systems vary in the proportion a social system assigns to each.

At its core, the Essentialist argument is based on culture and history. Other markers for the Essentialist framework are language, ancestry, and blood.

Constructivist/postmodernist. Constructivism posits that dominant groups create, manipulate, and dismantle identities for their specific gains (Beaune, 1991; Berezin, 1997; Brubaker, 1992; Corse, 1996; Fine, 1996; Gillis, 1994; Griswold, 1992; Hobsbawm, 1992; Hobsbawm, & Ranger, 1983; Kubik, 1994; Lane, 1981; Schudson, 1992; Schwartz, 1987, 1991; Spillman, 1997; Wagner-Pacifici, & Schwartz 1991; Zerubavel, 1995). Within this paradigm, there are two very interesting viewpoints, with the characteristics of paradigm shifts.[3]

The first viewpoint is embodied in the work of Anderson (1991) who posits that identity is an imagined construct. It is imagined because individuals in a given geopolitical entity do not and cannot interact with one another—there are simply too many people to allow for such activity. So symbols, rituals, and other ceremonials are used as means for bonding, and individuals thus *imagine* they have a community with other members of society. In Anderson's model, print Capitalism was crucial for building this imaginary identity. People in different parts of a nation were able to read the same documents in the same language that maximized sales and circulation. Readers began to understand one another and thus formed the basis for an imagined community. Anderson argues that the first European nation-states were founded around their national print languages.

The second viewpoint is advanced in the work by Hobsbawm and Ranger (1983)—national identity is invented for political reasons. Invented traditions are created in order to ensure continuity with the past. Indeed, a sure sign that there has been a break with the past or where existing modern norms and values are not effective in maintaining stability and order, is the utilization of traditions toward this end. Such instability may be brought on by rapid social change or other axial events, such a wars or economic crises. There are several instances where the invented traditions paradigm has been used in research. Sievers (2007), for example, uses invented traditions in studying the Highland Myth in Scotland as a reaction to Scotland's union with England in 1707; Vlastos (1998) uses the concept to study the tradition of martial arts in Japan; also studying Japan using an "invented community" paradigm is Fujitani's (1996) superb study about pageantry in modern Japan. Despite these interesting studies, it appears to us that one of the earliest uses of the concept was conducted in 1912 by Basil Hall Chamberlain. In his little essay, Chamberlain (1912) looked at the role of "Mikado-worship" in Japan. In point of fact, Chamberlain succinctly captures an important reason for the invention of tradition.

> But the twentieth-century Japanese religion of loyalty and patriotism is quite new, for in it pre-existing ideas have been sifted, altered, freshly compounded, turned to new uses, and have found a new centre of gravity. Not only is it new, it is not yet completed; it is still in process of being consciously or semi-consciously put together by the official class, in order to serve the interests of that class, and, incidentally, the interests of the nation at large. (Chamberlain, 1912, p. 4)[4]

Not all is well within the Constructivist camp. While Postmodernists support the Constructivist model, they have serious problems with its approach. To begin with, they argue that Constructivism seems to be a simple cataloguing of identity construction processes, devoid of content. Secondly, they argue that the paradigm underestimates the central role of power (Connell, 1987; Gilman, 1985), and that such an error leads them to incorrectly suggest that influence and agency are "a multidirectional" (Calhoun, 1995, p. 199). Power for *Postmodernists* is the crucial concept.

At its core, Constructivism/Postmodernism is based on politics and the use of power by dominant groups in order to gain and maintain their privileged status in society.

Civic identity. Civic identity is a form of identity where membership in a geopolitical entity is unfettered by ethnicity or culture. Instead, it is based on a set of shared values about rights and the legitimacy of State institutions to govern. The State's political legitimacy is derived from citizens' participation in many social institutions, such as politics, voluntary associations, unions, and so on. The notion of civic citizenship is closely aligned with Jean-Jacques Rousseau's *The Social Contract* (1762).[5] Others who espouse a civic approach to national identity include Habermas (1994), Miller (1995), Tamir (1993), Greenfeld (1992), Canovan (1996), and Marshall (1949).

Challenges to National Identity: A Model for Analysis

Factors Affecting National Identity

Guibernau (2007) proposes a number of dimensions about national identity. There are, according to Guibernau, at least seven dimensions to national identity: psychological, cultural, antiquity, original, historical, territorial, and political. To be sure, these dimensions are related to national identity as Guibernau argues. However, the list is not complete because there are at least two other factors that appear to affect national identity: Economics and social demography. Scholars can debate what other factors might influence national identity, however the chapters included in this volume highlight the following factors: Social demography, economics, national hegemony related to a specific governance regime, and politics.

Social demography. Demography affects national identity. Whatever the causes might be for demographic changes, emigration and immigration appear to be exerting pressure on national identity in many Western countries.

Demographic factors affect population size and composition and thus cultural content in a geopolitical entity. As the size of the immigrant population increases, natives appear to have serious questions about their culture and what it means to be a member of their society. In essence, there are concerns about the sustainability of native culture and its way of life.

Economics. Generally, the better the economic situation, the more positive is national identity. Loss of work, economic depressions, and other negative economic factors lowers identity. Keep in mind that identity is a sense of belonging to a geopolitical entity, and citizens expect their leaders to protect their basic rights and needs. Failing to do so leads a citizenry to question their government, their leaders, and the meaning of membership in their society.

National hegemony. By hegemony, we mean a framework of governance or dominance. A change in hegemony creates confusion, and depresses national identity. If change is drastic, it changes roles and statuses in a social system. For example, going from Communism and a planned economy to a form of Democracy and Capitalism is a major change if the cultural and structural apparatus are not in place to support such a change. Another example would be changing from an absolute Monarchy toward greater freedom for a population. Changes in hegemony challenges national identity. A related issue is constant hegemonic change. A social system that is in relatively frequent hegemonic change also taxes national identity. In fact, it may be that the more frequent hegemonic changes occur, the more likely invented traditions are used in stabilizing a social system.

Politics. Politics are a broad concept, and our use of it refers to the acquisition and maintenance of power. Some examples include wars, conquests, imperialism, colonialism, and other forms of aggression where a geopolitical entity is involved in some conflict. State policies are another marker.

The effects on the nation are significant. Politics influence the social demography, composition, and distribution of achieved and ascribed statuses, such as ethnicity, race, social class, or religious groups. The ability of a host society in integrating immigrants or a conquered people challenges national identity. If a country has been conquered or colonized, it is a complex problem as to whether its population will develop a sense of belonging with the conquering country.

Each chapter in the present volume is driven by an historical view and develops its analyses around many of the issues briefly raised in the preceding sections, and more in some cases. In doing so, they not only add to national identity research, but raise questions for additional research. Table I.1 formalizes our thinking about these factors, national identity, and the level of analysis affected by these factors: national and individual.

TABLE I.1 Theoretical Model of Factors Affecting National Identity: National and Individual Levels

Factor/Finding	Country	Effects
Social Demography: The primary Demographic factors related to national identity are immigration and emigration. Significant emigration reduces the native population and greater immigration increases the presence of immigrants in a nation and diversity.	Ireland Level: National	Mass emigration and later immigration led to concerns about the Irish culture.
	France Level: Individual	Mass immigration, especially from former colonies led to questions about the meaning and continued existence of French culture.
	Belgium Level: Individual	The increased presence of immigrants and their children in Belgium has led to Turks being treated as outsiders. Such a status opens them up for discrimination and other forms of ostracism. Consequently, such treatment affects their identifying as Belgium.
	UK Level: Individual	Immigrants are raise issues about their not being accepted by their British acquaintances based on their own appearance and their ability to speak English.
	Russia Level: National	Imperialism and later conquests led to greater diversity and questions arose about what it meant to be Russian.
	BH Level: National	Various ethnic and religious groups within BH have led to much discord.

(continued)

TABLE I.1 Theoretical Model of Factors Affecting National Identity: National and Individual Levels (continued)

Factor/Finding	Country	Effects
Economics: The economic status of a nation is positively related to national identity. The better the economy, the more favorable views a population has about its leaders and nation, and the better the national identity.	Ireland Level: National	Poor economy led to mass emigration and a distrust of national leaders and an inferior national identity. In contrast, prosperity during the Celtic Miracle led to positive national identity, returning migrants and important immigration. The presence of immigrants led to questions about Irish culture.
	Russia Level: National	Economic stagnation during Gorbachev's liberalizing led to questions about leadership, and poor national identity. After the fall of the USSR, and the open market (Capitalism) approach, national identity fell as did a distrust of Russian leadership. In any event, economics and national identity are positively related.
Hegemony: denotes leadership and the power of superordinates to impose their views and world views on subordinates. We use a version of hegemony that focuses on world view characterizing a governance regime, e.g., Communism, Democracy, Monarchy Welfare State	Russia Level: National	Continual change in the governing hegemony has been followed by confusion about what it means to be Russian—a member of a monarchy, a Communist, a member of a Democracy, a Federation
	BH Level: National	Conflict over an imposed or attempted imposition of a hegemony by Serbian leaders has caused much discord in the BH region.
	France Level: Individual	Hegemony has influence social policy regarding tests for citizenship and also has raised questions about what it means to be French
	Germany Level: National	After re-unification and the movement of Eastern Germans into Western Germany has caused problems about expectations for both groups of Germans. The confusion is succinctly captured in the following comment by an East German—"we expected justice, but got the rule of law."
	Scotland Level: National	National identity is based on making "British" the "Other." Scotland has its own hegemony and has no desire to be under the world view of Britain.
Politics: Events and strategies followed for acquiring and maintaining power.	Scotland Level: National	In Scotland, politics and political party membership has no effects on national

(continued)

TABLE I.1   Theoretical Model of Factors Affecting National Identity: National and Individual Levels (continued)

Factor/Finding	Country	Effects
Included are wars, colonialism, state policies, etc.		identity. For example, while the Scottish people have their own unique identity based on history and culture, they have no desire to break away from British.
	Ireland Level: National	State policies in Ireland have affected the perception of identity. In this case, the state has included a forced choice question in asking respondents how they identify ethnically. The "White" and "Other" choices lump together different White ethnics, such as Polish, and gives the impression of more Irish in the country than there actually are.
	Russia Level: National	Politics has played an important part of Russian identity, in one form or another. Its imperialism increased diversity and adversely affected the country's ability to form one unified national identity; its constant change in governance regimes challenged national identity; and its war time exploits also challenged national identity. It debacle in the Sino-Russian War caused much consternation among the population and questioned whether Russia was as great at most had assumed.
	BH Level: National	The attempted power grabs by Serbs, and other factors, such as a history of ethnic and religious discord, and increased nationalism/identity, led to civil war in the BH region.
	Germany National	Reunification has caused some discord between East and West Germans. It is equivalent to the merging of two cultures. There does not appear to be a unified version of being "German."
	France/ Individual	France's colonial past has affected current national identity issues. Specifically, a large proportion of its immigrant population originated from its former colonies. In addition, given this growing diversity, issues among the native French population and its leaders have begun to ask what it means to be "French." One result has been to test "Frenchness" among those applying for citizenship.

NATIONAL IDENTITY: NATIONAL AND INDIVIDUAL LEVELS

Theoretical Overviews of National Identity

Chapters 1 and 2 provide theoretical overviews about the state of national identity research. In Chapter 1, Largueche presents a broad review of major theories, issues, and summaries of some examples of how selected social systems are addressing the issues surrounding national identity. In addition, the author raises some difficult topics surrounding national identity, such as rising nationalism, populism, and multiculturalism. These are important issues and need careful and thoughtful attention by decision makers.

In Chapter 2, Luong focuses on State policies and how these attempt to integrate its immigrant populations. The chapter reviews and critiques theories about identity and strategies for integrating immigrants, and concludes that none is satisfactory. The proposed solution is Constitutional Patriotism, a program that decouples national identity from citizenship. The focus is for immigrants to respect and obey their host country's Constitutional laws, yet they are not obligated to accept these laws on an ethical or moral basis. As the author indicates, one cannot legislate national identity.

National Level

Economics

Economics play a significant role in developing and maintaining national identity among a population. Economic downturns lead a population to mistrust its leaders and call into question the pride they have for their country. The more prosperous a country, the greater is national identity. Several countries in the present volume have witnessed the rise and fall in national identity depending on the status of their economies.

Trust and meeting basic needs. During its economic downturns, thousands left Ireland. It was during this period that the Irish population held many negative views of their leadership and their country. Their negative views were aimed at the ability of their leaders to provide economic safety.

The economy rebounded during the Celtic Tiger years, and Ireland welcomed back many who had emigrated and it was also a period when Irish national pride rose to pitch levels. However, with the global recession of 2008, Irish pride once again declined (Guillaumond, Chapter 4).

Russia also experienced some significant economic downturns prior to the breakup of the USSR and after its leaders pursued an open market economy. Unfortunately, the latter strategy failed and Russia seems to have morphed into a semi-planned economy. Nonetheless, during the economic downturn, Russian national identity seems to have suffered (Karnaukhova & Verdugo, Chapter 5).

Lifestyle differences. Economics played a different role in Germany. Prior to reunification, East and West Germans lived in two diametrically opposed systems—Social Democracy in the West, and Communism in the East. In the West, the economy was Capitalistic and open; in the East the economy was planned and centralized. The West eventually enjoyed prosperity, whereas in the East, though staples were available at fairly reasonable prices, other items were scarce. East Germans learned the art of bartering and getting by with little; West Germans expected more. With reunification, both populations experienced their new situation differently: West Germans were disdainful of their Eastern counterparts and viewed them as lower class, whereas East Germans viewed their Western counterparts as conspicuous consumers and greedy. A unified national identity was going to be a challenge (Martin & Verdugo, Chapter 7).

Corruption and basic needs. Economics may also lead to corruption, and not only challenge the trust a population has with its leadership, but also have the population question their own national identity. This appears to have been the case in Russia. When Gorbachev took power, he began liberalizing the Russian empire, but soon realized that the country could not survive under its existing social structure. He eventually dissolved the USSR and introduced Capitalism in Russia. Upon the introduction of a Capitalist system and the breakup of the USSR, leadership began selling off large portions of government held assets. Unfortunately, they were sold to existing Oligarchs at bargain basement prices. The level of social inequality, corruption, poverty, unemployment, and underemployment in the USSR challenged national identity and protests were frequent (Chapter 5).

Social Demography

Demographic changes, mostly by increasing a society's ethnic/racial makeup, raise challenges about one's national identity, and leads to signifi-cant concerns among the native population about the fate of their society. Indeed, ethnic/racial diversity as expressed in the presence of immigrants in a nation is arguably the single most important factor affecting national identity.

Ethnicity and culture clash. An increase in the number of immigrants (especially from Turkey) in Germany has raised issues about national identity, citizenship, and German culture (for a discussion see Verdugo & Mueller, 2008). In Chapter 7 the authors focus on another issue regarding lifestyles. Basically, reunification merged two different cultural groups, if we view culture as a way of life among a people. The merging of East and West created significant discord between both populations. East Germans developed skills at bartering and the ability to get by with little, whereas West Germans grew accustomed to a given level of prosperity and expected and demanded such a lifestyle. Such cultural differences challenged the ability of forging a united Germany.

The same may be said of Russia (Chapter 5) and the Bosnia Herzegovina region (Vukovic, Savanovic, & Vranjes, Chapter 6). Demographic diversity brought on by Russian imperialism created significant diversity and challenged a unified Russian identity. In fact, a united Russian national identity never occurred because most frontier societies had their own unique cultures, social systems, and identities. In the BH region, the attempt to create one nation was doomed from the beginning, not only because of politics, but because each country within the region also had its own cultural and historical backgrounds that were fiercely protected.

Migration and labor shortages. Demography is related to migration—both emigration and immigration—and to labor shortages. This seems to have been the case in Ireland. During economic downturns, thousands of Irish citizens left the nation for jobs in other countries. In contrast, during economic prosperity, not only did Ireland attempt to lure some emigrants back to the island, it also witnessed significant immigration because of its increasing labor shortages resulting from its economic prosperity. Predictably, the presence of large numbers of immigrants from other nations created national identity issues (Chapter 4).

Politics

Politics are a broad concept, and our use refers to seeking and maintaining power. Several types of political activities are noted in this volume that affect national identity: attempts at gaining power, changing governance regimes, merging two populations from different governance regimes, and our use of politics also refers to State policies concerning the current and future organization of society and its relations with other nations. Finally, politics, as used here, refer to the dominant hegemony used in organizing a Nation/State, such as Communism, Social Welfare State, or Democracy.

The effects of politics on a social system are significant. Political activities raised in the present volume touch on three topics: attempts at gaining power, change in governance regimes, and the attempt in merging two different governance regimes.

Attempts at gaining power. National identity may be affected by one nation attempting to force its regime on another. In the Bosnia Herzegovina region, this seems to have been the case. There was an attempt by Bosnia/Serbia to bring Croatia into a BH regime. In contrast, Croatia seems to have been receptive to such a union if it could maintain its autonomy, and if such a union was equitable. Unfortunately, Croatia did not feel it would be fairly represented in such a union and sought independence. Serbia moved first and civil war ensued (Chapter 6).

Interestingly, as research has suggested, the war created strong national identity feelings among the combatants. It was an extreme form of "Them versus Us" feelings.

Changing governance regimes and various forms of aggression. Russia has experienced many changes in its governance regime, and such changes affect national identity. Russia has moved from a Duchy, Tsarist, Socialist/ Communist, and eventually to a Federation. These were not smooth changes and were often violent as competing groups sought dominance. These frequent changes, historically speaking, affected national identity and various generational leaders took control and imposed its view of Russia (Chapter 5).

Merging populations from two different governance regimes. Individuals residing a specific governance regime are raised under unique world views and a set of roles they are expected to fulfill (Chapters 5 and 7).

In Communist regimes, the community takes priority; the government controls politics, the economy, and other social institutions; and social structure is, theoretically, flat. In Communist systems, there is the danger of totalitarianism and rule by an elite. In Democracies, in contrast, the priority is on individual freedom within limits. Property may be owned by individuals, the economy is generally open, and there tends to be less government intervention in the lives of citizens. However, there are the dangers of rule by the majority, or tyranny of the majority, and significant social inequality (Piketty, 2013).

In Germany, reunification merged two populations raised in two different political regimes: Communism and Social Democracy. Differences in world views, roles, and expectations about quality of life were major points of contention. These differences are captured in a comment by one East German: "We expected justice, we got the rule of law."

In Scotland (Duclos, Chapter 3), the population distinguishes the "Other" as the British. Scots have their own unique history and culture, and have no desire to become British. Interestingly, the majority of Scots have no desire to completely break away from Britain. There are certain benefits from continuing the alliance.

State Policy

State laws and other policies that regulate the behavior of persons residing in a country affect national identity. Four State policies are good examples: (a) policies about immigration, (b) policy about annexing/colonizing another country, (c) policies about citizenship, and (d) policies that seem to define a population.

Immigration and immigrants. Many western nations that are or have been experiencing significant inflows of immigrants have taken steps to reduce the number entering their borders. Once immigrants are residing within their borders, additional immigration integration policies have been enacted. The focus of immigrant integration policy has been either acculturation or assimilation. The former strategy is to accept immigrants and their culture yet also with the proviso that immigrants live amicably in both worlds. The latter strategy, in contrast, expects immigrants to shed their native culture and blend into their host culture. Needless to say, the latter has caused much controversy.

A strategy in assimilationist policy restricts or limits the practice of immigrant culture. In France, the State decided that it was against French law for Muslim women to wear the Hijab in public schools. The Hijab is a scarf worn by Muslim women as a symbol of modesty and privacy and part of the Muslim faith. The rationale behind the ban was France's adamant conviction of the separation between Church and State, and the banning of all religious symbols and signs from public schools. The specific laws were enacted by then President Jacques Chirac on March 15, 2004.[6]

Annexing a nation. In the BH region, the role of Bosnia in attempting to maintain a unified area enacted State policies and pursued strategies that created discord and raised national identities in the camps of all combatants. Indeed, conflict between nations is a major factor in raising national identity and nationalism (Conway, 2001; Kreisberg, 2003) (See Chapter 6).

Policy about citizenship. State policies regarding citizenship also affect national identity among immigrants. The approaches taken by some countries may be viewed as *Essentialist* because the content of many national citizen exams are heavily weighted toward historical events and symbols, rather than civic issues such as laws and policies. The French citizenship examination is a prime example as described in this volume (Milne, Chapter 8). Not only does Milne show how the exam is Essentialist, but he goes on to show that French university students and a sample of the general public are unable to pass the exam. French citizenship exams create boundaries for immigrant inclusion and are a source of "Othering" immigrants.

Defining a population. In Chapter 4, we see how Irish State policy has a hand in defining national identity or the perception of such an identity. The State has used its authority in creating a forced choice question about ethnicity in its Census. As a result, the data suggest that the size of the native population has been stable for years. What the data hide is that included in the "White" population are Polish and other respondents who indicated their race as "White." The result is that it presents a picture of Ireland as a country with a stable Irish population, which is good for business and brings to mind the famous Thomas Theorem: "If men define their situation as real, it is real in its consequences" (Thomas & Thomas, 1928, p. 572).

Individual Level

Two chapters examine some important issues about social acceptance and the national identity among immigrants. These studies demonstrate is how the native host population creates "Them vs. Us" distinctions by not fully accepting immigrants and thus challenging immigrants' ability at identifying with their host country. To be fair, the data are all from an immigrant's perspective, yet if they are to develop positive national identities with their host country, their assessments are valid.

In chapters about immigrants in Belgium (Van Kerckem, Chapter 9) and in the United Kingdom (Anjum, McKinlay, & McVittie, Chapter 10), the authors discuss how immigrants in each country perceive their being the "Other" and how this affects their sense of identity. In Belgium, the Turkish population faces considerable discrimination and is relegated to the status of the "Other." The "Othering" of the Turkish population is based on two objective factors: language and physical appearance. Both factors tend to identify Turks as non-Belgians, and places them in the precarious position of the "Other."

Muslim immigrants in the United Kingdom are the focus of Chapter 10. The authors use a semi-structured interview methodology in gathering data on the views from first and second generation Muslim respondents. Among first generation Muslims the authors find that, while they are able to balance their British-Muslim-Pakistani identities, they tend to reveal two traits not found in the second generation. First, their Pakistani identity is the strongest among the three identities. This makes sense not only because it is their place of birth, but also because to acknowledge otherwise would place them in an awkward position of not honoring their place of birth. Secondly, the first generation tends to care about what British citizens think about them and their status as immigrants in Britain. Being the "Other" is a negative for them. The situation is different for the second generation.

Second generation respondents also balance their British-Muslim-Pakistani identities, but their strongest identity is British. Interestingly, their British identity works as a facilitator for the other two. Their British identity creates a level of confidence that helps them balance all their three identities, while also being indifferent to what other British citizens think or say about them. Being the "Other" is irrelevant to the second generation.

Both studies tend to confirm Hoetink's (1967) theory about somatic distance. In a segmented social system the dominant group develops and maintains an idea about the somatic norm—their own somatic appearance. The greater a specific group's somatic distance from this norm, the greater will be its social distance. Social distance is reflected in a dominant group failing to accept groups not reflecting this somatic norm. It would be worthwhile to study social distance issues among these populations using such measures as the Bogardus Social Distance Scale.[7]

CONCLUSIONS

National identity research has been a much debated topic. On one side of the debate are those who argue that national identity is traditional and based on ethnicity, blood, a common history, and other cultural markers such as language. In contrast, another group posits that national identity is constructed, imaged, or invented for political reasons. These debates have not only frustrated scholars, but have stalled research from moving forward.

The chapters included in the present volume are both theoretical and research case studies about national identity. To begin with, two levels of analyses are pursued. One level is national, where a nation's identity is viewed historically. Questions and issues raised include discussions about the roles conflicts, imperialism, State policies, and changes in national governance regimes have in a population's national identity.

At an individual level the focus is on immigrants' views of their status in a host society. Results from two studies indicate that immigrants struggle in balancing three identities: their host country, their religious identities, and identifying with their sending country, or the country of their ancestors. In addition, these studies indicate that the behavior of the native population is important as to how much immigrants feel accepted and their sense of identifying with their host country. Generation plays a key role: the first generation is sensitive to the views of the native population. The second generation could care less. In addition, it appears that national identity among immigrants facilitates the identity of both religion and the homeland of their ancestors. There is a strong correlation among all three identities.

A third contribution is that this research contributes to theory development. Pursuing testable hypotheses or theories contributes to a research field and to its major theory(s). The chapters in this volume make the following contributions: national identity is based on both Essentialist and Constructivist ideas, many factors contribute to national identity—both macro and micro, and one should consider differences between macro issues and micro issues of national identity. The next step, in our view, is to synthesize factors affecting national identity into one general model—if that is at all possible.

There are at least three conclusions that we can draw from the studies included in this volume. First, the old dichotomy of Essentialism-Constructivism is not productive. National identities are based on both, and the strength of one over another depends on a State's history, culture, and governing ideology.

Second, the level of identity is significant. In the present volume two levels of identity research are presented: national and individual. Factors affecting identity at the national level, to be sure, may affect an individual's sense of belonging, but those affecting immigrants' identity varied by Generational status and feelings of being accepted by members of the host society. Important markers for immigrants are their physical appearance and their ability to speak the language of their host society. But this is only one strand of research at the individual level, another would be to study the views and factors affecting national identity among native populations and how this process differs by immigrant status

Third, of course, we believe there is more research to be done. We have several suggestions for future research.

- Research among non-immigrants and immigrants and how factors affecting each differ.
- Research about how societal transitions affect national identity. Max Weber noted the three types of authority that fit well into how societies have changed over time: from charismatic (familial and religiously based) to traditional (patriarchal, patrimonial, feudal) to legal/rational (legal and bureaucratic) social systems.[8]
- Recall that we suggested that factors affecting national identity may be viewed as a set with many subsets, $NI = \{\cdot\}$. Chapters in this volume have introduced factors that may comprise subsets of NI, and for further theoretical development we suggest grouping these factors into broader concepts for analysis. For example, Hegemony may logically be included in politics. Further theoretical development would greatly enhance research on national identity.

NOTES

1. Note that ethnicity has different definitions: in America, ethnicity is associated with a minority group, or some other ethnic group. In Europe, especially in Eastern Europe, ethnicity refers to a people or peoplehood. It has greater community or group connotations
2. Though we identify Smith's strategy as middle of the range, it is not to be confused with Merton's (1957) definition of middle of the range theories, which contrast Talcott Parson's Grand Theorizing or Minor theories. Merton defines middle of the range theory as "...theories that lie between the mi-

nor but necessary working hypotheses that evolve in abundance during the day-to-day research and the all-inclusive systematic efforts to develop a unified theory of social behavior, social organization, and social change" Merton (1957, p. 39).

3. Paradigm shifts are associated with T. S. Kuhn's masterwork, *The Structure of Scientific Revolutions.* (1970) The shift refers to a revolutionary change in how scientific problems are viewed and framed. Kuhn's work was heavily influenced by the earlier work of Ludwik Fleck (1935[1979]). Fleck argued that scientific truth was situational to a specific scientific community, and that truths and falsehoods could never truly be established. Fleck's notion of a scientific community predated Kuhn, and is an especially important concept that led to the emergence of the Sociology of Science discipline, in which scientists are studied much like other communities.

4. The page number is different from the original document because it was downloaded into Microsoft Word document. The download was from http://www.gutenberg.org/files/2510/2510-h/2510-h.htm

5. Rousseau's vision of identity is in contrast to J. G. Fichte's, which is based on ethnicity, blood, and social traits such as language. See Fichte (2013/1808). *Reden an die deutsche Nation.* The German version may be downloaded from www.gutenberg.or, or in English from www.ghi-dc.org.

6. The official name of the law is "*loi n° 2004-228 du 15 mars 2004 encadrant, en application du principe de laïcité, le port de signes ou de tenues manifestant une appartenance religieuse dans les écoles, collèges et lycées publics*" (literally "Law #2004-228 of March 15, 2004, concerning, as an application of the principle of the separation of church and state, the wearing of symbols or garb which show religious affiliation in public primary and secondary schools").

7. The Bogardus Social Scale was created by Emory S. Bogardus as a Guttman Scale (a logically ranked ordered scale) that asks respondents about how likely they would accept a group based on the following questions: As close relatives by marriage, as close personal friends, as neighbors on the same street, as co-workers in the same occupation, as citizens in my country, as non-citizen visitors to my country, would they *exclude* a group from entry into my country. See Bogardus (1926).

8. See Mommsen (1992) for a discussion and description.

REFERENCES

Anderson, B. (1991). *Imagined communities: Reflections on the origins and spread of nationalism.* London, England: Verso.

Armstrong, J. (1982). *Nations before nationalism.* Chapel Hill: University of North Carolina Press.

Beaune, C. (1991). *The birth of an ideology: Myths and symbols of nation in late-medieval France.* S. R. Huston (Trans.). Berkeley: University of California Press.

Berezin, M. (1997). *Community of feelings: Culture, politics, and identity in fascist Italy.* Ithaca, NY: Cornell University Press.

Bogardus, E. S. (1926). Social distance in the city. *Proceedings and Publications of the American Sociological Society, 20,* 40–46.

Brubaker, R. (1992). *Citizenship and nationhood in France and Germany.* New York, NY: Cambridge University Press.

Brubaker, R., & Cooper, F. (2000). Beyond identity. *Theory and Society, 29,* 1–47.

Calhoun, C. (1995). *Critical social theory: Culture, history and the challenge of difference.* Oxford, England: Blackwell.

Chamberlain, B. H. (1912). *The invention of a new religion.* Retrieved from www.gutenberg.org/files/2510/2510-h/2510-h.htm

Checkel, J. T. (2006). *Constructivists approaches to European integration.* Centre for European Studies: University of Oslo.

Connell, R. W. (1987). *Gender and power: Society, the person and gender politics.* Cambridge, England: Polity Press.

Connor, W. (1994). *Ethno-nationalism: The quest for understanding.* Princeton, NJ: Princeton University Press.

Conway, S. (2001). War and national identity in the mid-eighteenth century British Isles. *The English Historical Review, 116*(468), 863–893.

Corse, S. (1996). *Nationalism and literature: The politics of culture in Canada and the United States.* New York, NY: Cambridge University Press.

Fichte, J. G. 2013/1808. *Addresses to the German nation* [Translated with introduction and notes by Isaac Nakhimovsky, Bela Kapossy, and Keith Tribe]. Indianapolis, IN: Hackett.

Fine, G. A. (1996). Reputational entrepreneurs and the memory of incompetence: Melting supporters, partisan warriors, and images of President Harding. *American Journal of Sociology, 101*(5), 1159–1193.

Fleck, L. (1935 [1979]). *The genesis and development of a scientific fact* (T. J. Trenn, Ed., Foreword by T. Kunh). Chicago, IL: University of Chicago Press.

Fujitani, T. (1998). *Splendid monarchy: Power and pageantry in modern Japan.* Berkeley: University of California Press.

Geertz, C. (1973). *The interpretation of cultures.* London, England: Fontana.

Gillis, J. (1994). *Commemorations: The politics of national identity.* Princeton, NJ: Princeton University Press.

Gilman, S. L. (1985). *Difference and pathology: Stereotypes of sexuality, race, and madness.* Ithaca, NY: Cornell University Press.

Greenfeld, L. (1992). *Nationalism: Five roads to modernity.* Cambridge, MA: Harvard University Press.

Griswold, W. (1992). The writing on the mud wall: Nigerian novels and the imaginary village. *American Journal of Sociology, 57*(5), 709–724.

Guibernau, M. (2007). *The identity of nations.* Cambridge, England: Polity Press.

Habermas, J. (1994). Struggles for recognition in the Democratic constitutional state. In A. Gutman (Ed.), *Multiculturalism* (pp. 106–184). Princeton, NJ: Princeton University Press.

Hobsbawm, E. (1992). *Nations and nationalisms since 1780: Programme, myths, and reality.* New York, NY: Cambridge University Press.

Hobsbawm, E., & Ranger, T. (1983). *The invention of tradition.* Cambridge, England: Cambridge University Press.

Hoetink, H. (1967). *Caribbean race relations: A study of two variants.* London, England: Oxford University Press.

Huntington, S. (1996). *The clash of civilizations and the remaking of world order.* New York, NY: Simon and Schuster.

Kreisberg, L. (2003). Identity issues. In G. Burgess & H. Burgess (Eds.), *Conflict research consortium.* Boulder: University of Colorado. Retrieved from www .beyondintractabilittty.or

Kubik, J. (1994). *The power of symbols against the symbols of power: The rise of solidarity and the fall of state socialism in Poland.* University Park, PA: Penn State University Press.

Kuhn, T. S. (1970). *The structure of scientific revolutions* (2nd ed.). Chicago, IL: University of Chicago Press.

Lane, C. (1981). *The rites of rulers.* Cambridge, England: Cambridge University Press.

Marshall, T. H. (1973). *Class, citizenship and social development.* Westport, CT: Greenwood Press. (Original work published 1949)

Merton, R. K. (1957). *Social theory and social structure.* New York, NY: Simon and Schuster.

Miller, D. (1995). *On nationality.* Oxford, England: Clarendon Press.

Mommsen, W. J. (1992). *The political and social theory of max weber: Collected essays.* Chicago, IL: University of Chicago Press.

Piketty, T. (2013). *Capital in the 21st century.* Cambridge, MA: Harvard University Press.

Rousseau, J. J. (1762). *The social contract or principles of political right* (G. D. H. Cole, Trans.). Retrieved from www.ucc.ie

Schudson, M. (1992). *Watergate in american memory: How we remember, forget, and reconstruct the past.* New York, NY: Basic Books.

Schwartz, B. (1991). Mourning and the making of a sacred symbol: Durkheim and the Lincoln assassination. *Social Forces, 30*(2), 343–364.

Schwartz, B. (1987). *George Washington: The making of an American symbol.* Ithaca, NY: Cornell University Press.

Sievers, M. (2007). *Invented tradition of 18th and 19th century and its significance for the image of Scotland.* Norderstedt, DE: Verlag.

Smith, A.D. (1991). *National identity.* Reno, NV: University of Nevada Press.

Smith, A.D. (1986). *The ethnic origins of Nation.* Oxford, England: Blackwell.

Spillman, L. (1997). *Nation and commemoration: Creating national identities in the United States and Australia.* New York, NY: Cambridge University Press.

Tamir, Y. (1993). *Liberal nationalism.* Princeton, NJ: Princeton University Press.

Thomas, W. I., & Thomas, D. S. (1928). *The child in America: Behavior problems and programs.* New York, NY: Alfred Knopf.

Van den Berghe, P. (1981). *The ethnic phenomenon.* New York, NY: Elsevier.

Verdugo, R. R., & Mueller, C. (2008). Education, social embeddedness, and the integration of the Turkish community in Germany: An analysis of homeland identity. *European Education, 40*(4), 3–22.

Vlastos, S. (1998). *Mirror of modernity: Invented tradition of modern Japan.* Berkeley, CA: University of California Press.

Wagner-Pacifici, R., & Schwartz, B. (1991). The Vietnam veterans memorial: Commemorating a difficult past. *American Journal of Sociology, 97*(2), 376–420.

Weber, M. (1949). *The methodology of the social sciences.* (Edited and translated by E. A. Shils & H. A. Finch). New York, NY: Free Press.

Zerubavel, Y. (1995). *Recovered roots: Collective memory and the remembering of Israeli national tradition.* Chicago, IL: University of Chicago Press.

PART I

THEORETICAL CONSIDERATIONS

CHAPTER 1

IDENTITIES IN EUROPE

Past and Present

Aladin Larguèche

In the aftermath of terrorist attacks in Norway perpetrated by the right-wing extremist Anders Behring Breivik on July 22nd 2011, his 1,518-page manifesto entitled *2083: A European Declaration of Independence* was broadly distributed through the Internet and generously quoted by most of the media worldwide in order to describe and understand the ideological and personal motives of its author.

Beyond the brutality and unexpectedness of a tragedy that struck a small, peaceful, and wealthy land, the violence of the pamphlet actually crystallizes several trends in today's Europe. One of the most important trends has been the rise of right-winged populism in the last decade. Many exclusionary ideas in Breivik's pamphlet are not his own; some have been presented and discussed by other political militants and leaders throughout Europe, especially since the 9/11 attacks in America. Former French president Nicolas Sarkozy (2007–2012), for example, attempted to create a Ministry for Immigration and National Identity, while German Chancellor Angela Merkel firmly declared in October of 2010 that multiculturalism

National Identity, pages 25–54
Copyright © 2016 by Information Age Publishing

was a failure. Of course, this growing populism has not taken place in every European country with the same form or intensity. The most common form is a "low-level populism," expressing itself diffusely in traditional political parties, through Internet, mass media, public debate, and private conversations.

I have two objectives in this chapter. First, I wish to underline the similarities in the national identity problem in Europe; though I do see that there are also differences. My questions are: Who are we? How do we live together and how do we deal with increasing cultural differences when we have to cope with the long-lasting presence of foreigners and newly naturalized fellow citizens, many who come from the far ends of former European empires in Africa, Asia, and America? A second objective is to point out an historical irony: the quite unexpected growth of nationalistic, and sometimes radical, views in 21st century Europe, a continent which has been the epicenter of two world wars, as well as a continent that has committed itself into an innovative, attractive process of supranational integration since 1949. Indeed, Ernest Gellner has written about the weakness of nationalism, pointing out that failed nationalist movements are far more numerous than those that actually managed to supplant other ideologies and establish the almost unquestionable legitimacy of a Nation-State (Gellner, 1983). To illustrate his argument, he remarks that there may be around 8,000 languages in the world, but only 200 States.

THE IMAGINED COMMUNITY IN EUROPE: POLITICS, TRADITION, AND GROUP IDENTITY

National Identity: A Brief Overview

Breivik's manifesto shows that challenges around national identity in the 21st century can be perceived as a European concern with a European identity; "an imagined community," to use the expression by social scientist Benedict Anderson.[1]

National identity is commonly seen as a fundamental frame for any forms of political participation. It is the unavoidable ground for the general organization of human communities and it has mostly proven to be a remarkably effective way for creating a sense of being a "we" through modern times. The modern era is a time when personal or social differences between individuals and citizens have widened, and when economic globalization and technological improvements have neutralized geographical distances and traditional frontiers. In spite of all the simplifications, identities are not inevitably "criminal identities."[2] They are of valuable, ethical, and psychological significance in the processes of individuation and identification. But there also appears to be a paradox.

The effectiveness of national identity has created a paradox. On the one hand, national identity pretends to create a Self and consequently refers to several archetypes, intending to define "the ancestral spirit" of European nations, as many intellectuals did in the 19th century. From that point of view, identities are essences, a kind of metaphysical bond between humans, or the virtual and mysterious nucleus of origins, ideals, behaviors and hopes that give meaning to the environing world. On the other hand, far from actually being immutable, identities are also historical constructions in constant evolution, interacting within a complex set of events or phenomena. Historian Anne-Marie Thiesse is one among the very few to approach these matters from a genuinely European point of view:

> Nothing is more international than the formation of national identities. This paradox is huge since the irreducible singularity of each national identity has been a pretext for bloody confrontations. Yet, these identities really stem from the same model, which has been implemented within the frame of intense international exchanges. (Thiesse, 1999, p. 11)[3]

The cult of tradition and the celebration of an ancestral patrimony have been effective counterweights for making the radical economic, technological, and social mutations of European countries since the 19th century more acceptable. A nation opens the doors of a secular brotherhood and formal solidarity between the members of the same community, who are the heirs of a specific cultural legacy, and thereby share a common interest (ibid.). This is by no means a peculiarity of European nations—a similar pattern is at work in other communities, such as the United States, where the mythology of "the Frontier" and the New World, or the idea of being a promised land for immigrants have had a powerful effect in creating a "we."[4] In other words, it is necessary to explore this fundamental opposition between simplistic discourses about identity. One needs to examine its actual features, practices, and social realities, past or present, that may have fostered or contradicted modern forms of political allegiance. Such a strategy is necessary in order to disclose the rhetorical, symbolic, and strategic part of these discourses. Indeed, creating or asserting a "we" seems to be a necessary step toward ensuring political allegiance and participation in a political unit.

Nonetheless, the task seems extremely difficult for one reason: human action may ultimately be described as a conscious quest for identity. Identities reflect the contradictions of the human mind and its multiple world experiences; they are both static essences and evolving constructions. They can lead to a destructive narcissism, a blind self-contentment, a fierce hatred of difference, and an inability to act reasonably in the world. National identities can also be a source of self-confidence or a pre-condition for survival in a hostile or complex environment. Extrapolating Dr. Stockmann's declaration in *An Enemy of the People* (1882) by Henrik Ibsen (1828–1901), one can perhaps say that, morally speaking, "the compact majority" is always wrong, and it may be tempting to sort out righteous minority identities from potentially threatening majority identities by distinguishing between the oppressors and the victims. It may be that strong may always be wrong, and the weak may always be right, but in many cases, one may say that restless, unsatisfied identities have a natural tendency to victimize themselves.

Research on national identities has been structured around two elementary and common perceptions: identity as essence (essentialism); identity as construction (constructivism). Perhaps the right path is somewhere in the middle.

Sociologists, philosophers, ethnologists, and historians have often assumed that the easiest way to create a Self is to find the image of the Other. Let me quote the French historian Lucien Febvre and his discerning observation about "civilization": the issue of the frontier is somehow put at the center of his superb lecture delivered at the Collège de France in 1944–1945:

> In each civilization, there are two kinds of elements: sedentary peoples and travelers. And their proportion shifts singularly from a civilization to another. Poor, primitive, back-ward civilizations are not only those where elements of civilization are small and where the inventory of the material and the spiritual creations is quickly made; it is also the civilizations where the sedentary elements dominate from afar, that are unable of provoking desire and envy from the neighboring civilizations, and consequently that do not travel [...] Rich civilizations, on the contrary, brilliant civilizations, great civilizations are those where there are plenty of traveling elements and where spiritual and material elements are able to provoke desire and to be borrowed from the outside. (Febvre, 1999, p. 68)[5]

This can be the first step in defining a European identity: the EU's motto of "Unity in diversity." However, it is insufficient to depict European identity and Europe's national identities with this statement alone. The Old World is a place of impressive diversity, a genuine Babel tower, "a mosaic of cultural micro-spaces of great variety. National territories have become small cultural reserves, with different contents and styles. Within these territories, some ethnic cultures survive, among which some like Brittany, Catalonia, Euskadi, Scotland could have become nation-states, notwithstanding History's hazards" (Morin, 1987, p. 171).[6] So, if ethnicity is not going to be the factor that binds Europe, what is the alternative?

From Ethnicity to Citizenship

Social scientists tend to consider national identities as a product of late-modern time. Many historians continually underline that the modern definition of the nation was created in the aftermath of the Enlightenment, the French Revolution in 1789, and the Napoleonic Wars. These are seen as structural events that deeply changed the fate of Europe by shifting the aristocratic legitimacy through a new national sovereignty. Nationalism is the crystallization of new political units. Nationalism arises from new social conditions and occurs through the public use of legacy of religion, history, and culture which stem from earlier historical periods. Nationalists wanted people to believe that nations were part of a natural order given by God to human communities.

Nationalism appears to be a modern phenomenon, transforming pre-existing cultures into nations, sometimes inventing them. In fact, nation-states are not the natural and ultimate destiny of ancient ethnic groups (Gellner, 1983). Historian Miroslav Hroch made a similar observation by using a comparative method to analyze the birth of nationalist movements in smaller European nations like Bohemia (the main region of today's Czech Republic), Norway, and Flanders. Hroch was able to distinguish three pertinent stages in the formation of national identities (Hroch, 1985).

- In the first stage, the people have no national identity, but intellectual and cultural elites unveil a forgotten nation. Founding myths of a supposed former ethnic community are created or rediscovered. History and philology become important as academic fields, and most of the artistic or scientific artifacts contribute to this national revival. There is not yet any political claim related to the emergence of a new identity.
- In the second stage, national self-conscience rises among educated and active minorities that organize themselves through associations and patriotic groups. They are pioneers with an explicit political agenda, where a sense of nation is ranked the highest.
- In the third stage, nationalist programs and propagandas manage to gain mass support and to establish a Nation-State, through institutions like the school and the army. As British historian Eric Hobsbawm stated, the crucial point here is to understand the transition from stage 2 (identity as politics) to stage 3 (establishment of Nation-State), because it can virtually include any kind of situation.

At the end of the 18th century, Nationalism was a new idea, best reflected by the French Revolution, an essentially non-ethnic idea—language or religion were not explicitly considered markers of national citizenship. The common good and welfare were the most important interests of the nation. Such views were in accordance with the liberal view of the world held among the educated elite and the bourgeoisie, especially in France and in the United Kingdom (Hobsbawm, 1992).

However, asserting the novelty of nation and nationalism does not mean that nations have no real continuous bonds with earlier times. After all, one also has to consider that most historians study late-modern periods rather than ancient, medieval, or early-modern societies. Such a focus blinds them to those factors leading to the emergence of nations. What is the relationship between old ethnic identities and modern nations? Is there a causal link between ethnicity and the formation of nations?

"Historical nations" in the Middle Ages became, during the 19th century, the most effective way to legitimize various political rights for liberal/nationalist minorities in Germany, Norway, Italy, Ireland, Bohemia, and Hungary. The same is true of the many countries that had to bear foreign domination, national division, or both, such as Poland and Italy; this was especially the case in the European periphery. However, is this fact alone enough to foster the emergence of new Nation-States? Probably not.

One should not neglect the importance of ethnicity as a major component of national identities. These are some of the questions raised in 1986 by historian Anthony D. Smith, who wished to modify the "modernist" idea that European national identities are mostly late-modern creations. It Smith's strategy in distancing himself from the "perennial" school of thinking which claimed that modern nations were merely updated versions of ancient, natural kinships:

> Nationalism, as an ideology and movement, is a phenomenon that dates from the later 18th century, while a specifically national sentiment can be discerned little earlier than the late 15th or 16th centuries in Western Europe. The nation-state, too, as a political norm is quite modern. If the system of European states came into being at the Treaty of Westphalia in 1648,[7] it was not until the 19th century that these states began to be converted into nation-states, and hence a system of nation-states came into being. Even the nation and its national character would appear to be modern: certainly, it was not until the early modern period in Europe (the late 17th century), that the idea of populations being divided by national character and possessing a common identity became widespread among European educated classes. Yet, there are also difficulties with this view. For we find in pre-modern eras, even in the ancient world, striking parallels with the modern idea of national identity and character, in the way Greeks and Romans looked on people who did not share their cultures or come from their city-States. (Smith, 1994, p. 11)

What can we learn from these discussions around the idea of national identity? Modern nations can be seen as the result of fusions between pre-modern, ethnic identities, and civic elements translated into law and citizenship, or nationality. Ethnicity has been transmitted through historical records and has contributed to shaping individual and collective experiences. According to Smith, ethnicity is mainly constituted by myths, memories, values, and symbols, and it has proved particularly important in generating a sense of solidarity and purpose among members of a national community (Smith, 1994, p. 16).

The Ethno-Cultural Nation

The debate between *Modernist* scholars and *Perennialists* reflects an inner tension that tears apart two facets of national identities: ethnicity versus citizenship, or to put it otherwise, *jus sanguinis* versus *jus soli*.

In Eastern Prussia, linguist and Lutheran clergyman Johann Gottfried Herder[8] contested the superiority of reason and the moral domination of rational philosophy. The rediscovery of Europe's ancestral roots began at the end of the 18th century. It was an aesthetic and philosophical rebellion against the cultural hegemony of France, the stronghold of classical models, inspired by Greek and Roman antiquity, as well as the most influential countries in European aristocratic courts from Spain to Russia. Herder was not alone.

Swiss writer Paul-Henri Mallet (1730–1807), and Scottish poet and politician James Macpherson (1736–1796) had already collected fragments of poetry in the 1750s–1760s that strongly enhanced European cultural plurality (Thiesse, 1999). Later, historians, clergymen, and linguists from the German countries, Scandinavia, and the British Isles began taking a genuine interest in Norse mythology and medieval literature. Yet, Herder was the first to explicitly discredit the universal for the sake of the particular, enhancing culture and knowledge in a specific national legacy with a language of its own. Herder depicted societies as the natural state of mankind, as organic, objective, and primordial units put on Earth by Providence. Each society developed its own features and customs through history and, most of all, language (Hermet, 1996). An ethno-cultural nation (or *Kulturnation*) had the highest political legitimacy: nation transcends the state. This assertion has to be understood in the peculiar German context of that time: a broad linguistic community in the heart of Europe, although divided into 300 independent States![9] For Herder and for his followers,[10] the goal of their work was to restore the self-awareness of the German nation.

The prevalence of ethnic bonds in human communities may be rooted in ancient times, yet it is a modern phenomenon fostered by intellectuals like Herder. Any ethnic community that aspires to nationhood must become politicized and assert its claims if it wishes to influence international affairs (Smith, 1994). National identity is a matter of resistance, dignity, and an affair of empowerment.

Nationhood involves a philosophical base. Herder's ethno-cultural vision had a deep influence elsewhere on the continent. In 19th century Eastern Europe, several communities had retained a sense of uniqueness and staked out claims for autonomy from the old continental empires of Austria, Russia, and Turkey. For example, there were national liberation movements in Finland, Poland, Hungary, Croatia, Serbia, Bulgaria, Albania, and Romania, but this vision also legitimated xenophobia in 20th century Europe. Herder did not advocate of any sort of race hierarchy, he considered all nations as equal in dignity due to their uniqueness. Herder spoke of the *Volksgeist*, or "Spirit of the People."

Nevertheless, after having been combined with later statements like social Darwinism, the *Kulturnation* would open the way to the conviction of an Aryan superiority, an idea which became popular in Germany[11] from the 1890s on and gave rise to Nazism. Here again, we find the permanent contradiction inherent to identity-oriented movements (Hermet, 1996).

The Emergence of Liberal Citizenship

The notion of liberal citizenship represented another factor in Europe's national identities, as epitomized by the French Revolution. After the *Declaration of the Rights of Man and of the Citizen* (August 1789), politics would be built on the national sovereignty of citizens, defined by natural rights, universal human rights, the right to political participation, and civil liberty (Ellis, 2010). Religious freedom became a reality. During the 19th century, "the question of the relationships of dependency between the various nationals and their State (nationality in its present meaning) is not yet distinguished from the problem of political participation of citizens in public life (citizenship). The abstract reality of a 'national community' (including millions of individuals who are unacquainted with each other, and are extremely diverse in regard to language, customs, resources etc.) has not really been thought out" (Noiriel, 1997, pp. 25–54).

Ernest Renan summed up the philosophical principle of liberal citizenship. Renan's view was affected by the loss of Alsace and Northern Lorraine to the newly founded German Empire in 1871. He delivered his conception of the nation in a well-known lecture that contested the ethno-cultural vision of nationality. According to the ethno-cultural vision, the regions of Alsace-Lorraine were actually of German descent, and belonged to Germany. The same view was applied to Southern Denmark (Schleswig-Holstein) or in some parts of Bohemia-Moravia or Silesia.[12] Therefore, they were meant to fall under German rule. Renan adamantly denied this idea and, instead, advanced the idea of choice and subjectivity against ethnic, objective determinism:

> Nation is consequently a great solidarity, constituted by the conscience of sacrifices that were made and those that will be made later. It implies a past; yet, it is summed up in the present through a tangible idea: consent, a desire clearly expressed to resume together the common life. The existence of a Nation is ... a daily plebiscite. (Renan, 1992, pp. 54–55)[13]

Though people from Alsace and Lorraine were Germans in the past, they did not wish to belong to the new German Empire. According to Renan, they preferred to live under French rule. This idea of liberal citizenship implies the freedom of choosing one's political allegiance according to an identity that is not mainly determined by language or other ethnic or cultural markers. Today it is possible to roughly divide European countries into two categories. In the first one, there are countries with an old liberal tradition and relatively long-established democratic institutions (the United Kingdom, the Netherlands, Belgium, France, Scandinavia), as well as some countries that have benefited of a broad diffusion of their language throughout the world (Portugal, Spain). That is nationhood as a political choice; a result of a will to act together for the common good through democratic institutions, independently from language, regional belonging, or religion, and under the condition that citizens are actually born in the territory of the State (*jus soli*). In the second category, that is Central, Oriental, and Southern Europe, states with a specific state-construction (Germany, Italy), or younger nations that emerged between 1830 and 1918 (from former Yugoslavia to Greece), have had a tendency to enhance *jus sanguinis*. That is, nationhood based on an ethnic community using the same language, or practicing the same religion and identifying itself through a range of specific myths.

Jus Sanguinis and *Jus Soli* have influenced the translation of identity into national laws. One example is the French Nationality Act of 1889, which combined both an open conception of citizenship (*jus soli*) with restrictions against naturalized persons as well as most inhabitants of the French Empire (*jus sanguinis*). French colonial subjects (very often Muslims) remained generally excluded from the assimilationist statement of the newly founded French Republic; though there were a few exceptions like Algerian Jews, people from small-hold colonies, and people residing in four Senegalese cities (Ellis, 2011). The balance between one principle and the other has changed several times in the past century: the distance between legal ideals and actual practices in daily life can be large because law is not enough to define national identity.

Layers of Territorial Identities

It seems useful to give a short account of the different layers of territorial identities and the idea of Europe. For some, the continent may, for example, look like "An old garden Europe, wholly filled with disused erotic and rapacious mad men."[14]

In reality, there are striking similarities between European networks of towns, as well as similar, authentically transnational urban experiences from one country to another. For instance, the Roman and Gothic architectures, the heritage of the Renaissance, public squares in old city centers that manage to give a feeling of intimacy and openness, and train stations that are surprisingly alike from Austria to Bosnia-Herzegovina. Since the Middle Ages, Europeans have developed the conscience of living in a shared, common space, and with much interdependency between regions and societies (Berting, 2002).

Foreigners view Europe as a cultural unit with an identity of its own, while Europeans view Europe as diverse, like a mosaic of cultures. Yet, there is no real European identity; European identity exists only as an outcome of national identities. Each European country has a particular perception of Europe stemming from its own national identity. This is another paradox of Europe: it refers to a defined geographical space and a historical unit, more or less identical from one country to another. Naturally, these visions have changed, and a question emerges: What does Europe represent for its people today? To unveil some answers, one might give a brief look at the contemporary situation for selected countries.

National Identity: Some Case Studies

France: Europe as a Global Power
The French territory is sited between the North Sea and the Mediterranean coast, between the Atlantic coast and the Alps in the heart of the Continent. Historically, France has benefited from a high level of geopolitical unity and stability since the Middle Ages, something which may explain its unusually high level of centralization compared to other Western democracies. France was the most influential continental power in this part of the world, at least until the end of the 20th century. Economically, the country has been substantially weakened in the last decade in contrast to the rise of the new, reunited Germany. Moreover, Germany has been the economic heart of Europe since the 1950s and is one reason why the European unification was largely based on a pact between France and West Germany. These facts are essential in understanding how the French perceive Europe today: the vision is ambivalent, and Europe is seen as a potential tool for

regaining global influence, and as a possible threat against French identity; an identity where the claim for universalism has often been implicit.

"Among nations, France had a particular vocation: she was great because of her glorious past, the continuity of her action and her influence in the world. So great that when her glory seemed to vanish, the future and peace in the world could seem to be threatened" (Olivi & Giacone, 2007, p. 63).[15] This self-image is at the core of France's action within the EU. The image explains the powerful and effective commitment of France in the geopolitical reconfiguration of Europe after World War II. We can think of several examples.

In 1952, the European Defense Community (EDC) was to establish an integrated pan-European army, later combined with a European Political Community. The idea was originally proposed by French Prime Minister René Pleven (1901–1993), and the treaty was signed in Paris by five other countries (Belgium, Italy, Luxemburg, the Netherlands, and West Germany), but was rejected in 1954 by a French Parliament that feared an unacceptable loss of sovereignty (Olivi & Giacone, 2007, pp. 39–41). More recently, the *Treaty Establishing a Constitution for Europe* (Rome, 2004) was broadly written and negotiated within a European Convention chaired by former French President Valéry Giscard d'Estaing. It was also rejected in France, and a few days later, in the Netherlands, after a referendum in 2005, while ratified in 18 other countries. German philosopher Jürgen Habermas, who was writing before this referendum took place, expresses his views about this rejection:

> From the point of view of all other nations, a "no" coming from France will have, if it happens, a specific significance. It is from France that came, with a beautiful largesse, the initiative of reconciliation with Germany. It is hereby France that put Europe's unification on the tracks, a unification that she has continuously stimulated by constantly renewed impulses. Should it occur that France takes her distance from the path she has followed until now, while we all are standing at the crossroads, it is certain that depression will fall on Europe for a very long time. (Habermas, 2006, pp. 53–54)[16]

Belgium: The Split Heart of Europe

If France can be labeled as a geographical allegory for Europe, Belgium is certainly a metaphor for the identity subtleties and uncertainties of the European way. The Kingdom of Belgium was founded in 1830. During the Middle Ages, this region was actually politically indistinguishable from the Netherlands and was then known as the Low Countries, divided between several mighty merchant cities of Bruges, Ghent, Ypres, Tournai, Antwerp, and Namu, that made these lands one of the most industrious parts of Europe. Feudalism had its consequences: fostering several principalities, some counties and duchies looked successively towards the German area

or the Kingdom of France, and some areas fell into foreign dominion either by war or heritage (Dumont, 2005). The Southern Low Countries
became sequentially Burgundian (1384–1482), Spanish (1482–1713), Austrian (1713–1795), French (1795–1814), and Dutch (1815–1830). In 1830,
Belgium seceded from the United Kingdom of Netherlands, partly due to
religious differences: the North was mostly Protestant after the Reformation in the 16th century, but the South remained faithful to the Catholic
Church.[17] The Belgian Revolution was acknowledged by the Great Powers
in London in 1831, and a new State was established upon a community
that was still to be built.

The aristocratic elite and the bourgeoisie spoke French, and the Dutch
language did not have any official status. Yet, the remainder of Belgian society was segmented into several linguistic communities using various French
or Dutch dialects. This linguistic diversity was not a major issue at the beginning of Belgium's modern history. However, it became a problem, which
may have been the result of the country's secularization in the 20th century,
but it may also have been the result of the economic weakening of the
French-speaking region, which had dominated the country from its independence to the 1960's. It is for these reasons that some refer to Belgium
as a "*demos,*" or a community of citizens, without an "*ethnos,*" a weak Belgian
identity (Castano and Tousignant, 1999).

The current institutional construction of Belgium has resulted from
negotiations and arduous compromises between three federative regions
(Wallonia, Flanders, Brussels) and three linguistic communities (the
French, the Flemish, the German), while the central government mainly re-
tains its core functions (defense, representation, justice, and social affairs).
Belgium is thus composed of four linguistic areas, Brussels being the only
bilingual one: a French-speaking island surrounded by the Dutch-speaking
Flanders (Dumont, 2002). It is not by chance that this city was chosen to
host the main institutions of the European Communities after 1958. Indeed, Brussels is located on major trade roads in the industrial heart of
Western Europe, and is a country with a weak historical identity and at the
crossroads of major foreign influences. The city is crossed by an invisible,
transnational frontier between Latin and Germanic Europe and is at the
strategic center for European unification.

The United Kingdom "The Continent Is Just a Spot on the Sea"[18]

If there is one country in Western Europe whose bonds to "the Continent" have been ambiguous throughout history, it is the United Kingdom
of Great Britain and (Northern) Ireland. Geography has had a clear influence in this ambiguity. Great Britain is an island, and in spite of the very
short distance to the coasts of France and Belgium, insularity has helped to
foster the idea of a supposedly impenetrable, natural frontier: the English

Channel. This idea is deeply rooted in the English national conscience, whose mythology enhances the belief that Great Britain has been protected from foreign invasions for several centuries. Some may proudly say that this has been a fact since 1066, although historians will argue otherwise: pointing to foreign influences of political events (Doyle, 1999). After the loss of Calais, the last possession of England on the continent, in 1558 England turned her back on Europe and took to the seas of the world, fighting back the maritime pretentions of Spain (1588), the Netherlands (1654–1674) and France (1763–1805) between the 16th and the 19th centuries. In the process, it built an extraordinary global supremacy that reached its apogee with the crowning of Queen Victoria as Empress of India (1877) and the establishment of the British Empire, "on which the sun never sets." In the same period, the United Kingdom tried to maintain a "balance of power" on the Continent in attempting to prevent the resurgence of any hegemonic state (successively Austria, France, Russia and Germany).

Great Britain's persisting suspicion towards the European Union can largely be understood as completely alien to Great Britain's national political *habitus*. Though Great Britain still wishes to maintain strong ties with the Anglophone world, this does not mean that it is outside Europe. On the contrary, London is inside the network of prosperous European cities stretching from Northern Italy to South-East England, and it is one of the main centers of power in the world.

British identity has other singularities. More than other languages in Europe, English is a hybrid of Germanic, French, and Latin. In terms of religion, one finds specific, national confessions, not really represented elsewhere in Europe (Chassaigne, 1999, p. 227): Anglicanism and Presbyterianism in Scotland.[19] The noteworthy stability of British institutions is another singularity. The UK is not only one of the oldest States in Western Europe, but it has managed to integrate genuine liberal changes in the course of its long history, without challenging the monarchy, which has proved to be a powerful symbol of British identity. Yet, divisions between Scotland, England, Wales, and Northern Ireland are real and it is therefore tempting to compare these "would-be" nations to similar regional nationalisms elsewhere in Spain, Belgium, or Italy.

Ireland: The Small Island in the Shadow of the Big One

Insularity has had a tendency to enlarge the gap between Great Britain and Europe. In the case of Ireland, its insularity and living in the shadow of England have driven its attempts at getting closer to the continent. Its future independence may be tied to its asserting a European identity. Thus, Ireland played an important role in sending missionaries throughout "Barbarian" regions of the continent during the Middle Ages. The island also developed cultural and military relations with major Catholic countries in the early-modern period: Spain, France, and Austria. Later, the influence of the continental revolutions in Europe played a major role in fostering the modern Irish identity and shaping its nationalist movement (Jouannon, 1999).

The Irish singularity relies on a strong geographic and historical identity in spite of the weakness of Gaelic, its original language. Faith has played an even more important part in the creation of an Irish identity—Ireland remains a Catholic stronghold in Northern Europe. At last, we can mention the heavy weight of British colonialism on the Irish national conscience and the long-lasting dominance of a rural society in the shaping of this identity.

The Republic of Ireland officially became independent in 1922, and remained neutral during the Second World War Afterwards, the adhesion to the EEC in 1973 was a clear opportunity to diminish the economic dependency on England. Ireland became a fervent State-member of the EU and implemented the euro in 1999, becoming henceforth the EU country with the fastest growth, the so-called "Celtic Tiger." It should also be noted that Ireland became a land of immigration rather than a country of emigration, as it was in the previous centuries.

Irish identity is no longer defined by a set of traditional normative system, shaped by a rural, Catholic, and Gaelic-speaking people, that for so long opposed to all things British. During the Celtic Tiger years, the Irish were proud of their identity, proud of their country's economic achievement and success story symbolized by the Spire in Dublin. Ireland was no longer an economic laggard, and emigration, another element of the country's history that had shaped Irish character and identity, was a thing of the past. Instead, Ireland experienced much immigration from returning Irish, but also many immigrants from Asia, Africa, and Eastern Europe after 2004. The arrival of so many immigrants lead to acts of racism and violence, and the State began questioning its own definition of Irish identity in different terms, leading to the use of expressions such as "cultural diversity." However, it is not clear if such a definition successfully changed the definition of Irish identity.

The arrival of the IMF and European experts, after the economic crisis hit Ireland in 2008, was strongly resented by the Irish. Not only did it challenge Ireland's world status and the ability of Irish politicians in shaping economic policy, it also questioned the society the Irish population had collectively agreed upon. The world economic slow-down and the later recession challenged the viability of the Celtic Tiger's economic model. Ireland was one of many nations facing hard economic times and challenges to their national identities.

Russia: A European Empire or an Oriental Frontier?[20]

After the fall of Constantinople in 1453 and the swift progression of the Ottoman Turks through Balkan Europe onto the gates of Vienna in 1529, Russia became the heart of the Christian Orthodox world. Moscow became "the third Rome," a conservatorium for the defunct Byzantium Empire. These obvious links with Christianity's fate at that time did not prevent the Great Duchy of Muscovy from looking Eastward and gathering "all Russian lands" under its dominion during the reign of Ivan III the Great (1462–1505). There is a certain historical and geographical symmetry with Western Europe: while Spanish conquistadores explored and colonized America, Cossacks[21] patiently pushed Russia's frontiers to Siberia (from 1581–1584), reaching the Kamchatka Peninsula in the 17th century and the passage to Alaska in 1727 (Szùcs, 1985). If America was then the Western appendicle of Europe, Asiatic Russia was its Oriental extension.

At that time, the Russian empire was almost as large as it is today. It was, however, less impressive than states like the Polish-Lithuanian Republic or the Kingdom of Sweden, that managed to contain Russian expansion in Europe until the 1720s. To some Europeans, Russia was more barbarous than the Ottoman Empire.

During the early-modern period, several Tsars were able to build an effective Absolutist State upon a society that never really renounced serfdom before 1861. Ivan III, Ivan IV the Terrible (1533–1584) and Peter the Great (1682–1725) had progressively implemented a bureaucratic revolution in order to modernize the State, thus forming a mighty army. The reign of Peter the Great, first Russian emperor, is considered the most important because he implemented several reforms inspired by European counselors (Riasanovsky, 1963). Russia became a European power to the detriment of Sweden (1700–1721). As Szùcs noted: "Now we need Europe for some decades in order to be able to even better turn our back on her" (Szùcs, 1985, p. 89).[22]

Among these reforms was the construction St-Petersburg in 1703, a new capital city, on shores of the Baltic Sea. St-Petersburg represented an exceptional authoritarian will to Europeanize Russia.[23] There was a paradox, though: Peter maintained the "Oriental logic of power concentration" (Hermet, 1996, p. 28). While serfdom was vanishing from Western Europe, it was an institution in Oriental Europe at the end of 17th century, especially in Russia (Hernet, 1996). In spite of the opposition of the Orthodox Church to many of Peter's reforms, Russia remained on its European path, getting its first Academy of Sciences (1725), its first university in Moscow (1755), and a Russian Academy of its own, dedicated to national humanities and founded in 1783 (Riasanovsky, 1963).

The reign of Catherine II the Great (1762–1796) marked an apogee in forging a genuine European civilization in Russia. During the Napoleonic Wars, the European fate of Russia was consecrated by military victories and by renewed political influence in the pan-European Congress of Vienna (1815). "If a mighty barbarian State like Russia generously decides to take the lead of a league whose goal is the balance of power in Europe, this country will save the world."[24]

Yet, in the course of the 19th century, the inability of the Absolutist regime to implement significant liberal reforms before 1905, combined with brutal economic and social changes (and the shockwaves of the First World War), led to the collapse of the autocracy and the establishment of a totalitarian despotism (1922). The frontier between the USSR and the rest of Europe became sealed, and this Iron Curtain moved into the heart of Europe after the Second World War and the subsequent Soviet expansion. After the collapse of the USSR (1991), Russia experienced a small liberal intermission in the 1990s, symbolized by the adhesion of the country to the Council of Europe in 1996. However, recent political events show that Russia has largely remained an authoritarian State with the formal appearances of a democracy, where the powerful Orthodox Church goes on sustaining an official national-identity building, in a radically different manner than elsewhere in Europe (Delsol & Mattéi, 2010). Meanwhile, massive nationalistic "Russian marches," where Breivik is regarded as "a hero of our time," are organized in Moscow (Dyrnes, 2013).[25]

Bosnia and Herzegovina: The European Dream of Balkan Europe

The existence of one national identity in Bosnia and Herzegovina is doubtful. The oriental frontier between Bosnia-Herzegovina and Serbia is one of the oldest in Europe, and it coincides with the demarcation between the Western Roman Empire and the Byzantine Empire that were operated by the sons of emperor Theodosius in the year 395. During the Middle Ages, this frontier symbolized the crossroads between two civilizations: the Greek Orthodox world and the Roman Catholic World (Béhar, 1999).

As the Ottoman Turks moved into the heart of Europe in the 16th century, politics were simplified, but religion and culture were complicated. A massive portion of the local population converted to Islam—a unique occurrence in Europe. Though the Ottoman conquest led to religious conversions, it did not threaten the territorial integrity of Bosnia nor its Slavonic identity (Mudry, 1999). The conversions were not meaningful.

The western frontier of Bosnia became a major political and military strategic point between the Kingdom of Hungary and the Ottoman Empire. Following the Austro-Ottoman Wars, the Turkish reflux of the 17th and 18th centuries made the religious map of Balkan Europe all the more intricate, and explains the extraordinary Bosnian religious mosaic, an intriguing "imperial vestige" in Europe (Béhar, 1999). It is no wonder that Bosnia and Herzegovina did not experience any kind of common national awakening in the course of late-modern history. The province remained under Ottoman dominion until 1878, and its organizing system was based on the 'millets,' or legally protected confessional minorities, with much autonomy (Mudry,

1999). These millets were not only examples of the acceptance of religious pluralism; they also became the basis for a national awakening that relied on religion in the broadest part of Balkan Europe. The integration of Bosnia and Herzegovina into the Habsburg Empire did not challenge religious tolerance. However, the growing nationalism and instability at the borders of both empires threw Europe into the First World War. On June 1914, the Austrian Archduke Franz-Ferdinand was assassinated in Sarajevo by a young Serbian nationalist, and signaled the start of WWI.

The combination of elaborate layers of identities and global geopolitical change in these borderlands also had terrible consequences later in the 20th century. Why do the three largest ethnic groups (defined under the Constitution of Bosnia and Herzegovina as "constituent peoples" and identifying themselves as Bosniaks, Croats, or Serbs) do not have Bosnian national identity? A number of factors are at play. One factor is that there are different interpretations of their own historical legacy. A second factor is the different attitudes these groups have towards the current State and its future prospects. Moreover, there are such issues as the status of Bosnia and Herzegovina in the former SFRY, the civil war (1992–1995), mass migrations of the population, and the creation of near mono-national geographical units within the new established country. The demographic configuration of the state changed, which further strengthened differences in attitudes towards their own national identities. There is no one reason, but a complex configuration of issues.

Currently, the Balkans are the last significant European region excluded from the EU. The promise of joining the European Union has presumably been a stabilizing factor, but political instability, linked to religion, may be a major obstacle toward gaining EU membership. Bosnia and Herzegovina is heavily assisted by the EU because it is concerned about the long-term viability of the State-building process in a country without any clear national identity and a society where religion has been dominant.

Germany: Europe and the Price for Global Peace

Modern German identity is caught in an unavoidable relationship with European identity, perhaps more than any other European country. There are deep historical reasons. Germany has had a definite way of national identity, based on a broad linguistic community (the largest in Europe) with no unified State before 1871. The German *Sonderweg* (exceptionalism) is based on ethno-cultural nationalism (*jus sanguinis*) and has another side to it: Nazism in a country with a rich cultural and spiritual heritage. At the end of the 19th century, Germany proudly saw herself as one of the most civilized, prosperous, and industrious nations in the world. And yet, it became a symbol of criminal identity and barbarity, and threw Europe into an era of doubt and long-lasting self-questioning that exists to this day.

Philosophers like Hannah Arendt (1906–1975) and Raymond Aron (1905–1983), as well as many other intellectuals and writers from the continent, have reflected and debated over the issues of Democracy, Totalitarianism, and the decline of European civilization.

For German social scientists, the question has been particularly inescapable since 1945. Why 1933? Is National-Socialism a phenomenon that was meant to happen in Germany, and nowhere else, even if similar tendencies were at work in several European countries? Is 1933 a historical accident? Is it possible to ask the question regarding the long-term historical continuity in German history in explaining the emergence of Nazism and Hitlerism? Some may underscore the permanency of an authoritarian and imperialistic State since 1871, the predominance of willing militarist and nationalist conservative elites, as well as the passivity of German "mandarins" in the administration (Gauzy, 1999). It is thus no surprise that discussing current German identity has proven to be particularly tricky, and this is clearly a result of the division of the country between 1945 and 1990. Today, German identity reflects the complex realities of the 21st century.

Discussing a European identity is a problem because of the complex interaction between geography, history, and "the exhaustion of European culture" (Mattéi, 2007). Some philosophers suggest that the great paradox of today's European identity would be precisely the rejection and negation of identities as a response to its totalitarian past. National identity is a complicated issue with both negatives and positives. Indeed, Levi-Strauss makes an accurate observation: "Any utilization of the notion of identity begins with the critic of this notion" (Lévi-Strauss, 1983, p. 331).[26]

For these reasons, The Federal Republic of Germany seems to be at the heart of Europe more than ever, and not only in this symbolic manner. "Germany's new 0 year became ipso facto Europe's 0 year, and both are equally caught in a no man's land between their past and their future, by the very fact of getting back their own, outdated past and their still unknown future" (Morin, 1987, p. 32).[27]

The European Union seems to serve chiefly German economic and political interests. Recall that the foundation of the European Union in 1993, and the subsequent implementation of a European currency, were the political consequences of German reunification, and the desire by France to see Germany abandon its national currency, as a gesture of a good will towards other European nations. Historically, the German commitment in the EU is inexplicable if one does not keep in mind the peculiarities of German history and the necessity for Germans constantly to define their self-being and identity in a European context, in order to achieve peace in Europe.

EUROPE AND THE WORLD: MIGRATIONS, RESISTANCES, AND THE ORDEAL OF MULTICULTURALISM

Is it possible to talk about a single plural national identity in Europe? Certainly, it is preposterous to talk about one national European identity. Indeed, the sense of being a "we" does not work well at the supranational level because the "European way" is the result of unaccountable and challenging compromises between leaders of European States and EU institutions. Saying that there is a European identity is more of a hope than a reality. A European identity still needs to be constructed, and will probably take two generations to do so. Europe has its flag, its anthem, its currency, and even a formal citizenship, but its identity remains uncertain, while territorial citizenship should be derived from an identity. Still, Europe has several commonalities among its nations, and most nations within Europe see immigration as national crises.

National Identity in Europe: A Common Experience Since 1945?

Though national identity in Europe is complicated, it is possible to distill common experiences from cultural and historical factors. Consider the thoughts of the Swiss historian Jacob Burckhardt (1818–1897) writing at a time when European nations held high status and power:

> Europe, the ancient and modern household of a multiform life, the original place of the most magnificent creations, the fatherland of all contrasts resolving themselves into a single unity and giving to all the tendencies of the mind, here and nowhere else, the possibility to express themselves. What is European is indeed the collective and individual manifestation of all human faculties through monuments, paintings, words, institutions and parties, it is the fullness of intellectual and moral life, from all sides and into every direction, it is the ambition of the mind letting the testimony of everything inside itself, as well as the ambition of not submitting itself silently to universal monarchies or theocracies like the ones from the Orient. (Burckhardt, 1965, p. 142)[28]

Religious and Cultural Commonalities
More recently, the French philosopher Edgar Morin wrote that

> the Jewish, Christian, Greek and Latin sources seem to have met and created a harmonious synthesis which is simultaneously the specific substrate and the common denominator of Europe. This is the base upon which Europe has produced an original civilization influenced by spirituality, humanism, rationality, democracy, that is to say values superior to anything comparable

in other civilizations. This is at least the myth that Europe believes. (Morin, 1987, p. 81)[29]

Historians and philosophers have tried to sketch out the characteristics of Europe's cultural legacy: the specificity of Christian religion, the subsequent tension between temporal authorities and spiritual powers, the creation of modern Nation-States, a rationalistic approach towards economy, the rise of relativistic thought since the 16th century, the rise of modern ideologies in the 19th century, and individualism as a common practice within civil society. As a system of values, Europe is characterized by the respect for individuals; their autonomy and liberty, the acceptance and tolerance of lifestyles, minorities and religious beliefs, the recognized superiority of reason, and social solidarity and political participation in public life. In spite of the many unique national and intranational cultural traits, the European heritage has a common frame based on legal and political history.

Group and Individual Rights

The Treaty of London, signed in 1949 by ten European nations, established the Council of Europe. Today, it is the largest and the oldest pan-European organization, with 47 member states, representing more than 800 million inhabitants. The Council was conceived as a direct answer to the tragedies of the Second World War, namely an attempt to defend human rights, democracy, and the *Rechtsstaat* ("Rule of Law"). To do so, a *European Convention on Human Rights* was negotiated in 1950 and entered into force in 1953. Its main innovation was a European Court of Human Rights, which can be appealed to by individuals, something which is unique in the field of international law where only sovereign States are given this opportunity. To a large extent, the European Union stems from the same historical trend, although it has been more politically ambitious.

The Copenhagen criteria were formulated in 1993. It was the EU's first official response to the necessity of defining a common political identity beyond the formal and practical dispositions of citizenship that were written into the Treaty of Maastricht. For the first time, it was stated that membership required the achievement of stable institutions that guarantee democracy and the rule of law, respecting human rights and protection of minorities. Some years later, a larger and more systematic process was launched and achieved by the proclamation of a *Charter of Fundamental Rights of the European Union* (December 2000). The Charter listed all civic and social rights of European citizens or all inhabitants living on the EU's territory. It was implemented in 2009 and applied to all state members with the exceptions of the UK, Poland, and the Czech Republic. This text is based on several previous European protocols or decisions (among which is the European Convention of 1950[30]) and divided into 6 sections: dignity, liberty, equality, solidarity, citizenship, justice.

There is no need to delve into the details of these agreements. However, there is a need to underline that the details constitute a framework for defining a common experience of national identity based on humanistic principles. Since 1945, there has been a pattern of putting human rights at the core of rebuilding Europe. A key problem in this process has been multiculturalism, and at least two other issues. To begin with, these texts can be seen as a legal pact imposing rules for the relationships between European nations. Second, the texts pretend to defend multiple kinds of minorities: linguistic, ethnical, religious, and sexual. Yet, it is uncertain if they are sufficient to protect recent migrant minorities, and to answer the challenges of identity crises and reemerging populism. In a specific historical context there is a tendency of decoupling citizenship from nationality. That is, the sense that allegiances and identities are now invested in communities larger than the state (the European Union) or smaller than (or transversal to) the state, such as ethnic groups, regions, and cities.

The Rise of Nationalism in Europe

However, this decoupling is losing its acceptance by the public and by political elites throughout the continent. The reason of its losing its acceptance is the current crisis of the Nation-State. We are seeing the emergence of re-nationalizing citizenship in the post-2001 period, the introduction of language and integration tests as a condition for naturalization and citizenship. But in present multicultural Europe, the only identity that newcomers could legitimately be expected to adopt is a liberal identity consisting in the general rules and principles of liberal democracy (e.g., the principles of equal rights, democracy, respect for fundamental freedoms of the individual, and the rule of law). Such identity is *a fortiori*, devoid of any particular cultural content. National identity cannot be imputed on people by liberal states. This is to say that identity belongs to the realm of feeling and passion, whereas citizenship belongs to the domain of reason, law, and enlightenment.

Immigration, Multiculturalism, and the Crisis of Nation States

Multiculturalism

Identity building in Europe must address immigration and multiculturalism. Multiculturalism is, however, a relativistic concept, having different meanings according to the social, political, and historical characteristics of each European nation. Recently, the term has been used to describe various policies implemented in Canada and in the United Statess to protect and enforce the human and civil rights of minorities. Similar policies have been implemented in countries like the UK and the Netherlands, while in countries like France, the traditional assimilationist statement has prevailed in the name of national unity and equality before the law. The underlying premise of multiculturalism is that any culture is worthy of respect, because all cultures fundamentally share the same values. Quite ironically, this abstract and theoretical conception has also been very much criticized for its inability to foster a genuine sense of community within European societies.

One criticism is that multiculturalism is an ideological concept. Multiculturalism may be inadequate in coping with the social and practical realities of everyday life because it weakens the role of the State as the enforcer of law and reason in society. The concept, as a social policy, also may weaken the function of citizenship in a democratic system by giving to communities (ethnic, religious, and so forth) collective rights that contradict or limit unavoidably individual freedom, thus challenging the possibility of creating authentic plural identities. There are valid criticisms of multiculturalism when it leads to cultural differences, and hence deteriorates the conditions of multiculturalism as a private freedom. Thus, one hermeneutic difficulty is to distinguish the sometimes blurred frontier between the public sphere and the private sphere.

A second criticism is the challenge of comprehending each particular society and state construction, implementation, and enforcement of multiculturalism: public responsibility and management of multicultural societies have extremely diverse implications whether one talks about France or Belgium. It is impossible to ignore the impacts multiculturalism has on fragile state constructions. In those contexts, multiculturalism may be the only adequate solution to replace deficient citizenships and to obtain civil peace.

The Muslim Problem

Multiculturalism in Europe brings to mind the "Muslim" problem. Many European countries are becoming increasingly diverse in terms of ethnicity, but few—if any—embrace this growing ethnic diversity. These anti-immigrant sentiments have especially targeted Europe's Muslim immigrants, who are increasingly categorized by the native population as the "essential other" that fails to integrate. There has always been some tension between Oriental and Western societies, but this tension widened with the terrorist attacks in America on 11th September 2001 by a group of persons claiming to be Muslims. Thus, it often looks as though Islam is at the heart of identity crises in Europe. However, Delsol and Mattei note that

> Islam is not at the heart of Europe's identity crisis. It is rather one of its symptoms. The crisis is actually more profound and more endogenous. Its' a cri-

sis of politics degenerated into 'impolitics.' It's a crisis of the denationalized Nation-State. It's the crisis of a secularized Europe. It's the crisis of a disincarnated Christianity. It's the crisis of a perverted secularism. It's the crisis of a disoriented modernity. It's the crisis of a dehumanized humanism, cut off from any kind of divine transcendence. It's the crisis of a hedonist and self-centered globalization. It's the crisis of a burnt-out consumerism. It's the crisis of an exhausted civilization. (Delsol & Mattéi, 2010, p. 119)[31]

The rise of Islam in Europe does not reflect a religious quest in societies under profound spiritual crisis. Rather, it is an element of "belonging" asserting its distinctive identity against dominant national identities. Why so? Tunisian theologian Mezri Haddad has conjectured an explanation: it is the difference between Europe as a civilization and Islamic political practices that separate temporal powers and spiritual authorities. Christianity is indeed supposed to be the religion of an ontological separation between "the sacred and the profane" in politics, while Islam is a religion of a primitive and impassable coalescence between these two instances (Delsol & Mattéi, 2010, p. 115). In other words, Christianity, as a theology, would naturally open the doors of democracy and secularization, while Islam would be fundamentally theocratic. Any European identity cannot be solely founded on religion, although Christianity has undeniably been the first solid ground for the forging of a common civilization in Europe. In the West, the separation of Church and State is a fundamental principle.

The Discovery of Globalization

Europe's discoveries of the wider world and Globalization have changed national identity. It is crucial that we look into these issues. Consider the status of White South African migrants in the UK. Following the end of apartheid, there has been an increase in South African migration. South Africans make up one of the largest foreign national groups in the UK to date. However, it is noteworthy that in South Africa itself, White South Africans make up only about 10% of the country's population, while as many as around 90% of the South African population who reside in the UK are White. White South Africans have not only benefited from their ancestral ties to the UK or other European countries, but also have successfully negotiated their legal access to the UK by drawing on their privileged socio-economic status as a legacy of the racial inequalities during apartheid. Nonetheless, we have recently seen the introduction of policy restrictions imposed upon non-EEA immigrants, including some White South Africans. In this context, it is argued that policy restrictions can have an impact upon White South Africans' access to the "British nation."

There are clear British ancestral ties between English-speaking rather than with Afrikaans-speaking White South Africans. It is also clear that even the possession of ancestral ties might not be sufficient for membership in the UK. In the current restrictive immigration position of the UK, even for privileged and "White" migrants with ancestral ties, boundaries are erected. Some White South Africans argue that they are more "deserving" than other immigrant groups, and eve that they "add more value" to British society than certain groups in the UK. But this is mere rhetoric and a strategy for coping with exclusionary boundaries in British society.

Other Barriers to European Integration

There are other, legal-administrative barriers to immigrant integration in Europe. For example, there are civil tests that are used in order to determine whether or not an immigrant has reached a sufficient level of integration within French society to acquire French citizenship. Civic tests mainly focus on values and symbols of French culture and history. However, it is essential to have some sort of test to evaluate integration of those who might wish to acquire citizenship. Current administration policies in France are driven by a singular view integration. Integration or identity is, I would argue, multi-faceted and double-hinged. Also, if the values and symbols are important for integration, then it is essential that there be an official manual that one can use to acquire such knowledge. Such a document does not exist.

Creating normative/ideological boundaries affects national identity. It has been argued that in Europe, religious boundaries function in the same way as racial boundaries[32] in the United States: in Europe, religion marks Muslim immigrants and their descendants as "the others." Such processes of categorization and exclusion have a far-reaching impact on ethnic minorities' self-identification. Such categorization supports the notion that there is a distinction between "being," "feeling," and "doing" when it concerns national (as well as ethnic) identification. Secondly, a sense of exclusion and being "the other" often coincide with a strong assertion of "being" a member of a society, but a low or absent sense of "feeling" to be a member of a society.

Muslims are an interesting case study of national identity. Muslim loyalties have demands placed upon them and are scrutinized by their host societies. While first generation Muslims talk about their identity dilemma of being an immigrant and a citizen of their host society, second generation Muslims have a more balanced and valued identity as part of their life. They are not confused; in fact, they present themselves as fully aware of all facets of their identities, and seem to create a balance between their religious and citizenship identities.

The ability of second generation Muslims to integrate and elaborate their own balanced "multiple" identities can be seen as a success of the liberal democratic systems in Europe. It seemingly shows that the experience of national identity has proven positive in spite of the citizenship crisis.

These silent successes are probably underestimated when one faces the recurrent noise of "integration's failures" in the public debate.

CONCLUSION

To conclude, national identity appears to be an issue at several scales, implying different challenges. At the individual level, the issue is formulated differently if one is an immigrant or not, and it can be summed up as acceptance of implicit or explicit social rules and behaviors, language, national policy, and somatic appearance. If one is a member of the native population, the challenge is in the acceptance or the rejection of new citizens or foreigners in the national community, depending on the perception that one may have of national identity. This perception can be dynamic, accepting the process of global cultural change, or it can be static and idealized, especially in moments of moral crises. Indeed, populist movements in Europe have not only been the result of the economic crises since the 1970s, they have deeper roots, as they are simultaneously a crisis of globalization, and a crisis of the Nation-State. At this level, the issues around national identity have been revealed by changes of political regimes and significant axial events, such as wars and various ideological movements (the Enlightenment and the French Revolution, the rise of far-right regimes in the 1930s . . .).

Today, the question of fighting against right-winged populisms in Europe remains a challenge. As time goes by, Europeans' relationship to recent history loosens, and political elites are ineffective in their fight against the rise of intolerance. Indeed, if political decision makers do not cynically exploit these feelings, they usually just rely on the worn out rhetoric about "democratic and humanistic values" that has obviously little appeal, especially among the younger generation. If the foundation of pan-European institutions was a direct response to these potential disorders and has proven to be an effective tool in promoting and protecting the rule of law and pluralism, recent history shows that international agreements about human rights are not always sufficient to prevent European states and societies from drifting beyond this legal and moral framework. Intolerant identities are never far away.

NOTES

1. Anderson has proposed an anthropological definition of the nation, as an imagined political sovereign community, intrinsically limited by frontiers. See Anderson, B. (1983), *Imagined communities: Reflections on the origin and spread of nationalism.*

2. This expression is the translation of a book by Amin Maalouf: *Les identités meutrières* (Paris, 1998). The philosopher begins his argument by noticing that the contemporary notion of identity may engender conflicts, especially because identities, as "imagined communities," can easily exclude each other, while individual identities are much more complex and can combine elements from different human communities and individual histories. Against the prevalence of such uniform collective identities, Maalouf defends Enlightenment ideals and humanism as a solution against simplistic categorization of mankind. Identities are also put in perspective with globalization and religion. The book has been translated in English under the title *In the name of identity: Violence and the need to belong* (2000).

3. "Rien de plus international que la formation des identités nationales. Le paradoxe est de taille puisque l'irréductible singularité de chaque identité nationale a été le prétexte d'affrontements sanglants. Elles sont pourtant bien issues du même modèle, dont la mise au point s'est effectuée dans le cadre d'intenses échanges internationaux." Translation by A. Larguèche.

4. American cultural critic and historian Richard Slotkin has written about the forge of American identity since early-modern times. See for example *Regeneration through violence: The mythology of the American frontier 1600–1860*, (2000) first published in 1973.

5. Translation by A. Larguèche.

6. Translation by A. Larguèche.

7. The Peace of Westphalia ended the Thirty Years' War (1618–1648) opposing two European coalitions: on one side, France, Sweden, Protestant German princes, and the Dutch Republic; on the other side, Spain, the Habsburg Emperor in Vienna, head of the Holy Empire, Catholic German princes, and the Papal States. These treaties were meant to end wars of religion in the Holy Empire between the Catholic Emperor and the Protestant princes. The defeat of the Catholic coalition led to a considerable reduction of the Austrian Emperor in Western Europe, while the idea of balance of power between fully sovereign independent states was asserted like a fundamental principle in what we can call European public law. At the same time, feudal structures and the religious ambitions of the Catholic Church were politically weakened. These treaties were concluded in the German cities of Munster and Osnabruck, and they are sometimes regarded as the result of the first pan-European peace congress: indeed, there was a genuine attempt to resolve a multitude of conflicts, and the clear intention to formulate principles for ensuring global peace. To that extent, historians and jurists often say that the Peace of Westphalia inaugurated a new era in international relations.

8. The original title of the four volumes was *Ideen zur Philosophie der Geschichte der Menschheit* (1784–1791).

9. Many of these States were formerly gathered in a feudal confederation founded in 962 and presided over by the Austrian House of Habsburg since the 15th century: the Holy Roman Empire, which was not a genuine state, but rather a political relic from the Middle Ages, was to be abolished under the pressure of Napoleon in 1806. Covering the largest part of the German countries, this powerless-institutional structure had already included many minorities in its

marches and in throughout the course of its long history; for example in cities and regions in Northern Italy, Eastern France, Flanders, Southern Denmark, Switzerland or Bohemia-Moravia. After 1815, it was replaced by a similar structure called the German Confederation, with a simpler map of 39 States.

10. The most significant among them was the philosopher Johann Gottlieb Fichte (1762–1814), author of the *Addresses to the German Nation* (original title: *Reden an die deutsche Nation*, 1808), a series of speeches declaimed in Berlin under the Napoleonic occupation.

11. The first theoretician of Aryan superiority was a French diplomat and essayist, Count Joseph-Arthur de Gobineau (1816–1882). He published in 1853–1855 *An Essay on the Inequality of the Human Races*, which is still labeled as one of the first examples of scientific racism, and had a significant influence in the United States and Germany, where it was translated and reedited several times from the 1890's on. Let us also note that this work was supposedly admired by the prominent anthropologist Claude Lévi-Strauss, although not for its contents, but rather for its formal qualities.

12. In fact, a large part of Northern Lorraine was still majorly French-speaking, like in the city of Metz. The same could be said about the region of Schleswig-Holstein, where the Danes were far from being an insignificant minority at the same period. Yet, both regions were integrated into the German Empire after short, bloody wars against the Kingdom of Denmark (1864) and the French Empire (1871).

13. Translation by A. Larguèche.

14. "Vieux jardin l'Europe, tout rempli de fous désuets, érotiques et rapaces." In Céline, L-F. (1990), *Voyage au bout de la nuit*, Paris: Gallimard, p. 273. First published in 1932; translation by Aladin Larguèche.

15. Translation by A. Larguèche.

16. Translation by Christian Bouchindhomme, Alexandre Dupeyrix, and Aladin Larguèche.

17. Between 1482 and 1648, both countries were under Spanish dominion and were then known as the Imperial States of the Habsburg Netherlands, or the Seventeen Provinces. Following the Reformation, the Republic of the Seven United Netherlands was founded (1579) and recognized as an independent Protestant State after the Eighty Years' War and the Peace of Westphalia (1568–1648), while the Southern provinces were recovered by Spain or had remained Catholic. Thus, the "reunification" of the Low Countries under Dutch rule in 1815 did not seem natural anymore, in spite of a long history of political homogeneity in this region during the Middle Age. Consequently, religion was certainly the most visible factor of the Belgian uprising in 1830, but it is uncertain if it really was its main cause: since their separation in the 17th century, both countries had become more and more estranged to each other. In the early 19th century, this antagonism was also economical and cultural, as given that the French-speaking bourgeoisie did not have any influence in the affairs of the Dutch State. Finally, the Dutch king William I (1815–1840) was an authoritarian sovereign that managed to gather liberals and Catholics against his rule (Dumont, 2005). Let us note that the Belgian

uprising opened the way to one of the most liberal constitutions in Europe in those years, inspired by the French Revolutions of 1789 and 1830.

18. "Le continent n'est qu'un point sur la mer." These words are quoted from a text by Benjamin Biolay, "Les insulaires," in *Négatif* (2003, Virgin Music). Translation by Aladin Larguèche.

19. Both confessions stemmed from the Reformation. Anglicanism is often considered as a middle ground between Catholicism and Protestantism, or a sort of non-Roman Catholic Church.

20. For detailed information on Russia and national identity see Karnaukhova and Verdugo in the present volume.

21. Cossacks were originally East Slavonic communities, often employed as mercenaries, border guards, or soldiers, acting quite independently from central states until the 18th century. A military and rural class as well as a nation, they played a major role in Russia's history, especially regarding territorial expansion. (Riasanovsky, 1963).

22. Translation by Ibolya Virag and Aladin Larguèche.

23. Other examples were clothing laws that were meant to Europeanize Russians by taxing the wearing of beards in the years 1698–1700.

24. These words are pronounced by Abbot Morio, a fictional character created by count Leo Tolstoy (1828–1910) in the novel *War and Peace* (Война и миръ), published in 1869. Translation by Boris de Schloezer and Aladin Larguèche.

25. See Steinar Dyrnes, "Breivik er vår tidshelt," in *Aftenposten*, 5.11.2013. In http://www.aftenposten.no/nyheter/uriks/—Breivik-er-var-tids-helt-7361968.html

26. Translation by Aladin Larguèche.

27. Translation by Aladin Larguèche.

28. Translation by A. Larguèche.

29. Translation by A. Larguèche.

30. Article 53, "Charte Européenne des droits fondamentaux," in *Journal Officiel des Communautés européennes*. http://www.europarl.europa.eu/charter/pdf/text_fr.pdf

31. Translation by A. Larguèche.

32. The issue of race-based boundaries is discussed in the racial stratification literature. Essentially, racial stratification systems have two components: an ideological system of norms and values, and a structural component that isolates minorities, both physically (e.g., separate communities, jobs, schools) and in the social consciousness. The ideological part is used as a rationale for structural isolation/separation (see Verdugo, 1995; 2008).

REFERENCES

Anderson, B. (1983). *Imagined communities: Reflections on the origin and spread of nationalism*. London, England: Verso.

Béhar, P. (1999). *Vestiges d'empires: La décomposition de l'Europe centrale et balkanique*. Paris, FR: Éditions Desjonquères.

Berting, J. (2002). Les concepts de l'Europe depuis le temps des Lumières (1776–2000). In C. Villain-Gandossi (Ed.), *L'Europe à la recherche de son identité* (pp. 41–69). Paris, FR: CTHS.

Burckhardt, J. (1965). *Fragments historiques*. Genève, CH: Droz.

Castano, E., & Tousignant, N. (1999). La Belgique et l'Europe. Un demos sans ethnos ? In G-F Dumont (Ed.), *Les racines de l'identité européenne* (pp. 99–123). Paris, FR: Economica.

Delsol, C., & Mattéi, J-F. (Eds.). (2010). *L'identité de l'Europe*. Paris, FR: PUF.

Doyle, W. (1999). Brouillard dans la Manche, continent isolé: Les hésitations britanniques face à l'Europe. In G-F. Dumont (Ed.), *Les racines de l'identité européenne* (pp. 232–238). Paris, FR: Economica.

Dyrnes, S. (2013). "Breivik er vår tidshelt," in Aftenposten. Retrieved from http://www.aftenposten.no/nyheter/uriks/–Breivik-er-var-tids-helt-7361968.html

Dumont, G-F. (2002). *La Belgique : hier et aujourd'hui*. Paris, FR: Presses Universitaires de France.

Dumont, G-F. (2005). *Histoire de la Belgique: des origines à 1830*. Brussels, BE: Le Cri.

Ellis, S. G. (2010). Towards a citizenship of the European Union. Perspectives on European integration and European Union history. In A-K. Isaac (Ed.), *Citizenships and identities: Inclusion, exclusion, participation* (pp. 173–193). Pisa, IT: University Press.

Febvre, L. (1999). *Europe: genèse d'une civilisation*, Paris, FR: Perrin.

Gauzy, F. (1999). L'exception allemande et l'identité européenne. In G-F. Dumont (Ed.), *Les racines de l'identité européenne* (pp. 49–63). Paris, FR: Economica.

Gellner, E. (1983). *Nations and Nationalism*, New York, NY: Cornell University Press.

Habermas, J. (2006). *Sur l'Europe*, Paris, FR: Bayard.

Hermet, G. (1996). *Histoire des nations et du nationalisme en Europe*. Paris, FR: Seuil.

Hobsbawm, E. (1992). *Nations and nationalism since 1780: Programme, myth, reality*. Cambridge, England: University Press.

Hroch, M. (1985). *Social preconditions of national revival in Europe. A comparative analysis of the social composition of Patriotic groups among the smaller European nations*. Cambridge, England: University Press.

Joannon, P. (1999). De la verte Erin au Celtic Tiger: Crises et mutations de l'identité nationale irlandaise contemporaine. In G-F. Dumont (Ed.), *Les racines de l'identité européenne* (pp. 173–193). Paris, FR: Economica.

Lévi-Strauss, C. (1983). *L'identité*. Paris, FR: Grasset.

Maalouf, A. (1998). *Les identités meurtrières*. Paris, FR: Grasset.

Mattéi, J-F. (2007). *Le regard vide: Essai sur l'épuisement de la culture européenne*. Paris, FR: Flammarion.

Morin, E. (1987). *Penser l'Europe*. Paris, FR: Folio.

Mudry, T. (1999). *Histoire de la Bosnie-Herzégovine: faits et controversies*. Paris, FR: Ellipses.

Noiriel, G. (1997). Socio-histoire d'un concept: les usages du mot nationalité au XIXe siècle. *Genèses. Sciences Sociales et Histoire, 27*, 25–54.

Olivi, B., & Giacone, A. (2007) *L'Europe difficile: Histoire politique de la construction européenne*. Paris, FR: Gallimard.

Renan, E. (1992). *Qu'est-ce qu'une nation ? et autres essais politiques*. Paris, FR: Presses Pocket.

Riasanovsky, N. (1963). *A history of Russia.* Oxford, England: Oxford University Press.

Slotkin, R. (2000). *Regeneration through violence: The mythology of the American frontier 1600–1860.* Norman, OK: University of Oklahoma Press.

Smith, A. D. (1994). *The ethnic origins of nations.* New York, NY: Blackwell.

Szùcs, J. (1985). *Les trois Europes.* Paris, FR: L'Harmattan.

Thiesse, A-M. (1999). *La création des identités nationales en Europe XVIIIe-XXe siècles.* Paris, FR: Seuil.

Verdugo, R. R. (2008). Racial stratification, social consciousness, and the education of Mexican-Americans in Fabens, Texas: A socio-historical study. *Spaces for Difference, 1*(2), 69–95.

Verdugo, R. R. (1995). Racial stratification and the use of Hispanic faculty as role models: Theory, policy, and practice. *The Journal of Higher Education,* 669–685.

CHAPTER 2

THE CRISIS OF WESTERN DEMOCRACIES AND NATIONAL IDENTITY

Citizenship, Immigration, and Constitutional Patriotism

Francis Luong

The confluence of citizenship and national identity are complex issues, especially in this era of mass immigration. Citizenship has often been used as a synonym for nationality, denoting legal membership in a nation-state. However, since the end of World War II this specific meaning of citizenship has faced many challenges. In the present context of universal human rights and anti-ethnic discrimination there is a tendency of separating citizenship from nationality. Membership, allegiances, and identities are now invested in collectivities either larger or smaller than the state, such as global citizenship, ethnic groups, and cities. Given several worldwide events (immigration,[1] a crisis of the nation-state, a crisis of national identities in the post-2001 period, and the global economic crisis), Western

National Identity, pages 55–79
Copyright © 2016 by Information Age Publishing

liberal democracies are redefining the meaning of citizenship by instituting passing State constructed tests as a pre-condition for citizenship. But a paradox has emerged.

Western democracies find themselves in the "paradox of universalism" (Joppke, 2010a). The paradox is based, on the one hand, on the localization of identity and, on the other hand, the espousing of identity as a universal concept, and resembling the precepts of "political liberalism" (Rawls, 1993). The only particular identity that newcomers could logically adopt is one based on the general principles of liberal democracy, such as equal rights, democracy, individualism, and the rule of law. Such principles are *a fortiori*, devoid of any cultural content. The purpose of my chapter is to propose that national identity cannot be imposed on a population residing in liberal states, and that nation-building should be founded on the concept "constitutional patriotism" (Habermas, 1998), which separates citizenship from national identity. In advancing my proposal, I have organized this chapter in the following manner:

- I examine citizenship, its philosophical underpinnings, and how it addresses multiculturalism.
- I then discuss the paradox currently facing liberal states, examine the meaning of liberalism as identity, and compare it to a non-liberal viewpoint in discussing new criteria for citizenship.
- Finally, I introduce and suggest that constitutional patriotism is the logical paradigm for citizenship and identity in Western democracies.

THEORETICAL BACKGROUND: CITIZENSHIP, IDENTITY, AND MULTICULTURALISM

What Is Citizenship?

Loading citizenship with the semantics of nationalism creates a framework for merging integration and social cohesion. States aspire to mold their populations into something more than mere congeries of individuals; they attempt to create a homogeneous and cohesive population. Membership is not just "state membership," but "nation membership," in which "the political community should be simultaneously a cultural community, a community of language, mores, or beliefs" (Brubaker, 1989, p. 4). Only thus can a state be a *nation's state*—the authentic expression and legitimate representative of a nation.

In the early secular, modern state, there was a need to legitimate the state in order to foster the loyalty of its members. However, the somewhat abstract notions of popular sovereignty and democracy, according to

Habermas (1996), needed a catalyst and a mobilizing force in order to "activate the people." A national identity—that is, the awareness of belonging to the same cultural community—was an important strategy that created feelings of political responsibility; and it was national identity that "provided the socially integrating substrate of the political identity of the republic" (Habermas, 1996, p. 130). But there was always a challenge; immigrants.

Immigrants have been a challenge in constructing a national identity. Historically, the manner by which states incorporated immigrants varied from country to country due to different "philosophies of integration" (Favell, 2001). Such philosophies were "based on contrasting understandings of core concepts such as citizenship, nationality, pluralism, autonomy, equality, public order and tolerance" (Favell, 2001, p. 2). Consequently, national debates about immigration and citizenship were informed by different "traditions of nationhood" (Brubaker, 1989) and distinctive views about what constitutes a nation and its identity. In this section, I review the theoretical underpinnings of discussions surrounding citizenship and national identity. I also discuss how multiculturalism emerged as an important factor in these discussions and how it represents challenges for those wishing to build citizenship and national identity.

Brubaker and Two Views About Nationality

There are, essentially, two views about nationality: universal and exclusive. Brubaker (1992) explains how different national histories have generated both views: universal, expansive, and assimilationist among French elites; and exclusive, particularistic, and ethno-culturally among Germans. The author suggests that the politics of citizenship, and the boundaries that limit access to citizenship, are better understood by examining national traditions and ideals. These ideals and traditions form an "idiom of nationhood" (Brubaker, 1992)—that is, "a manner of thinking and talking about cultural and political belonging at the level of the nation-state" (Brubaker, 1992, p. 162). Accordingly, the idiom of nationhood can be used as symbolic capital in examining national identity.

Nation-state formation is key in understanding the different approaches of integrating immigrants in France and Germany. Brubaker argues that Germany's view of nationhood is "an essentially ethno-cultural fact, prior to and independent of the state" (Brubaker, 1992, p. 56). The formation of the German nation-state is a history of searching for a common state: a story of subnational entities that were territorially scattered, but ethno-culturally bonded. It is this history that explains why German traditions of cultural and national belonging were characterized by many conflicts in fragmented nineteenth century central Europe.

It was different in France. The French Revolution established norms and ideals of national citizenship *before* any conception of a nation emerged.

While fragmentation characterized the formation of the German nation-state, the path in France was marked by a unitary center, moving towards the periphery. Republican ideologies stressed civic equality and generalized political rights, and were spread through universal military service and secular education, the two main instruments of assimilating populations in outlying areas. France's successful practice of socializing immigrants and peasants with French national and cultural ideals accounts for its assimilationist tradition.

There are, thus, two views about citizenship laws: based on blood or territory. France's penchant for *jus soli*, according to which citizenship is a function of the state's territory into which one is born, is a civic conception of nationhood. By contrast, Germany's inclination for *jus sanguinis*, according to which citizenship is inherited from one's parents, is based on an ethnic tradition of nationhood.

In explaining the debates in France and Germany, Brubaker concentrates on the elites' interpretations of their own cultural traditions in order to explain what constitutes the primary elements in debates on national identity. He states that "the idiom of nationhood...[belongs to] the French political and cultural elite, [who hold]...dominant positions in the institutions and access to (as well as habits of using) the media of public expression" (Brubaker, 1992, p. 161). Brubaker does not accept the idea that inertia and tradition account for the resilience of the politics of citizenship. Like Pierre Bourdieu, Brubaker considers tradition a form of symbolic capital:

> To present a policy or practice as traditional can contribute to its preservation by investing it with normative dignity and thereby raising the political cost of challenging it. Tradition is therefore a contested category. Policies and practices are the object of representational struggles that seek to deem them 'traditional' or to deny them this dignity—instances of general and perpetual struggle over representation and characterization of the social world. (Brubaker, 1992, p. 186)

Brubaker's focus on elites is too rigid to account for conflicting conceptions about the significance of culture and tradition. He admits to the discordance between the meanings of symbols and representations, but he fails to take this into account when describing broad consensus on national self-understanding. Thus, this conceptualization of nationhood is monolithic, homogeneous, and invariant in terms of economic interests, occupational fields, or geographical location. Further, the concept fails to explain the social conditions that result in national immigrant policies.

The least convincing part of Brubaker's argument is his claim about the inertia in French and German citizenship policies. In fact, some important changes occurred in German citizenship law: while immigration has been strongly reduced since 1992, naturalization regulations have been liberalized and were put on an as-of-right basis in 1993. Another change occurred in 1999, when *jus soli* for second-generation immigrants was implemented. This liberalization of the politics of citizenship in Germany, which actually follows a larger liberalizing tendency in Europe, is not captured in Brubaker's "idiom of nationhood" analytical approach of citizenship. Brubaker's essentialist argument regarding Germany fails to explain the change in historical events that have allowed Germany to re-think its past positions and pursue change. Another paradigm was needed.

Yasemin Soysal: State Institutional Disposition and Immigrant Integration

Yasemin Soysal (1994) challenges the idea that the cultural background of immigrants drives their strategies of adapting to their host society. Soysal claims that it is the institutional dispositions of the host state that determine immigrants' adaptation:

> Migrant organisations...define their goals, strategies, functions, and level of operation in relation to the existing policies and resources of the host state. They advance demands and set agendas vis-à-vis state policy and discourses in order to seize institutional opportunities and further their claims. In that sense, the expression and organisation of migrant collective identity are framed by the institutionalised forms of the state's incorporation regime. (Soysal, 1994, p. 86)

Examining the Netherlands, Germany, France, Switzerland, Sweden, and the United Kingdom, Soysal distinguishes between nations that deal with immigrants as individuals, or as cultural minorities. The latter strategy tends to create a structure of immigrant organizations that are viewed as representing the interests of immigrants. Soysal also distinguishes between states that deal with immigrants through a centrally organized and formal system, or through decentralized local voluntary or public agencies.

Soysal finds significant commonalities among many nations. Borrowing liberally from the analytical framework developed by sociologist John W. Meyer (see, e.g., Meyer, Boli, Thomas, & Ramirez, 1997), Soysal finds a worldwide convergence among the concepts of citizenship. Where citizenship becomes "post-national," peoples' rights are not defined by the nation-state, but are universal rights granted to citizens qua *individuals*. In this context, European countries are facing substantial international pressure to grant universal rights to their immigrant populations. These pressures are epitomized by the development of an international corpus of *fundamental rights*, reflected in the European Convention of Human Rights.

Soysal's argument is illustrated by examining the rights that were granted to "guest workers" in Europe during the post-war period. During the 1950s and early 1970s, Northwestern European nations experienced significant economic growth and were in need of extra labor because of their high dependency ratios, meaning the number of retired and elderly persons to employed workers was high. A common strategy for addressing this problem, for assumed short periods of time, was to enter into bilateral agreements with other countries for guest workers. However, many guest workers decided to remain in their host countries and have progressively obtained legal status, as well as gaining the civil and social rights that were equal to those of native citizens. Soysal's notion of citizenship closely resembles a view by T. H. Marshall (1992)—citizenship is internally inclusive, and involves having rights and making claims about these rights. In contrast to Marshall, though, Soysal claims that civil and social rights are no longer located at the national level, but rather invested in a concept of universal "personhood," and thus announcing the advent of a "post national model of membership" (Soysal, 1994, p. 3).

Two "transnational" sources of post-national membership are found in Soysal's argument. First, there are "universalistic rules and conceptions regarding the rights of the individual" (Soysal, 1994, p. 145). Second, there is a growing number of interdependence between international and transnational political structures which "constrain the host states from dispensing with migrant population at will" (Soysal, 1994, p. 144). Though nation-states are still responsible for "providing and implementing individual rights" (Soysal, 1994, p. 143), their "legitimacy for these rights now lies in a transnational order" (Soysal, 1994).

Also, Soysal argues that "rights" and "identity" are tenuously related, because rights have become institutionalized as human rights on a global level, and make citizenship a challenge. In contrast, identities remain specifically defined because national identity has to compete with other types of identity. While rights are "defined and legitimated at the transnational level" (Soysal, 1997, p. 512), identities are proliferating and challenging the classical definition of national identity and "authorising ethnic nationalisms and non-ethnic subcultures of various sorts (youth, feminist, gay and lesbian, and deaf culture)" (Soysal, 1997, p. 513). These are Soysal's main contributions.

Soysal's argument leaves us at an impasse—where do we go from here in describing citizenship and identity in a liberal society? If rights are universal, while identities are specific, what, exactly, is the meaning of integrating immigrants?

Kymlicka: Diversity and Minority Rights

Kymlicka (1995) aims to reconcile citizenship with ethnic diversity by supplementing the traditional notions of human rights with a theory of minority rights. Kymlicka argues that modern democracies must ensure the fair recognition of different cultures by reforming their institutions and providing individuals with the means of cultivating and transmitting their cultural differences.

Kymlicka challenges the liberal concept of individualism by noting that liberal values stress a non-individualistic concept—the management of cultural minority groups. He questions the presumed neutrality of the liberal state and argues that liberal Western democracies can never be completely neutral. Indeed, state neutrality is a myth, and, in reality, it conceals the state's granting privileges to its majority group. For example, "the state can (and should) replace religious oaths in courts with secular oaths, but it cannot replace the use of English in courts with no language" (Kymlicka, 1995, p. 111). Not recognizing minority cultures leads directly to their discrimination and exclusion within liberal democracies. As a result, Kymlicka favors the promotion of collective rather than individual rights so that minority cultures may enjoy equal recognition.

Kymlicka's multicultural citizenship is particularistic, stressing the deficiencies of generalized citizenship rights for national and ethnic minority groups. However, his argument is a liberal viewpoint because, in pursuing a view of equality and freedom, it grants rights to "societal cultures" which then frames the context for individual free choice; an important liberal concept. A societal culture is defined as "synonymous with 'a nation' or 'a people'—that is, as an intergenerational community, more or less institutionally complete, occupying a given territory or homeland, sharing a distinct language and history" (Kymlicka, 1995, p. 18). Accordingly, the modern state, which tends to be multinational, must ensure access for all its inhabitants to *their* societal culture.

In order to explain the complexities of cultural and ethnic pluralism, Kymlicka distinguishes national minorities from immigrants. Immigrants are generally expected to "participate within the public institutions of the dominant culture" (Kymlicka, 1995, p. 14) and are not supposed to be "asking for a parallel society" (Kymlicka, 1995, p. 15). Immigrants' demands for accommodation and recognition of their religion and ethnicity are made so they can better integrate into the host society. In Kymlicka's terminology, immigrants should be granted "polyethnic" rights—for example, exemptions from the law, funding of ethnic minority associations, anti-discrimination policies, and changes to the educational curricula. National minorities and indigenous groups, however, usually put forward claims for territorial and/or political autonomy and should be accorded "self-governmental" rights and, in certain case[s] of historical exclusion of disadvantaged groups, special representation rights that are seen as "corollary to self-government rights" (Kymlicka, 1995d, p. 32).

In the liberal paradigm, culture is paramount for the *individual* and not for a given culture. Kymlicka argues that liberal democracies should promote "external protections" against discrimination for ethnic and religious minority cultures. Liberal states also should concomitantly reject "internal restrictions" (Kymlicka, 1995, p. 37) in order to ensure that the fundamental freedoms and basic liberties of individuals are not endangered at the intragroup level.

To summarize, Kylmicka's (1995) analysis is important for normative theory because it espouses three key elements. To begin with, multicultural citizenship promotes state recognition of many cultures. Second, multiculturalism is a contemporary invention specific to liberal democratic societies that have witnessed the transformation of "cultural differences" into an issue of "social justice." Supporters of the multicultural ideal argue that it is not enough to simply recognize the equality of individuals in their *similarity;* one also must recognize the equality of their *differences.* Third, multicultural citizenship implies institutional changes and an active role of public authorities in providing individuals with the means for cultivating and transmitting their cultural differences.

Criticisms of Multiculturalism

Multiculturalism has its critics. For opponents of multicultural citizenship, it is this idea of giving collective rights to cultural groups that seems to be problematic (see, e.g., Barry, 2002; Fourest, 2009; Ollier, 2004; Sartori, 2003; Taguieff, 2005). Giving specific equal rights and privileges to certain minorities does not guarantee civic equality between *individuals,* but promotes equality between different *ethnic groups.* By recognizing the legitimacy of collective cultural rights, multicultural policies may run the risk of reinforcing communitarianism and restricting individual freedoms. Also, there is the pessimistic view that such policies would drive citizens into their different cultural identities and lead to an endless fragmentation of society and eventually to its dissolution.

There are three criticisms of multicultural citizenship. First, giving collective rights to cultural groups is a form of "cultural" bias. By considering cultures as homogeneous, one can overestimate the stability and reproduction of cultures, while underestimating cultural evolution and its capacity to adapt to different situations. Cultures actually become subjects of complex processes of *acculturation* (Cuche, 2004, Chapter 4). Second, multicultural theories also tend to ignore the *individual.* Individuals are never the passive reflection of culture, but, on the contrary, they are able to interpret cultural legacies in new social contexts (Cuche, 2004, Chapter 6). Human identity extends beyond the field of culture, which means that individual identity is not primarily cultural, but takes shape at the intersection of different circles of belonging and socialization which vary on many criteria such as age, sex, residency, education level, and professional activity. Finally, multiculturalism tends to *essentialize* cultures—that is, to assign them a proper existence.

It is necessary to distinguish between cultural differences and social inequalities. The issue of identity tends to hide fundamental power relations. What may matter most is not the need of belonging to a cultural community, but rather the processes of social exclusion and domination. This view is supported by Jean-François Bayart (1996), who asserts that global cultural identification processes and identity claims do not result from any actual increase in cultural diversity, but in fact hide social relations of inequality and domination; and thus represent an "illusion of cultural identity." In contrast to Samuel Huntington (1996) and Benjamin Barber (1996), who theorize about the development of civilizational consciousness and identity, Bayart (1996) asserts that politics and power relations override cultural factors. In this sense, particular cultural affiliations are not primordial, but rather reflect a social stratification system, while identity affirmation becomes a strategy to achieve prosperity and social prestige. Consequently, if cultural diversity is not the problem, multicultural citizenship is not the solution.

For a variety of reasons there has been a retreat from multicultural policies. A list, though not exhaustive, of these reasons includes the following—

- Many socioeconomic reasons, such economic crises
- The emergence of right-wing groups that fuel anti-Islamic hatred
- The threat to national identity
- The chronic lack of public support for multicultural policies
- A new assertiveness of the nation-state in implementing centrist policies of civic integration with respect to immigrants

Moreover, many tend to denounce multicultural citizenship as a strategy that has not only prevented the integration of minority groups, but also which has led to "Islamization" of Western societies. Multiculturalism prevents the emergence of a national identity and leads to a cultural relativism that is harmful for social cohesion.

Re-Nationalizing Citizenship

Programs and Tests for Citizenship

Integration programs and tests have proliferated in Europe since the beginning of the 21st century. Between 2002 and 2008, Austria, Belgium, Denmark, France, Germany, the Netherlands, and the United Kingdom have introduced language and integration tests as a condition for naturalization. In order to become citizens, candidates for naturalization must demonstrate sufficient language competences and knowledge of their host state. These policies reflect an association between citizenship, national sovereignty, and the cultural self-interpretation of a political community.

The legal counter-reactions to the cultural diversity brought on by immigrants may be interpreted as an attempt by much of Europe at defending its cultures. Moreover, they appear to be indicators of much confusion and anxiety in Western liberal democracies about the meaning of national identity in the wake of globalization and their own internal differentiation. Further, they reflect the politics of turning citizenship into a tool for national integration and represent a process of "culturalizing" immigration rules in which culture increasingly becomes an essential factor for the selection of immigrants. In Dora Kostakopoulou's words:

> Multiculturalism and the politics of recognition have been superseded by a model of integration that shifts the attention away from issues such as equal treatment, non-discrimination and social inclusion towards conditional sociopolitical membership, the preservation of core national norms and values and towards social cohesion. In the eyes of government elites, social cohesion, national unity and belonging can be bolstered by requiring migrants to learn to speak the language of the host state and by re-educating them so that they embrace a country's history and institutions, its values and the national way of life. (Kostakopoulou, 2010, p. 1)

Social cohesion and national identity are important. Security concerns, terrorist attacks, the introduction of obligatory civic integration courses, and tests for newcomers all may be explained as attempts in promoting social cohesion and national unity. The assumption is that a society with too much diversity may lose its solidarity, whereas social stability is the result of a culturally homogenous population (Macedo, 2007). Historically, the host state adapted to immigrants and to support their settlement. Currently, however, it is the responsibility of immigrants to acculturate or assimilate.

Thin and Thick Conceptions of Citizenship

One can see a shift from a "thin" liberal conception of citizenship, in which citizenship is simply a legal status and where complete national identity is not required, to a "thicker" communitarian notion of citizenship with a solid and coherent identity that has been established by the majority culture. In this communitarian model of citizenship, the state personifies the national community and it has the responsibility of determining who may enter and reside in its territory. Whereas in the liberal model naturalization is seen as a right, and should be easily available to all long-term residents (Bauböck, 1994, p. 102); in the communitarian model, naturalization is complex and involves assimilating. In a communitarian society, not only must immigrants adopt and share the behavior and rules of the host society, but they also must prove an adequate level of loyalty prior to becoming citizens. Citizenship in a communitarian model is an "end point" of an integration process (Entzinger, 2004).

In a communitarian model, language tests are legitimate because language is a determining element of national identity (Neuman, 1994, p. 264). In thinking about communitarian social systems, Kostakopoulou remarked that "resident aliens must learn and appreciate the traditions and values of the majority community, and must earn their membership by showing commitment and working hard in order to familiarize themselves with the constitutional history and the nation's traditions" (Kostakopoulou, 2003, p. 102). The content of a citizenship test may thus include more than simple questions about a national political system and its Constitution, but also questions concerning history, values, and mores.

Since the end of the 1990s, citizenship and integration programs have proliferated throughout Europe. For example, Germany introduced *Integrationskurse* (which are partly based on the Dutch model), France launched *Contrats d'accueil et d'intégration*, and Austria implemented *Integrationvereinbarungen*. Integration programs and tests are a necessary intermediary step, not only for becoming a citizen, but also for obtaining long-term residence. Undoubtedly, these efforts are partly the result from the 9/11 terrorist attacks in America. Western liberal states fear that they have failed in adequately integrating their immigrant populations. There is a feeling that immigrant integration is not simply the outcome of informal socialization and long-term residence, but must be fostered, supervised, and—in the case of integration failure—penalized by specific state policies.

THE PARADOX OF UNIVERSALISM

The Neo-Liberal Paradox

Attempts at creating identity and citizenship as universal concepts by liberal nations have created a paradox. Christian Joppke (2010a) concedes that in order to make citizens of immigrants, states require them to adopt their host society's national identity. Traditionally, national identity has been rooted in a nation's normative structure: language, mores, traditions, and customs. However, Joppke's argument is that by trying to "bind immigrants into a particular nation-state" (Joppke ,2010a, p. 33), Western democracies are getting caught in the *paradox of universalism*: national particularisms that ethnic minorities and immigrants are being asked to adopt and respect are local versions of the universalistic idiom of liberal democracy: a universal identity rooted in the liberal-democratic creed. Their inability to define a distinctively common identity is due to their inability at finding specific answers to the kind of identity expected from immigrants. "Citizenship identity," then, is a universalistic notion of political liberalism.

Why does this paradox of universalism exist? The answer lies in the liberal character of the Western states. Political liberalism is founded on the principles of *individual autonomy* and *state neutrality*. Such principles, in Rawls' words, distinguish between law and morals that lead to the compatibility of many competing conceptions of the good life ("comprehensive doctrines" in Rawls' terminology) within the existence of a "well-ordered society." According to this ideal of a neutral state, "nation or nationalism" cannot integrate a liberal society:

> The hope of political community must indeed be abandoned, if by such community we mean a political society united in affirming a general and comprehensive doctrine. This possibility is excluded by the fact of pluralism together with the rejection of the oppressive use of state power to overcome it. (Rawls, 1987, p. 10)

This is another way of saying that social unity in a liberal democracy cannot be derived from a notion of the national "good," but only through a consensus on the "rights" that should accrue to each individual. The bonds that tie people to the political community cannot be substantive and thick, but only procedural and thin. Otherwise, individuals could not be free: "It is precisely because we are free and independent selves, capable of choosing our own end, that we need a framework of rights that is neutral among ends" (Sandel, 1994, p. 1769). In a complex liberal society, characterized by significant differentiation, and in which constitutional principles are paramount, it is impossible to define a distinctive sense of collective identity. Or, if such a collective identity may be found, it is bound to be a shared consensus on a minimal amount of rights. As Jonathan Sacks puts it, the liberal state "is a system in which politics makes no claim to embody the true, the beautiful and the good. Political involvement promises neither salvation nor redemption; it claims merely to keep the peace between contending parties" (Sacks, 2007, p. 221).

In the liberal state, there is a need for a common minimum consensus ("overlapping consensus") about a set of rights and freedoms that determine the manner in which a society addresses its many conflicts. Thus, within a liberal political regime, what is *right* must override what is *good*, and the state must remain neutral towards the incommensurable moral choices of each individual (Rawls, 1993).

Citizenship tests in Europe may assess future citizens' cognitive knowledge, but may not scrutinize their "inner dispositions." In other words, citizenship tests are liberal, in the Rawlsian sense, because they concentrate on basic rights and freedoms, the political system, and factual knowledge of "what is right." However, it should not assess issues about "what is good."

Accordingly, being devoid of any particular cultural content, citizenship tests in liberal democracies tend to converge towards a single universalistic model. Some brief examples might help.

In Britain for example, this paradox of universalism is particularly visible in the government statements of what it means to be British:

> To be British seems to us to mean that we respect the laws, the elected parliamentary and democratic political structures, traditional values of mutual tolerance, respect for equal rights and mutual concern; and that we give our allegiance to the state (as commonly symbolised in the Crown) in return for its protection. To be British is to respect those over-arching specific institutions, values, beliefs and traditions that bind us all, the different nations and cultures together in peace and in a legal order. (Home Office, 2004, p. 15)

Obviously, except for "the Crown," this definition of the essence of "Britishness" is actually shared by most liberal democracies. Respecting the democratic political structure and the rule of law is not a specific British feature; it is British just as it is Dutch, French, or German. Consequently, Joppke rightly argues that:

> The British state, like all Western states trying to upgrade citizenship for the purpose of more successful immigrant integration, is caught in the paradox of universalism: it perceives the need to make immigrants and ethnic minorities parts of *this* and not of *any* society, but it cannot name and enforce any particulars that distinguish the "here" from "there." (Joppke, 2010a, p. 130)

Another illustration of this paradox of universalism is the new Australian citizenship test that was introduced in October 2007. In Australia the citizenship test resembles the test of other Western European states: growing security concerns about domestic Islamic terrorism, the need to reassure Australian citizens about immigration, and a crisis of the multicultural ideology. Surprisingly, a major factor that explains the use of the citizenship test in Australia was the bombing of the London Underground in July 2005 (Cheng, 2009).

As is the case in Western Europe, citizenship in Australia is viewed "as a privilege, not a right." Accordingly, the acquisition of "English skills" and "understanding the Australian way of life and our shared values" are deemed essential elements for immigrants to acquire citizenship in Australia (Australian Government, 2006, p. 5). However, the Australian citizenship test exhibits the typical liberal inability of offering anything but universalistic views about "Australian values" which newcomers are expected to adopt. Although obtaining Australian citizenship is defined as "joining a distinct national community" (Australian Government, 2007, p. 1), the main "Australian values" that have to be adopted by candidates for citizenship are "freedom of religion and secular government," "respect for the equal worth, dignity and freedom of the individual," "freedom of speech," "equality under the law," and "support for parliamentary democracy and the rule of law" (Australian Government, 2007, p. 5). As Cheng puts it, Australian national values are nothing but "the liberal values of democracy, freedom of religion, freedom of speech, and the equality of men and women" (Cheng, 2009, p. 62). These are values shared by all liberal democracies.

In France, in contrast to Britain, there seems to be a clear sense of national identity. Such an identity is associated with the Republican civic ideology, which stresses generalized political rights and civic equality. However, Republicanism is *framed in universalistic terms*, and French symbols (such as the flag, the national anthem, *Marianne*, etc.), are all symbols of human rights. As Todd appropriately states, French Republican particularism is enabled (fortunately for France) by the specific circumstance that "our particularism is universalism" (Todd, 1994, p. 194).

The common solution to the problems of national identity and cultural integration in Europe today seems to be the one pioneered by Republican France; to be national is defined in universalistic principles of democracy, liberty, respect for human rights and fundamental freedoms, and the rule of law. Consequently, a worldwide "review of state pronouncements of what it means to be 'French,' 'British,' or 'Dutch' reveals them all to be identical. In sum, citizenship identities... have become universalistic." (Joppke, 2010a, p. 33)

Liberalism as Identity

Universalism can be particularistic and exclusive. William Galston (1995) and John Gray (2000) remind us that liberalism has always had two different sides: one that limits itself to noninterference and toleration, and that allows many diverse ways of life to coexist peacefully without the presumption of overarching common values; and a second view that prescribes reason and autonomy over faith and heteronomy, and thus enables the achievement of the best way of life for all humankind.

Trapped in a paradox of a specific identity, which seems necessary for integration and yet cannot be supplied because of the commitment to universalism, Western states call upon a certain idea of liberalism. While the tolerant version of liberalism prevailed during the period of multiculturalism in the past few decades, episodes of Islamic terrorism are seen as reasons for replacing a multicultural paradigm with a variant of liberalism. The new liberalism prescribes a shared way of life, a potential identity that separates illiberal from liberal people. By displaying aggressive integrationist policies, it resembles what Triadafilos Triadafilopoulos calls a "Schmittian" liberalism that "aims to clarify the core values of liberal societies and use coercive state power to protect them from illiberal and putatively dangerous groups" (Triadafilopoulos, 2011, p. 863).

In the Netherlands, the change from multiculturalism to assimilation has expanded from an institutional *modus vivendi* (Gray, 2000) to a way of life based on a "thick" liberal identity. Accordingly, the Dutch require that newcomers adopt and share a "progressive" liberal attitude, which stresses gender equality, the acceptance of homosexuality, and the marginalization and privatization of religiosity. The message is that the Netherlands is a progressive and liberal society.

A second illustration of liberal exclusion is the decision taken in June 2008 by the highest French administrative court, the *Conseil d'État*, which confirmed the denial of citizenship to Faiza Silmi, a *niqab*-wearing woman. The *Conseil d'État* recognized that Silmi "possessed a good mastery of the French language," and that she had a French husband as well as three French-born children. Nonetheless, the denial of citizenship was based on Silmi's "insufficient assimilation"[2] into the French Republic, and was legitimated by the fact that she had adopted "a radical practice of her religion, incompatible with the essential values of the French community, especially the principle of the equality of sexes."[3] The *Conseil d'État* referred to a recent modification in the French Civil Code which stipulates that "the government may, on grounds of indignity or lack of assimilation other than linguistic, oppose the acquisition of French nationality by foreign spouse," and that "no one may be naturalized unless he proves his assimilation in the French community."[4] This was the first time that the *Conseil d'État* refused to grant citizenship on the basis of religious expression, and—paradoxically—the court invoked a fundamental liberal principle, sex equality, in order to undermine another core liberal norm, freedom of religion. Therefore, the court took an illiberal decision in order to protect liberal identity.

In contrast with liberal multiculturalism, repressive liberalism sees "the task of immigrant integration as part of a broader campaign to preserve 'Western civilisation' from illiberal threats, particularly those based on 'fundamentalist Islam'" (Triadafilopoulos, 2011, p. 863). Echoing older strains of liberalism, and associated with a colonialist vision that established the superiority of Europeans and their way of life, this new "enlightened fundamentalism" (Fekete, 2006) views the preservation of liberal regimes as sufficient ground for pursuing aggressive and coercive measures. Thus, nations pursue illiberal policies in order to preserve what it perceives as an endangered Western civilization.

Liberal Versus Illiberal Citizenship Tests

As discussed above, liberalism can transmute into an identity and become exclusive. It also can become repressive and illiberal. In order to avoid this illiberal bias, citizenship tests in Western liberal democracies, which are inspired by the logic of political liberalism, should be conceived in a way so they are not *intrusive*. Liberal citizenship tests should abandon their focus on "moral obligations," and focus on "legal commitments." Such a test should concentrate on the "external" respect for core constitutional principles, such as democracy and human dignity, and not on the "internal" perceptions of applicants. Immigrants seeking citizenship should demonstrate knowledge and understanding of the state's fundamental constitutional principles and accept and respect them as the law of the land, but they are not morally required to be in agreement with these laws. After all, liberalism also includes the freedom to choose *not* to be liberal, as long as one's way of life is democratic and legal.

As an example of a repressive liberal policy, consider the *Gesprächsleit-faden*, which were issued by the regional *Land* government of Baden-Württemberg in September 2005. The test inquires about the "true" beliefs and values of an applicant for citizenship, and inadmissible as a true liberal policy. Even if it focuses on the fundamental rules and principles of liberal democracy, by touching the intimate sphere of the person, it raises many doubts about its compatibility with the principles of equality, freedom of religion and expression, and especially of freedom of thought. As the legal commentators Wolfrum and Röben put it, "the mere holding of an opinion is no threat to the liberal democratic order, if it is not expressed in concrete actions that are directed against this order" (Wolfrum & Röben, 2006, p. 15).

It is a fundamental principle of liberalism that public policy and law may not regulate the "inner motivations" of people, but only their "external behavior." The threshold of unacceptability is exceeded whenever citizenship tests transgress "the thin line that separates the regulation of behavior from the control of beliefs" (Joppke, 2010b, p. 3). As David Miller puts it:

> Liberal states do not require their citizens to *believe* liberal principles, since they tolerate communists, anarchists, fascists, and so forth. What they require is that citizens should conform to liberal principles in practice and accept as legitimate policies that are pursued in the name of such principles, while they are left to advocate alternative arrangements. (Miller, 2004, p. 14)

The border between liberal and illiberal citizenship tests within Western liberal democracies lies in the Kantian distinction between "legality" and "morality." Legal commitments involve recognition, respect, and acceptance of a state's constitutional principles, while moral obligations imply adherence and identification with these principles. The former can be required in the process of obtaining citizenship, while the latter are illiberal policies, since they convey the idea that the liberal democratic state is only reserved for liberal people. Thus, we have a paradox of universalism.

CONSTITUTIONAL PATRIOTISM

Theoretical Foundations

Joppke (2010a) argues that contemporary nation-building is limited by non-discriminatory norms and liberal equality, so national identity cannot be imposed on people in liberal states. Consequently, the political will to renationalize citizenship in Western liberal democracies has failed, while liberal citizenship identities, which cannot be reproduced in nationally distinctive manners, have become "universalistic."[5] Nonetheless, liberal citizenship identity can be exclusive, expressing the view that only liberal people may enter and reside in the liberal community (which is a profoundly illiberal idea).

In this potentially repressive liberal context, the paradox of universalism has challenged Western liberal democracies seeking to reinvent national identity. European states face the fact that renationalizing citizenship identity is impossible, and that decoupling national identity and citizenship is the only viable solution for integrating immigrants. As Joppke puts it, "the decoupling of citizenship and nationhood in plural societies is the incontrovertible exist position for contemporary state campaigns for unity and integration, especially with respect to immigrants" (Joppke, 2010a, p. 143).

What other framework would be useful for Western liberal states? Constitutional patriotism is a concept which argues that the association between citizenship and national identity is the result of history and empirical contingencies, and that it is possible for them to be separated.

Jürgen Habermas (1992) has developed a perspective that decouples politics and culture; he argues that social bonds in a liberal society should be political and juridical rather than historical and cultural. The motives for becoming attached to a political community should be universalistic and not particularistic.[6] Accordingly, any blind identification with an inanimate object, such as a nation, becomes anathema; democratic citizenship does not require a national identity, but only a *shared political culture.*

The relationship between citizenship and national identity gives rise to a common sense of belonging and to the emergence of democratic citizenship (Habermas, 1992). There is a "circular process" of mutual reinforcement that unites these two elements: the common feeling of belonging has facilitated the establishment of democracy which, in turn, has strengthened solidarity between citizens. In a democracy, it is political participation, and the principles that justify this participation, that create the social bonds between societal members rather than belonging to the same cultural entity. Habermas stresses that these two dimensions of the nation-state may be potentially contradictory: the political and legal dimension are based on universal principles and reflected in the institutions of the democratic state, while the national dimension is affective and particularistic (Habermas, 1998).

These two dimensions explain the dual aspects of a nation-state. In a democracy, the rule of law and the welfare state are derived from universalistic principles, and nationalism justifies invasions, exclusions, and oppressions. It is because of the lucid understanding of the historical link between nationalism and citizenship, that Habermas developed his theory of constitutional patriotism. His theory refers to a sense of belonging that is no longer based on a common cultural identity, but rather on universal constitutional principles. Such allegiance is political rather than cultural, since it is based on the ideals of democracy and the rule of law. Allegiance is rational rather than primordial.

Western liberal states should abandon their efforts at promoting "national values," which are culturally based, and should turn to constitutional patriotism and its fundamental constitutional principles. This is the only way for Western liberal democracies to be *consistent* with their liberal principles, while also recognizing, accepting, and respecting their core constitutional principles.

Constitutional Patriotism, Cultural Diversity, and European Integration

Habermas has applied the concept of constitutional patriotism to the growing cultural diversity within Western liberal societies. He deems it essential to mobilize a citizenry around the state's core constitutional principles. His conceptualization of constitutional patriotism dissociates citizenship and national identity, and allows for the coexistence of different cultures while promoting shared feelings of belonging.

This universalistic approach of integration may be very useful in the present context of rising xenophobia. Indeed, it would be beneficial to clearly distinguish between identity and citizenship when approaching the question of integrating different cultures. Contemporary liberal states should only use the language of shared political values, without attempting to complement them with communitarian references. There is no need to promote a common national identity.

Constitutional patriotism implies the full recognition of citizenship rights (civic, political, and social) to cultural and religious minorities, but not the recognition of collective rights. These collective rights are problematic in several respects: they reify cultural groups, they jeopardize and endanger the internal evolution of cultures, and there may be a contradiction between these collective rights and the fundamental freedom of the individual (Habermas, 1998). Constitutional patriotism bypasses these issues entirely.

By the end of the 1990s, Habermas believed that the process of economic globalization required the enhancement of post-national consciousness and constitutional patriotism on a Europe-wide basis (Habermas, 2000). In his view, a nation-state could not control economic globalization. It was only at the European level that globalization could be contained.

A post-national perspective implies that it is possible and desirable to develop social and democratic institutions at the European level. However, the institutions should not be based on a common European identity, but rather on political principles. Habermas denounces the opponents of building a Europe because they mobilize a "national-communitarian" rhetoric, which establishes an intrinsic link between nation and citizenship. On the contrary, he claims that the absence of a European nation is not in itself a barrier to political European integration (Habermas, 2000). Instead, post-national membership could lead to European constitutional patriotism based on political, rather than cultural, principles.

Constitutional patriotism is supposed to prevent oppression and exclusion by mobilizing citizens around democratic principles and the rule of law. Nevertheless, according to Habermas, this perspective does not imply the disappearance of national identities, but rather their reinterpretation, which involves their constant submission to the criticism of constitutional principles. Cultural aspects of social cohesion should be abandoned in favor of civic principles. National cultures would not disappear under this model, but would function as interpretation grids for universalistic principles. Moreover, cultural beliefs, mores, and values should be examined on a consistent basis.

According to Habermas, European integration is readily open to the development of this type of post-national membership. On the one hand, European nation-states have begun to develop some predispositions for post-national consciousness. The disastrous effects of nationalism during the 20th century have led to much thought about the ambivalent and dangerous aspects of "national tradition," and a critical view of national history (Habermas, 2006). On the other hand, the creation and development of the European Community and the European Union have political, rather than ethical, foundations. The European Union is already based on constitutional principles and not on a common national identity (Habermas, 2006). This process was a step toward constitutional patriotism.

Constitutional Patriotism and Citizenship Tests

Every society has a specific ethical culture that influences the interpretation of its prevailing political principles. Though ethical principles are constantly evolving, an important factor in such change is the cultural/demographic composition of the population. A society that has become plural as a result of immigration should expect its structure of ethics and its political principles to change (Habermas, 1992). However, even if this political community is open, changing, and democratic, a common political identity, shared by all citizens, is deemed essential by Habermas.

Western liberal democracies are rooted in long-standing legal frameworks and in broadly shared ideas of citizenship and national identity. Favell (2001) points out that the same ideas have different legal interpretations in different states. Universal concepts such as freedom, equality, pluralism, autonomy, and tolerance have no standard universal meaning, and they must be understood in the context of a state. In this sense, the nations' political solutions to the problem of ethnic and cultural diversity, although apparently similar in their formulation, must actually be read as *distinct and different applied versions of political liberalism.*

As Liav Orgad states, "every state has a constitutional uniqueness reflecting its history, developments, traditions, and contextual background" (Orgad, 2010, p. 99). This specific constitutional identity is not apparent if one looks at the questions of citizenship tests. Rather, national culture appears if one looks at the system *as a whole.* Orgad states, "what makes the German Constitution *German* is not any single constitutional principle, but the entire Constitution, the whole package, and the particular way Germans express and implement these principles" (Orgad, 2010, p. 100).

Immigrants should accept and adopt a state's fundamental constitutional principles before obtaining citizenship. Viewing constitutional patriotism in this manner, when looking at citizenship tests, should allow each nation-state the possibility of preserving its own history and constitutional identity. Constitutional exceptionalism, or "national constitutionalism" (Orgad, 2010), leaves room for constitutional particularity, while at the same time it is being distinguished from cultural and ethnic conceptions of citizenship. It is less universal than political liberalism (Rawls, 1993) because it does not seek to formulate universalistic principles of justice, but rather to retain the essential constitutional principles of a specific nation-state without requiring cultural nor emotional allegiance. In Orgad's words, "it is a necessary stipulation for a legal, non-emotional belonging in a particular political body" (Orgad, 2010, p. 100).

Citizenship tests in Western liberal democracies should establish whether applicants for citizenship are familiar with, and are accepting of, the essential constitutional principles of a specific nation-state. States can then formulate questions in accordance with their unique constitutional contexts. For example, one could imagine that the British citizenship test includes questions about British constitutional history and documents, such as the Glorious Revolution, the English Civil War, the Bill of Rights, the Petition of Rights, and the Magna Carta. It might also include questions about great jurists, such as William Blackstone or Edward Coke, who have had a large influence as English Law commentators. However, it should not formulate questions on issues that are not essential to British constitutional principles, such as "where does Father Christmas come from?," "what should people do if they are involved in a car accident?," or "suppose you spill someone's pint in the pub. What, according to the book, usually happens next?"[7] As Orgad puts it:

> [The British citizenship test] should set down the threshold needed to become British; this threshold needs to check whether migrants know and accept British national constitutionalism, and not whether they can spit back trivia about the Grand National or the Notting Hill Carnival. (Orgad, 2010, p. 103)

Under constitutional patriotism, citizenship tests should eliminate figures, events, principles, or values that have no or only little relation to a state's Constitution. Therefore, if a specific knowledge is normative or factually significant to a state's Constitution, it may be legitimate to require such as a condition for obtaining citizenship. In Germany for example, requiring the applicant for citizenship to have knowledge about Germany's path to democracy is legitimate because it transmits the message that applicants are seeking citizenship not of *any* community, but of the *German* political community. Indeed, constitutional patriotism is, next to language requirements, the single most important particularism that Western liberal democracies may legitimately require for citizenship. As Joppke states:

> With respect of the contents of the citizenship test, to ask for host-society language competence and knowledge of the principles and procedures of liberal democracies is an incontrovertibly legitimate core component of all citizenship tests in Europe and other Western states. And few would doubt that asking for knowledge of historical key events in a country's road to becoming a liberal democracy, along with knowledge of liberal democracy's peculiar institutional form in the respective country, is equally legitimate. (Joppke, 2010b, p. 1)

CONCLUSION

In this chapter, I have discussed the kind of citizenship identities that European states currently promote in integrating their immigrant populations. The recent proliferation of integration programs across Europe require that immigrants follow native customs and mores, including native language, as a prerequisite for acquiring citizenship status. By implementing their programs, Western states are attempting to create a culturally homogeneous population that shares the same language and mores. The simple message is that European states are dominated by one group, and it will be that group's culture that is the state's culture.

Some object to such a program. Joppke, for example, points out that such policies are narrowly limited, mainly by the principles of political liberalism. Identity cannot be legislated, and the actual content of citizenship identities fostered by states resemble the generic precepts of the universalistic idiom characterizing liberal democracy.

However, this is not to say that universalism cannot be exclusive. In fact, particular universalism is the main form in which Western liberal democracies practice exclusion. In this context, liberalism "thickens" from a procedural framework of tolerance into a substantive way of life in which diversity is accepted. This is an ethical way of life, to which immigrants are expected to conform.

In the context of "repressive liberalism," one needs to define the threshold above which states' policies become illiberal by raising cultural restrictions on immigrants and access to citizenship. I have argued that citizenship tests in Western liberal democracies should not be intrusive—that is, that public policy and law should not seek to regulate the "inner motivations" of people, but only their "external behavior."

If the liberal state wishes to remain liberal, it must admit, on one hand, that national identity cannot be legislated and, on the other hand, that it cannot force individuals to adhere and identify morally with a liberal way of life. Therefore, I have suggested that one might turn to "constitutional patriotism," which decouples citizenship from national identity. Following this logic, it is legitimate for citizenship applicants to recognize, respect, and accept a state's fundamental constitutional principles, though it is unacceptable to compel them to morally adhere with them. Furthermore, by separating civic integration from ethical integration, constitutional patriotism allows for the coexistence of diverse cultures while fostering a shared feeling of belonging. Finally, focusing on the content of the Constitution may provide a framework on how citizenship tests should be conceptualized, and offer to Western liberal democracies the possibility of preserving their own history and constitutional identity.

NOTES

1. The United Nations (2013) reports that there were 230 million migrants world-wide.
2. Interestingly, the *Conseil d'État* use the term "assimilation" rather than "acculturation." This clearly sends a signal that immigrants must become French and lose the culture of their sending country.
3. See Conseil d'État, 27 June 2008, Mme Faiza M., req. no 286798.
4. See French Civil Code, book I, title I, Ch. III, Sec. I §3 Arts. 21–24.
5. Of course, citizenship identity has become universalistic only insofar as it falls within the scope of state policy. This is an important reserve, since it is not argued, for example, that common German people do not identify Germanness with Christianity.
6. Of course, this universal attachment to the political community should not be exclusive, but inclusive. In that sense, a citizenship test inspired by the logic of constitutional patriotism should not be intrusive, as discussed in the previous section
7. These questions appear in the *Life in the UK Test*. Details on the test are available at http://lifeintheuktest.ukba.homeoffice.gov.uk/.

REFERENCES

Australian Government. (2006). *Australian citizenship: Much more than a ceremony* (Discussion Paper). Canberra, AU: Dept of Communications, Information Technology & the Arts.

Australian Government. (2007). *Becoming an Australian citizen.* Canberra, AU: Author

Barber, B. (1996). *Jihad VS McWorld: How globalism and tribalism are reshaping the world.* New York, NY: Ballantine Books.

Barry, B. (2002). *Culture and equality.* Cambridge, England: Polity.

Bauböck, R. (1994). *From aliens to citizens.* Aldershot, England: Avebury.

Bayart, J-F. (1996). *L'illusion identitaire.* Paris, France: Fayard.

Brubaker, W. R. (1989). Introduction. In R. Brubaker (Ed.), *Immigration and the politics of citizenship in Europe and North America* (pp. 1–27). Lanham, MD: University Press of America.

Brubaker, R. (1992). *Citizenship and nationhood in France and Germany.* Cambridge, MA: Harvard University Press.

Cheng, J. (2009). Promoting "national values" in citizenship tests in Germany and Australia: a response to the current discourse on Muslims? In R. Zapata-Barrero (Ed.), *Citizenship policies in the age of diversity* (pp. 53–69). Barcelona, ES: CIDOB Foundation.

Cuche, D. (2004). *La notion de culture dans les sciences sociales* Paris, France: La Découverte.

Entzinger, H. (2004). *Integration and orientation courses in a European perspective* (Expert report written for the Sachverständigenrat für Zuwanderung und Integration). Rotterdam, NL: Erasmus University.

Favell, A. (2001). *Philosophies of integration: Immigration and the idea of citizenship in France and Britain.* New York, NY: Palgrave.

Fekete, L. (2006). Enlightened fundamentalism? Immigration, feminism and the right. *Race and Class, 48*(2), 1–22.

Fourest, C. (2009). *La dernière utopie: Menaces sur l'universalisme.* Paris, France: Grasset.

Galston, W. (1995). Two Concepts of Liberalism. *Ethics, 105,* 516–534.

Gray, J. (2000). *Two faces of liberalism.* Cambridge, England: Polity Press.

Habermas, J. (1992). Citoyenneté et identité nationale: Réflexions sur l'avenir de l'Europe. In J. Lenoble & N. Dewandre, *L'Europe au soir du siècle: Identité et démocratie* (pp. 17–38). Paris, France: Esprit.

Habermas, J. (1996). The European nation-state. Its achievements and its limitations. On the past and future of sovereignty and citizenship. *Ratio Juris, 9*(2), 125–137.

Habermas, J. (1998). *L'intégration républicaine.* Paris, France: Fayard.

Habermas, J. (2000). *Après l'Etat-nation: une nouvelle constellation politique.* Paris, France: Fayard.

Habermas, J. (2006). *Sur l'Europe.* Paris, France: Bayard.

Home Office (UK). (2004). *Life in the United Kingdom: A journey to citizenship.* Norwich, England: The Stationery Office.

Huntington, S. P. (1996). *The clash of civilizations and the remaking of world order.* New York, NY: Simon and Schuster.

Joppke, C. (2010a). *Citizenship and immigration.* Cambridge, England: Polity Press.

Joppke, C. (2010b). How liberal are citizenship tests? In R. Bauböck & C. Joppke (Eds.), *How liberals are citizenship tests?* (working paper RSCAS) (pp. 1–4). Florence, IT: European University Institute.

Kymlicka, W. (1995). *Multicultural citizenship.* Oxford, England: Clarendon Press.

Kostakopoulou, D. (2003). Why naturalisation. *Perspective on European Politics and Society. 4*(1), 85–115.

Kostakopoulou, D. (2010). Introduction. In R. van Oers, E. Ersbøll, & D. Kostakopoulou (eds), *A redefinition of belonging? Language and integration tests in Europe* (pp. 1–23). Leiden, NL: Martinus Nijhoff Publishers.

Macedo, S. (2007). The moral dilemma of U.S. immigration policy: Open borders versus social justice. In C. M. Swain (Ed.), *Debating immigration* (pp. 63–81). Cambridge, England: Cambridge University Press.

Marshall, T. H., & Bottomore, T. B. (1992). *Citizenship and social class* (Vol. 2). London, England: Pluto Press.

Meyer, J., Boli, J., Thomas, G. M., & Ramirez, F. O. (1997). World society and the nation-state. *American Journal of Sociology, 103*(1), 144–181.

Miller, D. (2004). *Immigrants, nations, and citizenship.* Paper presented at the conference on Migrants, Nations, and Citizenship. New Hall, Cambridge, England, July 5–6.

Neuman, G. (1994). Justifying U.S. naturalization policies. *Virginia Journal of International Law, 35,* 237–278.

Ollier, F. (2004). *L'idéologie multiculturaliste en France.* Paris, France: L'Harmattan.

Orgad, L. (2010). Illiberal liberalism—Cultural restrictions on migration and access to citizenship in Europe. *The American journal of comparative law, 58,* 53–106.

Rawls, J. (1987). The idea of an overlapping consensus. *Oxford journal of legal studies,* 7(1), 1–23.

Rawls, J. (1993). *Political liberalism.* New York, NY: Columbia University Press.

Sacks, J. (2007). *The home we build together.* London, England: Continuum.

Sartori, G. (2003). *Pluralisme, multiculturalisme et* étrangers. Paris, France: Editions des Syrtes.

Sandel, M. (1994). Review of political liberalism, *Harvard Law Review, 107,* 1765–1794.

Soysal, Y. (1994). *Limits of citizenship: Migrants and postnational membership in Europe.* Chicago, IL: University of Chicago Press.

Soysal, Y. (1997). Changing parameters of citizenship and claims-making: Organized Islam in European public spheres. *Theory and Society. 26*(4), 509–527.

Taguieff, P-A. (2005). *La* république *enlisée: Pluralisme, communautarisme et citoyenneté.* Paris, France: Editions des Syrtes.

Todd, E. (1994). *Le destin des immigrés.* Paris, France: Seuil.

Triadafilopoulos, T. (2011). Illiberal means to liberal ends? Understanding recent immigration integration policies in Europe. *Journal of Ethic and Migration Studies. 37*(6), 861–880.

Wolfrum, R., & Röben, V. (2006). *Gutachten zur Vereinbarkeit des Gesprächsleitfaden für die Einbürgerungsbehörden des Landes Baden-Württemberg mit Völkerrecht* (discussion paper). Heidelberg, DE.

PART II

NATIONAL IDENTITY: CASE STUDIES

CHAPTER 3

THE IDIOSYNCRASIES OF SCOTTISH NATIONAL IDENTITY

Nathalie Duclos

"I'm a Scotsman!" replied Sean Connery when asked if he was Irish, so strong is his Scottish identity. In Scotland and throughout the United Kingdom, it is a widely shared belief that Scotland is a nation with its own identity, an identity which even has its own name: "Scottishness." Although Scotland is part of the United Kingdom, its status as a nation is not contested. British recognition of the UK's multinational nature makes relationships between the different British nations rather different from other multinational states, such as Spain or Belgium. As noted by Dodds and Seawright, "the debate in Scotland is not over the existence of the Scottish nation. . . . All the political parties assume that the Scottish nation exists and will play the 'Scottish card' to varying degrees—although their readings of Scottishness may vary" (Dodds & Seawright, 2004, p. 91). The aim of this chapter is to explore the varied "readings of Scottishness," through the idiosyncrasies of Scottish national identity.

My central argument developed is that from a European point of view, Scottish national identity and, by the same token, nationalism present some

National Identity, pages 83–112
Copyright © 2016 by Information Age Publishing

rather unorthodox characteristics. Firstly, while a national identity is generally defined in opposition to an "Other," which is its rival for people's national loyalty, Scottishness is often characterized as being part of, or complementary to, Scottish people's other national identity: the British one. Moreover, Scottishness is even described as shaping Britishness and being shaped by it. Secondly, in Scotland there is no obvious correlation between national identity, constitutional preferences, and party preferences. A strong feeling of national identity does not indicate a desire to see Scotland become an independent state.

All political parties in Scotland use a Scottish-national frame of reference, and Scottish national identity finds expression in both nationalism and unionism, in both pro- and anti-independence movements. However, one party has greatly contributed to the politicization of Scottish identity, namely the Scottish National Party which is why this chapter will analyze the SNP's nationalism and its views on identity and citizenship. The SNP's nationalism can appear in some respects to be rather unusual, in that the party does not present Scottish independence as signifying the end of a common British national identity, nor does it argue that the aim of independence is to give political recognition to Scottish national identity. Moreover, the SNP does not emphasize such commonly shared national features as a common language or religion. So, a better understanding of Scottish national identity one needs to grasp the SNP's role on this topic. This chapter of mine is a case study of these issues.

NATIONAL IDENTITY IN SCOTLAND: IS IT UNPROBLEMATIC?

In answer to the question, "Is Scotland a country?" a geographical magazine humorously noted that:

> Scotland is as much of a country as England; more of a country than Wales, which is a principality; far more of a country than Ulster, which is a province; but less of a country than the United Kingdom, which is a sovereign state, and hence, unlike Scotland, able to pass the final test and compete in the Eurovision Song Contest. (Geographical Magazine, 1993)

If Scotland can be called a country, it is not a state: It has not been an independent state since 1707, when it was united with England to form the United Kingdom of Great Britain. Nevertheless, inside the UK, Scotland is almost unanimously considered to be a separate nation, as are England and Wales. Scotland's status as a nation is very uncontroversial in the UK.

Scotland's status as a nation *within* a wider state is equally uncontroversial; rather it is the UK's status that has been under question in recent years.[1] Several phrases have been coined to convey Scotland's particular nature as a nation within a state. The phrase "stateless nation" (Leruez, 1983), first coined in 1983 by Jacques Leruez, was later popularized by leading Scottish scholars, such as David McCrone (1992), Michael Keating (1996), or T. M. Devine (2003). Scottish political thinker Tom Nairn prefers to describe Scotland as a "state-nation," a phrase which allows him to stress that Scotland was a state before becoming a nation: "Scotland itself had been a state long before turning into a nation in [the] modern sense. It was (as it remains today) a state-nation, not the other way round" (Nairn, 2000, p. 121).[2]

Why is Scotland's status as a nation viewed as unproblematic inside the UK? It could be argued that there are *three* interlinked reasons for this. First of all, Scotland has at its disposal many symbols that are internationally seen as national identity markers. It has its own flag (the "Saltire") or even two flags, if one also counts the red and yellow Lion Rampant, a patron saint (St Andrew), a national day (St Andrew's Day), an emblem (the thistle), national sports teams, and even unofficial national anthems that sports fans sing during "international" matches. It also has a national capital, Edinburgh, where the National Library of Scotland, the National Museum of Scotland, and the Scottish National Gallery are located. Last but not least, Scotland's borders are uncontested and have not changed in centuries.

Secondly, the idea that Scotland has been a nation since the Middle Ages is very controversial, but it is a view which many historians have defended. In 1969, H. J. Hanham claimed that "Scotland has possessed all the characteristics of a distinct nation since the twelfth century" (Hanham, 1969, p. 15). In his history of Scotland, Michael Lynch stated that "before there was a kingdom, in the sense of a consolidated territory, there was a people and an intensely felt pride in being Scots" (Lynch, 1999, p. xiii). Even more clearly, he argued that a "sense of Scottish nationhood" was sharpened as early as the late 13th century by England's "attempt to erect an English empire throughout the British Isles," which "galvanise[d] the Scottish Kirk into a church militant and force[d] its 'multinational' nobility to decide where their first loyalties la[id]" (Lynch, 1999, p. xiv). In his Oxford Companion to Scottish history, Michael Lynch, in the entry "national identity," starts with the following warning: "It is anachronistic to talk of national identities in the early Middle Ages" (p. 437). However, he then goes on to say that "[n]ational identities are often reformulations of older identities, so it is appropriate to ask when and how Scottish identity first came into being, long before this became anything which may be recognized as a national identity" (p. 437). The part of the same entry on early medieval Scotland concludes on the idea that a "specifically and distinctly Scottish identity for the kingship" could be found from the end of the 13th century (p. 438). The part on late medieval Scotland notes that:

> [C]ollective self-awareness...is not necessarily the same as national consciousness and identity. In so far as the latter presupposes, not just a shared sense of the past, but also a community of language, culture, custom, and law, late medieval Scotland was only just beginning to acquire the defining characteristics of nationhood. (Lynch, 2001, p. 439)

Not all historians believe that Scottish national identity can be traced back to the Middle Ages. Modernization theorists like Ernest Gellner argue that nations are artificial, manufactured constructs that came into being in the era of industrialization in the late 18th and the 19th centuries, and rejects both the idea that they are natural and timeless and the idea that they are ancient and rooted in history. However, while recognizing the importance of factors linked to modernization other theorists, such as Anthony D. Smith, believe that nations could not have been created out of nothing in the 19th century, and argue that most European nations find their roots in *ethnies* (or ethnic communities) which took shape in the Middle Ages.

Whatever Scotland's status in the Middle Ages, most historians would agree that it was a nation as well as an independent state by the time that it united with England. The Treaty of Union which both kingdoms agreed to in 1707 led to the creation of a new state called the United Kingdom of Great Britain. This union saw the closure of the Scottish and English Parliaments and the birth of the British Parliament. It was also an economic union which gave Scotland access to the English market and to the English colonies. However, most historians argue that the terms of the Treaty allowed Scotland to remain a separate society and therefore to keep its distinct national identity.

It is undeniable that the Scots retained crucial forms of institutional and social identity, most notably their own Church (the Church of Scotland, or "Kirk") and religion (Presbyterianism), their own educational system (at all levels), their own legal system, and their own banking system. In the views of the vast majority of Scottish scholars, the survival of these autonomous institutions, especially the so-called "holy trilogy" of religion, law, and education, created an enduring sense of Scottish identity despite its integration into the United Kingdom. In attempting to identify how Scotland was distinct from the rest of the UK, H. J. Hanham noted:

> Today the Scots have their own national church, their own national education system, their own national legal system, their own national banking system, their own national system of central and local government, their own national way of speaking English—even their own Scottish Trades Union Congress. (Hanham, 1969, p. 15)

To Hanham, the breath of Scotland's distinctiveness meant that Scotland was more than a nation: It was a "state within the wider state of the United

Kingdom of Great Britain and Northern Ireland" (p. 15). Most would disagree with him on that point; however, his assertion illustrates the extent to
which it is generally believed that Scotland has remained different from the
rest of the UK. To illustrate Scotland's distinctiveness today, modern scholars mention the trinity of law, religion, and education, the system of administrative devolution that developed after the establishment of the Scottish
Office (in 1885), and those civil society institutions which, "although not
isolated from their counterparts elsewhere in the United Kingdom, operate
in a Scottish context" (Cameron, 2010, p. 354). Some also mention the fact
that Scotland has its own media (and in particular its own press) and its own
popular culture. It has sometimes been claimed that thanks to these visible
differences between Scotland and the rest of the UK, "Scottish identity is
well defined" (Brand & Mitchell, 1997, p. 41). However, it is argued here
that Scottish national identity is not as unproblematic and easy to define as
this claim suggests.

Just as Scotland's status as a nation is largely uncontroversial in Britain,
so is the fact that Scotland has a national identity which, in the words of
leading Scottish academics (Paterson et al., 2001), is "part of the taken-for-
granted world" (p. 102). Nevertheless, some have warned against analyzing
Scottish identity through a purely national lens. First of all, a Scottish national identity is just one of the many identities that the people of Scotland
maintain. As noted by Colley (2008), "Identities are not like hats. Human
beings can and do put on several at a time" (p. 6). An analysis of Scottish
people's identities is incomplete if it does not take into account class, gender, and other factors that make up those identities. People stress different
forms of identities according to the context in which they find themselves:

> What is on offer [today] is what we might call "pick 'n mix" identity, in
> which we wear our identities lightly, and change them according to circum-
> stance.... Hence, national identity does not take precedence over class or
> gender identities (or, indeed, vice versa) except insofar as these are subjec-
> tively ordered. (McCrone, 1992, p. 195)

Some scholars even call into question the very validity of national identity,
both as a concept and as an individual attribute. In the words of Bechhofer
and McCrone (who disagree with such a viewpoint):

> To some ... national identity is something of a con trick, worked by the state
> and its institutions to make the citizenry malleable and willing to do its bid-
> ding.... This has led some writers to be skeptical of national identity, seeing it
> as a form of what Marxists call "false consciousness," somehow not quite right
> as identities go, and certainly less "real" than social class, gender, ethnicity,
> because from these certain clear-cut life chances derive. (Bechhofer & Mc-
> Crone, 2009, p. 3)

Thirdly, even if one believes national identity to be one of the key identities among the Scottish people, it would be ahistorical to believe that this has always been the case. In his preface to a recent history of Scotland since 1880, which is the final volume of the *New Edinburgh History of Scotland*, the general editor of the series warned that:

> [T]o talk of the Scots—or the Scottish nation—is often misleading. Local loyalty and regional diversity have more frequently characterized Scotland than any perceived sense of "national" solidarity. Scottish identity has seldom been focused primarily, let alone exclusively, on the "nation." The modern discourse of nationhood offers what is often an inadequate and inappropriate vocabulary in which to couch Scotland's history. (Mason, 2010, p. xiii)

These caveats notwithstanding, analyzing Scotland through a national prism is legitimate, if only because (arguably) "[b]eing national is the condition of our times, even as the nation is buffeted by the subnational rise of local, regional, and ethnic claims, and the transnational threats of globalization, hegemonic American culture, migration, diasporization, and new forms of political community" (Eley & Suny, 1996, p. 32).

Despite all this research on Scottish national identity, my central argument is that "Scottishness" is an unorthodox, even paradoxical, form of national identity. Why? To begin with, it is generally conceptualized as being both distinct from, and part of another national identity: Britishness. Secondly, there is no obvious correlation between national identity and constitutional preferences. Whether people in Scotland are nationalist or Unionist, whether they support the independence of Scotland or its remaining within the UK, has no direct correlation with how strongly Scottish they feel. Thus, debates on Scotland's constitutional future have not been debates about Scotland's national identity. Both the debate on devolution and the current debate on independence have focused on the governance of Scotland and its social and economic health. Thirdly, even the Scottish National Party, which to many is the political embodiment of Scottish national identity, does not consider Scottish independence in terms of identity politics.

THE NATIONAL IDENTITY/IES OF SCOTTISH PEOPLE: SCOTTISHNESS AND BRITISHNESS

Most people accept that Scotland and Britain are nations. This raises the following question: Are Scottishness and Britishness two distinct forms of national identity, or is Scottishness a specific form of Britishness? Most British scholars agree that a Scottish national identity existed before the creation of the British State in 1707, which itself led to the birth of a British national identity. Where they disagree is on what national identity Scottish people have had since 1707. Has Britishness absorbed the old Scottish identity, or have Scottishness and Britishness been two distinct identities? Linda Colley (2008) has convincingly argued that:

> Great Britain did not emerge by way of a "blending" of the different regional or older national cultures contained within its boundaries as is sometimes maintained, nor is its genesis to be explained primarily in terms of an English "core" imposing its cultural and political hegemony on a helpless and defrauded Celtic periphery. (p. 6)

Rather, Colley sees Britishness as an overarching identity which was "superimposed" on Scottishness and other national identities, as well as regional identities within Scotland, Wales, or England (p. 6). Bechhofer and McCrone (2009) share this belief, and define "being British" as "a sort of umbrella identity sitting loosely upon the older territorial identities of England, Scotland and Wales" (p. 1). To them, the result of this "superimposition" of Britishness on Scottishness is that these may be seen as "nested identities, complementary, not contradictory, although in practice people sometimes see them as alternatives depending on context" (p. 1). Speaking of 19th century Scotland, Graeme Morton (1999) also defines the population's British and Scottish identities as "complementary" (p. 200), but disputes that Britishness is an overarching identity in which Scottishness is nested. Instead, he argues that "the idea of Britishness is distinct in each [of the British nations], built around a number of competing and intermixed identities. There is much commonality in the British experience, but it means something unique to each of the four nations" (p. 7). More than just complementary identities, some see the British and Scottish identities of the Scots as shaping each other. According to Neil Davidson:

> [F]or the Scots, their British and Scottish identities do not merely exist in parallel, but interpenetrate each other at every point. In other words, Scottishness as we know it today not only emerged at the same *time* as Britishness, but is *part* of Britishness, and could not exist (at least in the same form) without it. (Davidson, 2000, pp. 201–202)

However, even those who argue that British and Scottish identities are complementary or intermixed do not always argue that they are complementary or intermixed *national* identities. Several commentators do not see Britishness as a national identity at all. They envisage Scottishness, Englishness, and Welshness as properly "national" identities, and Britishness as a "state identity" or "supranational identity."[3] In such accounts, Britishness is nothing more than the sense of citizenship of the British State. Neal Ascherson, for instance, noted in 1996 that "[f]or the past few decades, at least, Welsh and Scottish subjects of the UK have found it fairly easy to define themselves as Welsh or Scottish by nation, but British by citizenship (or statehood)" (Ascherson, 1996, p. 85).

The peaceful coexistence and possible interpenetration of "local" national identities and of a state-wide British identity (whether this is a national identity too or just a sense of citizenship) is often considered to be one of the things that make the United Kingdom "peculiar":

> The United Kingdom certainly has some peculiarities. From the start it was a multinational state, dominated by the largest nation, the English. Yet there were only sporadic attempts to obliterate the national cultures and national allegiances of the four component nations, and create a new national culture in their place.... The kind of nation-building that was practiced in many other countries, aimed at rooting out older allegiances and identities, and constructing a single nation and a single national identity, did not succeed and was only partially attempted in the United Kingdom. Part of the explanation is that there was no need. Apart from the Irish, the other nations of the United Kingdom were full and willing participants, and accepted the British identity alongside their other national identity, seeing them as complementary rather than conflicting. (Gamble & Wright, 2009, pp. 1–2)

This "peculiar" history explains why, in the past decades, Scottish people's national identity has generally been conceptualized as a "dual" identity.[4] Tom Nairn has criticized this conceptualization, arguing that it has historically served a political purpose. After denouncing "dual identity" as a "fulsome (and still popular) mythology," Nairn goes on to say:

> In one sense dual or multiple identity is merely a standard human condition, more significant in modern or industrialized societies than previously. There is nothing at all amazing about (say) being a Serb, a "Yugoslav," a Communist, a football fan, an Orthodox Christian and an ardent philatelist all "at the same time."...But the ideological or heavy-duty sense of "duality" was quite different: this decreed that two or more key (national) allegiances were compatible, and that it was preferable to be thus enriched. This may be true, but it is an abstract truth, which has had limited relevance in modern history. Historically, such combinations have in practice been rare cultural balancing-acts, mainly designed for the sustenance of inequality and empire. (Nairn, 2000, pp. 232–233)

T. M. Devine (2006) also avoids the phrase "dual identity," and prefers to speak of Scottish people's "dual allegiance," as he does not believe that Britishness is a national identity. To him, after the 1707 Anglo-Scottish Union, Scottish élites gradually developed "a political loyalty to Britain" while maintaining a "continuing sense of identity with their native land" (Devine, 2006, p. 30).

However that may be, British scholars promoting the notion of "dual" identities have influenced the way feelings of national identity are measured in the UK. If we believe the latest population surveys, a significant proportion of people in Britain see themselves as having (at least) two national identities: a British one and a Scottish, English, or Welsh one. However, the respective degrees to which they feel British and Scottish, English, or Welsh can vary. If we focus on the Scottish case, the British Social Attitudes and Scottish Social Attitudes Surveys revealed the extent to which people in Scotland have felt Scottish and British in the past twenty years. The approach taken in Table 3.1 is the so-called "Moreno" approach, designed by Spanish sociologist Luis Moreno for an analysis of national identities in the Spanish and British contexts. As a recent British Social Attitudes report explains, instead of being asked to choose between a "Scottish" and a "British" identity, "[r]espondents are presented with a set of options that range from exclusively Scottish at one end to exclusively British at the other, while at the same time also offering various possible combinations of feeling both Scottish and British" (British Social Attitudes, 2012). In other words, "[r]espondents are not required to participate in a zero-sum exercise where they must choose one identity over another, but can potentially express the dual nature of national identity by expressing the latter in a comparative rather than categorical manner" (Bond, 2000, p.16).

Four striking conclusions can be drawn from Figure 3.1. (Data for Figure 3.1 may be found in Appendix A.) The first is that almost everyone in Scotland feels Scottish at some level: Never more than 6% of respondents have denied having any sense of being Scottish. The second is that the majority of Scots lean towards the Scottish end, as opposed to the British one. The total percentage of respondents who feel either more British than Scottish, or British only, has never been higher than 11%, whereas the total percentage of those who feel either more Scottish than British, or

TABLE 3.1   National Identity and Constitutional Preference, Scotland, 2005 (%)

	Scottish, Not British	Scottish More Than British	Equally Scottish and British	British More Than/Not Scottish
Independence	51	34	20	19
Sc. Parliament with tax powers	26	40	49	38
Sc. Parliament without tax powers	4	6	8	8
No parliament	7	14	16	32

Note: Scottish Social Attitudes Survey, 2005 (as cited in Bechhofer & McCrone, 2007).

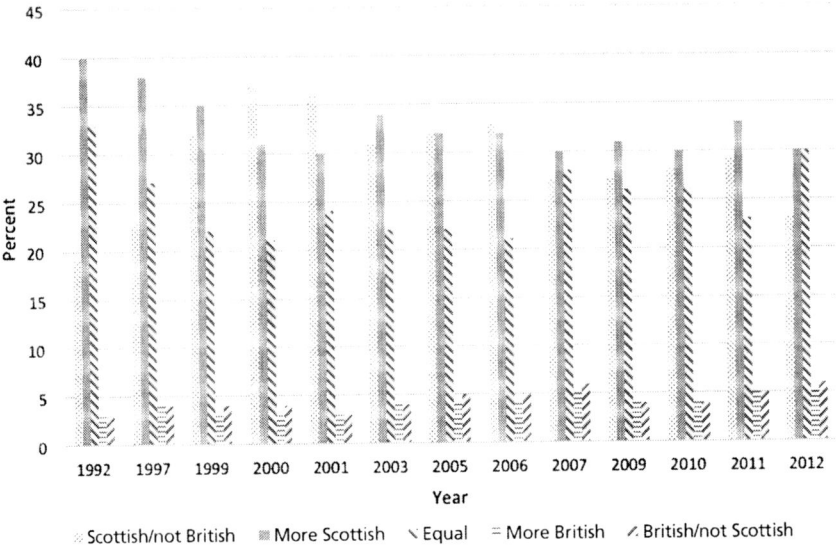

Figure 3.1 National identity in Scotland, 1992–2012.

Scottish only, has oscillated between 53% and 68%. Interestingly, the low of 53% was only reached in 2012 (the latest year for which data are available); until then, the proportion of Scots feeling more Scottish than British or exclusively Scottish had never gone below 58%. The third conclusion is that the category which people choose first is generally the "more Scottish than British."

There have been a few exceptions to this rule. On three occasions (in 2000, 2001 and 2006) more people chose the "Scottish only" category. In addition, in 2012, the same proportion of people (30%) chose the "more Scottish than British" and the "equally British" categories. However, the fact that the "more Scottish than British" category is generally the most popular points to the fourth conclusion which can be drawn from these surveys: The majority of people in Scotland feel British to some extent, though not in the same proportions as they feel Scottish. Those who do not feel British at all have represented 37% of the total at the most, and the proportion has not reached the 30% mark once since 2007. In summary, almost everyone in Scotland feels Scottish, but a majority of Scots feel British too, although a significant minority do not feel British at all.[5]

The theoretical debates over being Scottish, as well as the quantitative studies carried out in the British and Scottish social attitudes surveys, demonstrate that a discussion of national identity in Scotland needs to take into account the complex interrelations between national identities in the UK. This interpenetration explains why Scottish national identity does not solely find its political expression in Scottish nationalism, but can also take the form of unionism (or the defense of the Anglo-Scottish Union of 1707).

SCOTTISH NATIONAL IDENTITY, NATIONALISM, AND UNIONISM

Considering Scotland's status as a nation within a wider state, and given the existence of a structured, long established independence movement, one might think that having a strong feeling of national identity would entail supporting Scottish independence. In other words, there would be a strong correlation between national identity and constitutional preferences. One might also assume a strong correlation between national identity and electoral behavior, or party support. Feeling strongly Scottish might lead to supporting the pro-independence Scottish National Party. Let us now examine these two hypotheses.

This snapshot in Table 3.1 of 2005 shows what constitutional settlement Scottish people supported in 2005 according to their national identity (or identities). It reveals several things. First, as expected, a majority of those who feel exclusively Scottish support the independence of Scotland. However, it is a very short majority (51%) as slightly less than half of this category of Scots do not support independence. Moreover, supporters of independence can also be found in the "more British than Scottish" or "British only" categories, which is rather counterintuitive. As for those who feel a "dual" sense of national identity, most of them support a "Scottish Parliament with tax powers." In other words, stronger devolution of powers to the Scottish Parliament than is the case today. It is also notable that the more strongly Scottish one feels, the more one is likely to support independence; similarly, the more strongly British one feels, the more one is likely to oppose both independence and devolution. In conclusion, national identity is undeniably a predictor of constitutional preference. However, this snapshot of 2005 suggests that it is not as strong a predictor as one might imagine, since independence supporters and people opposed to devolution were to be found amongst all categories of Scots, whatever their feelings of national identity, and since almost half of Scots who did not feel British at all did not believe that Scotland should leave Britain.

Paterson et al. (2001) also conducted a study of the links between national identity and constitutional preference. In the Paterson et al. study, a twenty-year period was covered, and preceded the creation of the Scottish Parliament (from 1979 to 1999). They arrived at the same conclusions. The authors remarked that "knowing whether someone thinks of themselves as Scottish or British is a poor predictor of their preferred constitutional option" (p. 212). A direct comparison between this study and the one carried out in 2005 is difficult, as the latter used the Moreno question, when the former used a "forced choice question" (where people had to choose between feeling Scottish and feeling British). However, both studies make the same general point: One should not assume that there is a direct relationship between how people perceive their national identity and their attitudes to constitutional change. The latest Scottish social attitudes survey (conducted in late 2012) confirms this finding. Of those who see themselves as in no way British (29% of Scots), fewer than half (46%) wanted to leave Britain, a drop from 53% the previous year (Gardham, January 25, 2013).

Why is there not a stronger link between feelings of national identity and constitutional preferences in Scotland? A report analyzing the 2012 survey suggested that constitutional preferences were determined by economic arguments more than by identity politics (Gardham, January 12, 2013). Generally speaking, it has been argued that it is not whether one feels strongly Scottish or not that has the greatest impact on constitutional preference, but rather what meaning one gives to being Scot and what constitutional settlement will best allow this version of being Scottish to flourish (Reicher, Hopkins, & Harrison, 2009).

Or, as Kumar noted: "Scots can have an intense sense of Scottish identity but still feel that what they mean by Scottishness can best be served by remaining within the Union rather than opting out of it" (Kumar, 2010, p. 103). Hence the conclusion that whether Scotland becomes independent or not will not cause the disappearance of either the Scottish or the British dimensions to Scottish people's national identity (Gamble & Wright, 2009). We will see further on in this chapter that the Scottish National Party has recently been making the same point, presumably as a way of trying to convince a greater number of people to support independence.

Let us now consider the relationship between national identity and party support. I draw from data collected both in 1997 and in 2005, and instead of being presented with the preferences of people according to their national identity, data are arrayed by people's national identities according to their party preference. See Tables 3.2 and 3.3.

The table concerning the year 1997 shows first and foremost that supporters of each party, except the Conservative party, favored the "Scottish more than British" category. This might not seem very surprising as both parties were then campaigning for the creation of an autonomous Scottish Parliament within the framework of the UK. It is more unexpected of SNP supporters, who might be assumed to have exclusive feelings of "Scottishness," as the SNP favors Scottish independence. Yet, 44% of them chose to describe themselves as "Scottish more than British," with the "Scottish, not

TABLE 3.2 National Identity and Party Preference, Scotland, 1997 (%)					
	Scottish, Not British	Scottish More Than British	Equally Scottish and British	British More Than Scottish	British, Not Scottish
Conservative	10	23	47	7	6
Labor	24	41	26	4	3
Lib. Dem.	15	41	26	7	6
SNP	34	44	16	2	2

Note: Scottish Election Survey, 1997 (as cited in Bond, 2000, p. 19).

TABLE 3.3 National Identity and Party Preference, Scotland, 2005 (%)				
	Scottish Not British	Scottish More Than British	Equally Scottish and British	British More Than/Not Scottish
Conservative	21	29	26	20
Labor	31	35	24	7
Lib. Dem.	22	34	22	13
SNP	51	36	9	2

Note: Scottish Social Attitudes Survey, 2005 (as cited in Bechhofer & McCrone, 2007).

British" category only coming second (though a strong second at 34%). At a time when the Conservative party was engaged in a strong campaign against a Scottish Parliament (or "devolution") and in favor of the constitutional status quo, one might have expected its supporters to lean towards the British end of the scale. However, the majority of them preferred the "equally Scottish and British" tag. In summary, supporting one of the British-wide parties did not mean that one felt more British than Scottish, while supporting the Scottish pro-independence party did not necessarily mean feeling exclusively Scottish.

The table concerning the year 2005 generally confirms these findings. However, some changes are notable. First of all, the general balance had shifted towards the Scottish end of the scale. Whereas Labour and Liberal Democrat supporters still chose the "Scottish more than British" category, as did Conservatives. Moreover, SNP supporters now chose the "Scottish, not British" category before the "Scottish more than British," which still attracted 36% of SNP supporters. As a consequence, whatever the party they supported, Scottish people now mainly felt a strong Scottish national identity.

In 1997, as in 2005, supporters of the three main British-wide parties were less likely than SNP supporters to describe themselves as exclusively Scottish and more likely to describe themselves as exclusively British.

However, the relationship between national identity and party support was not straightforward. There were people who felt exclusively Scottish in each group of party identifiers (more than 20% in each group).

The previously mentioned study of the 1979–1999 period shows that the vast majority (84% to 94%) of SNP supporters chose a Scottish identity. Yet, this was true of every group of party identifiers. In all years, party supporters were more likely to identify as being Scottish than British, except for Conservative supporters on one occasion in 1979. However, even then, the percentage of Conservative supporters who described themselves as British was only slightly higher than the percentage describing themselves as Scottish (48% as opposed to 46%). In the 1992 survey, the balance had largely tipped in favor of being Scottish (58% as opposed to 38% for the British side).

There was an undeniable link between national identity and party preference. In 1999, 61% of Conservative supporters chose the Scottish identity, as opposed to 70% of Liberal Democrat supporters, 77% of Labour supporters, and 93% of SNP supporters. The meaning of these figures is that supporters of the Unionist parties were less likely than supporters of the Scottish nationalist party to have a strong Scottish identity. However, there was a "shift over time towards Scottishness among voters of all parties, including Conservatives" (Paterson et al., 2001, p. 109).

Scottish people's national identity, constitutional preferences, and party preferences are "non-aligned" (Bond, 2000). This is only unorthodox if we "conflat[e] 'upper case' and 'lower case' nationalism in Scotland," or nationalism as a political program and nationalism as a collective identity (Bond, 2000, p. 31). The three major British parties are the Labour Party, the Conservative Party, and the Liberal Democrats (previously the Liberal Party). They systematically produce separate manifestos for Scotland during "General Elections," even though these are British-wide parliamentary elections. Let us take the example of the 1997 General Election and examine the Scottish manifestos issued at the time by the four major parties in Scotland. Of the four party manifestos, the SNP's is the most clearly nationalist. A chapter entitled "a nation once again" reminded people that Scotland had remained distinct despite almost three centuries of Union with England. However, despite retaining its distinctive national characteristics, Scotland had not reached its full national potential, and only independence would make it into a "real" nation.

The Scottish manifestos of the three major Unionist parties were not nationalist. Yet, the Labor and Conservative manifestos demonstrated their awareness of Scotland's distinctiveness and even their patriotism. The Labour Party's Scottish manifesto reminded Scots that "Scotland ha[d] its own education system, its own legal system, its own structure of local government and a distinct and proud national identity" (Scottish Labour Party,

1997). The Scottish Conservative Party's manifesto was even more openly nationalist.

At the time, the Conservative Party was the only party opposed to devolution. Labour supported devolution in a context of wider constitutional reform, including reforming the House of Lords. Liberal Democrats supported devolution as the first step on the road to federalism, and the SNP supported it as the first step on the road to Scottish independence. Yet, the rhetoric used in the Scottish Conservatives' manifesto, entitled "Fighting for Scotland" (1997), was undeniably "lower-case nationalist." The manifesto opened on a foreword by Prime Minister John Major describing the Scots as "the World's greatest instinctive entrepreneurs," followed by a nationalistic message by Michael Forsyth, the Secretary of State for Scotland.

The Conservative Party clearly wanted to demonstrate that constitutional preference had nothing to do with feelings of national identity or with patriotism. Only the Scottish Liberal Democrats refrained from using nationalist rhetoric, though they did refer to the existence of a "Scottish people." It is common occurrence for British parties to use a Scottish frame of reference when addressing the Scottish population, and even put forward an openly nationalist viewpoint.

At times when constitutional issues do not dominate the political agenda, the tone of British parties' General Election manifestos is not so openly nationalistic. Let me now focus on the 2010 General Election. Naturally, the SNP boasted that it was the only national party of Scotland and thus the only one with Scotland's best interests at heart.

The other parties also claimed to defend Scotland's interests, but that Scotland's and Britain's interests were intimately bound. Scottish Labour had the following view, "[w]hile Britain brings strength to Scotland, Scotland brings breadth to Britain"; that is why both the British and the Scottish Parliaments needed to "examine how best they can work together in the interests of Scotland and the UK" (Scottish Labour Party, 2010). In the Scottish Conservatives' manifesto, Scots were reminded that this was "a British General Election about UK issues like debt, jobs, welfare, energy, defense, and our relationship with the wider world" (Scottish Conservatives, 2010). In this view, Britain's and Scotland's interests were conflated. As a consequence, defending the interests of Britain meant defending the interests of Scotland. The Conservative manifesto, though not as stridently patriotic as their 1997 Scottish manifesto, was still nationalist in that it was concerned with the defense of Scottish interests, defined in unionist terms.

The manifesto of the Scottish Liberal Democrats was similarly concerned with how best to defend Scottish interests, but it too conflated Britain's and Scotland's interests: "Set your sights on the Britain—and the Scotland—you want for your children and your grandchildren" (Scottish Liberal Democrats, 2010).

When constitutional issues are not at the forefront of the political agenda, the unionist parties' General Election manifestos are nationalist in a limited manner—they argue that the defense of Scottish are distinct from British interests. However, as the 1997 election campaign showed, the unionist parties can be openly patriotic when they feel that being Scottish is questioned.

THE SCOTTISH NATIONAL PARTY AND SCOTTISH NATIONAL IDENTITY

Brand & Mitchell (1997) argue that "Scottish identity may take on a political meaning only when there are features in the environment which make that political meaning important" (p. 36). To them, a typical "trigger of politicization" was "the existence of an institution—a party, perhaps—which draws attention to the political dimension of Scottish identity" (p. 36). McEwen (2003) makes the same argument.

Has the SNP acted as a "trigger of politicization" of Scottish identity? It could be argued that until devolution was granted to Scotland in the form of a Scottish Parliament, Scottish national identity had been politicized in two phases (McEwen, 2003, pp. 13–16). The first phase, from the mid-1960s to the failed 1979 referendum on devolution, saw the emergence of the Scottish National Party as a significant political force in Scotland. This emergence had economic as well as political roots. Scottish people were dismayed by the UK's economic decline and by Scotland's relatively steeper decline, as well as by the British government's inability to address these calamities. The discovery of oil in the North Sea off the Scottish coast in the early 1970s reinforced the SNP's credibility by allowing it to argue that Scotland had the means to survive independently of England. With the emergence of the SNP, Scottish national identity became politicized. All parties, and not just the SNP, now acknowledged Scottish distinctiveness, and both the Conservatives and the Labour Party supported Scotland's political and administrative autonomy.

The second phrase in the politicization of Scottish identity started towards the end of the Thatcher years, in the late 1980s, and continued until the introduction of devolution in the late 1990s. There was opposition to Thatcherite policies, introduced under Prime Minister Margaret Thatcher in the 1980s and her successor John Major in the 1990s (McEwen, 2003). A key reason for this opposition was Thatcher's neo-liberal attacks on the welfare state, which changed Scottish people's feelings of national identity. McEwen sums up the links between the welfare state and national identity by stating that the welfare state was a symbol of British solidarity, but

Thatcher introduced a neo-liberal ideology and policies that stressed individualism, enterprise, and so on. Scots could not identify with this picture.

Scottish identity was politicized in those years because being Scottish was redefined as being anti-Conservative and pro-Welfare State. In the 1990s, it was also progressively redefined as being sympathetic to home rule. Thatcher's government was felt to be a threat to Scottish identity, and devolution "seemed to provide the potential for a barrier to what was seen as an alien ideology" (Cameron, 2010, p. 338).

While collectivist values came to represent the core values of being Scottish, political autonomy came to be seen as the best way to defend the welfare state in Scotland. By the time a second referendum on devolution was organized, in 1997, the primary motivation behind support for the creation of a Scottish Parliament was a belief that it would improve the quality of public welfare in Scotland (McEwen, 2003).

Scottish identity has been politicized since the 1970s, something to which the SNP contributed, without being its only trigger. Since the birth of the Scottish Parliament, the SNP has been elected to power twice, in 2007 and in 2011, meaning that it has been the government party in Scotland since 2007. What has it had to say about national identity during its years in power?

The SNP does not consider Scottish independence in terms of identity politics. Firstly, it does not argue that the aim of independence is to give political recognition to Scottish national identity. Secondly, it does not present Scottish independence as ending a common British national identity.

Since its electoral rise in the late 1960s, the SNP has consistently claimed that its nationalism is not one based on a desire for Scottish national identity to be recognized, for one simple reason: It believes that there is no need for this, and that Scottish national identity is well established. Instead, independence has been promoted as the best way to defend Scottish interests. For instance, independence has been presented as the best way to achieve economic growth and social justice. Nicola Sturgeon, the current leader of the SNP has recently given several speeches and interviews in which she has repeatedly made the same point: The Scottish independence debate is not about identity politics.

Table 3.4 presents the aims of the SNP as stated in the different Constitutions that the party adopted over time. Whatever the period, independence (or "self-government") has been associated with the concepts of democracy and sovereignty, as well as with the defense of Scottish interests, but never with the concept of identity. The SNP is not alone in stressing that independence is not about giving political expression to Scottish national identity. Most Scottish intellectuals who are sympathetic to independence make the same case.

TABLE 3.4 SNP Constitutions: Aims of the Party	
1943 SNP Constitution	(a) Self Government for Scotland (b) The restoration of Scottish national sovereignty by the establishment of a democratic Scottish government whose authority will be limited only by such agreements as will be freely entered into with other nations in order to further international co-operation and world peace.
1967 SNP Constitution	(a) Self-Government for Scotland—that is, the restoration of Scottish National Sovereignty by the establishment of a democratic Scottish Government within the Commonwealth, freely elected by the Scottish people, and whose authority will be limited only by such agreements as will be freely entered into with other nations or states for the purpose of furthering international co-operation and world peace. (b) The furtherance of all Scottish interests.
2004 SNP Constitution	(a) Independence for Scotland; that is the restoration of Scottish national sovereignty by the restoration of full powers to the Scottish Parliament, so that its authority is limited only by the sovereign power of the Scottish People to bind it with a written constitution and by such agreements as it may freely enter into with other nations or states or international organizations for the purpose of furthering international cooperation, world peace and the protection of the environment. (b) The furtherance of all Scottish interests.

The relaxed attitude to identity that the SNP wishes to project has led its previous leader, Alex Salmond, to make surprising comments about Britishness. In a recent interview with the *New Statesman*, Salmond, whom one might expect to deny having a British identity, declared:

> One of the great attractions of Scottish nationalism is that it's very much a multilayered identity. It's never been sensible to tell people they have only one to choose. . . . I've got a British aspect to my identity. Scottishness is my primary identity but I've got Britishness and a European identity. (Eaton, 2013)

Like most Scots, the former SNP leader claimed to have a dual Scottish and British identity, despite being the embodiment of the policy of Scottish independence in the eyes of most Scots (and Britons). The message here was clear: If independence is not about recognizing Scottishness, neither is it about rejecting Britishness. It should be noted that most SNP members do not envisage their national identity in the same way as their party leader. A recent study of SNP members (Mitchell, Bennie, & Johns, 2012) revealed that when asked the "Moreno question," 80% of members choose the "Scottish not British" option. This means that only 20% of SNP members acknowledge having a British identity. Moreover, according to the same study, "very few" of the senior members or office-holders were "willing to acknowledge any British component to their identity and then only when prompted. The majority view of these senior figures was a rejection of Britishness in any shape or form" (Salmond, 2007 p. 104). It appears that Salmond's acknowledgment of his British identity goes against the feeling of most members of his party. However, this acknowledgment is one of the SNP's key political strategies, and is consistent with the SNP's claims that the independence debate should not be viewed in terms of identity politics.

Claims that Britishness would survive in the event of Scottish independence are reflected in the SNP's recurring argument that what it has termed the "social union" between Scotland and the rest of the UK would continue too. The concept of a "social union" has been defended and defined as such:

> Independence means running our own affairs in our own way. What it doesn't mean is losing our cherished links with the other nations of the United Kingdom. We've forged strong ties and built trust with our neighbours on these islands in the 300-plus years since the Act of Union. That's an important and valued legacy, a social union, and it will continue. (SNP, 2011)

We see here that what lies behind the SNP's concept of a "social union" is the will to dissociate independence and identity politics.

The SNP's position on Britishness is also reflected in what it says about citizenship in an independent Scotland. It believes that citizenship should be granted automatically for all Scottish residents at the time of independence, but also that it should be open to nonresidents of Scottish birth (SNP, 1995; 2005). Moreover, the SNP has suggested that having a dual Scottish-British citizenship would be possible:

> Citizenship in Scotland would be based on an inclusive model designed to support economic growth, integration and promotion of diversity. Given Scotland's close ties to the other parts of the British Isles a positive approach to dual citizenship would be essential; and given the existence of EU citizenship consideration could also be given to the creation of enhanced citizenship arrangements with the nations of the rUK (the remainder of the UK). (Scottish Government, 2009)

As a nationalist party campaigning for the independence of the nation, the SNP is rather unusual because it does not base its nationalism on identity politics. It can seem idiosyncratic for another reason: it avoids appealing to cultural identity markers such as language. We will now examine in more detail what types of identity markers have appealed to the SNP, and those that it avoids.

One of the distinctions made by scholars of nationalism is between civic and ethnic nationalisms. The ethnic nation, organic (or natural), rooted in history, and based on such shared characteristics as language or religion, is often opposed to the civic nation, which is contractual and defined by people's will to identify with it. Consequently, ethnic nationalism presents membership of the national community as a given (one is a member by birth or by blood), while civic nationalism is territorial and based on common values and institutions (one is a member by choice). This dichotomy finds its historical origins in the conflict between France and Germany over the Alsace and Lorraine regions (Dieckhoff, 2000). German historians argued that Alsatians' German culture justified their incorporation into Germany. French historians, in contrast, replied that Alsatians should remain French if that was what they chose to be (Dieckhoff, 2000, p. 65). It was popularized by German historian Friedrich Meinecke in the early twentieth century and then by American philosopher Hans Kohn after the Second World War. It is doubtful whether this distinction is analytically helpful because it could be argued that any nationalist movement may contain both civic and ethnic elements. However, the SNP is a firm believer in this dichotomy, and it often points out its "civic" credentials.

Michael Keating (2009) has described the SNP's ideology as "impeccably civic" (p. 217), and in his book on what he termed the "minority nationalisms" of Scotland, Catalonia, and Quebec, he argued that Scottish nationalism as a whole, just like Catalan and Québécois nationalisms, is civic and "modernizing":

> Minority nationalisms are dismissed as archaic, narrow-minded and "ethnic." I have already sought to combat this prejudice in my work on minority nationalisms and the state where I argued that in many cases they represent modernising and democratising movements in the face of archaic states. (Keating, 1996, p. xii)

Even more straightforwardly, in an article disputing that a parallel can be made between the successes of the Scottish National Party and the (limited) successes of the British National Party (a far right party), political journalist Iain Macwhirter stated that the SNP "is a civic nationalist party with strong social democratic leanings" (June 8, 2009).

Are such claims justified? Stephen Shulman has classified the "key components" of national identity into three groups: civic, cultural, and ethnic, as shown in Table 3.5.

An analysis of SNP literature reveals that the party appeals to all of the civic components of national identity, but not to ethnicity, and rarely to culture. Peter Lynch (1999) notes that two anti-English groups which briefly existed in the 1990s, Scottish Watch and Settler Watch, were opposed by the SNP which expelled its members when they were also members of these groups. In the same decade, "the SNP's non-ethnic appeal became more pronounced with the establishment of the groups New Scots

TABLE 3.5 Components of National Identity	
Content of National Identity	Key Components
Civic	• Territory • Citizenship • Will and consent • Political ideology • Political institutions and rights
Cultural	• Religion • Language • Traditions
Ethnic	• Ancestry • Race

Source: Stephen Schulman, "Challenging the Civic/Ethnic and West/East Dichotomies in the Study of Nationalism," *Comparative Political Studies,* Vol. 35, p. 559, 2002 (as cited in Mitchell et al., p. 108).

for Independence and Asians for Independence" (pp. 4–5). The SNP also prides itself on having provided the Scottish Parliament with its first and, to this date, its only minority-ethnic MSP.

A recent survey of SNP membership (Mitchell et al., 2012) asked SNP members how important were certain characteristics to be truly Scottish. Results reveal that having Scottish ancestry and being born in Scotland, ethnic markers of belonging, were considered important by more than half of SNP members. Yet, "few identified these as the *only* ways of being 'truly Scottish'" (Mitchell et al., 2012 p. 111), and living in Scotland was seen as more important. The authors concluded that "very few of [SNP] members would define Scottishness in exclusive ethnic terms" (Mitchell et al., 2012 p. 116).

That the SNP should define itself as a civic nationalist party is not surprising, and is consistent with an international trend that has seen "the ethnic definition of the nation give way in nationalist discourse to a civic one" (Keating, 2009, p. 215). However, the SNP's relative lack of appeal to the cultural components of national identity is unexpected given that at least one cultural element has been a major factor in other nations' national identity: language.

What makes the SNP's nationalism particularly unorthodox is that language is not a key issue. Scottish nationalism is often compared to nationalisms in other Western "stateless nations." Parallels have been drawn with Catalonia (in Spain) and Quebec (in Canada), sometimes with Flanders (in Belgium), and most often with Wales. However, in the Catalonian, Québécois, Flemish, and Welsh cases, linguistic issues have been central, which has never been the case in Scotland.

Scotland has three native languages: English, (Scottish) Gaelic, and Scots. English is the majority language, spoken by the whole Scottish population; yet, probably because it is the language that Scotland shares with the rest of the UK, it is not seen as a key part of Scotland's national identity. Gaelic is a Celtic language which, today, is only spoken by 58,000 people in Scotland, mainly concentrated in the Highlands and Hebrides. While this figure was described by the Scottish Government as "encouraging"—it only represented a 1.2% drop in the numbers of Gaelic speakers since the previous population census (in 2001), as opposed to an 11% drop between 1991 and 2001—Gaelic speakers only represent 1.1% of the total Scottish population.[6] Gaelic was never seen as a central component of Scottish national identity, as opposed to regional Highland identity. That is why, although the SNP has aimed at promoting and developing the Gaelic language, in the SNP's history it has never put the promotion of Gaelic at the heart of its nationalist program.

As for the Scots language, its very status is contested, as it is alternatively seen as either a fully-fledged language or as a group of dialects. The website of the government-supported Scots Language Centre (http://www.scotslanguage.com) explains that Scots and English are sister tongues which grew apart in the Middle Ages. Scots then became "the national language of Scotland, spoken by Scottish kings, and was used to write the official records of the country," but it was "displaced as a national language" when Scotland united with England. The Scots Language Centre (n.d.) notes that in Scotland most people do not know exactly what the Scots language corresponds to:

> Many people have heard about the Scots language but aren't sure what it is. Scots has been spoken in Scotland for several centuries and is found today throughout the Lowlands and Northern Isles. The name Scots is the national name for Scottish dialects sometimes also known as "Doric," "Lallans" and "Scotch" or by more local names such as "Buchan," "Dundonian," "Glesca" or "Shetland." Taken altogether, Scottish dialects are known collectively as the Scots language.... Scots is mainly a spoken language with a number of local varieties, each with its own distinctive character. (n.p.)

Not only is Scots a language divided into local dialects, but most people believe Scots to be "bad English" (as "the Scots language was for a long time discouraged by officials and schools"). This has made it only marginally a better candidate than Gaelic as a key component of Scotland's modern national identity. It is notable that the latest population census (2011) was the first ever to ask Scottish people whether they could "understand, speak, read and/or write Scots." There was the pervasive belief that people would find these questions difficult to answer, so the government sponsored a campaign (known as "Aye Can"; http://www.ayecan.com) to help.

For these reasons, Scottish identity is not based on any one of Scotland's national languages, which explains why Scottish nationalism has never given priority to linguistic issues. It is not to say that the SNP has not made any language-related demands, or that it has not implemented any language-related policies when in power. Aside from its 2009 Gaelic plan, in 2005, when the then Labour-Liberal Democrat Scottish Executive introduced a Gaelic bill in the Scottish Parliament to give recognition to the Gaelic language "as an official language of Scotland commanding equal respect to the English language," the SNP wanted to go a bit further than the government's plan. It proposed that Gaelic have "equal validity" with English. The proposal was rejected by the Parliament, mainly for fear that "a court might rule that the legislation conferred the right to demand the use of the language in a wider range of circumstances than is intended"; in particular, it might be ruled that "all public services should be made available in Gaelic in all places, to anyone who request[ed] that" (Scottish Parliament, April 21, 2005). Moreover, the SNP government recently prided itself in having "taken a number of important steps to support the Scots language," including:

> [A]n audit of Scots language provision, a national conference on the Scots language, the funding of two Scots bodies, a survey of attitudes to Scots, the introduction of a census question on Scots and the establishment of a ministerial Scots language working group. (Scottish Parliament, 2010)

However, language has never provided Scottish nationalists with a key for mobilizing and defending self-government.

The SNP's lack of reliance on linguistic distinctiveness has been interpreted as a strength, as it means that one does not have to speak a specific language to feel part of the national community, or to support independence. McCrone (1992), for instance, has hypothesized that "[p]erhaps the strength of nationalism in Scotland vis-à-vis that of Wales reflects the fact that, despite (or because of) a lack of linguistic differentiation, nationalism can present itself as more than protecting a cultural past under threat" (p. 29). Generally speaking, he notes that "cultural concerns provide some raw materials for [Scottish] nationalism, but are rarely its *raison d'être*. As a consequence, the tariff for being a nationalist is much lower" (p. 212).

Rather than saying that the SNP does not emphasize cultural issues, it would be more accurate to say that it does not place the emphasis on defending a traditional culture or way of life. The SNP strives to "be postmodernist in its cultural emphasis, valuing diversity, rather than modernist, committed to unity" (Aughey, 2001, p. 111). This is in fact true of all parties in Scotland. It became apparent in the Scottish Parliament's debates over the creation of a national day on St Andrew's Day.[7] Members of the Scottish Parliament (MSP) almost unanimously wanted to promote a multicultural vision of Scottishness, as opposed to a more traditional, past-oriented, "tartan-and-shortbread-tin" version (Scottish Parliament, March 17, 2004).

Dennis Canavan, an independent MSP and promoter of the bill, whose aim was to make St Andrew's Day into a bank holiday, declared that the bill would make St Andrew's Day into "a celebration of Scotland's multicultural and multiethnic traditions" (Scottish Parliament Consultation Paper, July 29, 2004). Before Canavan introduced his bill, Liberal Democrat MSP Donald Gorrie had already introduced a parliamentary motion on the celebration of St Andrew's Day. When that motion was debated in the chamber, he pointed at the pluralistic nature of Scottishness, insisting that "we are a mixed lot" and that "we have a varied history and culture." SNP MSP Linda Fabiani stated her belief that St Andrew's Day should be a "day of celebration of Scotland's cultural diversity" (Scottish Parliament, March 17, 2004).

CONCLUSION

The birth of a new Scottish Parliament in 1999, followed by the first ever Scottish independence referendum organized on September 18, 2014, have undoubtedly amplified the debate over national identity in Scotland. When the people of Scotland were asked for the first time in their history whether they believed Scotland "should be an independent country" in September 2014, a majority of them (55%) voted against independence, meaning that Scotland will remain part of the United Kingdom in the foreseeable future—although the planned organization of another referendum in 2016 or 2017, this time on the UK's membership of the European Union, could possibly jeopardize Scotland's future within the UK and provoke the organization of a second Scottish independence referendum. Why did Scottish people reject independence in 2014? Was the referendum result partly based on national identity issues, or only on social and economic concerns? In other terms, was it a sign of Scottish people's belief that their dual Scottish-British identity is best embodied in the UK multinational state, or was it just the result of a fear of "going it alone"? It is too early to say, but what is undeniable is that national identity issues were not a central part of the independence debate that preceded the referendum. The independence debate was centered not on the nature of Scottish identity, but on economic and social issues such as what currency an independent Scotland might adopt, or whether Scotland could avoid austerity measures by breaking away from a conservative- and liberal-dominated UK. What was under debate were Scotland's relations with London, the political and financial center of the UK, rather than its relations with England, its neighboring nation. In other words, Scottish people were asked by the pro-independence camp to rethink the center-periphery relations within the UK, rather than the relations between the different nations that make up the British State. While national identity issues clearly matter in Scotland, in the sense that there is an on-going debate about the nature of Scottishness and its link with, or imbrication in, Britishness, they do not matter so much (or at least not openly) to the SNP, the main pro-independence party in Scotland, or, for that matter, to any of the major pro-independence organizations.

APPENDIX A
TRENDS IN MORENO NATIONAL IDENTITY,
IN SCOTLAND, 1992–2012 (%)

	92	97	99	00	01	03	05	06	07	09	10	11	12
Scottish not British	19	23	32	37	36	31	32	33	27	27	28	29	23
More Scottish than British	40	38	35	31	30	34	32	32	30	31	30	33	30
Equally Scottish and British	33	27	22	21	24	22	22	21	28	26	26	23	30
More British than Scottish	3	4	3	3	3	4	4	4	5	4	4	5	5
British not Scottish	3	4	4	4	3	4	5	5	6	4	4	5	6

Note: British Scottish Attitudes Survey, 2013.

NOTES

1. One could for instance quote Graeme Morton: "Scotland and England came together in 1707, but commentators are becoming acutely aware this did not result in a *British* civil society. Each of the four nations [Scotland, England, Wales and Ireland] became united under a state, but there was no single British nation as a result, despite the banner 'United Kingdom.'" Morton, 1999, p. 6.

2. By defending the view that Scotland only became a nation in modern times, Nairn confirms that he is a modernization theorist and disagrees with the view that the Scottish nation finds its roots in the Middle Ages, a view which will be described further on in the chapter.

3. For examples of both phrases, see for instance Brown, McCrone, & Patterson, 1998, pp. 214–215.

4. Many examples could be given. See for example Bond (2000), Keating (1996), or Morton (1999).

5. While this chapter was being written (in September 2013), the results of the 2011 population census, the first to include a question on national identity, were made public. This confirmed that the vast majority of Scots (83% according to the census) feel some Scottish identity. Surprisingly, it also suggested that a majority of Scots do not feel British (with 62% of Scots describing themselves as "Scottish only"). However, it should be noted that the census did not offer Scots the same range of choices as the "Moreno question": people could only choose between "Scottish only," "Scottish and British" and several UK identities (or combinations of UK identities) excluding Scottish. This could account for the differences in results obtained. See *BBC News Scotland* (September 26, 2013).

6. As shown by the results of the 2011 population census. See for example http://www.bbc.co.uk/news/uk-scotland-highlands-islands-24281487.

7. To know more about those debates, read Duclos, 2013, pp. 169–185.

REFERENCES

Ascherson, N. (1996). National identity. In G. Radice (Ed.), *What needs to change* (pp. 79–97). London, UK: Harper Collins.

Aughey, A. (2001). *Nationalism, devolution and the challenge to the United Kingdom state.* London, UK: Pluto Press.

BBC News Scotland. (2013, September 26). *Census suggests most Scots 'only feel Scottish.'* Retrieved from http://www.bbc.co.uk/news/uk-scotland-24282271

Bechhofer F., & McCrone, D. (2007). *Being British: A crisis of identity?* Retrieved from http://www.institute-of-governance.org/publications/working_papers/being-british_a_crisis_of_identity

Bechhofer, F., & McCrone, D. (Eds.). (2009). *National identity, nationalism and constitutional change.* London, UK: Palgrave Macmillan.

Bond, R. (2000). Squaring the circles: Demonstrating and explaining the political 'non-alignment' of Scottish national identity. *Scottish Affairs, 32,* 15–35.

Brand, J., & Mitchell, J. (1997). Home rule in Scotland. The politics and bases of a movement. In J. Bradbury & J. Mawson (Eds.), *British regionalism and devolution: The challenges of state reform and European integration* (pp. 35–54). London, UK: Routledge.

British Social Attitudes. (2012). *Survey 30*. Retrieved from http://www.bsa-30.natcen.ac.uk/read-the-report/devolution/trends-in-national-identity.aspx

Brown, A., McCrone, D., & Paterson, L. (1998). *Politics and society in Scotland* (2nd revised ed.). London, UK: Macmillan.

Cameron, E. A. (2010). *Impaled upon a thistle. Scotland since 1880.* Edinburgh, SCT: Edinburgh University Press.

Colley, L. (2008). *Britons. Forging the nation 1707–1837* (2nd ed.). New Haven, CT: Yale University Press.

Davidson, N. (2000). *The origins of Scottish nationhood.* London, UK: Pluto Press.

Devine, T. M. (2003). *Scotland's empire 1600–1815.* London, UK: Penguin.

Devine, T. M. (2006). *The Scottish nation 1700–2007.* London, UK: Penguin.

Dieckhoff, A. (2000). *La nation dans tous ses etats. Les identités nationales en mouvement.* Paris, FR: Flammarion.

Dodds, A., & Seawright, D. (2004). The politics of identity: Scottish nationalism. In M. O'Neill (Ed.), *Devolution and British politics* (pp. 90–112). London, UK: Pearson Longman.

Duclos, N. (2013). Identité britannique et identité écossaise: Les débats sur la célébration de fêtes nationales au Royaume-Uni. In M. Mattioli, O. Muro, & M. Prum (Eds.), *"L'identité nationale" à l'épreuve des identités culturelles en allemagne, en France, au royaume-uni: Une approche critique* (pp. 169–185). Paris, FR: L'Harmattan.

Eaton, G. (2013, June 19). Alex Salmond on his youth jobs right, the bedroom tax and why he will win. *New statesman.* Retrieved from http://www.newstatesman.com/politics/2013/06/exclusive-alex-salmond-his-youth-jobs-right-bedroom-tax-and-why-he-will-win.

Eley, G., & Suny, R. G. (1996). Introduction: From the moment of social history to the work of cultural representation. In G. Eley, & R. G. Suny (Eds.), *Becoming national* (pp. 3–37). Oxford, UK: Oxford University Press.

Gamble, A., & Wright, T. (2009). Introduction: The Britishness question. In A. Gamble & T. Wright (Eds.), *Britishness. perspectives on the British question* (pp. 1–9). London, UK: Wiley-Blackwell & the Political Quarterly.

Gardham, M. (2013, January 12). Economics will decide referendum, research suggests. *Herald.* Retrieved from http://www.heraldscotland.com/politics/referendum-news/economics-will-decide-referendum.19889414

Gardham, M. (2013, January 25). Salmond "a victim of his own success." *Herald.* Retrieved from http://www.heraldscotland.com/politics/referendum-news/salmond-a-victim-of-his-own-success.20004339.

The Geographical Magazine. (1993, March). Is Scotland a country? *Geographical Magazine, 63,* 13.

Hanham, H. J. (1969). *Scottish nationalism.* London, UK: Faber & Faber.

Keating, M. (1996). *Nations against the State. The new politics of nationalism in Quebec, Catalonia and Scotland.* Basingstoke, UK: Palgrave.

Keating, M. (2009). Nationalist movements in perspective. In G. Hassan (Ed.), *The modern SNP. From protest to power* (pp. 204–218). Edinburgh, SCT: Edinburgh University Press.

Kumar, K. (2010). Review: National identity, nationalism and constitutional change. *Scottish Affairs, 73*, 102–105.

Leruez, J. (1983). *L'Ecosse. une nation sans etat.* Lille, FR: Presses Universitaires de Lille.

Lynch, M. (1999). *Scotland. A new history.* London, UK: Pimlico.

Lynch, M. (Ed.). (2001). *The Oxford companion to Scottish history.* Oxford, UK: Oxford University Press.

Lynch, P. (1999). *SNP. The history of the scottish national party.* Cardiff, WAL: Welsh Academic Press.

Macwhirter, I. (2009, June 8). Last night was the SNP's night. *Guardian.* Retrieved from http://www.theguardian.com/commentisfree/2009/jun/08/snp-bnp-european-elections-scotland.

Mason, R. (2010). General editor's preface. In E. A. Cameron (Ed.), *Impaled upon a thistle. Scotland since 1880* (pp.xiii–xiv). Edinburgh, SCT: Edinburgh University Press.

McCrone, D. (1992). *Understanding Scotland. The sociology of a stateless nation.* London, UK: Routledge.

McEwen, N. (2003). The depoliticisation of national identity? Territorial politics after devolution. In E. Longley, E. Hughes, & D. O'Rawe (Eds.), *Ireland (Ulster) Scotland: Concepts, contexts, comparisons* (pp. 11–27). Belfast, IRL: Queen's University Belfast

Mitchell, J., Bennie, L., & Johns, R. (2012). *The Scottish national party. Transition to power.* Oxford, UK: Oxford University Press.

Morton, G. (1999). Unionist-nationalism. *Governing urban Scotland, 1830–1860.* East Linton, SCT: Tuckwell Press.

Nairn, T. (1977). The break-up of Britain. *Crisis and neo-nationalism.* London, UK: New Left Books.

Paterson, L., Brown, A., Curtice, J., Hinds, K., McCrone, D., Park, A., Surridge, P., et al. (2001). *New Scotland, new politics?* Edinburgh, SCT: Polygon.

Reicher, S., Hopkins, N., & Harrison, K. (2009). Identity matters: On the importance of Scottish identity for Scottish society. In F. Bechhofer, & D. McCrone (Eds.), *National identity, nationalism and constitutional change* (pp. 17–40). London, UK: Palgrave Macmillan.

Salmond, A. (2007, October 12). *Speech to the council on foreign relations, New York.* Retrieved from http://www.cfr.org/business-and-foreign-policy/speech-alex-salmond-first-minister-scotland/p14497

Scots Language Centre (n.d.). *What is Scots?* Retrieved from http://www.scotslanguage.com/articles/view/id/3169

Scottish Conservative and Unionist Party. (1997). *Fighting for Scotland.* Scotland: Author.

Scottish Conservatives. (2010). *Invitation to join the government of Britain.* Scotland: Author.

Scottish Government. (2009). *Europe and foreign affairs: Taking forward our National Conversation.* Retrieved from http://www.scotland.gov.uk/Resource/Doc/283886/0086022.pdf.

Scottish Labour Party. (1997). *Because Scotland deserves better*. Scotland: Author.

Scottish Labour Party. (2010). *A Future fair for all*. Scotland: Author.

Scottish Liberal Democrats. (2010). *Change that works for you*. Scotland: Author.

Scottish National Party. (1995). *Citizens not subjects. The Parliament and Constitution of an independent Scotland*. Scotland: Author.

Scottish National Party. (2005). *Raising the standard*. Scotland: Author.

Scottish National Party. (2011). *Your Scotland. Your future*. Scotland: Author.

Scottish Parliament. (2004, March 17). *Official report*. Retrieved from http://www.scottish.parliament.uk/parliamentarybusiness/28862.aspx?r=4501&i=33100&c=819251&s=.

Scottish Parliament. (2004, July 29). *Consultation paper*. Retrieved from http://www.parliament.scot/S2_MembersBills/Draft%20proposals/DCanavanStandrewsday.pdf

Scottish Parliament. (2005, April 21). *Official report*. Retrieved from http://www.scottish.parliament.uk/parliamentarybusiness/28862.aspx?r=4577&i=34899&c=846619&s=

Scottish Parliament. (2010, November 25). *Official report*. Retrieved from http://www.scottish.parliament.uk/parliamentarybusiness/28862.aspx?r=6021&i=54024&c=1162275&s=

IS A NEW DEFINITION OF IRISH IDENTITY EMERGING IN THE REPUBLIC OF IRELAND IN THE 21ST CENTURY?

Julien Guillaumond

The world's economic slow-down and its late downturn had severe impacts on European economies. The social consequences of the financial crisis have also pressed nations to question the meaning of membership in their societies. Recently, many European states have been defining who does and does not belong, and who is entitled to State benefits and rights. In fact, many states have been implementing citizenship tests to gauge whether applicants have sufficient linguistic and other cultural knowledge of the host society (van Oers, Ersbøll, & Kostakopoulou, 2010).

In this context, national identity has taken center stage within a contradictory framework: on one side, the wall-building policies of numerous European states, and on the other side, the European Union, promoting diversity as a counter to ageing EU societies. National identity and the debates it has spawned have been serious questions in Europe. Indeed, national identity is being challenged. As Guibernau has argued, the identity of

National Identity, pages 113–145
Copyright © 2016 by Information Age Publishing

nations is being challenged from three major sources: a nation's minorities, supranational institutions, and a nation's immigrant populations (Guibernau, 2007, p. 189).

The Republic of Ireland[1] represents an interesting case study of national identity due to its economy, migration issues, and state policies. Ireland experienced tremendous economic and social changes over the last two decades triggered by an unprecedented economic boom from the mid-1990s until the devastating economic crisis after 2008, leading the Irish State to bankruptcy. Ireland also is known as a country of migration: emigration and immigration. The label is the result of the economic difficulties Ireland faced during the 20th century. During economic hard time, many of Ireland's population left; and during its economic good times, some Irish returned and immigrants from other countries entered to fill specific labor market needs.[2] The nation itself had little experience with immigration and immigrants. Both factors have challenged Irish identity.

In light of these challenges, how has Irish identity fared over the last two decades? Does Ireland have a new definition of its identity? To what extent is multiculturalism acknowledged and promoted? Is the "State-created myth of a culturally homogenous people living within its territory" (Guibernau, 2007, p. 26) being re-examined or re-assessed? The purpose of my chapter is to examine several issues about national identity in Ireland. While many factors affect national identity, economics, demography, and state policies are included in such a list. I examine the effects each has on Irish identity. Specifically, I examine the economic down turns and up turns in the Irish economy, immigration, and State policies on Irish national identity.

THEORETICAL BACKGROUND

National Identity: A Brief Overview of the Literature

Nowadays, a wide consensus seems to exist on the main features of National identity, such as that it is a modern, fluid, and dynamic phenomenon (Guibernau, 2007) central to nation building and the organization of society (Cole, 2010; Keating, 1997). Among the multiple identities human beings may share (Puhle, 1994), it still represents the most "fundamental and inclusive of all" (Smith, 1991, p. 143), and remains, even today, "widely attractive and effective and is felt by many people to satisfy their needs for cultural fulfilment, rootedness, security and fraternity" (Smith, 1995, p. 159).

What seems less definite, however, are its intrinsic dimensions and their respective interactions. Indeed, though national identity very often invokes the past to give the present meanings, its primary aim is towards the future, such as the type of society citizens collectively aim at. As such it touches more on "the process of becoming rather than being: not 'who we are' or 'where we came from,' so much as what we might become, how we have been represented and how that bears on how we might represent ourselves" (Hall, 1996, p. 4). If national identity as a question emerges when societies experience rapid transformations and when "old traditions" are being contested (Hobsbawm & Ranger, 1983, pp. 4–5), it can very often also operate as a "populist umbrella" term (Malešević, 2011, p. 272) for many a State willing to imagine (Anderson, 2006) or re-invent their nation (Gellner, 2006). Without a doubt, such a question does not have the same weight in various countries as the French national identity debate and subsequent sour demise can attest in comparison with the case studied here.

National identity is also deeply personal and subjective; it represents an individual feeling of being part of a larger community. It contributes to an individual's social identity and has a positive effect on personal self-esteem if the person's nation is evaluated positively (Arts & Halman, 2006, p. 74). Also, as a collective sentiment it makes a nation distinct from other nations (Guibernau, 2007, p. 11). It does not imply complete similarity as "not all citizens feel with the same intensity the emotional bond which connects them to their nation-States" (Guibernau, 2007, p. 29). That "affective dimension" (Harttgen & Opfinger, 2014, p. 347), the intensity of one's attachment to a nation (Malešević, 2011, p. 274), has a true importance in the value individuals give to it. The intensity of national identification can thus be studied through "identity markers" (Kiely, Bechhofer, Stewart, & McCrone, 2001) which are characteristics presented to others to support a national identity claim, but also looked to in others when seeking to attribute national identity (Kiely et al., 20016), but also through the ordinary reminders of one's membership to the nation (Prideaux, 2009) and the interactions such membership offers on a daily basis (Déloye, 2013).

History and Diversity in Defining Irish National Identity

Guibernau has argued that national identity possesses five dimensions: psychological, cultural, territorial, historical, and political (Guibernau, 2007, p. 11). Thus, any attempt at defining Irish identity becomes a strenuous exercise, rendered all the more difficult by Partition, but also because it seems that "what it means to be Irish and the discourse used to define Irishness have never been neatly defined" (Crowley, Gilmartin, & Kitchin, 2006, p. 19).

Partition is the existence of two opposite versions of the nation. Each version has its own definition of the Irish nation—a single nation in the Irish nationalist tradition, a two-nation framework in the unionist perspective (Gallagher, 1995). This difficulty gets more complex when the debate is extended to a three-nation framework: an Irish nation, an Ulster Protestant nation, and a part of the British nation (Gallagher, 1995).

The "imagined community" (Anderson, 2006) of the Irish nation, as defined by the Irish nationalist tradition and adopted by the Republic of Ireland, is all-encompassing, comprising the northern counties as part of Irish nationalism. It is one view of Irishness (Sinha, 1998, p. 21): a fetishized "Irishness" (Longley, 2001, p. 9), which was predominant until the end of the 20th century. It is a contested view (Crowley et al., 2006, pp. 19–20) because it tends to exclude travelers or Jews from both national imagined space and narrative (Fanning, 2002; Garner, 2004).

A very restrictive version of the "imagined community" has a long history (Crowley et al., 2006, p. 7). This version equates Irish identity with a common religion and a particular demographic profile. There are two interacting reasons for the longevity of this narrow view: colonization (Sinha, 1998, p. 21), and the role of Catholicism as a central element of resistance to non-Catholic Britain (White, 2010, p. 23). A true Irish person was Catholic, nationalist, a GAA member,[3] and absolutely *not* British. At the core of Irish identity in the Republic lay in a very rigid definition of "authenticity," thus negating any sense of diversity (Sinha, 1998, p. 21).

The same was true in the nationalist movement during the early part of the 20th century. *Sinn Féin* members had to learn the Gaelic language, write on paper made in Ireland, and demonstrate high moral qualities and respect for the family (Goldring, 1975). In nationalist discourse, relative homogeneity, whether in terms of religion or in skin color, is a goal (Loyal, 2011). Language had a similar function, and represented a commitment to the nation by distancing oneself from Britain and the influence of the English language.

Land was also part of Irish identity. Land demonstrated resilience in the face of historical events, and the roots of the nation. It represented place, a home, a geographic area where people could establish a community and their sense of peoplehood.

Being Irish as a mono-cultural status was promoted by the Catholic Church, Republican parties, and the GAA. Being Irish meant being against most everything British (Crowley et al., 2006). Being Irish leaves no room for non-white, non-Celtic peoples, or for those who are not part of Ireland's history (Loyal, 2003). This restrictive version of being Irish was reinforced by the strength of community life and values and viewed "Other" as a stranger to the community (McVeigh, quoted in Sinha, 1998, p. 21).

Finally, the historical dimension reinforces the perceived uniqueness of Irish identity since a shared history is another central element of being Irish (Davis, 2003). Such a view explains the negative reaction when the "Other," the foreigner, does not possess such a background (Sinha, 1998).

The Irish Economy: Boom and Bust

The Celtic Tiger Years

In the late 1980s, Ireland was in deep economic crisis. The unemployment rate was a major concern, emigration was a major problem, and it had a serious public debt.

Leaving Ireland seemed to be one solution. Many Irish left the country during economic hard times, and in 1989, the worst year on record for decades, Ireland saw approximately 70,000 people leave the country (Fahey, 2007, p. 27). This figure represented approximately 2% of its population. In the following decades, things changed.

The 1980s starkly contrast with the following decades when being Irish became synonymous with economic success. In the space of just a few years, the Republic of Ireland went from being bankrupt to a model of economic development—a Celtic Tiger with impressive growth rates, becoming, by the early 2000s, one of the most open economies in the world (Yester, 2002).

The Celtic Tiger era and positive Irish identity were synonymous. Ireland's European neighbors were bewildered with the country's "model of economic development" and its outstanding growth rates. Irish Economists were more than happy in presenting its recipes for success to their European colleagues (Sweeney, 1998; Barry, 1999). Unassailable statistical proof of Irish economic success caused intense satisfaction, particularly while recording how the Republic of Ireland was "economically more advanced than the UK" and other EU States (Coulter, 2003, p. 15).

Ireland's attractiveness is further demonstrated by migration statistics. A greater number of people were clamoring to get into Ireland than rushing to leave (Hughes, McGinnity, O'Connell, & Quinn, 2007)—net migration (in-migration—out-migration) was positive. The economy had an average growth rate oscillating between 8 and 10%, a huge surge in employment, and a substantial workforce growth rate of more than 80% between 1991 and 2005 (Mac Éinrí, 2007, p. 237).

There was no questioning the Irish identity. The Irish were proud of their country, and could collectively boast about the large growth in their GDP growth and their rising standard of living. Life was good in Ireland, but there were some concerns.

There were some concerns about the Celtic Tiger development model. Kieran Allen pointed out the large increase in the consumption of luxury vehicles (Allen, 2000). Ann Marie Hourihane, in her book, *She Moves through the Boom*, pointed out other dimensions of the boom and its impact on Irish society (Hourihane, 2000). Nonetheless, economic success bred Irish pride and positive national identity.

That particular confidence was confirmed by data collected in the 1990s, which reported a surge in pride in Irish identity: 71% of Irish respondents were "very proud" of their identity, a sharp increase from the 55% in the late 1980s (Fahey et al., 2006, p. 65; Davis, 2003). Being Irish in the early 2000s was slightly different from previous decades (Logue, 2000). Even former British Prime Minister, T. Blair proudly praised his Irish roots while reminiscing about his childhood summers in Donegal (Logue, 2000). But change was in the air.

The Fallen Tiger: The Economic Crisis

The 2008 global economic crisis changed everything.[4] The fall began with an initial economic slow-down, but soon the Irish State realized that it was more than that. The state realized it would be unable to face the economic global crisis, and was forced to accept a bailout and the presence of International Monetary Fund, EU, and Central Bank experts. The bailout announcement represented a huge blow for Ireland and, correspondingly, an even greater blow to Irish identity. The public perceived that they had collectively lost their country's economic and political independence. It was a desperate time.

The media in Ireland echoed the people's sentiments. There was complete loss of trust and confidence in political representatives and State institutions. Despair set in, and emigration, once again, seemed to be the only solution for many. Such low esteem in the country was captured in an opinion letter to the *Irish Times* in early 2013, where the author referred to a form of self-delusion in Ireland, was highly critical and disdainful of the country (Fennell, 2013).

Irish Demography in Perspective

Migration and the Irish Identity: An Emerging Diversity

Over the past decade, immigration has challenged definitions of national identity. In some ways, immigration has forced many European countries to question and strengthen what they mean by national identity. One lingering, and still contentious, issue in Europe is matching the free movement of people from other parts of Europe, including those whose nations have become EU members, and those from non-EU countries. Should these people be granted the same political, economic, and social rights associated with EU members?

Ireland has undergone significant demographic changes over the past two decades. Originally Ireland was viewed as a country of emigration (Mac Laughlin, 1994), but it has become a country of immigration. It is a new member among those nations experiencing significant increases in their immigrant populations (Segal, Elliott, & Mayadas, 2010). This fact is contrasted with the Irish depopulation for the greater part of the 20th century.

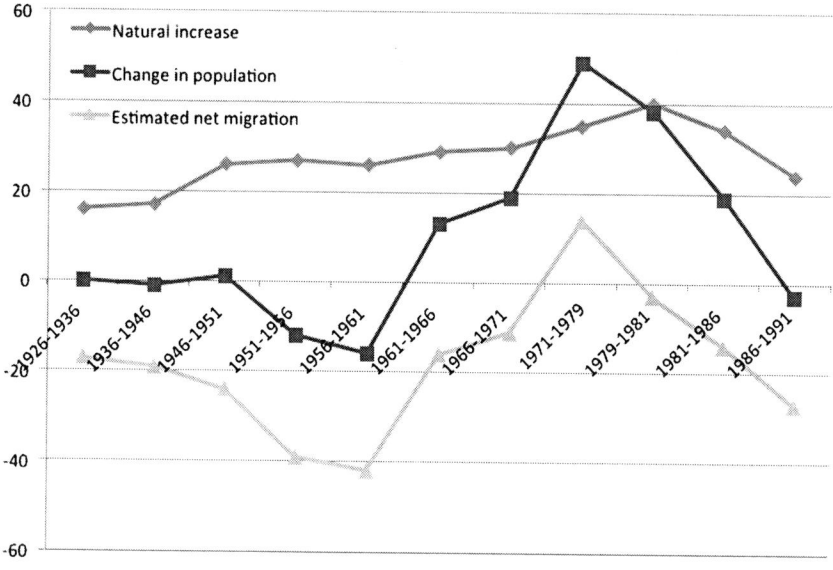

Figure 4.1 Natural increase, net migration and population growth in Ireland at different census years, 1926–1991 (in 000s).

Since the "Great Famine," one characteristic of Irish demography has been the continuous decline of its population. The effect of natural increase, the traditional component of population growth, was completely reversed by the sheer size of out-migration (see Figure 4.1).[5]

The Irish population reached an all-time low in the mid-1950s when many left the country. In their official report on the phenomenon, the members of the Commission on Emigration noted that the number of people who emigrated was "still large enough to absorb the whole, or almost the whole, of the natural increase and thus prevent population growth" (O'Brien, 1954, p. 130). John O'Brien's book, *The Vanishing Irish*, was published in 1954 and reflected the thinking of the time—that the nation of Ireland might become extinct as a result of emigration.

People had different views about emigration and immigration—though most viewed these events negatively. However, to some emigration was a positive (Delaney, 2000); it prevented all forms of social unrest and discontent in the young Republic. Throughout the 20th century, the population of the Republic of Ireland closely mirrored the State's economy: the Irish population grew in the 1960s when the economic situation improved, encouraging many men and women to return, while the situation was reversed when the economy worsened in the 1980s and emigration increased.

In the second half of the 20th century, emigration slowed, and immigration by non-Irish persons became relatively insignificant (Mac Éinrí, 2001).

In 1973, net in-migration occurred for the first time in Irish history, most likely the result of Ireland joining the EEC. Immigration was led by returning Irish migrants, many with their families, coming to fill jobs as Ireland was experiencing labor shortages in an emerging economy (Mac Éinrí, 2001).

Up until the 1980s, immigrants[6] to Ireland comprised four groups: returning Irish, high-skills immigrants working for foreign companies, retirees—especially from the United Kingdom, and "counter-cultural" immigration from Britain and European States (Mac Éinrí, 2001, p. 52). Before the mid-1990s, few non-Irish or non-British populations immigrated to Ireland (Mac Éinrí, 2001).

Since the 1990s there was a net increase in the Irish population, of which in-migration was a major contributor. The year 1996 was a turning point in Irish demography. It was the first year of net immigration to Ireland—an increase of about 8,000 people (Gilmartin, 2012, p. 2). During this period, Ireland became one of the last countries in the EU to display net immigration (Ruhs, 2009). Since then, net migration has contributed to Ireland's population growth (Hughes et al., 2007). In 2000, Ireland saw a net migration inflow of 26,000 persons (Tarantino, 2012, p. 5), and between 1999 and 2008 the population increased by 18%, the highest rate in the 27 EU countries (CSO, 2008).

In 2006, Ireland's population in 2006 was at its highest level since 1871, at 4.04 million; the growth over the past few years owes as much to in-migration as to natural increase (National Economic and Social Council, 2006, p. 12). Between April 2004 and April 2005 the country realized its highest level of immigration (70,000 persons) and lowest level of emigration (16,600) since records began, thus giving a net migration rate of over 50,000 persons. After an increase following the 2004 EU enlargement (Ruhs, 2009), inflows peaked in 2006–2007 at over 100,000 immigrants per year. The situation has since been reversed as net migration plummeted in 2007–2008 (see Figure 4.2), and by 2010 the levels of migration were at their lowest since 1994 (Gilmartin, 2012, p. 2). If migration currently appears to be an issue, it is very different from the past decade when levels of out-migration dramatically increased, from over 49,000 in 2008 to 87,000 in 2012.

Rapid economic growth created an unprecedented demand for labor across a wide range of sectors including construction, finance, information technology, and healthcare (Ruhs, 2009). Over the 1990s and early 2000s, there was a huge inflow of people to Ireland. A brief summary of these migration patterns the composition of immigrants is as follows:

- Between 1995 and 2000, approximately a quarter of a million persons migrated to Ireland, of whom about half were returning Irish (Mac Éinrí, 2001, p. 53). There was a positive trend in migration as

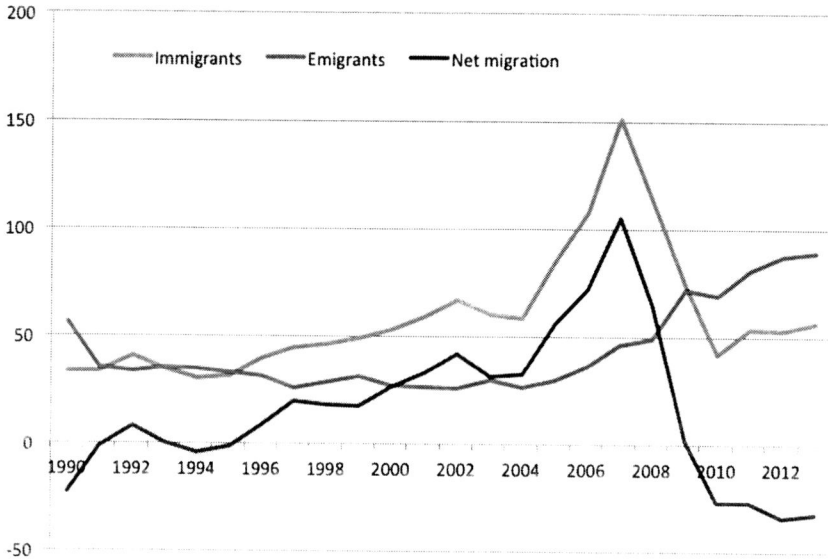

Figure 4.2 Immigration, emigration, and net migration in Ireland, 1991–2013 (in 000s).

more people were coming to Ireland than leaving. By 2001, some 20,000 people were leaving the country each year, but more than twice that number were arriving (NESC, 2006, p. 1).

- By the end of the 20th century, a change took place in the profile of immigrants arriving in Ireland. Among those who came, first were returning migrants, but soon thereafter people from other countries were arriving. Gradually, the number of returning migrants was offset by the number of other immigrants coming to work to Ireland. The increase in immigration has been accompanied by a steady fall in emigration. Even though the number of returning Irish migrants increased almost continuously between 1987 and 2002 (Ruhs, 2009); Irish people returning home represented about two-thirds of immigrants in 1991. They accounted for less than half of the gross inflow of 39,200 in 1996, and by 2005, they had fallen to 19,000 or about one quarter of the gross inflow of 70,000 (Hughes et al., 2007, p. 218).
- While 2002 was a peak year, their share in total immigration fell continuously from about 65% in the late 1980s to 44% from 2000 to 2002 (Ruhs, 2009). Between 2003 and 2005, their share fell again to 27%, and from 2006 to 2008, it fell to 18%, even though their number remained steady (Ruhs, 2009). As the share of returning Irish migrants fell, non-EU migrants came to dominate the flows

between 2001 and 2004 when they represented more than half of all non-Irish immigrants between 2001 and 2004 against one-third from 1992 to 1995 (Ruhs, 2009). In 2006, the ratio of foreign-born to the local population in Ireland was consequently deemed high compared with other industrialized countries, especially when considering immigration as a recent phenomenon in Ireland (NESC, 2006, p. 21). Since the accession of 10 new EU Member States in 2004, EU nationals have not only dominated migratory inflows, they have helped push flows to new heights. Between 2005 and 2008, an average 44% of the immigration flow and 54% of the non-Irish immigration flow was made up of nationals of the 10 EU States that acceded in 2004, together with Romania and Bulgaria, which acceded in 2007 (Ruhs, 2009).

One category of immigrants has challenged Irish national identity. Ruhs found that among the various categories of non-EU nationals coming to Ireland in the last decade, the great majority were workers (issued with work permits), followed by asylum seekers, students, and dependents (Ruhs, 2009). Asylum seekers have caused much trouble to the Irish State, and have definitely challenged past conceptions of Irish identity. The number of persons seeking asylum increased greatly between the mid-1990s and the early years of 2000, from 362 in 1994 to 11,364 in 2002, before falling off in 2003 and down to around 3,866 in 2008, and less than 1,000 in 2012 (Figure 4.3). Most asylum seekers are from African countries, such as Iraq and Nigeria, but also from Asia and Eastern Europe, such as Romania (ORAC, several years). Since joining the EU, the number of applications from Eastern Europe decreased since Ireland is not obligated to accept asylum applications from other EU Member States (Ruhs, 2009). In 2008, 26.1% of applications came from Nigerian nationals, 6.1% from Pakistani nationals, and 4.7% from Chinese and Georgian nationals.

As Ruhs has argued, "the increase and change in the composition of immigration to Ireland has significantly impacted the country's population" (Ruhs, 2009). Surveying the place of birth of its respondents, the Census of Population has revealed that among those born outside Ireland, three categories have continued to increase: the EU, Africa, and Asia. Among those residing in Ireland during the years 2002, 2006, and 2011, people born in the EU represented more than 70% of all foreign residents, and those from Africa between 6.6 and 7%. The most striking growth is among Asians, from 7.03% to 10.31% of all people born abroad. Moreover, the rate of growth of the population born outside Ireland between 2002 and 2011 represented half of the total population increase over the same period—55%.

Between 2006 and 2012 the Polish immigrant population grew the fastest. Their size increased from 63,090 to 115,193. Their average rate of

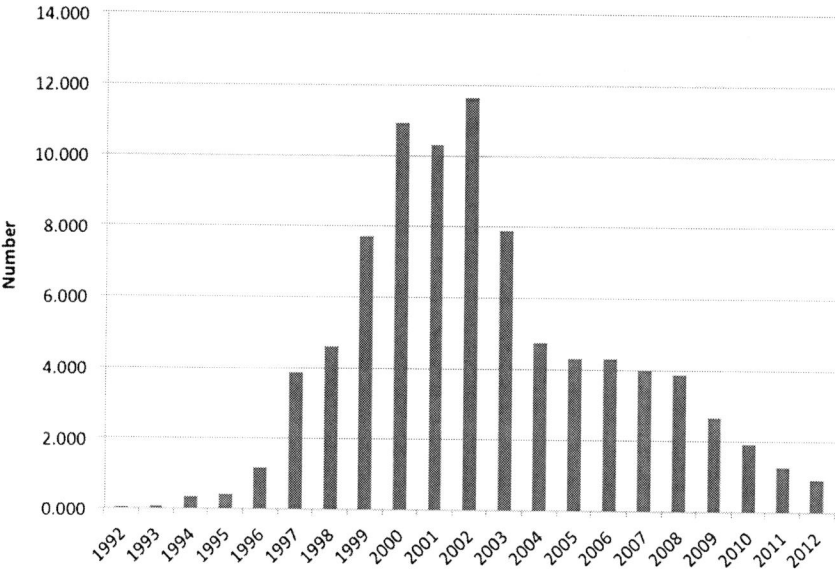

Figure 4.3   Number of applications for asylum received in Ireland, 1992–2012.

growth has been 1.6% per year (CSO, 2013, p. 1). In contrast, the number of non-Irish nationals has grown by 30% since 2006, representing 199 different nations. Ireland is a diverse nation.

Since 2002, the Census of Population asked respondents to self-identify their nationality. Though the data needs to be considered cautiously (Piola, 2007, p. 148), the findings show substantial growth of the "non-national" population in Ireland. In 2002, 5.8% of the total population resident in Ireland had non-Irish nationality. That share increased to 10.1% in 2006, and was 12% in 2011 (see Table 4.1).[7]

At the same time, the share of the population that are Irish nationals decreased over time: 92.9% in 2002, 88.8% in 2006, and to 86.8% in 2011. Their numbers did not decrease, but the increase in the non-Irish population reduced the share of the population held by those identifying as Irish nationals. The most significant increase (Ruhs, 2009) was seen in the EU nationality category, whose share rose from 3.5% in 2002 to 6.6% in 2006, and to 8.5% lately. Most EU nationals come from EU-10 countries:[8] over 120,500 people or almost 3% of the population counted in the 2006 census (Ruhs, 2009). Their number nearly doubled 5 years later, representing 8.5% of the Irish population.

According to the latest CSO statistics, the number of non-Irish nationals grew by 143% in 9 years (2002–2011).[9] In 2011, the largest group of non-Irish nationals were Polish citizens (Table 4.2). Between 2006 and 2011 the

TABLE 4.1 Persons Usually Resident and Present in Ireland by Nationality, 2002, 2006, and 2011[13]

	2002		2006		2011	
	Number	Share in Total Population	Number	Share in Total Population	Number	Share in Total Population
All Irish	3584975	92.9	3706683	88.8	3927143	86.8
UK	103476	2.7	112548	2.7	112259	2.5
EU15 excluding Irish and UK	29960	0.8	42693	1.0	48280	1.1
EU15 to EU25 States	—	—	120534	2.9	226225	5.0
Total EU	133436	3.5	275775	6.6	386764	8.5
Other European	23105	0.6	24425	0.6	16307	0.4
United States	11384	0.3	12475	0.3	11015	0.2
Africa	20981	0.5	35326	0.8	41642	0.9
Asia	21779	0.6	46952	1.1	65579	1.4
Other nationalities	11236	0.3	22422	0.5	22210	0.5
Multi/no nationality	3187	0.1	3676	0.1	2327	0.1
Not Stated	48412	1.3	44279	1.1	52294	1.2
Total non-Irish	224261	5.8	419733	10.1	544357	12.0
All nationalities: Total	3858495	100.0	4172013	100.0	4525281	100.0

Source: Census 2002, 2006 and 2011.

TABLE 4.2 Top Ten Nationalities Among Non-Nationals at Each Census Since 2002

Rank	2002		2006		2011		Rank
	Country	Number	Country	Number	Country	Number	
1	UK	103,476	UK	112,548	Poland	122,585	1
2	USA	11,384	Poland	63,276	UK	112,259	2
3	Nigeria	8,969	Lithuania	24,628	Lithuania	36,683	3
4	Germany	7,216	Nigeria	16,300	Latvia	20,593	4
5	France	6,363	Latvia	13,319	Nigeria	17,642	5
6	China	5,842	USA	12,475	Romania	17,304	6
7	Romania	4,978	China	11,161	India	16,986	7
8	Spain	4,436	Germany	10,289	Philippines	12,791	8
9	South Africa	4,185	Philippines	9,548	Germany	11,305	9
10	Philippines	3,900	France	9,046	USA	11,015	10
Total Non-Irish		224,261		419,733		544,357	

Source: CSO, Census statistics.

number of non-Irish nationals increased by 124,624 persons, or 29.7%. Polish nationals/residents increased by 93.7%: from 63,276 to 122,585, and account for almost half of the total increase among non-Irish nations and have overtaken UK nationals as the largest non-Irish group living in Ireland (CSO, 2013, p. 5).

Non-Irish nationals are a visible group. In 2002 5.8% of residents were non-Irish nationals, and by 2011 they accounted for 12% of the Irish population. In the table shown above, a gradual increase of people from Eastern Europe can also be observed (2006 Poland, Lithuania and Latvia, 101,323, or 24.1% of non-Irish nationals; 2011 Poland, Lithuania, Latvia, Romania, *i.e.*, 197,165, or 38.2% of non-Irish nationals, including Slovakia, not listed).

In 2011, a CSO publication entitled *Migration and Diversity* identified 199 nationalities residing in Ireland. The publication commented on the "remarkable diversity" (CSO, 2011a, p. 8), and provided the names of the top 12 nations with more than 10,000 nationals present in Ireland: China, Germany, India, Latvia, Lithuania, Nigeria, Philippines, Poland, Romania, Slovakia, UK, and USA. These 12 nations accounted for 74.4% of non-Irish nationals living in Ireland. The largest group is Polish nationals (amongst the biggest group of EU nationals living in another EU States) (Vasileva, 2011, p. 3), followed by UK nationals.

It has been argued that migration does have an impact on national identity. The number of immigrants received, the time-scale in which immigration occurs, immigrants' ethnic identity, their skills and socio-economic position within the host society are among the factors affecting national identity (Guibernau, 2007). In this respect, because immigration took place in so short a time in Ireland, it has had an impact on national identity. The attitude and legislation of the host country regarding immigration, the degree of difficulty in obtaining citizenship, and the level of willingness of immigrants to integrate into the host culture (Guibernau, 2007) represent a second set of factors influencing a nation's identity.

In the context of these demographic changes, how has Irish identity evolved? In 2007, Fanning and Mutwarasibo wrote that "a period of rapid economic expansion over the last decade [...] has changed Irish society into a visibly diverse one" (Fanning & Mutwarasibo, 2007, p. 440). So, how has the new status of Ireland—a country of immigration—been acknowledged, either in the actions of the state, or how has diversity been embraced? Has this newly discovered diversity been included in any definition of Irish identity? Does Irishness in the 21st century possess a multicultural dimension? How has Irish identity reacted to these challenges?

The State and Identity: The Irish Census, Irish National Identity,
and Homogenizing the Irish Population

Four elements will be considered in how Irish identity has evolved, demonstrating that strategies at maintaining Irish identity are defensive, stressing its history, and maintaining the main tenets of Irishness. First, however, let me point out the distinction between race and ethnicity. Race is a methodological construct, and ideal type, used to differentiate populations based on somatic and biological features, such as skin color, hair type, and other physical features. In contrast, ethnicity is another theoretical construct differentiating people based on culture. For example, Germans and Italians are of the same White race, but are different ethnic groups.

The state defining identity. Since 2006, the Republic of Ireland has included a question on race and cultural background (King-O'Riain, 2007). Officials argue that such questions are needed in order for the State to create and implement more effective policies.[10] But such data may also be used for political reasons.

There are two problems with the ethnic question. While census data provide a snapshot of the population at a given time, the same data help to "crystalise identities" (Cadogan, 2008, p. 52). Similarly, while collecting ethnic data, censuses "simultaneously help shape the emerging identities they seek to objectively record and document" (Cadogan, 2008, p. 50). In other words, not only do the census results provide the State's definition of national identity, but also logically contribute to the possible emergence or demise of other identities. The State has engaged in defining and creating national identity.

The 2011 census revealed that 94.3% of the population in Ireland had ticked the White box, a slight decline from 94.8% in 2006 (see Table 4.3). The two other main categories increased: "other background" and "not stated." These two categories declined from 2006 to 2011: 1.1% to 0.9% and 1.7 to 1.6%, respectively.

While such a question gives an official representation of Ireland's population, it also shows the Irish State's attempt at showing that Irish identity had not changed despite recent demographic trends. It thus gives the impression that Irish identity remains unaltered while at the same time denying diversity.

With its race question, the census instills a definition of race. In that sense, the "ethnic and cultural" question follows the trend which uses "ethnicity" to describe "race" (note that race is a concept based on physical traits, while ethnicity is culturally based). Though there was some consultation for using the question in the 2006 census (within some organs of the State, as well as within non-government and inter-government agencies), there was little or no consultation with experts or with non-Irish communities (King-O'Riain, 2006,). The census erased some distinctions between

TABLE 4.3 Persons Usually Resident in the Republic of Ireland by Ethnic or Cultural Background, 2006 and 2011

Category	2006		2011	
	Numbers	%	Numbers	%
White				
Irish	3 645 200	87.4	3 822 000	84.5
Irish Traveller	22,400	0.5	29,500	0.7
Any other White background	289,000	6.9	413,000	9.1
Black or Black Irish				
African	40,500	1	58,700	1.3
Any other Black background	3,800	0.1	6,400	0.1
Asian or Asian Irish				
Chinese	16,500	0.4	17,800	0.4
Any other Asian background	35,800	0.9	66,900	1.5
Other Including Mixed Background	46,400	1.1	40,700	0.9
Not Stated	72,300	1.7	70,300	1.6
Total	4 172 000	100	4 525 300	100.0

Source: CSO, Statistical Yearbook of Ireland, 2011 and 2013

nationalities by putting people from different ethnic groups, such as those from Eastern origins, with people of Irish origins and excluding others based on skin color. In the census, one is either white, black/black Irish, or Asian. Anderson stated that the "fiction of the census is that everyone is in it, and that everyone has one—and only one—extremely clear place" (Anderson, 2006, p. 166). It was a forced-choice question, and respondents had to tick a box with options imposed by the State.

The "White" category reinforces Ireland's traditional view, by putting people from different origins into the same category. Consequently, results indicate that approximately 94% of the Irish population is White, and gives the false impression about the actual size of the Irish population. Moreover, it incorrectly emphasizes the mono-cultural conception of Irish identity. People of English, Polish, or Russian origin are very likely to be found in the "White" category, thus leading to the notion of a large homogenous Irish population (Cadogan, 2008, p. 58), and a false impression of immutability (O'Keeffe-Vigneron, 2010).

The undifferentiated White category contributes to sustaining a myth about cultural unity and 'national integrity,' underlining the unquestioned centrality of Whites as the dominant identity group in Ireland (Cadogan, 2008, p. 59). At the same time, the use of other categories, such as Back African, also merges people from different African nations that would not be grouped based on ethnicity (Cadogan, 2008, p. 60). Such oversimplification is misleading, reinforces the mono-cultural identity of the country, and makes minority or ethnic groups less visible. Ultimately, it strongly implies that no new identity can be acknowledged.

The different subcategories, the "weird subcategory, under each racial group, of 'Others'—who, nonetheless, are absolutely not to be confused with *other* 'Others'" (Anderson, 2006, p. 166) are all social constructs. "[W]hiteness has become salient as an identity in the co-presence of non-white" (Cadogan, 2008, p. 57). This is also an important element when considering the "White" category and the Polish people, for example, who are not fully Irish, but are counted in the "White" category and not in the "Other" category. This is corroborated by one participant in Yau's study when the person asserts that "if you don't fit white Irish then you're not really Irish" (Yau, 2007, p. 64).

By pigeon-holing people, the situation for those not part of the White group, even immigrants from the second or third generation, leads to their non-recognition. Indeed, the ethnicity question implies that ethnicity is something one has, something inherited (Cadogan, 2008, p. 55). One is either Irish or of Irish descent, or one is in the "Other" category. That position is further strengthened by the 'background' element, which further implies that what matters is the place where one or one's ancestors were born, leaving no space for other generations of immigrants, for instance, to assert another identity. The Chinese community, one of the largest visible minority ethnic groups within Ireland, still remains pretty much invisible in Irish society (Yau, 2007, p. 49). Members of that community, when interviewed, equate White with Irishness, and anything else being other (Yau, 2007, p. 58), providing new comers with a "restrictive" definition of Irishness (Yau, 2007, p. 60). There appears to be a dual perception of immigrants or non-Irish nationals in Ireland. Even though second generation Chinese respondents identified as Irish because they felt like it was their national identity, they were racialized as the Other (Yau, 2007, p. 61).

The race question is a forced choice question, and does not leave much room for other responses. This emphasis on the "White" category in the Irish census contributes to a traditional conception of Irishness, and prevents any questioning about cultural homogeneity in Ireland (Cadogan, 2008, p. 62), thus reinforcing a traditional conception of white Irishness. It is an example of a constructivist's strategy in creating national identity for specific political purposes.

Citizenship and identity. Nationality laws and access to citizenship constitute a second element of national identity. How has access to Irish citizenship evolved, and to what extent does its evolution restrict Irish identity?

Citizenship refers to "the particular legal bond between an individual and his or her State" (Vasileva, 2011, p. 7). Over the past decades, immigration policies have served as government policies on nationality (Symmons, 1999). This also seems to be the case in Ireland. Citizenship represents the State's prerogative of inclusion and exclusion: It covers passport, all rights and privileges accruing to citizens such as the right to vote and many other protections (Symmons, 1999).

From 1922 up to 2004, Irish citizenship was accorded either through ancestry or through birth, *ius soli* (King-O'Riain, 2006, p. 283). Thus, the children of immigrants were granted citizenship, and immigrants could be naturalized relatively easily (Honohan, 2010). The *ius sanguinis* principle applied to the children and grandchildren of Irish born citizens.

Access to Irish citizenship has been radically transformed. The transformation is due to Ireland changing from a nation of emigration to a nation of immigration. The *ius soli* principle has been restricted and is no longer unconditionally given to children born in Ireland. In contrast, *ius sanguinis*, initially influenced by emigration, has remained unaltered.

There are three modes of acquiring citizenship in Ireland: acquisition by *ius sanguinis*, by *ius soli*, and by naturalization. Each mode has its own peculiarities.

The first mode, *Ius Sanguinis Citizenship*, known as "citizenship by descent," states that a person is an Irish citizen from birth if at the time of birth, either parent was an Irish citizen or would, if alive, have been an Irish citizen. It also applies to persons whose parent(s) is entitled to Irish citizenship. "Irish nationality" can be acquired especially for children of the diaspora, provided there is an unbroken ancestry chain to Ireland.

The second mode, *Ius Soli Citizenship*, is limited to those who have, at the time of birth, at least one parent who is an Irish citizen or is entitled to be an Irish citizen (Handoll, 2012, 11). An important change in the granting of Irish citizenship occurred as a direct consequence of the Belfast Agreement in 1998. I will discuss this at some length.

In the 1937 Constitution, citizenship had a rather broad definition in accordance with the aspiration of the Irish State for a united Ireland. In addition, there was a desire of protecting and including former generations of Irish, who were either living on the other part of the island or had left Ireland altogether. Therefore, all persons born on the island of Ireland and those born of Irish parents and thus part of the diaspora had automatic citizenship. The 1956 Nationality Act legally enshrined the *ius soli* principle to all those born on the island of Ireland, and citizenship through descent was possible if either parent was an Irish national (Loyal, 2011, p. 143). Other generations could possess Irish citizenship on demand (Symmons, 1999).

Following the Good Friday Agreement, an Amendment to the Constitution declared that: "It is the entitlement and birthright of every person born on the island of Ireland, which includes its islands and seas, to be part of the Irish nation. That is also the entitlement of all persons otherwise qualified in accordance with law to be citizens of Ireland. Furthermore, the Irish nation cherishes its special affinity with people of Irish ancestry living abroad who share its cultural identity and heritage" (Constitution of Ireland). This amendment to the Irish Constitution was approved by a majority (94%) in a referendum in June 1998, taking effect on December 2, 1999.

The amendment had two consequences: it put on an equal footing access to citizenship for people from both parts of Ireland (Handoll, 2012). At the same time, it also reasserted the diaspora dimension of Irish nationality (Symmons, 1999). For some like Garner, the Irish State has used the peace process as an opportunity to redraw the boundaries of being Irish (Garner, 2007).

The amendment opened a "loophole," as the Minister of the time had labelled it, through which people tried to gain Irish citizenship. With the Republic of Ireland becoming a country of in-migration, the new provisions conferred entitlements on children born in Ireland to non-Irish parents (Handoll, 2012). This was further reinforced by the interpretation of the family clause, where the Supreme Court stipulating that non-national parents had the right of residency because their children had been born in Ireland.

The law was criticized in the early 2000s because if offered a form of "carte blanche" of staying in the country for non-national parents who had children in Ireland (Handoll, 2012). In 2001, the Irish government considered the possibility of a constitutional amendment to close that loophole and remove the unconditional *ius soli* (Ryan, 2004). Though the Supreme Court's decision was reversed in January 2003 (with the Supreme Court decision in the Lobe case) it was "a surprise" that the government proposed restricting the constitutional provision of birthright citizenship to children of non-nationals (Ryan, 2004).

Three reasons were presented by the then government to justify the proposed referendum. First, there was a fear of people coming to have babies in Ireland, practicing "citizenship tourism" ("Citizenship Tourists," 2004) because too many non-national women were giving birth in Dublin maternity hospitals. It was shown later that the reactions of the heads of different maternity hospitals had been used to defend this argument, whereas they only meant to alert the government to the difficulties the health services had coping with such large numbers of birth (Brandi, 2007).

A second reason was that the loophole meant that Ireland remained open for immigrants, and this would cause relationship problems with other European countries. These two elements have to be set against a context of growing anti-immigrant attitudes in Ireland (King, 1998). The last argument was that such a loophole questioned the "integrity" of Irish citizenship, and led to the "common sense" citizenship campaign (Ryan, 2004, p. 17).

The campaign around the referendum exhibited the Irish State's views about immigration. There was government consensus, and with the main opposition party, on restricting citizenship rights to the children of foreigners (Brandi, 2007). The commonsense citizenship campaign and the perception of immigrants "fixed and 'essentialized' Irishness, highlighting the threatening 'Other,' constructing immigrants as suspect" (Crowley et al., 2006, p. 2). There were issues surrounding the debate: important concepts were simplified in order to evade the complex nature of the issues (Brandi, 2007; Breen & Devereux, 2003; Conway, 2008) and the timing was inappropriate, not allowing much time for questions (Ní Chiosáin, 2007).

After the Referendum, a person born in Ireland no longer had an automatic constitutional right to be an Irish citizen (Becker & Cosgrave, 2013). Some argued that the 2004 attempt was aimed at removing a constitutional problem that was created by previous constitutional reforms (Handoll, 2012). Ryan (2004) argued that Ireland is no exception as the abandonment of unconditional *ius soli* is significant but not unusual in a comparative perspective, in line with an increase in immigration. However, such a change validates Honohan's contention that the Irish nation is in complete opposition with its citizenry, "being both more inclusive—of those who had left Ireland, and more exclusive—of those who did not share a Catholic and Gaelic background" (Honohan, 2010, p. 8).

While access to citizenship has been curtailed through the *ius soli* principle, the last mode for acquiring Irish citizenship is being naturalized. Naturalization entails obtaining a certificate from the Minister for Justice and Equality. Lately, it has not been a strongly promoted program. Irish authorities do not promote naturalization, whether through a full informative website or through information on benefits that may be obtained by becoming an Irish citizen (Becker & Cosgrave, 2013). Moreover, there are challenges for those applying to naturalized citizens. To begin with, the fee for an application acts as a "deterrent for certain applicants" (Becker & Cosgrave, 2013, p. 3). Furthermore, the process of providing documents for application can be strenuous, and in the end, all applications remain at the discretion of the Minister for Justice and Equality.

The labor market and identity. Compared to other European countries, the Irish State did not attempt to protect its citizens by closing its borders in the 1990s to economic migrants. On the contrary, it sought additional workers to fuel the boom during the Celtic Tiger period. Rapid economic growth created significant labor shortages across many sectors of the Irish labor market (Kuhling & Keohane, 2007). Consequently, there was an increased demand for migrant labor, especially outside the EU. However, the economic policies of the Irish State have been used as a *de facto* immigration policy through the recruitment of extra labor. In the 1990s, the first part of the strategy was to attract specific migrant workers: first, from the Irish diaspora, second, returning Irish, and then labor from the European Economic Area (EEA) and other countries. Throughout the two decades, economic necessity drove migration policy (Boucher, 2008; Hughes et al., 2007).

In the first phase, the Irish State tried to attract members of the Irish diaspora. The state was proactive in its drive to draw people to Ireland to fill its labor shortages; there were many "globetrotting employment fairs" sponsored by the state (Fanning, 2009). One example was the "Jobs Ireland" campaign targeted to a special diaspora between 1999 and 2002 with roadshows and exhibitions in major cities throughout Europe and overseas. These fairs looked for young skilled Irish expatriates. Some elements of the campaign especially targeted people of Irish descent, taking into account the elements of "primordial Irishness" (Hayward & Howard, 2007). The underlying idea was that "members of the Irish diaspora, no matter how far removed in terms of distance and time, will fit in better to life in Ireland than those with no connection in the country" (Hayward & Howard, 2007, p. 53). The policy of recruiting people abroad was to some extent a way of creating a particular profile of the Irish population, and consequently to Irish identity. Certain workers were targeted for their Irish identity rather than their skills. In that sense, one cannot but agree with Hayward and Howard when they write that the campaign "to recruit skilled Irish professionals abroad indicates a desire to control immigration and thus to control the extent and nature of social change that it would engender" (Hayward & Howard, 2007, p. 58).

The second element of the Irish State's economic policy was granting work permits. The program's administrators assumed that permit holders would leave Ireland when their skills were no longer required; it was supposed to involve work for specific amount of time, and permits were linked to one employer (Hughes et al., 2007). Access to Ireland for many migrants was "shaped through formal recruitment programs set up by companies based in Ireland, such as McDonalds or Tesco, who placed adverts in Lithuanian newspapers as part of a strategy of acquiring labour" (Loyal, 2011, p. 34).

Until April 2003, Ireland's labor migration policies were almost entirely "employer-led" (NESC, 2006, p. xii). There were few restrictions imposed on employers when recruiting workers from the non-European Economic Area (EEA). There was one condition—"labour market test" to encourage employers to make efforts at filling existing vacancies with EEA workers before looking to employ non-EEA workers.[11] In other words, employers could legally recruit as many non-EEA workers as they wished, from any country, and to employ them in any job, regardless of the skill level required (Ruhs, 2009). The number of work permits issued to non-EEA nationals increased dramatically between 1999 and 2003, by more than 650%. Most of these permits were issued for low-skilled occupations in sectors such as catering, agriculture, and other services (Ruhs, 2009). After EU enlargement, all low-skilled labor had to be sourced from EEA countries, and certain categories became ineligible for work permits (Ruhs, 2009). The service sector remained one of the main sources of recruitment post 2004 for non-EEA nationals, mainly immigrants from India and the Philippines (Ruhs, 2009).

This policy was truly part of the official position. The National and Economic Social Council (NESC) retrospectively praised the "flexibility of the immigration system" and "its responsiveness to demands of employers for migrant labour" (NESC, 2006, p. 41). These two elements helped generate "benefits, both for individual employers and the Irish economy as a whole" (NESC, 2006, p. 41). Immigration was seen as an essential factor for the success of the Irish economy, present and future.[12] "[With] the domestic labour pool drying up, immigration has played a critical role in meeting significant labour shortages at both the high and low-skill labour market segments. This has clearly helped maintain Ireland's rapid economic growth since the mid-1990s. Immigration is also considered a key requirement to maintaining high levels of economic growth in the future" (NESC, 2006, p. 41). In that sense, immigration was favorably presented as it had "increased economic growth, eased labour market shortages, improved output" and reduced earnings inequalities (NESC, 2006, p. xiii).

Paradoxically, in its appraisal of immigration over the 1990s, NESC only mentions migration composed of "returning skilled Irish" or "Irish" immigrants is acknowledged as having "played a key role in expanding the productive economy," influencing growth, easing skill shortages, and helping to reduce long-term unemployment (NESC, 2006, p. xiii).

Immigration did seem to have upgraded the Irish labor market with the return of skilled Irish workers. Immigration also triggered population growth and consumer demand: "increased the size of the domestic market and resulted in increased demand for a variety of goods and services" (NESC, 2006, p. xiv). It is also "reasonable to generalize that, in the majority of cases, employment in Ireland leads to a financial gain for the individual migrant that may not have materialized had that worker stayed home." (NESC, 2006, p. xiv) Migration to Ireland had many positive results, but only Irish migration was acknowledged. There was an untold assumption in this praise of immigration: the focus was mostly on skilled people, preferably of Irish origin.

Diversity and national identity. Over the last decade, diversity has become a fashionable topic in Europe (Guillaumond & Martin, 2013). Ireland is no exception. To what extent has diversity been included in political discourse? Has Irish identity been able to feed on such a newly discovered and proclaimed diversity?

An important factor to consider is that the Irish government began addressing immigrant integration rather late. A Ministry for Integration was created in 2007; its strategy for integration involved several institutions, mainly the school and workplace. Prior to 2007, a series of official publications presented the vision of Irish society regarding the "Other." In these publications, economics established a code of good diversity practices, undoubtedly driven by the presence of several multinationals in Ireland. In the mid-1990s, it was important to market Ireland abroad in a positive light (Mac Laughlin, 1997).

The rhetoric of interculturalism is a key element to consider in those documents. Such rhetoric gives the impression that the State and its institutions are responding to racism by fostering a "more inclusive Ireland." However, "its underlying logic of celebrating, embracing and respecting diversity reinforces power inequities" between majority group and ethnic minority groups (Bryan, 2010). One factor celebrates difference, while the latter defines how minorities benefit or enrich the host culture (Bryan, 2010). In *Integration: a Two-Way Process* (DJELR, 1999), demographic diversity is acknowledged, but the document in itself only deals with political refugees.

Integration refers to elements that improve refugees' living conditions. Interculturalism is a key element of integration in which the host and sending cultures acknowledge and respect both cultures (Guillaumond & Martin, 2013). However, Interculturalism is a weak form of multiculturalism— a focus on cultural coexistence rather than cultural exchange (Longley, 2001). In a second document, *Planning for Diversity: The National Action Plan Against Racism* (DJELR, 2005), the position of the Irish State on integration is ambiguous. The publication stresses cultural diversity that avoids a formal recognition of diversity. Moreover, although diversity is presented as value added for the host society, and should be celebrated, the primary focus is on economics. In dealing with racism, Minister at the time, Michael McDowell, stated that the success of the plan presented in the document "will be a key factor for the continued economic and social prosperity of our country and for the wellbeing of the society we pass on to future generations" (DJELR, 2005, p. 11). Again, interculturalism becomes the key word of the Irish State's policy regarding integration of its immigrant population. "Interculturalism is essentially about creating the conditions for interaction, understanding, equality of opportunity and respect" (DJELR, 2005, p. 42).

The rationale behind the *National Action Plan Against Racism* is about promoting an intercultural society. The justifications for establishing the EU recommended policies on anti-discrimination and integration policies (Garner, 2009), two of the three reasons are oriented towards the well-being of the Irish economy. The strategy is threefold: for business, for social cohesion, and for Ireland's international reputation. In a globalized world, "Ireland must continue to ensure it plays an important role in this process. This requires greater understanding of the needs and greater interaction with our existing and potential international trading partners." (DJLER, 2005, p. 41)

The document singles an economic rationale for integration: the positive benefits that will accrue to economy, and that the promotion "an intercultural workplace" will increase work effectiveness for multinationals in Ireland (DJLER, 2005, p. 41). Social cohesion case is alluded to in one sentence, and stresses that racism has the "potential to become a major challenge to social cohesion and stability within a country or a region."

Ireland's international reputation is closely associated with it as a place to invest and visit (IDA, 2010):

> Ireland has an international reputation built on proactively supporting human rights and speaking out on human rights abuses at a global level. Ireland has an international image of being a warm and welcoming place to visit and to live. It is important that racism is not allowed to undermine or tarnish this reputation. (DJLER, 2005, p. 41)

In that respect, migrants are defined in terms of how they economically benefit the majority culture and the State, while non-economic benefits take the form of vague pronouncements (Bryan, 2010). Moreover, the very expression of acceptance of "the other" implies that it is conditional and that it could be withdrawn, were migrants to be deemed undeserving (Bryan, 2010).

The last document articulating official State thinking on interculturalism is *Migration Nation* (Office of the Minister for Integration, 2008). The document celebrates and specifies interculturalism. For example, immigration laws are focused on welcoming "skilled migrants with a contribution to make" (OMI, 2008, p. 9). "A clear commitment to Immigration Laws that control and facilitate access to Ireland for skilled migrants with a contribution to make." (OMI, 2008, p. 9). *Migration Nation* rests on the kinds of immigrants the country is ready to welcome, skilled migrants mostly, hardworking as well (Hughes et al., 2007). For Bryan (2010), such a position has the effect of entrenching power relations between majority and minority groups and legitimizing negative responses towards those less skilled or who do not have a contribution to make to society.

There are also roles attributed to the population—the host population and the new communities. The former must respect cultural differences, inform itself "about the new communities rather than accepting stereotyped and mythical views," and encourage "integration in local communities" (OMI, 2008, pp. 17–18). The latter must respect cultural differences and make "every effort to understand and learn core aspects of Irish society and way of life," maximize "the contribution to overall prosperity through work and social engagement with the host community," undertake "and commit to the basic integration skills such as language acquisition and skills development," and encourage "integration in local communities" (OMI, 2008, p. 18).

One has to agree with Bryan that the above examples "reveal the extent to which concerns about global competitiveness and productivity are central to influencing the particular vision of interculturalism and anti-racism promulgated by the Irish State" (Bryan, 2010, p. 259). The focal of these documents and the marketing strategy of the State is to assure trading partners and tourists that Ireland has a friendly environment and welcoming nature. At the same time, it constructs the illegitimate and undeserving as the "Other" within the Irish national space (Bryan, 2010). Moreover, for Bryan, the Celtic Tiger period had some influence on the shaping of multiculturalism—a corporate-style multiculturalism that espouses the main contributions of immigrants purely in terms of their labor (Bryan, 2010).

There is a discrepancy between Ireland's international and the reality. The multicultural image of Ireland is pure marketing, existing in the brochure of the Industrial Development Authority to attract investors. The word "multicultural" is also mentioned in tourist brochures but is soon followed by the usual pictures and text describing an historical, unaltered Ireland. Ireland looks to Britain as a model for addressing multiculturalism and drawing a parallel between contemporary Ireland and Britain in the 1950s, when both countries required immigrants to fill labor shortages. Hickman argues that the period was an occasion for reconfiguring the nation as a White host (Hickman, 2007). Hickman's contention is that current discussions of diversity are predicated not on the acceptance of plurality but on a notion of a 'host' that is being subjected to diversification (Hickman, 2007). While the discourse about interculturalism stresses a diverse population, it leaves the social order intact.

CONCLUSION

Following the country's changing status from a land of emigration to one of immigration over the last decades, Irish identity has become more restrictive and less inclusive. Such a position, however, has not applied equally to all migrants entering Ireland. Following constitutional reform after 2004, returning migrants belonging to the Irish diaspora have been granted a separate position regarding citizenship and, consequently, Irish identity, compared to other migrants. While Ireland has become a more visible diverse society, the Irish State has also tried to play down and mitigate the societal consequences of such diversity, implementing a weak multiculturalism principle or adopting a categorization of its population to taper off recent demographic changes and offer a vision of stability. Indeed, the addition of an ethnicity question to the official census demonstrates the State's attempt to show that Irish identity has remained unaltered despite recent demographic trends. It also shows that Irish identity is a social construct in which the State actively develops a "mode of imagining" the Nation (Anderson, 2006, p. 166). Ultimately, safeguarding Irish economic growth and its capacity to attract investors has been, without contest, the State's underlying motive against which these developments have unfolded.

At that stage, one cannot but wonder why Irish identity needs to remain unaltered. Has the return from the 1990s onwards of so many "sons and daughters" of Ireland triggered the need for an unchanging version of Irishness since these homing pigeons were also coming back expecting to find their roots? Have Ireland's international economic imperatives annihilated any collective endeavors to change the way Irishness was envisioned? Can the apparent stability of Irish identity be explained by religious sameness where Polish people would be more easily accepted than other migrants since the "romantic character of Christianity" to love thine neighbor as yourself works better when the other (he/she) is a Christian (Kiberd, 2005, p. 309)? On that particular point, Census 2011 found that on a population of 3.8 million Catholics, 92% were Irish while Poles and UK nationals accounted for over half of all non-Irish Catholics (CSO, 2011). Or, do Irish people as a whole fear some form of "hybridity" (Kiberd, 2005, p. 303) in which several foreign identities could weaken their own identity and lead to its subsequent demise?

Two challenges seem to arise from then on. The first one is to overcome present resistance, building and maintaining a "real connection between communities so that groups will not seek freedom *from* a secular society so much as freedom *in* a multicultural endeavor" (Kiberd, 2005, p. 319, emphasis in original). The second challenge is to overcome the founding myth of Irishness, the country's traditional self-portrayal, and promote a new *imagining* for the Irish nation in the 21st century, while offering a reappraisal of the concept of diversity. These are two huge and pressing challenges, all the more so as the Republic of Ireland might also be tempted, in some not so distant future, to adopt citizenship tests which offer for all to see, in a less concealed form as an ethnicity question does in a Census, a State's conception of its national identity.

NOTES

1. Ireland refers to the Republic of Ireland or Éire in the Irish language. In the following pages, the two terms will be used interchangeably.
2. See figure in appendix A for population data in Ireland from 1500 to 2009. Data are from Angus Maddison's Historical Statistics website: http://www.ggdc.net/MADDISON/oriindex.htm. For an excellent discussion of Ireland's economic situation see O'Grada (2011): https://ideas.repec.org/p/ucn/wpaper/201112.html.

3. The Gaelic Athletic Association (GAA) was created in 1884 for the promotion of national pastimes such as Gaelic football and hurling.
4. To be sure, the global financial crisis hurt the Irish economy, but there were issues that, in hindsight, could have been handled better. By 2007, the housing market had topped out. That year, tax revenues began to decline and new home completions fell for the first time since 1988 (it should be noted that the housing market was the major component of Ireland's GDP), and in 2008, Ireland's unemployment rate increased for the first time in 15 years. Irish banks began reporting defaults and loans in arrears. With confidence evaporating, banks were faced with customers withdrawing their funds. Also, banks have been heavily reliant on short-term inter-bank loans for their funding, but in the new economic times, these became difficult to access.

   The Irish government responded issuing blanket guarantees of the banks' liabilities and to re-capitalize banks with public funds. These large costs exacerbated the budget deficit, which the collapse of the housing market had revealed.

   Bank debt added to a significant budget deficit, and led international investors to question the ability of Ireland to manage its debt. In November 2010, the Irish government debt reached 9%, an unsustainable%, and meant that the government was locked out of international bond markets. The country was unable to borrow money to fund the deficit. Ireland had to make devastating and quick adjustments to public services because spending had to be aligned with revenue immediately.

   On November 29, 2010, Ireland negotiated a package with the EU and the IMF for €85 billion and €17.5 billion from its own resources. The funds were to be used to re-align spending with revenues.
5. The famine has been listed as lasting from 1845 to 1852. By 1854, about 1.5 to 2.0 million Irish had left their country. Some also estimate that between 1845 and 1852 about 1 million died from disease or starvation, and another 1 million left Ireland. This loss amounts to about 20 to 25% decline in the Irish population. For excellent histories of the Famine, see Daly (1986), Gray (1995), Woodham-Smith (1968), O'Grada (2000), and Coogan (2012). See also Bouvier and Gillissen (2014).
6. For a good discussion on indicators used by the Irish State to measure migration to Ireland, see Gilmartin, 2012.
7. In addition to these data, the following are indices of diversity based on Simpson's Index. There are three indices: Simpson's Index (S), Simpson's Diversity Index (D), and the Reciprocal of Simpson's Index (R).

   Simpson's Index was computed with the following formula and only among the population that provided a national identity— $S = \Sigma (n/N)^2$. Where n = number of a specific group, N = total population providing their national identity; $D = 1—S$; $R = 1/S$.

   S varies from 0 to 1. When $S = 0$ there is infinite diversity, when it equals 1 it means no diversity. D ranges from 0 to 1, and the greater the D, the greater the diversity. Finally, R starts from 1, and its maximum is the number of categories being examined. In our case, the number of categories is eight (8).

Index	2002	2006	2011
Simpson's Index (S)	.842	.771	.742
Diversity Index (D)	.157	.229	.258
Reciprocal (R) of S	1.187	1.291	1.347

Thus, while Ireland is not a terribly diverse society, it is becoming more diverse, based on these indices.

I would like to thank Richard R. Verdugo for making these calculations.

8. Until 2004, « EU » referred to the 15 member States (Austria, Belgium, Denmark, Finland, France, Germany, Greece, Italy, Ireland, Luxembourg, Netherlands, Spain, Sweden, Portugal, and United Kingdom). From May 1, 2004, the EU also includes the following 10 States: Cyprus, Czech Republic, Estonia, Hungary, Latvia, Lithuania, Malta, Poland, Slovakia, and Slovenia. From January 1, 2007, the EU also includes Bulgaria and Romania. Therefore, from May 1, 2004, EU-15 is used to refer to the original 15 member States, EU-10 or EU-12 to identify the new member States, EU-27 to refer to all of them.

9. Note that percent increase is different from percent age point increase. The 143% increase is based on the following formula: $((Yj—Yi)/Yi)*100$. Where Yj = most recent year, Yi = base year.

10. The 2011 Census is presented as such: "The census will give a comprehensive picture of the social and living conditions of our people in 2011. Only a census can provide such complete detail. The census is not, however, an end in itself! Rather the results are essential tools for effective policy, planning and decision making purposes." In Your Questions, Census 2011 website, http://www.census.ie/The-Census-and-You/Your-Questions.90.1.aspx (4 January 2014)

11. This policy changed in April 2003 when the Employment Permits Act made it easier for nationals of the EU-10 accession countries to work in Ireland. After May 1, 2004, EU-10 nationals could travel to Ireland and work without having to rely on Irish employers to obtain work permits for them. (NESC, 2006, xii)

12. This assumption, as Gilmartin and Migge have argued, is not challenged in recent academic work (Gilmartin & Migge, 2013, 4). Immigration remains perceived as a variable of adjustment, and some argue that it can be seen as a chance for Ireland as it releases pressure on the Irish labor market. Barret & Kelly write that "if employment loss has indeed resulted in outflows, Ireland can be said to have enjoyed a benefit to its economy from immigration. An inflow allowed labor demand to be met in the boom and then for that labor to be released in the downturn. In this way, Ireland's openness to immigration has been rewarded" (Barret & Kelly, 2012, p. 109).

13. Please note that figures have been rounded by the CSO. In some cases, percentages might not exactly match.

REFERENCES

Allen, K. (2000). *The Celtic tiger. The myth of social partnership in Ireland.* Manchester, England: Manchester University Press.

Anderson, B. (2006). *Imagined communities. Reflections on the origin and spread of nationalism.* London, England: Verso.

Arts, W., & Halman, L. (2006). National Identity in Europe Today. What the people feel and think. *International Journal of Sociology, 35*(4), 69–93.

Barret, A., & Kelly, E. (2012). The impact of Ireland's recession on the labour market outcomes of its immigrants. *European Journal of Population, 28,* 91–111.

Barry, F. (Ed.). (1999). *Understanding Ireland's economic growth.* London, England: MacMillan Publishers.

Becker, H., & Cosgrave, C. (2013). *Naturalisation procedures for immigrants Ireland.* EUDO Citizenship Observatory, Italy. Retrieved from http://eudo-citizenship.eu.

Boucher, G. (2008). Ireland's lack of a coherent integration policy. *Translocations, 3*(1), 5–28.

Bouvier, A-C., & Gillissen, C. (2014, September 2013). The great famine in Ireland, 1845–1851. *French Journal of British Studies. 19*(2). Retrieved from http://rfcb.revues.org/194

Brandi, S. (2007). Unveiling the ideological construction of the 2004 Irish citizenship referendum: A critical discourse analytical approach. *Translocations, 2*(1), 26–47.

Breen, M. J., & Devereux, E (2003). No racists here: Public opinion and media treatment of asylum seekers and refugees. In N. Collins & T. Cradden (Eds.), *Irish political attitudes today.* Manchester, England: Manchester University Press (pp. 168–188). Retrieved from http://hdl.handle.net/10395/304

Bryan, A. (2010). Corporate multiculturalism, diversity management, and positive interculturalism in Irish schools and and society. *Irish Educational Studies. 29*(3), 253–269.

Cadogan, M. (2008). Fixity and whiteness in the ethnicity question of Irish census 2006. *Translocations, 3*(1), 50–68.

Central Statistics Office. (2008). *Measuring Ireland's progress.* Dublin, Ireland: Stationery Office.

Central Statistics Office. (2011a). *Profile 6—Migration and diversity.* Dublin, Ireland: Stationery Office.

Central Statistics Office. (2011b) *Statistical yearbook of Ireland.* Dublin, Ireland: Stationery Office.

Central Statistics Office. (2011c). *Press statements census 2011— Profile 7.* Dublin, Ireland: Stationery Office.

Central Statistics Office. (2013). *Statistical yearbook of Ireland.* Dublin, Ireland: Stationery Office.

Citizenship tourists: Harder to be Irish. (2004, June 3). *The Economist.* Retrieved from http://www.economist.com/node/2734580

Cole, P. (2010). Introduction: 'Border crossings'—The dimensions of membership. In G. Calder, P. Cole, & J. Seglow (Eds.), *Citizenship acquisition and national belonging: migration, membership and the liberal democratic State* (pp. 1–23). New York, NY: Palgrave Macmillan.

Conway, B. (2008). Who do we think we are? Immigration and the discursive construction of national identity in an Irish daily mainstream newspaper, 1996–2004. *Translocations. 1*(1), 76–93.

Coogan, T. P. (2012). *The famine plot: England's role in Ireland's greatest tragedy.* New York, NY: Palgrave.

Coulter, C. (2003). The end of Irish history? An introduction to the book. In C. Coulter & S. Coleman (Eds.), *The end of Irish history? Critical reflections on the Celtic Tiger* (pp. 1–33). Manchester, England: Manchester University Press.

Crowley, U., Gilmartin, M., & Kitchin, R. (2006). "Vote yes for common sense citizenship": Immigration and the paradoxes at the heart of Ireland's 'Céad Míle Fáilte.' NIRSA WP 30.

Daly, M. E. (1986). *The famine in Ireland.* Dundalk, Ireland: Dundalgan.

Davis, T. C. (2003). The Irish and their nation: A survey of recent attitudes. *Global Review of Ethnopolitics, 2*(2), 17–36.

Delaney, E. (2000). *Demography, state and society. Irish migration to Britain, 1921–1971.* Liverpool, England: Liverpool University Press.

Déloye, Y. (2013). National identity and everyday life. In J. Breuilly (Ed.), *The Oxford handbook of the history of nationalism* (pp. 615–631). Oxford, England: Oxford University Press.

Department of Justice, Equality and Law Reform. (1999). *Integration: A two-way process.* Dublin, Ireland: Author.

Department of Justice, Equality and Law Reform. (2005). *Planning for Diversity—the National Plan Against Racism 2005–2008.* Dublin, Ireland: Author.

Fahey, T. (2007). Population. In S. O'Sullivan (Ed.), *Contemporary Ireland. A sociological map* (pp. 13–29). Dublin, Ireland: University College Press.

Fahey, T., Hayes, B. C., & Sinnott, R. (2006). *Conflict and consensus. A study of values and attitudes in the Republic of Ireland and Northern Ireland.* Boston, MA: Brill.

Fanning, B. (2002). *Racism and social change in the Republic of Ireland.* Manchester, England: Manchester University Press.

Fanning, B. (2009). *New guests of the Irish nation.* Dublin, Ireland: Irish Academic Press.

Fanning, B., & Mutwarasibo, F. (2007). Nationals/non-nationals: Immigration, citizenship and politics in the Republic of Ireland. *Ethnic and Racial Studies, 30*(3), 439–460.

Fennell, D. (2013, January 25). Ireland has become a nothing mosaic with no binding identity. *Irish Times.* Retrieved from http://www.irishtimes.com/opinion/ireland-has-become-a-nothing-mosaic-with-no-binding-identity-1.966266

Gallagher, M. (1995). How many nations are there in Ireland? *Ethnic and Racial Studies. 18*(4), 715–739.

Garner, S. (2004). *Racism in the Irish experience.* London, England: Pluto Press.

Garner, S. (2007). Ireland and immigration: Explaining the absence of the far right. *Patterns of Prejudice, 41*(2), 109–130. Retrieved from http://oro.open.ac.uk/38780/

Garner, S. (2009). Ireland: From racism without 'race' to racism without racists. *Radical History Review, 104,* 41–56.

Gellner, E. (2006). *Nations and nationalism* (2nd ed.) Oxford, England: Blackwell.

Gilmartin, M. (2012). *The changing landscape of Irish migration, 2000–2012.* NISRA working paper series, no. 69.

Gilmartin, M., & Migge, B. (2013). European migrants in Ireland: Pathways to integration. *European Urban and Regional Studies, 22,* 285–299. doi:10.1177/0969776412474583

Goldring, M. (1975). *Irlande: Idéologie d'une révolution nationale*. Paris, FR: Éditions Sociales.

Gray, P. (1995). *The Irish famine*. London, England: Thames and Hudson.

Guibernau, M. (2007). *The identity of nations*. Cambridge, England: Polity Press.

Guillaumond, J., & Martin, D. (2013). Double portrait: La "diversité" en Irlande et en Allemagne depuis les années 2000, entre discours et réalités. In A. Ghouati & E. Agbessi (Eds.), *Diversité et innovation en milieux socioprofessionnels* (pp. 45–65). Clermont-Ferrand, FR: Presses universitaires Blaise Pascal.

Hall, S. (1996). Who needs 'Identity'? In S. Hall, & P. du Gay (Eds.), *Questions of cultural identity* (pp. 1–17). London, England: Sage.

Handoll, J. (2012). *Country report: Ireland*. EUDO Citizenship Observatory, Italy. Retrieved from http:://eudo-citizenship.eu.

Harttgen, K., & Opfinger M. (2014). National identity and religious diversity. *Kyklos, 67*(3), 346–367.

Hayward, K. & Howard, K. (2007). Cherry-picking the diaspora. In B. Fanning (Ed.), *Immigration and social change in the Republic of Ireland* (pp. 47–62). Manchester, England: Manchester University Press.

Hickman, M. J. (2007). Immigration and monocultural re(imaginings). *Translocations. 2*(1), 12–25.

Hobsbawm, E., & Ranger, T. (1983). *The invention of tradition*. Cambridge, England: Cambridge University Press.

Honohan, I. (2010). Citizenship attribution in a new country of immigration: Ireland. *Journal of Ethnic and Migration Studies, 36*(5), 811–827. Retrieved from http://www.ucd.ie/norface/papers/maa_honohan.pdf

Hourihane, A. M. (2000). *She moves through the boom*. Dublin, Ireland: Sitric Books Ltd.

Hughes, G., McGinnity, F., O'Connell, P., & Quinn, E. (2007). The impact of immigration. In T. Fahey, H. Russell, & C. T. Whelan (Eds), *Best of times? The social impact of the Celtic tiger* (pp. 217–244). Dublin, Ireland: Institute of Public Administration.

Industrial Development Agency (IDA) (2010). *Ireland. Where else?* Dublin, Ireland: Author.

Keating, M. (1997). *Les défis du nationalisme moderne. Québec, Catalogne, Écosse*. Montréal, CA: Presses de l'Université de Montréal.

Kiberd, D. (2005). *The Irish writer and the world*. Cambridge, England: Cambridge University Press.

Kiely, R., Bechhofer, F., Stewart, R., & McCrone D. (2001). The markers and rules of Scottish national identity. *The Sociological Review, 49*(1), 33–55.

King, J. (1998). Porous nation: From Ireland's 'haemorrhage' to 'immigrant inundation.' In R. Lentin (Ed.), *The expanding nation: Towards a multi-ethnic Ireland* (pp. 49–54). Dublin, Ireland: Dept. of Sociology, Trinity College.

King O'Riain, R. C. (2006). Re-racialising the Irish State through the census, citizenship and language. In A. Lentin & R. Lentin (Eds), *Race and state* (pp. 275–293). Newcastle, England: Cambridge Scholars Press.

King O'Riain, R. C. (2007). Counting on the 'Celtic Tiger': Adding ethnic census categories in the Republic of Ireland. *Ethnicities, 7*(4), 516–542.

Kuhling, C. & Keohane, K. (2007). *Cosmopolitan Ireland. Globalisation and quality of life.* London, England: Pluto Press.

Logue, P. (Ed.), (2000). *Being Irish: Personal reflections on Irish identity today.* Dublin, Ireland: Oak Tree Press.

Longley, E. (2001). Multi-culturalism in Northern Ireland. In E. Longley, & D. Kiberd (Eds.), *Multi-culturalism: The view from the two Irelands.* Cork, Ireland: Cork University Press, 1–44.

Loyal, S. (2003). Welcome to the celtic tiger: Racism, immigration and the state. In C. Coulter, & S. Coleman (Eds.), *The end of Irish history? Critical reflections on the Celtic Tiger* (pp. 74–94). Manchester, England: Manchester University Press.

Loyal, S. (2011). *Understanding immigration in Ireland. State, capital and labour in a global age.* Manchester, England: Manchester University Press.

Mac Éinrí, P. (2001). Immigration policy in Ireland. In F. Farrel, & P. Watt (Eds.), *Responding to racism in Ireland* (pp. 46–87). Dublin, Ireland: Veritas.

Mac Éinrí, P. (2007). Immigration: Labour migrants, asylum seekers and refugees. In B. Bartley, & B. Kitchin (Eds.), *Understanding contemporary Ireland* (pp. 236–248). London, England: Pluto Press.

Mac Laughlin, J. (1994). *Ireland: The emigrant nursery and the world economy.* Cork, Ireland: Cork University Press.

Mac Laughlin, J. (1997). Ireland in the global economy: An end to a distinct nation. In E. Crowley, & J. Mac Laughlin (Eds.), *Under the belly of the tiger: Class, race, identity, and culture in the global Ireland* (pp. 1–19). Dublin, Ireland: Irish Reporter Publications.

Malešević, S. (2011). The chimera of national identity. *Nations and Nationalism, 17*(2), 272–290.

National Economic and Social Council. (2006). *Managing migration in Ireland: A social and economic analysis.* Dublin, Ireland: NESDO.

Ní Chiosáin, B. (2007). Passports for the new Irish? The 2004 citizenship referendum. *Études Irlandaises. 32*(2), 31–47.

O'Brien, J. (1954). The vanishing Irish. *The enigma of the modern world.* London, England: W. H. Allen.

Office of the Minister for Integration. (2008). *Migration nation: Statement on integration strategy and diversity management.* Dublin, Ireland: OMI.

Office of the Refugee Applications Commissioner. (2012/2013). *Annual reports.* Dublin, Ireland: ORAC.

Ó'Gráda, C. (2000). *The great Irish famine.* Cambridge, England: Cambridge University Press.

Ó'Gráda, C. (2011). *Five crises.* Retrieved from https://ideas.repec.org/p/ucn/wpaper/201112.html

O'Keeffe-Vigneron, G. (2010). Les Irlandais en angleterre et les polonais en Irlande: Chemins convergents ou parcours divergents? In L. Germain, D. Lassalle, M. Prum, F. Binard, & B. Deschamps (Eds.), *Identités et cultures minoritaires dans l'aire anglophone, entre "visibilité" et "invisibilité"* (pp. 169–185). Paris, FR: L'Harmattan. Retrieved from http://hal.archives-ouvertes.fr/hal-00612719 12 July 2013.

Piola, C. (2007). La politique d'immigration en Irlande. In C. Maignant (Ed.), *Le tigre celtique en question* (pp. 147–172). Caen, FR: Presses Universitaires de Caen.

Prideaux, J. (2009). Consuming icons: Nationalism and advertising in Australia. *Nations and Nationalism, 15*(4), 616–635.

Pulhe, H-J. (1994). Nation states, nations, and nationalisms in Western and Southern Europe. In J. G. Beramendi, R. Máiz, & X. M. Núñez (Eds.), *Nationalism in Europe. Past and present, II* (pp. 13–38). Santiago de Compostela, ES: Universidade de Santiago de Compostela.

Ruhs, M. (2009). Ireland: From rapid immigration to recession. *Migration Information Source.* Retrieved from http://www.migrationinformation.org/Feature/display.cfm?ID=740.

Ryan, B. (2004). *The Celtic Cubs: The controversy over birthright citizenship in Ireland,* Retrieved from http://kar.kent.ac.uk/1677.

Segal, U. A., Elliott, D., & Mayadas, N. S. (2010). *Immigration worldwide. policies, practices, and trends.* Oxford, England: Oxford University Press.

Sinha, S. (1998). The right to Irishness: Implications of ethnicity, nation and state towards a truly multi-ethnic Ireland. In R. Lentin (Ed.), *The expanding nation: Towards a multi-ethnic Ireland* (pp. 21–25). Dublin, Ireland: Dept. of Sociology, Trinity College.

Smith, A. D. (1991). *National identity.* London, England: Penguin Books Ltd.

Smith, A. D. (1995). *Nations and nationalism in a global era.* Cambridge, England: Polity Press.

Symmons, C. R. (1999). Le Droit de la Nationalité en Irlande. In P. Weil, & R. Hansen (Eds.), *Citoyenneté et nationalité en Europe* (pp. 307–328). Paris, France: La Découverte.

Sweeney, P. (1998). *The Celtic Tiger: Ireland's economic miracle explained.* Dublin, Ireland: Oak Tree Press.

Tarantino, F. (2012). Ethnic entrepreneurship. *Case study: Dublin.* Retrieved from http://www.eurofound.europa.eu/publications/htmlfiles/ef11218.htm. Dublin, Ireland: European Foundation for the Improvement of Living and Working Conditions

van Oers, R., Ersbøll, E., & Kostakopoulou, D. (Eds.). (2010). *A re-definition of belonging? Language and integration tests in Europe.* Leiden, NL: Martinus Nijhoff Publishers.

Vasileva, E. (2011). Population and social conditions. *Eurostat statistics in focus 3/4/2011.* Retrieved from http://epp.eurostat.ec.europa.eu/cache/ITY_OFFPUB/KS-SF-11-034/EN/KS-SF-11-034-EN.PDF

White, T. J. (2010). The impact of British colonialism on Irish catholicism and national identity: Repression, reemergence, and divergence. Études *Irlandaises. 35*(1), 21–37.

Woodham Smith, C. B. (1968). *The great hunger.* London, England: New English Library.

Yau, N. (2007). Celtic tiger, hidden dragon: Exploring identity among second generation Chinese in Ireland. *Translocations, 2*(1), 48–69.

Yester, K. (2002, January). Globalization's last hurrah? *Foreign policy review.*

CHAPTER 5

RUSSIAN NATIONAL IDENTITY

Oxana Karnaukhova and Richard R. Verdugo

To the Finland station.[1] The young man had been exiled and was living in Switzerland. On March 15, 1917, as he planned to go to the Altstadt library, a fellow exile, Mieczyslav Bronski, burst in and exclaimed, "Haven't you heard the news? There's a revolution in Russia!"

It was crucial that Vladimir Ilyich Ulyanov return to Russia immediately. But there was a war in progress, and Switzerland was surrounded by the warring parties: France, Germany, Austria-Hungary, and Italy. The seas were controlled by Russia's ally, Britain. Air travel was out of the question. What to do?

On March 31st, Fritz Platten, a Swiss Communist, got permission from the German Foreign Minister via Baron Gisbert von Romberg, ambassador to Germany from Switzerland, for Ulyanov and other Russian exiles to travel through Germany into Russia in a sealed one-car train. Germany financed the trip because they fully knew that Ulyanov would foment much trouble in Russia. Their goal was to spread unrest in Russia so it would stop Russian resistance during WWI.

Just before midnight on April 16, 1917, V. I. Ulyanov's (otherwise known as V. I. Lenin) train pulled into the Finland Station in Petrograd. He was

National Identity, pages 147–185
Copyright © 2016 by Information Age Publishing

147

greeted to the sound of La Marseillaise and a crowd of workers, sailors, and soldiers waving red flags. Once in Russia, Lenin and Trotsky began a revolution that shook the world.[2] First, though, they had to get rid of Kerensky's provisional government.

The ensuing Communist regime, begun after the October Revolution, redirected Russia, affecting all aspects of life in the country, and created a problem about national identity. Yet, it was clear that the paradigm driving Communism in Russia was a monumental historical event that had emerged much earlier—the Enlightenment. The Enlightenment is one of three historical events which, arguably, have had profound effects on Russian national identity. The other two are Russian Imperialism and the breakup of the Soviet Union. But the Enlightenment was the force behind these events. The Enlightenment altered world views about social organization, the role individuals take in their own lives within social systems. The Old World was in retreat and would soon be buried; the seeds of its demise were the ideas to be found in the Enlightenment. The great German social scientist, Max Weber, referred to this change as the "disenchantment of the world." The effect on Russia was to be significant.

* * *

In 2002, the international community was keenly interested in Russia's new configuration. The interest was expressed by The Telegraph in the following questions: For Russia's ill-defined boundaries, open spaces and indeterminate, mid-continental geography are the source of much confusion. Is Russia part of Europe or of Asia? Is the "real" Russian capital westward-looking St Petersburg or inward-facing Moscow? Are the "real" Russians the peasant inhabitants of the northern forests, the settlers of the Siberian open spaces, or the cosmopolitan aristocrats who created Russian literature, music and painting (Applebaum, 2002)?

The questions posed by Applebaum are relevant, but hardly touch upon the complexities involved in what is meant by national identity or how and why government leaders seek to develop and maintain such an identity among their constituencies. Scholars have examined these complexities, and the results are contradictory and confusing. So, Applebaum's questions about national identity in general, and Russia in particular, are part of ongoing research and political debate.

The extant literature addresses some of these questions by focusing on the meaning and status of national identity, and by attempting to identify those factors affecting its development and maintenance. However, scholars have different views about these issues. For example, one group of scholars argue that national identity is fixed and based on ethnicity or culture. Another group argues that national identity is flexible, involves social agency, or is an imagined concept (because it is developed and manipulated by politicians for their own benefit), or the result of industrial Capitalism. There appears to be little consensus in the field.

National identity, as used in our chapter, is a feeling of attachment to one's nation or State.[3] It is a concept different from *Patriotism* (devotion and attachment to one's country), *Ethnicity* (a group of people who identify with one another in terms of a common ancestry, culture, or national experience), or *Nationalism* (an ideology that a binds persons to their nation and supports the belief that their nation is superior to all others). National identity is about how citizens, especially generations, interpret the past and contemporary events in developing and maintaining their feelings of attachment to their nation (a group of people sharing a common language, culture, ethnicity, descent, or history) or *State* (a political community living under a government). In our theoretical model, generations are crucial and the missing link that molds national identity into one coherent model. The purpose of our chapter is to examine the role three events have had on Russian national identity: the Enlightenment, Russian Imperialism, and the breakup of the Soviet Union.

THEORETICAL BACKGROUND

Theories of National Identity

National Identity: A Continuum

Existing theories of national identity may be placed on a scale from one where the concept is fixed (one that is lodged in a common, ethnic group history) to one where the concept is flexible (involves social agency, malleable, and is imagined). The four dominant theories and their views about national identity may be displayed in a National Identity Scale; they are Essentialist/Primordialist vs. Postmodernists/Constructivists. See Figure 5.1.

Essentialists. *Essentialists* believe that national identity is fixed, and based on ethnicity. Nations are defined by their heritage and history, which include a common language, a common faith, and a common ethnicity. A variation of the Essentialist view is the work of *Primodialists*. Among *Primorialists* nations are ancient, natural phenomena, based on language learned in the community. The implication is that the community is fixed

Essentialists/Primordialists ◄────────────► Postmodernists/Constructivists
Fixed/common culture   *Flexible/human agency/imagined*

Figure 5.1 National identity scale: Fixed to constructed.

over time (Huntington 1991; Smith 1986; Armstrong 1982; Greenfeld 1992; Geertz 1973).

Postmodernists. Identities are fragmented into a diverse set of competing identities. *Postmodernists* reject absolute truth; what we believe to be true is constructed or an interpretation of reality; an imagined identity or community according to Anderson (1991).[4a]

Society is constantly changing, and so too are traditional social roles. Changing roles creates confusion of who we are as a people and thus affects national identity.

Postmodernism has removed any sense of objective reality, and with it the notion of an objective self. Since there is no truth, there can be no true me, only a version of me. Since there is no essential identity, I can be whatever I construct myself to be. *Constructivism* is a variant of *Postmodernist* theory. Identity for them is relative, stable, involves role specific understandings, and understandings are expected from oneself as well. These then are the general theories about national identity and belonging. As will be evident in the next section, Russian discourse on national identity may be organized around these theoretical categories.

Russian Theories of National Identity

The debate among Russian scholars on national identity map nicely onto our National Identity Scale.

Essentialist/primordialist theories: Western views about national identity. Since the mid-XIX century among Russian scholars in this category, identity is defined in terms of European identity. Their argument has its roots in German intellectual traditions and legal practices, Christianity, and the legitimacy of the Royal dynasty (Kavelin, 1989). The latter two were obsessed with the uniqueness and great spiritual mission of Russia[4b] (Khomyakov, 1835/1994; Dostoyevsky, 1876/1976).

National identity debates during the second half of the XIXth century went hand in hand with the expansion of the Russian empire. At the threshold of the XIX–XXth centuries, and facing stiff competition from European nations,[5] Russian intellectuals returned to the idea of the "Other." There was a push for returning Russia to its cultural and ethnic origins, and an identity centered in the East against Western individualism, which can be traced to the Enlightenment (Buchanan & Tullock, 1962; Mokyr, 2009). Russian intellectuals, while compared Russia with European society, felt the postponed social development of the country. At the same time in clash with the East Russia was considered as the West. The highest level of the "Eastern motive" could be seen in the so called "Eurasian movement" in 1920s. The history of Russia, its social structure, governmentality, and traditions are predetermined by geography and specificity of Eurasia as a peculiar geopolitical space. According to Nicolai Trubeczkoy (2000), "any state is alive only if it can fulfill those tasks, which are settled by the geographical nature of its territory."[6] Coming from this statement, the basis and the source of the Russian governmentality is seen not in the Kiev Rus', but in the Mongolian Empire of Genghis Khan. Later on, imperial ideas of Genghis Khan have been raised up again in the form of Byzantium Christianity. As Leo Gumilev (2007) stated, Russians must realize their traditional boundaries–temporal and spatial—of their ethnic community, clearly understand where "we," and where "strangers," are located. Otherwise, they cannot hope to maintain the ethno-social integrity, which was created by ancestors.

Some liberal Russian scholars based their ideas of a civic-nation on the American example, which was itself influenced by the European Enlightenment. Some intellectuals, such as Petr Struve (2004), insisted on building a unified imperial Russia on the foundation of the dominant ethnic Russian population. At the same time he was against forcing Russian culture on other nations and cultures. The role of Russian culture in the process of building an imperial nation was to be through open competition.

Other intellectuals, such as Paul Milyoukov (1906), argued for cross-cultural interactions and exchanges in the process of civic-identity building. Such an identity would be a commonly held imperial consciousness. Moreover, a common language was to be the basis for such a nation.

Postmodernist/constructivist theories. The primordialist position was the most wide-spread position during the Soviet period, fixed in classical ethnographic works of Bromley (1983), while from the beginning of the 1990s, Western academic influence (Anderson, 1991) was demonstrated in the process of academic self-identification and raising constructivism. As Valery Tishkov (2008) supposes, identity is a sense of belonging or connection with one or another community (nation, country, team, nationality, race, language group, party, etc.), culture, tradition, or ideology (religious belief, location, social movement, etc). Such identity is formed not only a historical basis, but also under influence of elites. Vladimir Malakhov (1998) suggests separating individual and social levels of identity. If at the individual level, we have a set of psychological reactions, or the most stable modes of behavior; then at the social level, identity is structured and intensively constructed, mostly through setting the direct linkage of identification and a nation-state. In this case "national" is used as the predicament. So the background of the construction process is political.

A Theory of National Identity: Merging Extant Theories

A Theoretical Model

Theories about national identity seem to agree on a set of factors that influence national identity (see Rodney, 1999). Disagreement is about the

TABLE 5.1 Specific Historical and Cultural Factors Affecting National Identity

Topic	Specific Factors
History	*Political:* wars, change in political regimes, mass movements/protests, distrust of political leaders, imperialism/colonialism *Economic:* Change dominant role of production, depression, high poverty rates
Culture/ Societal	Change in mores, norms, values, challenge to myths, traditions, and icons; change in language or diverse language base, or the eradication of a language

permanence of national identity. These factors may be organized around two topics: history and culture/society, as displayed in Table 5.1. We do not claim this to be a complete list.

Our theory of national identity is depicted in Figure 5.2. In this figure, historical events affect society, which, in turn, affects national identity. However, note that we have added the concept "Generations" mediating the effect of history on society. This is a crucial part of our theory, and we will spend a little time providing a rationale as to why Generations account for both societal stability and change.

Generations are an aggregate of persons born around the same time and are viewed collectively. The term "Generations" has an interesting history. In 1863, the French lexicographer, Emile Littre used the term generations in the following manner: "all men living more or less at the same time" (Wohl, 1979, p. 203).

But it was during the 19th century that the concept was expanded as a result of substantial social and economic changes that would affect the West: modernization and industrialism. The Enlightenment proposed the idea that society could be changed; and one of the change agents was youth. Social and economic change meant that the young were not as dependent on their parents or other adults as they were in traditional society. The skills and wisdom of their fathers and other adults were less relevant in a modern, industrializing society. Also, during their youth, young men went off to university or the military, and these experiences would shape their views.

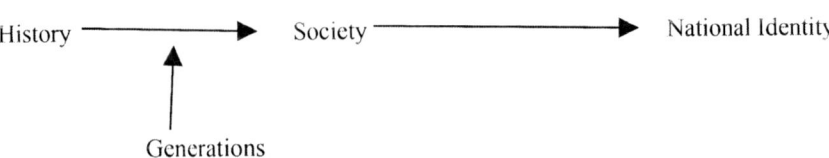

Figure 5.2 A theoretical model of national identity.

Moreover, the breakdown of traditional society and regional identifications lead to nationalism and a broader view of belonging.

August Comte (2009) was the first to seriously undertake a study of generations. Comte argued that social change was brought about by generational change and generational conflict. Other important theorists at the time were John Stuart Mill and Wilhelm Dilthey.

Karl Mannheim (1923/1952) is a seminal figure in studying generations. Mannheim argued that there were two schools of thought about generations. First, there was Comte's view about social change in the life span. Mannheim thought such a view reduced history to a time table and was thus not very productive. Romantics were a second school of thought as represented by Wilhelm Dilthey and Martin Heidegger. Mannheim felt they focused too much on individual experiences to the detriment of the social structure. Mannheim then argued that the tempo of social change affected the formation of generations. Thus, the more rapid the social change, the greater the likelihood the formation of a generation.

People are shaped through lived experiences as a result of social change (Mannheim, 1923), and society persists through what Ryder (1965) termed "demographic metabolism": mortality and fertility. Younger generations, though somewhat internally differentiated, develop their own set of ideas net of older generations. They threaten the existing social order because they question and push against it (Grenier, 2007; Mannheim, 1923; Ryder, 1965).

This is not to say that younger generations are a homogeneous group, but they have a point of view about themselves and society that is different, for the most part, than their parents or other adults. Their tendency to challenge the system and be innovative not only ensures the persistence of society, but its transformation as well (Mannheim, 1923; Ryder, 1965). It is the role of younger Generations in a social system that has eluded theories about national identity. Young generations are the purveyors of both change and stability.

In our study, it will become evident that new generations, and key figures within each generation, have significantly affected Russian history, and thus national identity. For example, some key figures of younger cohort were Peter the Great, Tsarina Catherine, V. I. Lenin, L. Trotsky, J. Stalin, M. Gorbachev, B. Yeltsin, and V. Putin.[7] The moral character of these persons is not an issue, only that they were/are key figures from specific generations, led social change, and contributed to the persistence of Russian society.

Russia: History and Social Change

In its long history, many events have shaped Russian national culture. In our study, we focus on three such events: the Enlightenment, Imperialism, and the breakup of the Soviet Union. Table 5.2 describes these events along with brief hypotheses about their effects on national identity.

TABLE 5.2   Significant Russian Historical Events and Their Effect on National Identity: Conjectures

Historical Event	Description
The Enlightenment	Change in values, views about life, democratic, Republican. Lead, eventually, to the end of Serfdom, and the end of a regime based on an Aristocracy, and the rise of Communism. Those raised under the shadow of a Monarchy, and the Oligarchs are now under a regime of a different set of norms, values, and governance under Peter the Great and then Catherine the Great. Such change throws older Generations into confusion about their identity; younger Generations are not so affected, and developed their own views.
Imperialism/ Colonialism	Created greater cultural diversity; not only were people in the Frontier different, but they had their own cultures, and it taxed the Russian government to maintain control, which infuriated ethnic Russians. In the Frontier, older Generations are not pleased, younger Generations are the prime movers of rebellions. Ethnic Russians wonder what such expansion will mean for a true Russian identity; Younger Generations must reflect and form about their own national identity.
Breakup of the USSR	The original social system was not working in the 20th century. There was a push for breaking up the USSR, and opening up Russia to a Free Market ideology if Russia was to become a modern society. By all accounts the Free Market framework was not working for various reasons; such as corruption at the highest level of government, the inability of old norms, values, traditions, etc., to work in a Free Market framework. Also, the wholesale of State resources at very low prices to oligarchs led to much anger and social protests.

The remainder of our chapter is an examination of each specific historical event and how it might have affected Russian national identity. Our hypotheses are as follows:

H1: *The Enlightenment set in motion a set of ideas that challenged traditional governance regimes and how one looked at the world. These ideas were brought into Russia, slowly, by Peter the Great and then Catherine the Great. Under Communism these ideas became radical, and when Communism as practiced in Russia ended, Enlightenment ideas developed even more, especially under Gorbachev and Yeltsin. How Putin handles these Enlightenment ideas will be seen later. Thus, the Enlightenment issued in a new set of ideas about social structure, which led to different types of governance regimes and how Russians would identity with their system, such as faithful followers of the Monarchy, as Russians, Communists, as Russian citizens in the Russian Federation, or in other ways.*

H2: *Russian Imperialism lead to greater diversity. In the Frontier, annexed nations had their own traditions, cultures, and thus identities. Becoming Russian was not a simple question, nor was an idea of changing identity easily accepted. This becomes clear when one examines the reasons for the many uprisings and revolts in the Frontier. Moreover, after the breakup of the Soviet Union, former states reverted to their own symbols, flags for instance, and declared this autonomy from the former Soviet Union. Thus, imperialism challenged the notion of an all-Russian identity.*

H3: *The breakup of the former Soviet Union was followed by a system based on some radical interpretations of modernist ideas, traced back in the Enlightenment: the free market, autonomy, and privatization. In short, Russians were now embedded in a Hobbesian[8] Capitalist system and all that it entails. The safety nets ended, Russians became private citizens as opposed to members of a larger community, and corruption was rampant.[9] Moreover, the breakup highlighted another important issue—the consistent instability of Russia's governance regimes. The greater the instability of governance regimes, the greater the challenge to national identity.*

RUSSIAN NATIONAL IDENTITY: THE ENLIGHTENMENT, IMPERIALISM, AND THE SOVIET BREAKUP

The Enlightenment: Reason, Individual Freedom, Citizenship, and Russian National Identity

The Enlightenment: Overview

Victor Hugo once said something to the effect that, "Nothing can stand in the way of an idea whose time has come." The Age of Enlightenment was an epic changing cultural and social movement that appears to have begun in 17th-century Western Europe.[10] The paradigm emphasized reason and individualism over tradition and religion on many aspects of individual and social life; it thus challenged existing paradigms that were grounded in tradition and faith. Knowledge was to be based on the scientific method and human reason. The Enlightenment was a revolutionary paradigm in human thought, a new paradigm (see Kuhn, 1962 for a discussion of paradigms). It rallied against superstition, tradition, and religion. Our basic argument, though, is that the Enlightenment had important effects on many nations (see Jaeger, 1985; Wohl, 1979; Zafirovski, 2001).

The Enlightenment paradigm developed against traditional and religious views and was later used, selectively, as a rationale for political reasons. Russell (1945), for example, borrows ideas of Max Weber (1930) and argues that the Enlightenment was based on a Protestant backlash against

Catholicism. He further argues that many other philosophical views—such as democracy against monarchy—started among Protestants in the early 16th century as rationales for their breaking away from the Catholic Church. Chartier (1991) proposes that the Enlightenment was created by leaders of the French Revolution who used selected scholars in order to legitimize their Republican political agenda.

Prior to the Enlightenment, the twin towers of tradition and religion were used to maintain social order. Historian Jonathan Israel (2002, p. 3) notes that, until the 1650s, Western civilization "was based on a largely shared core of faith, tradition and authority." Up until this date most intellectual debates revolved around the "confessional"—that is Catholic, Lutheran, Reformed (Calvinist), or Anglican issues, and the primary aim of these debates was to establish which bloc of faith ought to have the "monopoly of truth and a God-given title to authority."

This period also saw the shaping of two distinct lines of Enlightenment thought: First, the *radical enlightenment,* largely inspired by the philosophy of Baruch Spinoza, who believed in "democracy; racial and sexual equality; individual liberty of lifestyle; full freedom of thought, expression, and the press; eradication of religious authority from the legislative process and education; and full separation of church and state." A second strain of Enlightenment thought was *moderate enlightenment,* which was reflected in a number of different philosophical systems, like those in the writings of Descartes, John Locke, Isaac Newton, or Christian Wolff; moderates supported a critical review and renewal of the old modes of thought and sought to accommodate the old systems of power and faith. Both views were met negatively by conservatives who espoused a Counter-Enlightenment viewpoint with traditional beliefs.

The Enlightenment changed views about governance and rights. These views clashed with the old ways and eventually fomented revolutionary behavior by displacing monarchies and the dominance of religion in explaining the world. The divine rule of monarchs or kings, and the privileges of nobles, would cease. Reason was a tool that allowed individuals to find explanations and take control of their lives.

Other relevant Enlightenment views were that government needed checks and balances in order that one branch would not rise to dominance,[11] free speech, and freedom from religious persecution. These were major changes in how the world should be interpreted and structured. The Russian monarch would eventually feel the power of these ideas whose time had come.

Peter the Great and Tsarina Catherine

The Grand Embassy. Peter the Great's sweeping reforms were made in order to modernize Russia and were greatly influenced by his Western

European advisors. He faced considerable opposition to his policies, but he would brutally suppress any and all rebellions against his authority.

In 1697, Peter undertook the Grand Embassy, traveling incognito to Europe on an 18 month journey in the hope of obtaining assistance against the Ottman Empire. However, he was crushed upon learning that France was an ally of the Ottoman Sultan, and that Austria sought peace in the east while conducting its own wars in the west. The journey appeared to be for naught.

However, the "Grand Embassy" was not a complete failure, because Peter was to acquire a considerable amount of knowledge about life in Western Europe. In Amsterdam, he studied shipbuilding in Zaandam, and visited many individuals who provided him with experiences and views that would affect his rule in Russia. Nicolas Witsen, mayor of Amsterdam and an expert on Russia, gave Peter four months of access to the largest shipyard in the world, belonging to the Dutch East India Company. In the shipyard, Peter helped with the construction of an East Indiaman, and gained skills from workers such as builders of locks and fortresses, shipwrights, and seamen—including Cornelis Cruys, a vice-admiral who would later become Peter's advisor on maritime affairs. Later, the Tsar would put his knowledge of shipbuilding to work in building the Russian navy. Peter visited Frederik Ruysch, who taught him how to pull teeth and catch butterflies. Ludolf Bakhuysen, a painter of seascapes, and Jan van der Heyden, the inventor of the fire hose, also received Peter.

In England Peter met King William III, visited Greenwich and Oxford, was painted by Sir Godfrey Kneller, and saw a Royal Navy Fleet Review at Deptford. He travelled to Manchester where he learned the techniques of city-building that he would later apply in building Saint Petersburg. The Tsar's visit proved fruitful after all. Peter, a member of a new generation, saw Europe and its ways of life and would later attempt to implement some of these ideas in Russia.

Tsarina Catherine. Catherine ruled Russia from July 9, 1762 until her death in 1796 at the age of 67. She came to power following a *coup d'état* and the assassination of her husband, Peter III, at the end of the Seven Years' War. Under Catherine's rule, Russia grew larger and emerged as one of the great powers in Europe. The Tsarina was also a member of a new generation and introduced many reforms into Russia, especially reforms she would lift from Enlightenment thinkers.

The Russian Empire rapidly expanded by conquest and diplomacy. In the south, Russian forces crushed the Crimean Khanate following victories in the Russo-Turkish wars; it also colonized the vast territories of Novorossiya along the coasts of the Black and Azov Seas. In the west, the Polish-Lithuanian Commonwealth was ruled by Catherine's former lover, King Stanisław August Poniatowski, and it was eventually partitioned, with Russia obtaining the largest share. Also, Russia began colonizing and establishing Russian America.

Catherine reformed the administration of Russia, and many new cities and towns were founded. The Tsarina modernized Russia along Western European lines. However, she failed to end serfdom, and the increasing demands of the military, the economy, the state, and private landowners' reliance on serfdom led to rebellions, including Russia's largest peasant rebellion: the Pugachev's Rebellion.[12]

In Russia, Catherine, the ever present enlightened despot, backed the arts and sciences. The era produced the first Russian university, library, theatre, public museum, and independent press. Like other enlightened despots, Tsarina Catherine played a key role in fostering the arts, sciences, and education. She had her own interpretation of Enlightenment ideals, communicated with notable scholars such as Voltaire, and had in residence renowned scientists, such as Leonhard Euler, Peter Simon Pallas, and Fedor Ivanovich Iankovich de Mirievo (also spelled Teodor Janković-Mirijevski).

While Enlightenment values in Russia focused on the individual rather than on changing Russian social structure, there were attempts to change some aspects of social structure, such as abolishing serfdom. But these were met with heavy resistance from the powerful Russian oligarch community. Never the less, the seeds of freedom, autonomy, science, and human rights had been planted, and the sense of belonging became a starting point for theorizing about what it meant to be Russian (Mezhuev & Gradirovsky, 2004).

Imperialism and the Expansion of the Russian Empire

As we noted, during the reign of Tsarina Catherine, the Russian empire expanded significantly via imperialism and colonialism.[13] Expansion created several problems for building an all-Russian national identity (Hosking, 1997).

1. It created greater diversity.
2. People in the frontier had their own culture, and had no wishes to be "Russian."
3. It created "Them and Us" differences, which seemed to have led to many rebellions.

Before continuing, we should define Imperialism, Colonialism, and post-Colonialism. We define the concepts in the following manner. *Imperialism* is a mode of annexing a territory by conquest or diplomacy purely for logistical or economic reasons. *Imperialism* is associated with *Mercantilism*, as an economic paradigm based on the notion of protecting a nation's economy and acquiring territory in improving the economy (see Heckscher, 1955).

The idea that economic progress could be achieved internally had not been fully realized. *Colonialism* is a framework of conquest based on the idea of exploiting a people, a territory's resources, and the idea of assimilating people by various methods, including erasing historical and institutional memory. *Post-Colonialism* is associated with several factors related to the results of colonizing a nation. Among these factors are the migration of colonized people to the host country and the colonized peoples' views about citizenship and their status. In short, Post-Colonial people become a challenge to the colonizing nation.

Expansion of the Russian Empire created much diversity; and the citizens of the Frontier were not exactly quick to become Russians and adhere to a Russian identity.[14] For example, the 1897 Imperial Russian Census lists the following as the most dominant languages. See Table 5.3, below.

TABLE 5.3 Languages Spoken in Russian Empire From 1897 Empire Census		
Language Rank	Percent of Total	Number
Russian	44.78125	55,667,469
Ukraine	18.00385	22,380,551
Tukic-Tatar	10.7585	13,373,867
Polish	6.380276	7,931,307
Belarusian	4.734581	5,885,547
Yiddish	4.073015	5,063,156
Finnic languages	2.817274	3,502,147
German	1.440344	1,790,489
Latvian	1.155128	1,435,937
Kartvelian languages	1.088036	1,352,535
Lithuanian, ex Samogitian	0.973785	1,210,510
Armenian	0.943688	1,173,096
Moldavian/Romanian	0.902318	1,121,669
Dagestani languages	0.878275	1,091,782
Bulgarian	0.138894	172,659
Zhmud (Samogitian)	0.360408	448,022
Greek	0.15037	186,925
Ossetian	0.138136	171,716
Tajik	0.281874	350,397
Total		124,309,781

Source: www.demoscope.ru

Note: The total from the website is listed at 125,640,021. However, upon summing, that number appears incorrect.

Expansion of the empire not only created diversity, but because the conquered people were not entirely willing to become Russian and be governed by Russia, there were constant rebellions and trouble in the Frontier. The resistance to becoming Russian can be seen in the many rebellions in the Frontier and the great effort made by Russia at controlling its vast empire.[15] We have already noted the largest of such rebellions, the Pugachev Rebellion. There were three waves of Russian colonialism: the Colonization of Siberia, the Colonization of Middle Asia, and a period of colonization during the Socialist regime.

First Two Waves of Colonization: Siberia, the Caucasus, and Middle Asia

The first wave of colonization occurred in the 16th century; the colonization of Siberia under the influence, and with the assistance, of pre-capitalist clans of Stroganovs, Demidovs, and more. The second wave saw the colonization of the Caucasus and Middle Asia in the XIX century. Today, these colonized people are viewed as the "Oriental Other" in Russia. Russian colonialism was a mixture of both Western and European models. Its Western links are to its geopolitical and economic interests, whereas its European character concerns modernity and a civilizing mission.

Russian colonialism had a religious tint. The Russian empire colonized different regions with diverse faiths. Typically, modern colonial empires developed spaces in two ways. First, there was the conquest of distant colonies and merging them into the metropolis. Second, there was the mission of spreading Roman Christianity. In acquiring new territories, a State guarded and diffused their notion of "civilization." Interestingly, citizenship was granted to those born inside imperial borders, and religious affiliation was not a factor.

Maintaining control of annexed territories was a challenge, and new ways of controlling the populace of the Frontier were developed. The idea of loyalty to the State was raised by Nikolai Karamzin (Karamzin, 1989). Karamzin described the State-building process as a feeling of usefulness; belonging to the royal dynasty, membership in the Russian empire meant "to be a perfect citizen." The idea of a civic nation in the early XIXth century was a non-violent form of control; it basically called for colonized people to assimilate. For instance, the general-governor of Turkestan Konstantin Kaufman (1867–1882) felt that making both Orthodoxes and Muslims equally useful citizens of Russia was a step toward belonging (Tolz, 2009). Mosques were built close to Orthodox churches and the settlement of a multicultural population began a custom of building neighborhoods and, as a final task, of promoting assimilation into the dominant ethnic culture. So structural allowances were made in order to ensure assimilation and a sense of belonging.

Yet, the Russian Empire lacked an overarching framework. Many Russian intellectuals based their ideas on European definitions and categories, and it was difficult to find words in order to express such ideas as "Translatio Imperii."[16] The time was ripe for a new orthodoxy; and indeed, one such framework surfaced. The new framework was reflected in the official slogan "Orthodoxy-Autocracy-Peoplehood" (in some translations—Nationality), which was developed, elaborated, and promoted by Count Sergey Uvarov in 1830–40 in response to the Decembrist Uprising of 1825.[17]

In 1832, Count Uvarov gave his notes containing the formula to Tsar Nicolay together with some suggestions. The formula begins with *Orthodoxy*. A view of Human Reason, elaborated by the European Enlightenment, that argued that governance should be based on reason and political liberalism. Orthodoxy should be the basis for the "Russification" of the newly colonized Western lands.

The second component in the formula was *Autocracy*. State guardianship was necessary as a mechanism for guiding Russia toward enlightenment, and only the State possessed the resources to successfully implement a system of education and science in meeting Russia's needs.

The final component, *Peoplehood*, appeared vague. Uvarov argued that the core problem was linguistic. The concept was popular, though a bit vague, and viewed as a valuable part of the formula.

The formula was a reaction to what many thought was irresponsible liberalism in Europe, and directed the Russian Empire Eastward. Language and knowledge became instruments in developing relations with the "Other" (Tolz, 2011; Tlostanova, 2008).

* * *

Russia began modernizing at the second half of the XIXth century. Modernization had a specific imperial character. Liberal ideas about identification were implemented, and a major task for Russia was to synthesize Western European ideas about the nation-state. There were issues about modernizing Russia:

1. A large imperial State based on the principle of exclusion, such as centre-periphery relations; centralizing government; and a policy of Russification for the empire.
2. A poly-ethnic population. According to the first Russian Census of 1897, Russia was populated by 125.6 million people speaking in 130 languages (Census, 1905). Such plurality demanded a plan for how best to organize relations between the centre and the periphery.
3. Increasing nationalism and separatism resulting from a State policy of Russification.

* * *

A liberal model was prescribed for reconfiguring relationships between the centre and peripheries within the Russian empire. In addition, the model proposed equal rights among nations and extended equal opportunities for all ethnic groups within the empire.

Equal rights and personal freedom are the foundation of liberal ideology that were extracted from the Enlightenment. So Russian liberals argued for Civic rights that would be equal for all nationalities within the Russian empire. In the first issue of the journal, "Liberation," an article entitled "From Russian constitutionalists" listed a number of factors that were crucial for a free, civic life in Russia: the abolishment of all national, social, and religious exclusions; accepting full freedom of beliefs, eliminating all barriers to personal and economic rights, especially those barriers erected against Jews and Poles.[18]

On September 1905, during the City and Regional Summit, liberals proposed discussing the problem of national self-determination and decentralization,[19] with the idea of keeping the unitary structure of the Russian empire. For F. Kokoshkin (Kokoshkin, 2010), political self-determination would fragment Russia. For people of different ethnic origin, he suggested that cultural self-determination should be pursued as policy. Self-determination, though, must involve creating autonomous cultural entities within the Russian State. Cultural autonomy is the ability for ethnic groups to solve their own educational and cultural problems. Interestingly, this sort of autonomy was only extended to Finland and Poland, while the Caucasus and Middle Asia were excluded.

Third Wave of Colonization

The third wave of colonization occurred during the XX century as part of the Socialist program. Since the XIX century, the logic of colonialism involved a system of controlling non-Western, non-Christian territories (Caucasus, Middle Asia, some part of Siberia). The third wave of colonization created a new form of domination. The new dominance involved reducing illiteracy, creating a body of knowledge in socializing the colonized population, implementing a push for belonging and citizenship, and erasing a peoples' historical memory (Arkturk, 2010).

Theoretically, such a plan might have worked were it not for the fact that colonized people objected to being assimilated. There was much resistance from the populations of colonized territories. Building an all-Russian identity was out of the question.

Breakup of the USSR and Russian National Identity

The Union of Soviet Socialist Republics (USSR) ended on December 26, 1991. The official document ending the State was number 142-H of the Soviet of the Republics of the Supreme Soviet of the Soviet Union. The document confirmed the independence of the twelve remaining republics of the Soviet Union, and led to the creation of the Commonwealth of Independent States (CIS). On the previous day, December 25, 1991, Soviet President Mikhail Gorbachev resigned: he declared his office extinct, and turned over the office to Boris Yeltsin.

That evening, at 7:32 p.m., the Soviet flag was lowered from the Kremlin for the last time. In its place, the Russian tricolor was raised. In previous months, 13 of the 15 republics withdrew from the USSR. The week before the dissolution, 11 republics, except the Baltic States and Georgia, signed the Alma-Ata Protocol and established the CIS, and declared the end of the Soviet Union.

* * *

Mikhail Gorbachev was elected General Secretary by the Politburo on March 11, 1985, approximately three hours after Konstantin Chernenko died. Gorbachev's primary goal was to improve a stagnant Soviet economy. However, early in his tenure he realized that improving the flagging Soviet economy would be impossible without changing the entire Communist social structure. His reforms began with personnel changes.

On April 23, 1985, Gorbachev brought two of his proteges into the Politburo as full members: Yegor Ligachev and Nikolai Ryzhkov. He was also able to maintain some peace by promoting KGB head Viktor Chebrikov from a Politburo candidate to a full member, and appointing Sergei Sokolov as Minister of Defense. But things got out of hand quickly, much to everyone's surprise. Gorbachev's liberalizing policies created a rush for more liberal reforms. The net result was, of course, complete freedom away from the USSR.

The breakup of the USSR generated a number of issues affecting national identity. Among the most serious challenges were ethnic conflicts, issues related to diversity and multiculturalism, the erosion of citizenship, and the relationship of ethnicity to group solidarity.

Ethnic Conflicts

The collapse of the Soviet empire opened up ethnic conflicts. Conflict situations on the territory of the former Soviet Union occur due to many reasons: political (centralism and unitary authorities, victimization and conquest of nations), economic (economic crisis, unemployment, poverty), psychosocial (inter-ethnic communication barriers, negative forms of national assertiveness, open nationalism, ambitious national leaders), territorial, and others. The weakening of the USSR in 1980–1990s exposed flaws of the previous regime and national policy, which caused latent ethnic tensions. Besides this, autonomization of the state with four unequal levels of the national government and national administrative units (federal republic, an autonomous republic, national region, national district) laid "the bomb" under the national question in the former USSR republics. Nationalists, striving for power and property groups in many autonomous republics, suddenly became national heroes, trying to explain all the troubles of the people by the policy of exploitative internationalism.

The uneven modernization of the society, social and economic inequality, competition on the labour market were substituted by ethnic conflicts. That is, the nature of conflicts of the late 1980s–early 1990s in Fergana, Dushanbe, and Osh (Middle Asian countries), as well as other similar events. Movement towards democratization accompanied by a struggle of old and new political elites in the society became a detonator. Such transformation in a multiethnic society has led to the fight with "ethno-political color." Inept, incoherent steps of governments toward transformation into a real federation exacerbated ethnic conflicts and attempts to grasp the disintegrative tendencies in the republics using direct force: events in Tbilisi in 1989, Baku in 1990 and Vilnius 1991 were the most feasible (Pustobaev, 1994; Coppieters, 1994).

Some researchers (Pain, 2007) offer a typology of internal ethno-territorial conflicts:

1. Conflicts, which arise from claims of pre-existing national territorial autonomy for the full state sovereignty (the Chechen conflict).
2. Conflicts that have developed in a consequence of proclamation of the ethnic communities for new national-territorial autonomy or unilateral increasing of their current status, but without a formal claim to create an autonomy within Independent States (conflicts in the Kabardino-Balkar Republic, Karachay-Cherkessia).
3. Conflicts between ethnic groups or neighboring republics, which are seeking to gain control over the disputed border areas (conflicts between the ethnic communities of Dagestan, the dispute between North Ossetia and Ingushetia).

Being based on the evaluation of events in the late 1980s–early 1990s, the following types of inter-ethnic conflicts could be distinguished (Pain, 2007; Tishkov, 2008). The first type is based on psychological stereotypes. This kind of conflict is characterized by a significant extent of spontaneity and lack of control, coming from rumors or incorrect interpretations of real events. In these actions, hidden instigators of conflict usually stay in the shadows, such as in Sumgait 1988, Ferghana 1989, New Uzen 1989, and other similar events.

The second type is ethnic conflicts based on ideological concepts (or doctrines). It contains some ideological (theoretical, conceptual) design, which may include various complaints and their justification (the idea of a "historical nation"; justificatory doctrine of "the great nation"). These and similar constructions have nothing to do with scientific theories.

The third type is associated with the clash of political institutions (organizations). Political institutions include parties, civil movements, public authorities, armed forces, and so on.

The fourth type is the selection of strategic goals of ethno-social movement (autonomist, separatist, ethno-egalitarian, anti-immigrant, selectivist, etc.).

The Republic of Tatarstan has demonstrated peaceful options for handling a complex constitutional conflict. The Constitution adopted in the Republic in 1992 has recorded its independence and associate membership in the Federation, but the Federal Treaty has not been signed in that time.

In February 1994, after a series of negotiations between government bodies of the Russian Federation and the Republic of Tatarstan, the treaty was signed, whereby the basic contradictions were resolved. Since that time relations based on the signed agreement became known as the "Model of Tatarstan."

Elements of institutional conflict occurred in Bashkortostan. This republic has signed a federal agreement, but under certain conditions. Conflict has been removed after the signing of the Treaty, where power-sharing with the federal center has been constituted.

Constitutional conflicts occurred in two republics–Sakha (Yakutia) and Tuva. They were prompted in the early 1990s by active national associations, especially in Yakutia, which was seeking more autonomy within the Federation.

In the beginning of the 1990s, Russia was very close to civil war based on these conflicts. There are several reasons why a civil war did not occur. To begin with, social activity was exceedingly low by the end of the XXth century. Adapting to the new system of social, political, and economic relations demanded significant efforts from Russian citizens. Social activity was focused on adapting to the new system, and more precisely, individual adaptation.

Second, there was little civic activity. Social protests of 1980s were of a specific nature and disappeared quickly by the 1990s. Related to less civic activity were the strategies of including activists into the decision making process. Russian elites had a historical role in stabilizing the country. For example, elites met informally on many occasions to discuss issues about Russia; it was an exclusive club. In 1993, B. Yel'tsin began incorporating leaders from the opposition, a younger generation, into the post-Soviet elite. It was an important decision of engaging oppositional elites into the decision making process. The decision was part of a new way of building solidary, and part of overall integration plan. The effect was to stabilize the system by reducing civil protest.

Third, there was an emergence of nationalism in Russian. Nationalism posed a serious challenge to civic identity. These nationalist uprisings reflected a disappointment with Western democratic values and free market reforms. Other sources of growing nationalism were Russia's negative persona in the world, social protest among immigrants from the former Soviet republics and Northern Caucasus (a result of post-colonialism), and Russia's "brain drain." Ethnic nationalism seems to have been a response to these tensions.[20]

National tensions raised yet another important question for Russia: would it attempt to become a great Eurasian state (Eurasian in the geographical sense of the word), or a small country queuing up in line to join the European Union. Russia is at an important crossroads regarding national identity: awareness of Russian "greatness," which is an important component of national identity.

The transition of cultural conditions, a sharply shortened territory, and decreased world power and influence have been a tragedy for Russian national identity. To some extent, Russia today is at an awkward point in its history as its core of national identity is being tested. All attempts at artificially creating a great Russia in the 1990s had no satisfying results. Russia is still at the crossroads of developing its sense of greatness. The effect on national identity is significant.

Russia and Multiculturalism

The confluence of the Enlightenment and Russia's imperialism emerged in Russian multiculturalism. Multiculturalism has become an important issue in Russia, and a significant issue in politics and research (Galston, 2005). By multicultural we mean a society composed of more than one cultural group and social policies that promote such diversity. In order to stabilize a manifold society the framework of multiculturalism suggests to accept, include, and respect all cultural groups through a specific policy and practice.

The framework has its critics (Goldberg, 1994).[21] For example, some argue that multiculturalism reifies ethnicity, that it substitutes individual social rights with group rights (Kymlicka & Norman, 2000). Also, there are some specifically "Russian" objections toward multiculturalism—that it leads to ethnocentrism and ethnic prejudices (see Malakhov, 2002; Nizamova, 2009; Chebankova, 2012). Some general criticisms are listed below:

- There is a benign coexistence when cultural groups remain distinct.

- Nation-states have a core identity, and this core is challenged when enforcing multiculturalism (Nagel, 2009).
- There is less group trust, the greater the diversity (Putnam 2007).
- The greater the homogeneity, the greater the altruism (Salter 2006).

Later, other scholars noted their dissatisfaction with Western practices of multiculturalism. Their main objection is that multiculturalism is an ideology that blocks democratic pluralism and substitutes civic society for cultural communities (Joppke, 2004). In some circles, multiculturalism is seen as part of a democratic society. Wieviorka (2001) calls it integrative multiculturalism or discursive democratic multiculturalism (Benhabib, 2002). In Russia, cultural pluralism is not important enough to pursue an assimilation policy and negate group differences on behalf of common values, as it is in the USA. Assimilation is a policy asking ethnic groups to change their identity for the common good; where the common good refers to the culture of a dominant group (see Wieviorka, 2001).

* * *

Russian scholars tend to view multicultural policy as a threat and not applicable in multinational Russia. In contrast, discourse on immigration is based on citizenship, an ethos of the nation, justice, universal rights, and identity. Moreover, this view is driven by a Eurocentric view of freedom, belonging, and democracy. The challenge posed by immigration is an excellent topic for understanding multiculturalism in Russia (Mukomel, 2005; Thakahov, 2009).

The State remains neutral on immigrant co-existence. The upshot of State neutral policy is the decentralization of equality and tolerance and thus any immigration policy is a local matter (Walzer, 1997). Such a strategy is a major component of Neo-Liberal ideology (see Verdugo, 2013 for a discussion of the Neo-Liberal paradigm), but does not mesh with Russian hegemony and social structure. In reality, Russia is a political community with a large ethnic-cultural majority of Russians (80% of the population consider themselves Russians), and the State is controlled by this majority.

Neutrality has rendered Immigrants an invisible minority.[22] By an "invisible minority," we mean they are not acknowledged and their needs do not need to be met; such a group fails to exist in the national psyche. For instance, media in Southern Russia demonstrates the unpopularity of providing immigrants with assistance in finding work—because they do not exist. In a 2006 public opinion poll, respondents were asked, "Could ethnic quarters (ghettoes) be founded in Moscow?" The vast majority answered "No." Most Russians believe that ethnic minorities are well "integrated" into the capital's life; thus, they are invisible as ethnic minorities.[23] Yet, data indicate otherwise.

Russia has a significant immigrant population. The 2002 Russian Census reported that there were 5.6 million immigrants in the nation.[24] By 2007, the number increased by about 43% to 8 million immigrants.[25] Immigration is a source of the new Russian multicultural identity, and yet at the same time it is associated with poly-ethnicity. The two concepts are vastly different—in the former, ethnicity is recognized, in the latter, ethnicity is not recognized. According to the 2010 Russian Census, the total population in Russia was 142.9 million, and of this number, 137.2 million provided their ethnic origin. Of those providing an ethnic origin, 111 million identified as Russian,[26] and the remainder, about 26 million, defined their origin as non-Russian (Tatar ethnic group is the largest among minorities). Approximately 40% of minority groups have their own administration, territory, and quasi-state governments. Such diversity is a major challenge for developing a Russian national identity.

Wieviorka (2001) identifies three ways of developing collective identities—assimilation, tolerance, and multiculturalism. Where multiculturalism refers to the recognition and implementation of cultural rights for minorities; of course, under the condition that minorities accept community values and laws. Thus, multicultural practices in Russia are inconsistent and selective. Russia ignores the benefits and rights claims from ethnic-cultural minorities. The presence of the "Other" is acceptable, but their complaints about collective rights fall on deaf ears.

Integration, then, means the unification of differences and formulating a homogeneous community. The bases for a unified political community are the principles of citizen's equal rights, liberal rights, and personal freedom. Negative results may surface when personal freedom is absent, and where cultural differences and group rights have priority over individual rights. But Russian discourse on democratic multiculturalism does not openly discuss such a problem, and it is clear that the priorities in a liberal framework are the principles of individual rights and individual membership in an equal co-citizenship.

Differences between Russia and the West about multiculturalism appear to be between liberals and communitarians. For liberals, empowering citizenship via law is paramount; for communitarians, citizenship is important for developing "exclusiveness" in a political community (see Berry, 1991; Barry, 2001; Bennet, 1998). Upon closer inspection, the debate is actually between these groups and postmodernists. The "narrow" conception is close to liberals and communitarians, the "wide" conception associated with a radical postmodernist perspective (Brubaker, 2004).

Both liberals and communitarians believe that law and citizenship are necessary for social stability. However, there are differences between both ideological groups. Liberals construct their paradigm by defining the "Other" as deviant (Balibar, 2009). The liberal conception of universal values contains an alienating component. And citizenship, despite its universal claims, is an important instrument for settling and defending preferences of identity. Communitarianism initially rose in their critical answer to the passage of John Rawls (1971) about the principle task of a government to secure and distribute fairly common goods among people with the need of individualistic free life. Communitarians (Taylor, 1989; Walzer, 1994) doubted the idea of a totally independent individual, emphasizing social nature of self, the role of the social and cultural context and traditions, as well as the influence of a community value system on life trajectory. In the second half of 1990s, communitarians paid attention to social responsibilities, political and cultural alienation, and erosion of communal life in the epoch of the dispersed and atomized society. For this reason they shift the focus from exclusiveness and personal fulfillment toward "family engagement." So the term "community" is exploited in discussions around citizenship and the problem of status of the Other.

Liberals and communitarians base their ideas on the fact that citizenship creates individuals who are equal political subjects. From the liberal point of view, political integration is secured by the ideas and values shared among all citizens. For communitarians, integration means social inclusion (community membership shared by all citizens). So, citizenship is simultaneously a legal status, coordinated with personal identity, and social status, meaning equal opportunities and societal acceptance. The most feasible extension of citizenship and belonging is the right to social assistance: the State provides social assistance in terms of disability, aging, or labour market changes.

Citizenship Erosion in Russian

Russia is not a State of ethnic nationalism. Indeed, the most important social-political influence in Russia has always been the relations between elites and the masses, and the perception of the State by elites.

There is a difference between State and civic self-consciousness. State identity is easier than civic awareness. Political leaders, elites, and political entrepreneurs provide definitions of "Stateness" as a form of territorial unity. In recent years, this sense of "Stateness" has increased in Russia. For instance, in 1992 a public opinion poll conducted in Moscow suggested that no more than one in five respondents identified as Russian.[27] Whereas, at the beginning of the XXI century, 80% of the population in outlying areas identified as Russian; and about 65% throughout the nation identified as Russian (Public Opinion, 2006).

Leokadia Drobizheva has undertaken a long-term research project about the process of constructing civic identity among Russians.[28] The ideas of a strong State are epitomized in strong personal leadership, ideas of a great State, maintaining a leading position in the world, and appeared as official ideology at the beginning of the XXI century. For example, in 1999 a

Russian survey asked, "What Russia needs most of all?" 71% of respondents answered "strong leader," and 59% mentioned a "strong state."[29] An understanding of the strong State varied; most respondents believe that Russia must be a State, which "merits [a] more acceptable position in the world."[30] In other data, respondents indicated that Russia should continue to be a member of "the Great 8" (69% answered in 2001).[31] The breakup of the Soviet Union has been traumatic and a majority of Russians appear eager to restore Russia's past, vaunted, geopolitical world position.

Ethnicity, Identity, and Group Solidarity

An important factor in forming a common State identity involves combining State and ethnic identity. However, when asked about the meaning of "We," ethnicity was preferred over civic identity. In a 2006 national survey, a national (ethnic) unity was preferred by 85.6% of respondents; the unity with all other citizens of Russia—65%; though only about 19.8% felt this way "very often."[32] For ethnic Russians, a common Russian civic identity is easily combined with ethnicity, but for Russians of other ethnic origins such a combination was complex.

None the less, ethnicity may be losing its grip in Russia. According to research conducted in 2006 in regions with dominant ethnic Russian populations, Russian civic identity has become greater than ethnic identity: 90–95% of respondents living in the Sverdlovsk, Tomsk, and Voronezh regions; and up to 77–82% of people living in Saratov, Kaliningrad regions felt they were citizens of Russia. An affinity for people from one's ethnic origin was felt by 86% of respondents in Yekaterinburgh, 61–77% from Saratov, and 55–57% of respondents in Kaliningrad, Voronezh and other outlying regions.[33] Civic identity, in its unique Russian version, maybe the dominant identity in the future. Such an event may have positive effects, because there is strength in the weak ties to an ethnic community (Granovetter 1973).

Republican discourse gives priority to community over universal or individual rights. Republicans have exploited the idea of responsibility toward other members of society and in developing strong links with community and nation. (Also, keep in mind that a focus on individual rights and freedom would be a challenge to the status and privileges of Russian oligarchs.) In their discourse, responsibility is set in contrast to rights. Rights are nothing without a strong presence of values, so their primary message is about loyalty, civic literacy, and service to community and state, and all are connected to civic responsibility. In this sense Russian discourse is very close to the general Republican viewpoint in emphasizing individual rights in spite of collective responsibility. Does such a view coincide with reality? We conclude our analyses with the following 2003 survey results. (See Table 5.4)

Among all respondents, slightly under one-third do not feel close to Russia. We can interpret this as not identifying with Russia. There is also variation

TABLE 5.4 How Close Do You Feel to Your Country? (Russia)					
Responses	Regions				
	Panel A				
	Total	Northwest	Central	North	Volga-Vyatka
Very close	26.4	43.6	27.2	25.8	37.9
Close	40.6	38.5	41.9	25.8	37.1
Not very close	22.6	16.7	20.0	32.8	19.0
Not close at all	10.3	1.30	10.9	15.1	6.0
Total	100.0	100.0	100.0	100.0	100.0
	Panel B				
	Black Earth	Volga-Region	N. Caucus	Urals	W. Siberia
Very close	25.9	26.7	22.0	20.7	28.4
Close	41.7	42.4	47.1	37.3	42.8
Not very close	25.0	18.0	21.5	30.1	17.9
Not close at all	7.4	12.9	9.4	12.0	10.9
Total	100.0	100.0	100.0	100.0	100.0
	Panel C				
	E. Siberia	Far East			
Very close	22.1	23.2			
Close	44.3	38.4			
Not very close	26.2	29.5			
Not close at all	7.4	8.9			
Total	100.0	100.0			

Source: Original calculations derived from International Social Survey Programe. www.zacat. gesis.org

by region. The highest percentage of respondents not identifying as Russian are those in the North (48%). The lowest are those residing in the Northwest (18%).[34] Clearly, there is a significant identity problem in Russia.

CONCLUSION

The history of Russia begins with the Eastern Slavs and the Finno-Ugric peoples. The state of Garðaríki ("the realm of towns"), which was centered in Novgorod and included the entire areas inhabited by Ilmen Slavs, Veps, and Votes, was established by the Varangian chieftain Rurik in 862. This date is considered to be the beginning of Russian history. Kievan Rus' was founded by Oleg of Novgorod twenty years later in 882. Christianity was adopted from the Byzantine Empire in 988 and led to a synthesis of Byzantine and Slavic cultures that would characterize Russian culture for over 100 years. Mongol invasions in 1237–1240 eventually destroyed Kievan Rus'.

By the 18th century, Russia was a vast empire, stretching from the Polish–Lithuanian Commonwealth eastward to the Pacific Ocean. Western expansion increased Russia's sense of isolation, and would lead to greater interaction with Europe and the assimilation of some of its values, especially those from the Enlightenment, which would eventually end the monarchy. Successive regimes during the 19th century responded to pressures for social change; the responses were superficial and repressive. Serfdom was abolished in 1861, though it proved to be unfavorable to the peasants. Increased dissatisfaction in the populace eventually led to revolution. The situation appeared to be changing after the abolition of serfdom and the beginning of World War I in 1914. Other changes included Stolypin reforms, the constitution of 1906, and the State Duma's attempts at liberalizing the economy and politics. But the Tsars were not much interested in relinquishing their status and privileges.

The 1917 Russian Revolution was the result of several factors—an economic breakdown, war weariness, and discontent among the populace with autocratic rule. A coalition of liberals and moderate socialists rose to power, but their program failed miserably, and power was seized by the Communist Bolsheviks on October 25—The October Revolution.

Between 1922 and 1991, Russian history is about the Soviet Union; a State linked with the Russian Empire prior to the Treaty of Brest-Litovsk.[35] The approach at building Socialism varied during different periods of Soviet history, from a mixed economy and a diverse society and culture of the 1920s, to a command economy and repressions during the Stalin regime, and then the stagnation of the 1980s.

By the mid-1980s, Mikhail Gorbachev realized that the USSR could not continue as it was then structured, so he embarked on major liberalizing reforms, which eventually, and unexpectedly, led to the fall of the Soviet Union.

The history of the Russian Federation (RF) officially starts in January 1992. The Federation was the legal successor to the Soviet Union, sans its superpower status after facing serious challenges in its efforts at forging a new post-Soviet political and economic system. Scrapping the socialist central planning and state ownership of property, the RF implemented a program of market capitalism in an attempt at building its flagging economy. The attempt failed. Since the new millennium, Vladimir Putin has been its dominant leader, and Russia continues to share many of the political and social structures with its Tsarist and Soviet past. There is the sense that the RF is a Kleptocracy, and, indeed, there is much corruption and inequality (see Dawisha, 2014).[36]

Marx is reputed to have said that "people make history, but not as they please." It seems to us that there are at least two interesting parts to his comment. First, that history has a role in its own making by limiting what people can and cannot do. Second, that history repeats itself. In the current Russian Federation, the nation is facing a number of historical events affecting national identity. First, there are remnants of the Enlightenment and its core values, which challenges its current social structure. Second, there is Russia's colonial past where it not only increased its diversity, but added significant administrative and economic costs. Also, people in the Frontier were and are less likely to feel "Russian." Third, Russia has shown remarkable instability in its governance regimes. Such instability creates challenges for creating national identity. Fourth, there is the issue of corruption which hurts the Russian economy, creates much social inequality, and hurts ordinary Russian citizens. As someone once stated, "corruption in Russia is not a problem, it is a business." Each of these factors, in combination or separately, makes national identity among those living in Russia complex.

For example, Tishkov argues that there is widespread ethnic and civic identity (Tishkov, 2008). Civil identity is usually combined with the ethos of responsibility, loyalty, a feeling of belonging, a shared vision of the past, a unified system of education, a system of symbols, and memorable dates. This type of identity is usually accompanied by ethnic (ethno-cultural) identity, embodying feelings of belonging to an ethnic community and being different from others. Both types of identity may coexist within the same nation-state. Being a mixture of ethnic communities, Russia provides a hybrid identity where its dominant Russian culture, religion, and language construct a national framework

There are several conclusions to be derived from our analyses. First, generations have played an important part in Russian national identity and in fostering change, and yet maintaining the stability and continuance of the State. Many members from younger generations have played key roles in contributing to change and stability, such as Peter the Great, Tsarina Catherine, Lenin and Trotsky, Stalin, Gorbachev, Yeltsin, and Putin.

Second, historical events have been crucial in Russian national identity. Three of the more important were the Enlightenment, Russian imperialism, and the breakup of the USSR. The Enlightenment was crucial because it introduced new ideas about governance, social structure, and individual freedom into Russia, which eventually ended the monarchy, led to Communism and a free market economy, and later to a new autocratic system. Enlightenment views fostered change, and its values continue to be a challenge to Russia

Imperialism not only increased diversity, but also increased administrative and economic costs of managing a large empire. Moreover, people in the Frontier, not having any desire to be Russian, were constantly rebelling.

Finally, the breakup of the USSR has been affecting national identity. Russia is currently struggling with a major factor in its national identity— will it return to its former international power as a great nation?

In conclusion, national identity and its development and maintenance is complex. It revolves around societal processes, structures, and social change.

APPENDIX A
Additional Data Regarding National Identity

Data are original computations from the International Social Survey Program (www.gesis.org). Data in percents. All distributions sum to 100%, though there might be some discrepancy due to rounding.

1. Proud to be a native of Russia
   Very proud, 37.9
   Somewhat proud, 47.5
   Not very proud, 11.3
   Not proud, 3.3

2. Regional or national identity
   Only regional, 12.0
   More regional, 6.4
   Equal, 40.9
   Greater national, 13.3
   Only national, 26.7
   Other, 0.7
   None, 0.0

3. I would rather be a citizen of Russia than any other country
   Agree strongly, 44.3
   Agree, 33.6
   Neutral, 13.5
   Disagree, 4.7
   Disagree strongly, 3.8

4. There are some things about Russia that make me feel ashamed.
   Agree strongly, 40.3
   Agree, 41.8
   Neutral, 11.2
   Disagree, 4.9
   Disagree strongly, 1.7

5. Are you willing to fight for Russia?
   Yes, 75.3

6. Democracy causes a bad economy.
   Strongly agree, 8.9
   Agree, 39.4

Disagree, 46.6
Disagree strongly, 5.0

7. Democracy cannot maintain order.
   Strongly agree, 14.4
   Agree, 47.1
   Disagree, 34.6
   Disagree strongly, 3.9

8. Democracy is the best political system.
   Strongly agree, 15.3
   Agree, 54.2
   Disagree, 25.8
   Disagree strongly, 4.6

APPENDIX B
Corruption Indices for Russia

Russian Corruption Indices and Rank per Number of Nations in Survey		
Year	Index Score: Russia/Other*	Rank/Number of Nations
2000	2.1/Finland, 10	82/90 = bottom 10%
2001	2.3/Finland, 9.9	79/91 = bottom 10%
2002	2.7/Finland, 9.7	71/102 = bottom 10%
2003	2.7/Finland, 9.7	86/133 = bottom 10%
2004	2.8/Finland, 9.7	90/145 = bottom 10%
2005	2.4/Iceland/9.7	126/158 = bottom 10%
2006	2.5/Finland, Iceland, New Zealand, 9.6	121/163 = bottom 10%
2007	2,3/Denmark, Finland New Zealand, 9.4	143/179 = bottom 10%
2008	2.1/Denmark, Sweden New Zealand, 9.3	147/180 = bottom 10%
2009	2.2/New Zealand, 9.4	146/180 = bottom 10%
2010	2.1/Denmark, New Zealand, Singapore, 9.3	154/178 = bottom 10%
2011	2.4/New Zealand, 9.5	143/182 = bottom 10%
2012	28* (2.8)/Denmark, Finland, New Zealand, 90	133/174 = bottom 10%
2013	28* (2.8)/Denmark, New Zealand, 91	127/175 = bottom 10%
2014	27* (2.7)/Denmark, 92	136/174 = bottom 10%

Source: Transparency International: www.transparency.org.
* Transparency International changed its scoring, however, we can interpret these larger scores by divided by 10. From 2000 to 2011, the maximum score is 10; thereafter the maximum score is 100.

Russia has been and continues to be one of the most corrupt nations in the world. Throughout the period covered, Russia is ranked in the bottom with some of the most corrupt nations in the world. We also have posted the number one ranked, and safest nations in the world.

NOTES

1. See Edmund Wilson. 1940. To the Finland Station: A Study in the Writing and Acting of History. New York, NY: Harcourt, Brace and Company.
2. For a popular account of the Russian Revolution, see John Reed (1990). Ten Days that Shook the World. New York, NY: Penguin Classics.
3. Note that national identity is highly related to such concepts as class consciousness, a sense of community, etc. Some of the classic scholarship include Marx and Engels' work on class consciousness (Marx and Engels, 1919); Tonnies (2001) on Gemeinschaft (community) and Gesellschaft (association); Weber (1978) who refined Tonnie's work; Durkheim (1997) on mechanical (based on the homogeneity of people) and orgqanic (based on the interdependence of people due to the division of labor in modern society) solidarity; and Hobsbawm and Ranger (1983) on invented tradition. See Verdugo and Mueller (2008) for a quantitative application of some of Durkheim's ideas.
4a. Note that Anderson's "imagined identity" owes its origins from Hobsbawm's "invented tradition."
4b. Alexey Khomyakov in his work "About the Old and the New" in 1839 has expressed this in follows words: "Russian ancient life forms...were based on the sanctity of family ties and unspoiled individuality of our tribe life..."(Khomyakov, 1994).
5. There was a reaction at this time against the ideas of the Enlightenment; the movement was called "Romanticism." Martin Heidegger (2002) was arguably the most famous of the Romantic writers. Romanticism basically argued that reason had failed in organizing society, and that intuition and tradition were better concepts and practices. They also argued that identity and community should be based on blood and race/ethnicity.

   The feeling was that the Enlightenment and its ideas favored an emerging Bourgeois class and threatened the peasant and aristocratic classes.

   Interestingly, Romanticism was largely based in Great Britain and Germany, while the Enlightenment was centered in France.
6. See in: Trubeczkoy, N. "Herritage of Genghis Khan" Moscow: Agraph, 2000, p. 224 (in Russian)
7. Leo Gumilev (2007) used the term "passionary" to describe a cohort of people who are able to absorb energy and use it for transforming human and natural environment.
8. In his masterpiece, Leviathan, Thomas Hobbes (2012) lays out a rationale for why society needs a good, strong government. It is to guard against evil and civil war. In one of the most important passages in political philosophy, he describes what would occur without such a government:

   "In such condition, there is no place for industry, because the fruit thereof is uncertain and, consequently, no culture of the earth; no navigation, nor use of the commodities that may be imported by sea; no commodious building; no instruments of moving, and removing, such things as require much force; no knowledge of the face of the earth; no account of time; no arts; no letters; no society; and which is worst of all, continual fear, and danger of violent death;

and the life of man, solitary, poor, nasty, brutish, and short. (Chapter 13, On the Natural Condition of Mankind, The Incommodities of such a war.)"

9. In 2013, Russia's Corruption Index was 28. Such a score ranked it 128 out of 177 nations in the world. Thus, Russia ranked as one of the most corrupt nations in the world. See Transparency International for data: www.transparency.org

10. Although there is reason to believe that its ideas can be traced to Greece during the halcyon years of Greek dominance ( ).

11. While the Greeks discussed the topic of mixed government, Montesquieu (1977) outlined the separation of powers in his book, The Spirit of the Laws. Berkeley, CA: University of California Press.

12. Pugachev's Rebellion (or the Cossack Rebellion) of 1773–75 was one in a series of rebellions that occurred after Catherine II seized power in 1762. The rebellion began as an organized insurrection of Yaik Cossacks led by Yemelyan Pugachev, a former officer of the Russian Imperial army. The motivation for the rebellion was peasant unrest and war with the Ottoman Empire. After an initial success, Pugachev became the leader of an alternative government and ended serfdom.

    The rebellion consolidated support from many groups including the peasants, the Cossacks, and Old Believers. It claimed to control most of the territory between the Volga River and the Urals.

    At first, government forces did not effectively respond to the insurrection, mostly due to logistical difficulties and a failure to appreciate the revolts magnitude. Nevertheless, the revolt was crushed near the end of 1774. Pugachev was captured soon after and executed in Moscow in January 1775.

    The event has generated much literature, particularly notable is Pushkin's historical novel The Captain's Daughter (1836). It was the largest peasant revolt in Russia's history.

13. At the beginning of the 19th century, the Russian Empire extended from the Arctic Ocean in the north to the Black Sea on the south, from the Baltic Sea on the west to the Pacific Ocean, and (until 1867) into Alaska in North America on the east. With 125.6 million subjects registered by the 1897 census, it had the third largest population in the world at the time, after Qing China and the British Empire. Like all empires, it was highly diverse in terms of economics, ethnicity, and religion. There were numerous dissident elements who launched numerous rebellions and assassination attempts; they were closely watched by the secret police, with thousands exiled to Siberia.

14. By the end of the 19th century, the size of the empire was about 22,400,000 square kilometers (8,600,000 sq mi) or almost 1/6 of the Earth's landmass; its only rival in size at the time was the British Empire. However, at this time, the majority of the population lived in European Russia. More than 100 different ethnic groups lived in the Russian Empire, with ethnic Russians comprising about 45% of the population (See Gilbert, 2007).

15. Russia spent time and money in safeguarding the frontier. Forts were built and maintained in various strategic territories. However, they were abandoned once it was clear that in the event of assault by new, superior weapons, they could not be maintained.

16. See: Svetlana Lourie, 2012, Imperium(Moscow: AIRO Press) (in Russian).
17. The Decembrist revolt or the Decembrist uprising took place in Imperial Russia on December 26, 1825. Russian army officers led about 3,000 soldiers in a protest against Nicholas I's assumption of the throne after his elder brother Constantine removed himself from the line of succession. The uprising occurred in the Senate Square in Saint Petersburg and was eventually suppressed by the Tsar, Nicholas I.

    There are, we believe, four important results from the aftermath of the Decembrist Revolt. First, the revolt was driven by a dissatisfaction with the form of governance regime in Russia and many leaders of the revolt were members of the high Russian aristocracy. They were motivated by the many reforms that were occurring throughout Europe.

    Second, it appears that the revolt was a precursor to revolts that would shake Russia to its foundations, and would eventually lead to the Bolshevik Revolution and Communism.

    Third, it forced Tsar Nicholas to look inward to Russia and introduce some liberalizing policies. Though, he would later end such liberalizing and return to his autocratic governance. But the seed had been planted.

    Finally, many of the leaders of the revolt were from the Russian high aristocracy, and their exile into Siberia changed that section of Russia forever. Exiles, founded schools, introduced new foods and farming into the area, introduced medical care, and new ways of thinking.

    With the death of Nicholas, exiles were allowed to return home, but many stayed because Siberia had become home. It is a fascinating piece of Russian history.
18. See in: Osvobozhdenie (1902). Liberation V. 1. p. 9 (in Russian).
19. See in: Kokoshkin F. (2010). Regional autonomy and unity of Russia. Moscow, p. 7 (in Russian).
20. See Bloor, K. (2010). The Definitive Guide to Political Ideologies. UK: Author House.
21. See Nagel, J. (2009). Multiculturalism's Double Bind: Creating Inclusivity, Cosmopolitanism, and Differences. UK: Ashgate Ltd.
22. For an excellent literary treatment of being Invisible, see Ellison (2010). In the prologue to his great novel, the protagonist begins with following comment, which is appropriate for immigrants in Russia.

    "I am an invisible man. No, I am not a spook like those who haunted Edgar Allan Poe; nor am I one of your Hollywood-movie ectoplasms. I am a man of substance, of flesh and bone, fiber and liquids—and I might even be said to possess a mind. I am invisible, understand, simply because people refuse to see me."
23. See in: Vendina, O. (2004). Can ethnic quarter appear in Moscow?, Bulletin of the public opinion. V. 3. pp. 52–64.
24. See: Report of the State Statistic Committee, available at www.gks.ru/PEREPIS/report.htm (in Russian).
25. As pointed in the report of director of the Federal Migration Service of Russian Federation K. Romodanovsky at the meeting of the Federal Migration Collegiums in January 31, 2008, available at www.fmsrf.ru (in Russian).

26. This data is available at http://www.perepis-2010.ru/results_of_the_census/results-inform.php.

27. These polls have been produced by the Department of ethnosociology of the Institute of ethnology and anthropology of Russian Academy of Science.

28. See in: Drobizheva, L. (2009). Rossiiskaya identichnost' v massovom soznanii, Vestnik rossiaiskoi natsii. No. 1 (3).

29. Dataset of Russian Centre of Statistics and Monitoring, the date of public opinion polls March, 2000, N=1595, available at: http://wciom.ru/database/.

30. Dataset of Russian Centre of Statistics and Monitoring, the date of public opinion polls August, 2000, N=1574, available at: http://wciom.ru/database/.

31. Dataset of Russian Centre of Statistics and Monitoring, the date of public opinion polls May, 2000, N=1600, available at: http://wciom.ru/database/

32. Dataset of the Monitoring of economic positioning and health of population (RLMS), 2006.

33. Dataset of the Project "Future of Russia: social sphere." The project has been implemented by CASEs ad sponsored by InoCentre. The Resource Centre was the Institute of Sociology of Russian Academy of Science. The authors of the project – L. Drobizheva, M. Chernysh, A. Chirikova.

34. Appendix A presents additional data on topics associated with national identity.

35. The Treaty of Brest-Litovsk was a peace treaty signed on March 3, 1918 between the new Bolshevik government of Russia and the Central Powers (Germany, Austria-Hungary, Bulgaria, and Turkey), that ended Russia's participation in World War I. The treaty was signed at Brest-Litovsk (now Brest, Belarus), after two months of negotiations. The treaty was forced on the Bolshevik government by the threat of further advances by German and Austrian forces. According to the treaty, Soviet Russia defaulted on all of Imperial Russia's commitments to the Triple Entente alliance.

   In the treaty, Bolshevik Russia relinquished the Baltic States to Germany, as well as its province of Kars Oblast in the south Caucasus to the Ottoman Empire. It also recognized the independence of Ukraine. In addition, Russia agreed to pay six billion German gold marks in reparations. Under the treaty, states in the Baltics were meant to become German vassal states under German princelings. When Germans later complained that the Treaty of Versailles of 1919 was too harsh on them, the Allies responded that it was more benign than Brest-Litovsk.

36. See appendix B for indices of corruption and human development in Russia.

REFERENCES

Akturk, S. (2010). Passport identification and nation-building in post-soviet Russia. *Post-Soviet Affairs*, 26(4), 314–341.

Anderson, B. (1991). *Imagined communities: Reflections on the origins and spread of nationalism.* London, England: Verso.

Applebaum, A. (2002, September 22). Russia's ongoing identity crisis. *The Telegraph.* Retrieved from telegraph.co.uk/culture/4728799/Russias-ongoing-identity-crisis.html

Armstrong, J. (1982). *Nations before nationalism*. Chapel Hill: University of North Carolina Press.

Balibar, E. (2009). Europe as borderland. *Environment and Planning: Digital Society and Space, 27*(2), 190–215.

Barry, B. (2001). *Culture and equality*. Cambridge, England: Polity Press.

Benhabib, S. (2002). *The claims of culture. Equality and diversity in global era*. Princeton, New Jersey: Princeton University Press.

Bennet, D. (1998). *Multicultural states. Rethinking difference and identity*. London, England: Routledge.

Berry, J. W. (1991). *Sociopsychological costs and benefits of multiculturalism*. Ottawa, Ontario: Economic Council of Canada.

Bloor, K. (2010). *The definitive guide to political ideologies*. Buckinghamshire, England: AuthorHouse.

Buchanan, J.M. and Tullock, G. (1962). The Calculus of Consent. Logical Foundations of Constitutional Democracy. Ann Arbor: Liberty Fund

Bromley, Y. (1983). *Essays on the theory of ethnic groups*. Moscow, Russia: Nauka.

Brubaker, R. (2004). *Ethnicity without groups*. Harvard, MA: Harvard University Press.

Census. (1905). The first Russian census. *Places of the Russian empire populated by more than 500 People*. St. Petersburg, Russia: The Common Good Press. Retrieved from http://www.prlib.ru/Lib/pages/item.aspx?itcmid=4952

Chartier, R. (1991). *The cultural origins of the French Revolution*. Durham, NC: Duke University Press.

Chebankova, E. (2012). Contemporary Russian multiculturalism, *Post-Soviet Affairs, 28*(3), 319–345.

Comte, A. (2009). *A general view of positivism* (R. Bridges, Trans.). Cambridge, England: Cambridge University Press. (Original work published in 1865)

Coppieters, B. (1994). *Contested borders in the Caucasus*. Brussels: VUBPress.

Dawisha, K. (2014). *Putin's Kleptocracy: Who owns Russia?* New York, NY: Simon & Schuster.

Dostoevsky, F. (1976). *Writer's notes, 1876. Full collection of F. Dostoevsky*. Saint Petersburg, Russia: Nauka. (Originally published 1876)

Drobizheva, L. (2002). Rossiaiskayaietnicheskayaidentichnost': protivostoyanieilisovmestimost,' *Rossiareformiruyushchayasya*. Moscow, Russia. (in Russian)

Drobizheva, L. (2009). Rossiiskaya identichnost' v massovom soznanii, Vestnik rossiaiskoi natsii. No. 1(3).

Durkheim, E. (1997). *The division of labor in society*. New York, NY: The Free Press. (Original work published in 1893)

Ellison, R. (2010). *Invisible man*. New York, NY: Knopf Doubleday. (Original work published in 1952)

Galston, W. (2005). *The practice of liberal pluralism*. Cambridge, England: Cambridge University Press.

Geertz, C. (1973). *The interpretation of cultures*. New York, NY: Basic Books.

Gilbert, M. (2007). *The Routledge atlas of Russian history*. New York, NY: Routledge.

Granovetter, M. S. (1973). The strength of weak ties. *American Journal of Sociology, 78*(6), 1360–1380.

Grech, N. (1990). *Zapiski o moeizhizni [Notes of my life]*. p. 268. Moscow, Russia. (in Russian)

Goldberg, D. T. (Ed.). (1994). *Multiculturalism: A critical reader.* Oxford, England: Blackwell.

Greenfeld, L. (1992). *Nationalism. Five roads to modernity.* Cambridge, MA: Harvard University Press.

Grenier, A. (2007). Crossing age and generational boundaries: Explaining intergenerational research. *Journal of Social Issues, 63*(4), 713–727.

Gumilev, L. (2007). *The black legend. friends and enemies of the great step.* Moscow, Russia: Airis-Press.

Heckscher, Eli F. (1955). Mercantilism. London: Allen&Unwin

Heidegger, M. (2002). *Time and being.* Chicago, IL: University of Chicago Press (Reprinted from 1927)

Hobbes, T. (2012). *Leviathan.* Oxford, England: Oxford University Press.

Hobsbawm, E., & Ranger, T. (1983). *The invention of tradition.* London, England: Cambridge University Press.

Hosking, G. (1997). *Russia: People and empire, 1552–1917.* London, England: Oxford University Press.

Huntington, S. (1991). *The third wave: Democratization in the late 20th century* (The Julian J. Rothbaum Distinguished Lecture Series). University of Oklahoma Press.

Israel, J. (2002). *Radical enlightenment: Philosophy and the making of modernity, 1650–1750.* New York, NY: Oxford University Press.

Jaeger, H. (1985). *Generations in History: History and Theory,* 273–292.

Joppke, C. (2004). Ethnic diversity and the state. *The British Journal of Sociology. 55*(3).

Karamzin, N. M. (1989). *History of the Russian state.* St. Petersburg, Russia. 1836 reprinted in 1989 (in Russian) (Istoriya gosudarstva Rossiyskogo). (Original work published in 1818)

Kavelin, K. D. (1989). *Russian national interest.* Moscow, Russia: Economicheskaya Gezeta Press (in Russian) (Russky Nacional'ny Interes). (Original work published in 1897)

Khomyakov, A. (1994). *About the old and the new. Full collection of works of A. Khomyakov.* Moscow, Russia: Nauka. (Originally published in 1835)

Kokoshkin, F. (2010). *Regional autonomy and unity of Russia.* Moscow, Russia. ("Oblastnaya avtonomia i edinstvo Rossii") (in Russian) (Original work published in 1906)

Kuhn, T. S. (1962). *The structure of scientific revolutions.* Chicago, IL: University of Chicago Press.

Kymlicka, W., & Norman, W. (Eds.) (2000). *Citizenship in the culturally diverse societies: Issues, contexts, concepts/ citizenship in diverse societies.* Oxford, England: Oxford University Press.

Lourie, S. (2012). *Imperium.* Moscow, Russia: AIRO Press (in Russian)

Malakhov, V. (1998). *Disadvantages with identity, Questions of Philosophy, 1998, V. 2* (in Russian).

Malakhov, V. (2002). *Zachem rossii multiculturalism, multiculturalism I transformacia-postsovetskikhobshchestv.* V. Malakhov, & V. Tishkov (Eds.). Moscow, 2002 (in Russian).

Mannheim, K. (1952). The problem of generations. In K. Mannheim (Ed.), *Essays on the sociology of knowledge.* New York, NY: Oxford University Press. (Republished from 1923)

Marx, K., & Engels, F. (1919). *The manifesto of the communist party.* (Samuel Moore, Trans.). Chicago, IL: Charles H. Kerr and Co.

Mezhuev, B., & Gradirovsky, S. (2004). *Anthropotok. strategy of Russia.* 4 (in Russian).

Milyoukov, P. (1906). *Russia and its crisis.* Chicago, IL: The University of Chicago Press.

Mokyr , J. (2009). *The invention of enterprise: Entrepreneurship from ancient Mesopotamia to modern times* (The Kauffman Foundation Series on Innovation and Entrepreneurship; with William J. Baumol and David S. Landes). Princeton, NJ: Princeton University Press.

Montesquieu, C-L. (1977). *The spirit of the laws.* Berkeley: University of California Press.

Mukomel, V. (2005). *Rossiiskie discursy migracii, Vestnik obshchestvennogo mnenia.* 1 (in Russian).

Nagel, J. (2009). *Multiculturalism's double bind: Creating inclusivity, cosmopolitanism, and differences.* Surrey, England: Ashgate.

Nizamova, L. (2009). R*ossiiskieizapadnyetractovkimulticulturalisma, Soziologicheskieissledovania. Vol.10 (in Russian).*

Osvobozhdenie (1902). *Liberation* V. 1. p. 9 (in Russian).

Pain, E. (2007). Rossia mezhdu imperiei i naciei, Pro et Contra. *Journal rossiiskoi vnutrennei I vneshnei politiki.* 2(3). (in Russian).

Public Opinion. (2006). *Obshchestvennoe mnenie–2006.* Analitichesky Centr Y. Levada. Moscow, Russia: WCIOM. (in Russian).

Pustobaev, M. (1994). *The chronicle of aggression.* Vilnius, Lithuania: Amzius Khronica agressii (in Russian).

Putnam, R. D. (2007). E Pluribus Unum: Diversity and community in the twenty-first century The 2006 Johan Skytte Prize Lecture. *Scandinavian Political Studies, 30,* 137–174. doi: 10.1111/j.1467-9477.2007.00176.x

Rawls, J. (1971). *A theory of justice.* Cambridge, MA: Harvard University Press.

Reed, J. (1990). *Ten days that shook the world.* New York, NY: Penguin Classics.

Rodney, B. H. (Ed.). (1999). *National collective identity. National collective identity: Social constructs and international systems.* New York, NY: Columbia University Press.

Russell, B. (1945). *History of western philosophy.* New York, NY: Simon & Schuster Press.

Ryder, N. (1965). The cohort as a concept in the study of social change. *American sociological review. 30*(6), 843–861.

Salter, F. K. (2006). On genetic interests: Family, ethnicity, and humanity in an age of mass migration. Piscataway, NJ: Transaction.

Shank, J. B. (2008). *The Newton wars: The beginning of the French enlightenment.* Chicago, IL: University of Chicago Press.

Smith, A. D. (1986). *The ethnic origins of nations.* Malden, MA: Blackwell.

Struve, P. (2004). *Intelligenziainazional'noelizo, in Naziai imperia v russkoimislinachala XX veka (Struve P. Intellectuals and national face, in Nation and empire in Russian thought of the beginning of XX century),* Moscow, Russia: Skimen. (in Russian).

Taylor, C. (1989). *Sources of the self: The making of the modern identity.* Cambridge, England: Cambridge University Press.

Thakahov, V. H., & Kogatko, D. G. (2009). Leokadia. *Rossiiskayaidentichnost' v massovomcoznanii, Vestnikrossiaiskoinatsii. 1*(3) (in Russian).

Therborn, G. (1995). *European Modernity and Beyond.* Routledge, England.

Tishkov, V. (2008). The Russian people and national identity: Ways to form a civic nation. *Russia in Global Affairs. 6*(3).

Tlostanova, M. (2008). *The Janus-faced empire distorting orientalist discourses: Gender, race and religion in the Russian/(post)Soviet constructions of the "Orient." Worlds & Knowledges Otherwise.*

Tolz, V. (2009). Russia: Empire or a nation-state-in-the making? In T. Baycroft, & M. Hewitson (Eds.) *What is a nation?* Oxford, England: Oxford University Press.

Tolz, V. (2011). *Russia's own Orient: The politics of identity and Oriental studies in the late imperial and early Soviet periods.* Oxford, England: Oxford University Press.

Tonnies, F. (2001). *Community and civil society.* J. Harris (Ed.). Cambridge, England: Cambridge University Press.

Trubeczkoy N. (2000). *Herritage of Genghis Khan.* Moscow, Russia: Agraph (in Russian).

Vendina, O. (2004). Can ethnic quarter appear in Moscow? *Bulletin of the Public Opinion, 3,* 52–64

Verdugo, R. R. (2013). School reform: Community, corporatism, and the social good. *International Journal of Education Reform, 22*(2): 118–128.

Verdugo, R. R., & Mueller, C. (2008). Education, social embeddedness, and the integration of the Turkish community in Germany. *European Education, 40*(4), 3–22.

Walzer, M. (1994). Comment, In A. Gutman, (Ed.), *Multiculturalism.* Princeton, NJ: Princeton University Press.

Walzer, M. (1997). *On toleration.* New Haven, CT: Yale University Press.

Weber, M. (1930). *The protestant ethics and the spirit of Capitalism.* New York, NY: Scribner.

Weber, M. (1978). *Economy and society: An outline of interpretive sociology.* G. Rother, & C. Wittich (Eds.). Berkeley, CA: University of California Press.

Wohl, R. (1979). *The generation of 1914.* Cambridge, MA: Harvard University Press.

Wieviorka, M. (2001). *La différence: Identités culturelles: Enjeux, débats et politiques.* Paris, France: Balland.

Wilson, E. (1940). *To the Finland station: A study in the writing and acting of history.* New York, NY: Harcourt, Brace, and Company.

Zafirovski, M. (2001). *The enlightenment and its effects on modern society.* London, England: Springer.

CHAPTER 6

THE IMPOSSIBLE STATE

National Identities in Bosnia and Herzegovina

Djordje Vukovic, Aleksandar Savanovic, and Aleksandar Vranjes

INTRODUCTION

National identity does not exist in Bosnia and Herzegovina (BH). The three largest ethnic groups, defined under the Constitution of BH as "constituent peoples," are Bosnians, Croats, and Serbs. According to the 1991 census[1] there were 4.37 million people living in Bosnia and Herzegovina, of whom 43.5% were Muslims (in 1993 they declared themselves Bosniaks), 31.2% were Orthodox Serbs, 17.4% Catholic Croats, 5.6% of citizens declared themselves as Yugoslavs (mostly those in mixed marriages), and 2.3% as "others" (Jews, Czechs, Ukrainians, etc.). Such diversity does not automatically lead to national identity.

In this chapter we describe how certain factors have contributed to a lack of a common identity in BH. Our main hypotheses are that external and internal factors have created barriers toward a common group identity in BH. External factors are the policies by Western powers that created

National Identity, pages 187–211
Copyright © 2016 by Information Age Publishing
All rights of reproduction in any form reserved.

severe economic, social, and political challenges dividing the states within BH. Internal factors are those unique to BH. In examining our hypotheses we begin with a historical overview of the BH area; we then discuss some theoretical issues about national identity which helps us in understanding the issues facing national identity in conducting an analysis of the consequences of the civil war and discussing the current situation in BH, including a discussion of recent survey data.

THEORETICAL BACKGROUND

Historical Overview

Early History

The Great Migration, during the first centuries AD, brought Southern Slavs to the Balkans territory, south of the Sava and Danube rivers, onto the Pannonia Plain and the Eastern Alps. The first ten centuries in the history of the area were characterized by significant antagonisms among the Slavic tribes. The first Serbian state was established in the 9th century (Ćorović, 2001, p. 88) and, having being constituted as a kingdom and later as an empire, it left a significant and long-term imprint in these regions.

Empires and religions clashed and laid the foundation for differences between inhabitants of the area. Under the influence of the Byzantine Empire, Serbs became Orthodox Christians, while Croats converted to Catholicism as a result of significant proselytizing by delegates of the Holy See. When the Ottoman Empire took control of the Balkans by the end of the 15th century (Ćorović, 2001, p. 365) it introduced Islam, a third major religion. Interestingly, Islam seemed to have been accepted by many Christians. Considerable diversity characterized the three largest nations of the current Bosnia and Herzegovina region.

Antagonisms between the three nations began in the Middle-Ages. In the period between the 16th and 18th centuries, the territory of the former Yugoslavia was ruled by three major powers: the Ottoman Empire, the Habsburg Empire, and the Venetian Republic (Đurđev, Grafenauer, & Tadić, 1959). Animosities between the Ottoman and Hapsburg regimes influenced the lives of the populations in the area. For example, the Ottoman rule established both bureaucratic and feudal systems. To be sure, there was well-developed trade, but there was no willingness on the part of the Ottomans of developing the territory. Many view this time as the "dark period" because Yugoslavia failed to experience the same social development as did the rest of Western Europe (Đurđev et al., 1959). This period also saw the end of the Ethnogenesis among Serbs and Croats; their ethnic affinity and common Southern Slavic roots were never to be prominent again.

Moreover, further divisions occurred under the Ottoman Empire when some members of these nations converted to Islam. The Middle Ages saw the origins of antagonisms that would plague the area to the present day.

After the dissolution of the Ottoman Empire, the Austro-Hungarian Empire took control of the Balkans. Until the First World War, the Habsburg Empire exerted important social and political influences in the area. According to Mirjana Kasapovic (2005), there was not a comprehensive secular constitution and formation of the three major religious and ethnic communities until the Austro-Hungarian occupation in 1878, at the same time when the political and social modernization of Bosnia and Herzegovina commenced (Kasapovic, 2005, p. 88). Moreover, Kasapovic argues that in late 19th and early 20th centuries, profound religious and historical discrepancies emerged, manifesting themselves in national communities. The three major religious and ethnic communities began forming separate social and political institutions and organizations at all levels of social life—separate schools, cultural institutions, publishing centers, business entities, trade unions and, of course, political parties (Kasapovic, 2005).

For Bosnia and Herzegovina, the beginning of the 20th century marked the national emancipation of Serbs and Croats (Kasapovic, 2005, p. 91). Kasapovic points out that the same process was slower for Muslims because Muslim deputies in the Parliament of the First Yugoslavia declared themselves as the Croats, rarely as Serbs (Kasapovic, 2005, p. 93). National emancipation of Muslims remained limited to their political and social elite. National emancipation during the Austro-Hungarian rule did not lead to open animosities; that would ensue later.

During and after WWI animosities surfaced. Also, between the two world wars this territory was part of the Kingdom of Serbs, Croats, and Slovenes. Later, it became part of the Kingdom of Yugoslavia, and was dominated by Serbs and the Serbian crown.

Modern History

During the Second World War, civil war broke out between the Communists/Partisans and loyalists to the Serbian crown. Led by Josif Broz Tito, the Communists had victories over the Nazis, and the former monarchy. These victories laid the foundations for Communist rule, and later for Socialist Yugoslavia. The ideological model behind the new regime was that of the USSR.

In the period between the end of the Second World War and the 1990s, BH was a socialist republic within the Socialist Federal Republic of Yugoslavia (SFRY). During this period, regional identities were set aside, and in their place Yugoslav identity was promoted. Leaders stated that a Yugoslav identity was accepted by all the citizens of SFRY. Yet, when the Yugoslavian state was dissolved, nationalistic fervor drove violence and the civil war. New states emerged, including Bosnia and Herzegovina.

The Dayton Peace Agreement of 1995 established the three constituent groups: Bosniaks, Serbs, and Croats. Muslims were renamed, and the Bosniak nation was created in the mid-1990s. The Bosniak nation then sought to distinguish itself from the other two groups and created much discord. In reality, there were only minor differences between the three groups because they spoke the same language and shared a common culture. Nevertheless, these differences were blown out of proportion and viewed as dogma that blocked the development of a Bosnia and Herzegovina state; it has been called "an impossible state."[2]

Civil War

The dramatic political and cultural events during the late 20th and early 21st centuries in Eurasia did not bypass the Balkans. The fall of the Berlin War and the end of the Cold War had consequences for Yugoslavia: the political defeat of the Yugoslav Unitarian power, the dissolution of the state union which led again to the civil war, mass killings, material destruction, including some other war repercussions such as ethnocentrism, populism, corruption, crime, the disappearance of the middle class, and more. All this encompassed nearly all newly established states of the former Yugoslavia.

When reflecting upon the civil war in the states of the former Yugoslavia, one can identify the main factors causing the war: the collapse of socialism and the "Brotherhood and Unity" slogan of the Communist Party; potential conflicts stemming from historical events; an increasing emphasis on differences between the Roman Catholics, Orthodox, and Muslims; the emergence of the religious fundamentalism; rearmament; support from external forces; the absence of democratic procedures; and a struggle for new ethnic borders, among other things. (Hantington, 2000). Consequently, new independent states emerged: Slovenia, Croatia, Serbia, Montenegro, Bosnia and Herzegovina, and Macedonia.

In 1992, Bosnia and Herzegovina gained recognition as an independent state, which ended the four-year civil war in 1995. Since then, BH has existed as a state with two entities, the Republic of Srpska, and the Federation of Bosnia and Herzegovina. These entities are home to three ethnic groups—Bosnians, Serbs, and Croats. The BH is a place of never-ending conflict, a divided social system with an unstable state (Halpert & Kajdikel, 2002; Kasapović, 2005; Kecmanović, 2007). There are no efforts at unraveling and reconciling the ideological differences and moving towards a "better future" (Majstorović & Turjačanin, 2011). At the same time, it is widely believed that there is an overemphasis on pointing out small differences between competing groups (Stojković, 2002). Such a view is supported by the theses of "split," "fabricated," even "murderous."[3] Maalouf (2003) also argues that cultural and historical group predispositions, which originally shared a group identity, unraveled and led to conflict after separation. In addition, tensions and the level of intolerance in the country are rationales for ideological confrontations and further complicates reconciliation.

The question of identity becomes problematic during times of social and political upheaval. Golubović (2006) warns that finding an identity is currently more challenging due to rapid social change. Identity crisis manifests itself in the "form of various psychopathological disorders which narrow the field of authentic individual identities, imposing pseudo-identities, by escaping on the one hand into extreme individualism, and on the other hand into extreme collectivism (racial, national/ethnic, confessional). At the same time, both forms lead to isolation and exclusion of the 'other' and establish both individual and collective identities" (Golubović, 2006, pp. 177–178).

After the dissolution of the SFRY, elites began constructing new national identities. Their efforts occurred during a period of much chaos: brutal warfare, political and media propaganda, and cultural terror. Burdened by an ideology of creating states founded on ethno-nationalism, the newly created entities were unsuccessful. Nationalism, as an expression of ethno-cultural and pre-political unification, and drawing its strength from a romanticized past, represents a foundation shaping the collective identity of a political community. Contemporary BH does not rest on such a foundation; it was not created by consensus among its three ethnic communities, but through a unilateral declaration of independence (with Serbian Croatian opposition), and under the strong influence of Western leaders.

Since independence, Bosnia and Herzegovina has experienced interethnic conflict. Bosniaks sought control of the entire territory, centralizing the power of the state and laying the foundation for Muslim-Bosniak dominance. Both Serbs and Croats opposed such a strategy, and looked for ways of expressing their concerns: the declaration of autonomous regions, regionalization, consociation,[4] secession, and peaceful dissolution. Their proposals were rejected and civil war ensued.

The war lasted four years and caused major demographic changes. The United Nations and the Hague Tribunal disclosed the final data on the number of victims in Bosnia and Herzegovina (Tabeau & Zwierzchowski, 2010). There were 68.1 thousand Bosniak victims, 22.8 thousand Serbian victims, 8.8 thousand Croats, and 5 thousand "Others." In addition, during the war and postwar years there were massive numbers of refugees and much internal migration. According to results from the 2013 Census,[5] there are 3,791,621 BH citizens, and approximately 500,000 refugees currently living in approximately 40 countries throughout the world. The two entities of the BH are inhabited by an ethnically homogeneous population: 2,371,603 people live in the Federation of BH (75% Bosniaks, 20%

Croats, 4% Serbs, and 1% others) and 1,326,991 in the Republic of Srpska (80% Serbs and 20% Bosniaks, Croats, and national minorities).[6] One part of the BH Federation (which consists of 10 cantons) is inhabited mostly by Bosniaks (the exact percentage will be known following the final results of the 2013 Census), while Croatians make up the majority in another part. The territory of the Republic of Srpska has a majority Serbian population (83.2%), with a significant number of displaced families from the territory of the contemporary Federation of BH. Moreover, there are tens of thousands of Serbs[7] who were expelled from Croatia in the early 1990s.

National Identity: Theoretical Discussion and Research Hypotheses

National identity is a slippery concept—hard to define, develop, and maintain. In this section we attempt to define and create some boundaries about national identity.

National Identity: Traditional and Modern Versions

National identity can be interpreted in at least two ways: *traditional* (individuals identify fully with the ethnic community), and *modern* (national identity is primarily equated with citizenship).

Traditional versions. Ethnic identity is founded on the concept of "blood and soil," on a common language, religion, set of customs, and tradition. Such a view was inspired by the original German idea of nation. The concept of citizenship, in contrast, is associated with the Republican idea of nationality and is associated with the French revolution; it is universal, rational, and unifying. In short, between the two approaches of national identity—one emphasizes cultural criteria and the other a social contract. In the Bosnia and Herzegovina area, the ethnic model is clearly dominant, and the question is whether such a model is relevant in the modern era, especially in an area that is attempting unification with much ethnic diversity.

National identity as a form of perceived group membership. Verba (1965) emphasized that national identity is not only central to the political integration of a people, but for the future stability of society. Thus, resolving this crisis of identity is crucial. Verba also adds that the problem of national identity can never be solved completely because it is an open and developing process. National and political identities are hardly ever experienced in the same way by all members of a community, both in terms of meaning and of recognition. National identity is perceived strongly and intensely by some, but others do not consider it important, some are indifferent, and others deny it.

Modern versions. Most modern Constitutions guarantee certain rights to its citizens, including the freedom to choose their political affiliation and cultural identity. Mirjana Vasović (2007) points out that identification is the basis of political identity, while the issue of national identity relies on generally accepted political values, political tradition, and political culture. Unlike ethnic identity, national identity in its broader sense implies the organization of the "nation" within the political community.

National identity, via civic identity, is rational. Civic national identity implies a political entity; a commitment to participating in shaping political processes and in protecting and promoting the public interest. According to Müller, Habermas proposes that the "principle of citizenship," which integrates the political community and legitimizes the political authority, is not reached solely through institutional formulas, but also through "constitutional patriotism" (*Verfassungspatriotismus*).[8] Such patriotism is founded on civic loyalty to the constitutional order and not to Essentialist traits such as culture, history, or ethnic allegiances. Habermas points out that multicultural societies, such as the USA or Switzerland, show that "political culture in which constitutional principles can be rooted does not have to depend on all its citizens speaking the same language or being of the same ethnic or cultural origin. Liberal political culture is only a general denominator for constitutional patriotism which reinforces the sense of differences as well as the sense of integration of different forms of life coexisting in a multicultural society" (Habermas, 1998, p. 550). Thus, the necessary conditions for the existence of civic identity are agreements among citizens with societal norms, state laws, rights of individuals, and the free will of citizens to exercise their basic human and political rights—a Social Contract.

The Role of Two Key Institutions: Mass Media and Education

Each collective identification requires the proper functioning of at least two societal institutions: the mass media, and the educational system. These institutions transmit a common "ideology" containing myths, rites, and rituals that contribute to the idealization, preservation, and expansion of national identity and to homogenizing the population. At the same time, these institutions encourage individuals to become politically involved in processes for the protection and promotion of the "public interest." Mass media and education are strong influences in the BH.

Hate propaganda is a constant in the BH. Members of the political, media, and scientific institutions within BH put forward daily insults and accusations against others ("aggressors," "fascists," "primitives," "genocidal nation," and similar), against individuals from their own or opposing social groups ("traitor," "foreign mercenary," "political adventurer," etc.), but also against the State ("artificial construct," "occupied territory," "result of ethnic cleansing," etc.). State and national leaders also take part in this hate propaganda, encouraging ethnic prejudices and political labeling. Such propaganda confirms a main feature of non-democratic societies—a lack of tolerance for dissent, the suppression of freedom of expression, stifling personal political autonomy, engaging in authoritarianism, servility, promoting fundamentalist religious beliefs, and political conflicts. BH is not a balanced state in which different cultures, religions, and political orientations are viewed as assets.

After WWII, it was widely believed that multinational and multi-ethnic societies would overcome national concepts and result in the disappearance of localized identities. It has not happened. No less an entity than the European Union has failed in its efforts at stopping the processes which emphasize national interests. For example, the Chancellor of Germany, Angela Merkel, and the Prime Minister of the United Kingdom, David Cameron, announced the death of "multiculturalism," not because they hoped for such epilogue, but simply as a way of admitting that cultural pluralism failed in their countries. The question arises as to how the BH can make cultural pluralism work when it has far less resources than either Germany or the UK? If a state fails to create clear and meaningful collective identities, says Andrew Heywood (2005), the results are particularisms based on ethnicity and religion. This is exactly what has happened in the former Yugoslavia and BH.

National Identity Typology

Milošević-Đorđević (2003) has a few key indicators for determining national identity: significant social mobility, a specific social character, language, set of customs, religion, collective memory, belief in common origin, and so on. The author points out the difference between the phenomena of nationalism and national identity—nationalism represents pronounced national identity. "Nationalism emerges when, through the process of identification, a nation as a group becomes too important to an individual, more important than any other form of identification" (Milošević-Đorđević, 2003). In the modern age, nationalism is the basis for a population's hegemony connected by language and cultural values. But in the Balkans, nationalism is based on blood and soil.

Milošević-Đorđević (2003) develops three categories of national identity: (a) Nature of national identity—coercion or choice, (b) Key determinants in defining national identity, and (c) Connecting political and economic power to national identity. A *Primordialistic* approach represents the view that national identity is given at birth and lasts throughout one's life. National feelings are not based on facts, objective relations, and needs, but are shaped by irrational forces, emotions, and instincts which cannot be chosen by individuals.

Criticisms of the Primordialistic view are widespread. Some of the criticisms are:

- National identities are not given and fixed but arise and change with life experiences of an individual and under the influences of social environment.
- Individuals can actually deny national identities, perceive them differently, and emphasize dual or multiple national identities.

Besides the *Primordsialitic* viewpoint, there are other approaches to national identity, such as instrumentalist, constructivist, situational, and functionalist. In the *instrumentalist* view, national identity is variable; it depends on circumstances since changes affect the intensity of identifications. The viewpoint does not exclude the affective component or interlocking of interests and irrational bonds, and it could serve as one of the possible explanations for the appearance and disappearance of the Yugoslav identity. The *functionalist* view of national identity is reflected in the territorial, economic, and political unification on which states rely. A *constructivist* approach is a combination of the previous two views. In the *constructionist* view, national identity is a matter of choice by individuals, and is developed and shaped throughout one's life. Also, its intensity is different for each individual, it ranges from very weak to very strong, is constructed in interaction with others, and is reflected in the fact that others see us as members of a specific national community. The *situational* approach to social circumstances affect the development, strength, and form of national identity. Intense national feelings are affected by many factors: war, the perceived threat by other ethnic groups, and the awareness that religious affiliation, name, and surname are key factors in identifying "friends and enemies." According to the *functionalist* approach, when national identity overcomes all other identities, and when one's own identity is subordinated to the nation, there is a risk of extreme nationalism. According to this view, the functions of national identity are the satisfaction of fundamental human needs for collective belonging, a reference to common interests, and a demarcation with other groups.

Majstorović and Turjačanin (2011) point out that one can discuss many types of national attachment. For example, *exclusive* national attachment (national, chauvinism, ethno-nationalism), *prominent* national attachment (patriotism and national identification, along with acceptance of other nations), *divided* national attachment (sense of belonging to one's nation, along with striving for transnational cooperation), *general* human attachment (cosmopolitism), and *a-nationalism* (lack of attachment to any nation, along with belief that nationalism is harmful and unnecessary). According to the results of an expert survey[9] on the territory of BH, belonging to the state is emphasized the most by Bosniaks; it is poorly represented among

Serbs and Croats, while belonging to the entity is most prominent for Serbs. Religious affiliation is the most important to Croats, ethnicity to Serbs. All three groups equally refrain from identifying with the broader European framework, and with the possibility of having a multiple national identity—that is, a national identity that includes Bosniaks, Serbian, or Croatian.

Similar results were obtained from surveys[10] conducted in 2011 and in 2012 about the national orientations among young people in the Republic of Srpska. These surveys show that young Serbs identify heavily with the Republic of Srpska, with the Serbian Orthodox Church, and with the Serbian language and tradition. In contrast, there is almost no sense of belonging to Bosnia and Herzegovina as a state. Moreover, 72% of respondents wanted the Republic of Srpska to declare its independence from Bosnia and Herzegovina. Even though the surveys show that the young population has no pronounced elements of ethnocentrism towards members of other ethnic groups, they also expressed no desire to live in the same state with other ethnic groups.

Thus, national identity represents a specific feeling and pronounced awareness of belonging to a political community based on common ancestry, language, culture, historical experience, same political values, and symbols. National identity also represents loyalty to the territorially organized government, a willingness to achieve social harmony, adherence to the laws and procedures that ensure the protection of personal and collective property, as well as affirming individuals and social groups. In addition, we theorize that the formation of national identity has numerous conditions based on social protection: the rights of its population, general protection, and cultural differences.

CREATING DIFFERENCES IN BH: EXTERNAL AND INTERNAL FACTORS

Traditionally, scholars have attributed antagonisms in the BH area to old conflicts and to the recent policies and behaviors of its inhabitants.[11] What is not as well-known, however, is the influence of policies from Western nations that exacerbated challenges and lead to conflict. In this section we discuss how both internal and external factors have driven differences and conflict in BH.

Internal Factors: Power, Policy, and the Tyranny of the Majority

Grabbing for Power

At the core of political struggles were different interpretations of the Dayton Agreement and the Constitution. Bosniak leaders worked against the

Dayton organization of the state, while the Serbian community developed a protective attitude towards the existing Constitution. The divisiveness was based on loyalty to the state, but as a result that the Constitution guarantees the preservation of the Republic of Srpska. The Republic ensures the political, national, ethnic, and cultural survival of the Serbian population west of the Drina River. Thus, patriotism was based on ethnicity, not on the state.

Croats, as the third constituent population in Bosnia and Herzegovina, manifest a contradictory attitude towards the constitutional order—a loyalty to certain legal provisions, and an insistence on changing other provisions.

Ethnic differences persist about geographical boundaries. Bosniak representatives sought to create a nation of "Bosnians" (such as the Americans, Swiss, etc.). Serbs and Croats did not accept the state imposed borders as boundaries of their national and political identities.

The media has had a hand in creating discord. The media in the Republic of Srpska have been promoting "entity patriotism," Serbian statehood, and nurturing Serbian culture, art, and history. The media's attitude towards Bosnia and Herzegovina often led to conflict between members of ethnic or political groups as old issues are rekindled. The result is that everything is questioned, including the Dayton Agreement.

Interpreting Policy

Interpretations of the Dayton Agreement also led to discord. The *spiritus movens* of the *"Dayton" Constitution* of BH is its attempt at finding a balance between national identity and other forms of identity. The key articles in the Dayton document are *Article II* and *Article IV*, as well as the *Preamble*, line 10. The basic thesis behind our presentation can be summed up as follows:

- The nationhood issues were, if not the primary, then surely the key issues in dissolving the former SFRY.
  - BH, as the only republic within the former state which had a tri-national structure, was particularly exposed to the risk of dissolution.
  - The independence of BH through the "civil" referendum completely ignored the importance and power of national identification. The referendum, then, was a direct cause of a crisis which eventually led to civil war
- *The Dayton Peace Agreement* is a peace treaty that emphasized the resolution of inter-ethnic antagonisms in Bosnia and Herzegovina.
- Post-war transformation of the *Constitution of Bosnia and Herzegovina Annex IV* of the *Dayton Peace Agreement* moved towards a "civic" concept, minimizing the importance of nationality in the *Constitution*.
  - In effect, the Agreement created a situation similar to that which led to civil war.

The crisis in BH is driven by national versus civic identity.[12] Unfortunately, leadership never quite understood this distinction during the dissolution of the SFRY. The referendum on the independence of BH was carried out as a "civil" issue, and a national view was ignored and thus failed to recognize the potential power that national identification may have had in the region. The BH, as an independent country, emerged from a "tyranny of the majority" framework as the Serbian population was outvoted by Bosniaks/Muslims and Croats. *Our hypothesis is that since BH emerged from a "tyranny of the majority" framework, it created much discord among the minority Serbian population.* Data from the referendum voter turnout confirm our hypothesis.

About 64%[13] (64.31%) of the population turned out for the vote. The overwhelming majority of those (approximately 99.40%) voted for independence. However, the problem was that the majority of voters were Muslims and Croats, and Serbs boycotted the vote. On November 9–10, 1991, the majority of Serbs voted to remain in Yugoslavia. In addition, the ethnic structure is almost entirely consistent with the results of the referendum (Savanović, 2013). According to the 1991 census, the ethnic structure of the state was as follows: Bosniaks[14] 43.47%, Serbs 31.21%, Croats 17.38%, Yugoslavs 5.54%, and others 2.38%. It is obvious that these numbers support the thesis that "non-Serbs" are the majority and would have dominated the vote at the *Referendum on Independence.* Moreover, during the first democratic elections, the national/nationalistic parties SDA, SDS, and HDZ completely dominated the "reform forces," led by the then prime minister Ante Marković. The number of votes won by these national parties was consistent with the ethnic structure of the population, and also with the *Referendum* results: SDA won 35.85% of votes, SDS won 30%, and HDZ won 18.35%.

Tyranny of the Majority

The "tyranny of the majority," regarding the referendum on independence, was a key cause of the war. The "minority" simply did not have an opportunity to protect its rights. It is common in such cases for the minority to undertake non-institutional and non-constitutional practices, termed "abnormal political behavior" by Dahl (Dahl, 1956, p. 138). In this case, the Serbian minority started practicing civil disobedience, and soon after that, military resistance. In essence, the Civil war was the result of "tyranny of majority."

Clearly, political decision makers did not fully comprehend that a "civil" or "majority" model of democracy does not function well in a highly divided, stratified society. The experience of BH confirms the thesis that pluralistic communities can be constituted in a Consociational governance model, at least in the first phase of their existence.[15] In order to understand the situation in BH, it is important to note that consociation is not necessarily conditioned by the existence of ethnically homogenous territories, since it can also exist as trans-territorial consociation.[16] This is particularly evident in BH which is an "asymmetric" creation. It is based on the model of "two entities and three constituent peoples," meaning that in the bi-national entity a FBH consociation would necessarily imply abstracting the territorial criteria.[17]

External Factors: Disagreement Over the Dayton Peace Agreement

The Agreement

Almost all of the key provisions of consociation are built into the Constitution of BH.[18] The most important involve institutional forms, which include issues of ethnic representation:

- The tripartite *Presidency*
- The bicameral *Parliament*
- The institution of vital national interests
- The election of delegates for the *House of Peoples*(Constitution of BH, IV/1)
- The elections for the *House of Representatives*(Constitution of BH, IV/2)
- The election of members of the *Presidency* (Constitution of BH, V/1)
- The composition of the *Council of Ministers*(Constitution of BH, V/4b)
- *Central Bank(Constitution of BH, VII/2)*

Article IX/3 of the *Constitution* states that employees in state institutions must be equally ethnically represented, "*Officials appointed to positions in the institutions of Bosnia and Herzegovina shall be generally representative of the peoples of Bosnia and Herzegovina.*" Such importance was given to national identity in the *Preamble of the Constitution*, line 10, which reads, "Bosniaks, Croats and Serbs, as the constituent peoples (along with others), and citizens of Bosnia and Herzegovina hereby establish the Constitution of Bosnia and Herzegovina."

The constituent peoples are defined as the source of the *Constitution of BH*. It was this line[19] that served as a basis for the well-known appeal 5/98[20] to the *Constitutional Court of BH*, which was used by former BH president Alija Izetbegović in challenging the constitutionality of *Article 1*[21] of the *Constitution of the Republic of Srpska* and of *Article I.1. The Constitution of the Federation of BH* defined constituent people as ethnic groups. Appeal 5/98 interpreted the "constituent" quality of the people as trans-territorial—that is, it covers the entire state, without limit to one entity. A strong basis for this appeal is that Bosnia and Herzegovina have never been ethno-territorially divided throughout its history. A counter-argument was that the provision of "being constituent" from line 10 does not mean that its requirement is not being met if one people is "constituent" only in one particular part of the territory. In case No. 4/05,[22] the *Constitutional Court of BH* accepted the appeal, and in referring to line 10, it proclaimed these articles of entity unconstitutional. The conclusion was that the division into entities does not imply the territorial division of the constituent peoples (5/98-III, item 69). Therefore, Serbs are a constituent people in the FBH with the same status as Bosniaks and Croats in the RS. (Steiner & Ademović, 2010). This is explicitly evident in the fact that "the electoral mechanisms do not reflect the ethnic, but a federal division. For instance, Serbian member of the BH Presidency is not elected by Serbs only, but by all citizens of the Republic of Srpska" (5/98-III, item 67) (Steiner & Ademović, 2010, pp. 63–64).[23]

The facts were clear:

- First, the *Constitutional Court of BH's* interpretation of the appeal 5/98-III was based on the principle of "being constituent" and led to a *de facto* proposition of general ethnic representation at all levels.
- Second, the argument about "trans-entity constituent peoples" is often used as an argument against the consociation perspective of the BH *Constitution*. However, consociation is not necessarily territorially based and it is possible that trans-territoriality is overlooked. It depends on specific circumstances within each community—if ethnic groups are territorially organized, consociation is by rule also territorially organized; yet, if ethnic groups are "mixed," consociation may reflect such a structure. In practice before the civil war, consociation in BH was to take a trans-territorial form.

Ethnic groups at that time were not organized into homogenous territorial units. The following map (Figure 6.1) illustrates this:

The consociation mechanism of protecting constituent peoples at the state level had to be trans-territorial.[24] However, after the civil war, this situation changed and the ethnic map of BH took the following character as shown in Figure 6.2.

This changed situation supports the territorial model of consociation. The war led to migrations, which, in turn, led to ethnically homogenous territories. For example, Serbs today, according to estimates, account for the majority of approximately 90% (or even higher) of the population in the RS (Nikolić, 2009).

The *Constitutional Court of BH* (5/98, item 86-98) defined ethnic based territorial segregation as a conscious continuation of the peacetime politics of ethnic cleansing. Item 88 states: "The conclusion drawn from these data is supported by the comparison of figures referring to the total return of refugees and displaced persons in the Republic of Srpska with those referring to

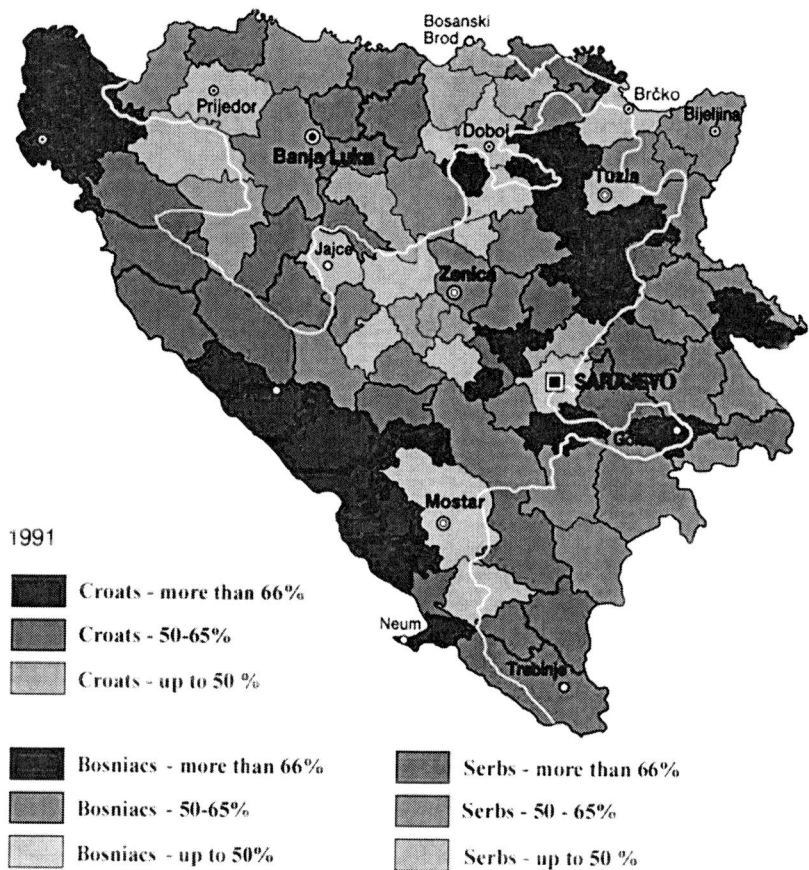

Figure 6.1 Bosnia and Herzegovina: Ethnic composition before the war (as of 1991).

the so-called 'minority' return. Before 31st January 1999 (UNHCR, statistical package of 1st March 1999), 97,966 refugees and displaced persons returned to the Republic of Srpska. Analyses reveals that only 731 Croats and 9,212 Bosnians returned, as opposed to 88,003 Serbs. Hence, the so-called return of 'minority' amounts to 10.17% ... of those who have returned." The conclusion is given in item 90: "These figures, therefore, provide sufficient evidence of a 'discriminatory effect' in terms of Article I/3.(a) of Annex VII, which means that the results of the previous de jure discrimination by means of ethnic cleansing were supported in the Republic of Srpska."

Such a conclusion is reinforced by a range of verdicts from the *Human Rights Chamber* regarding violations of the *International Convention on the Elimination of All Forms of Racial Discrimination*.[25] Most appeals refer to *Article II* of the *Constitution of BH*, as well as documents and conventions in the

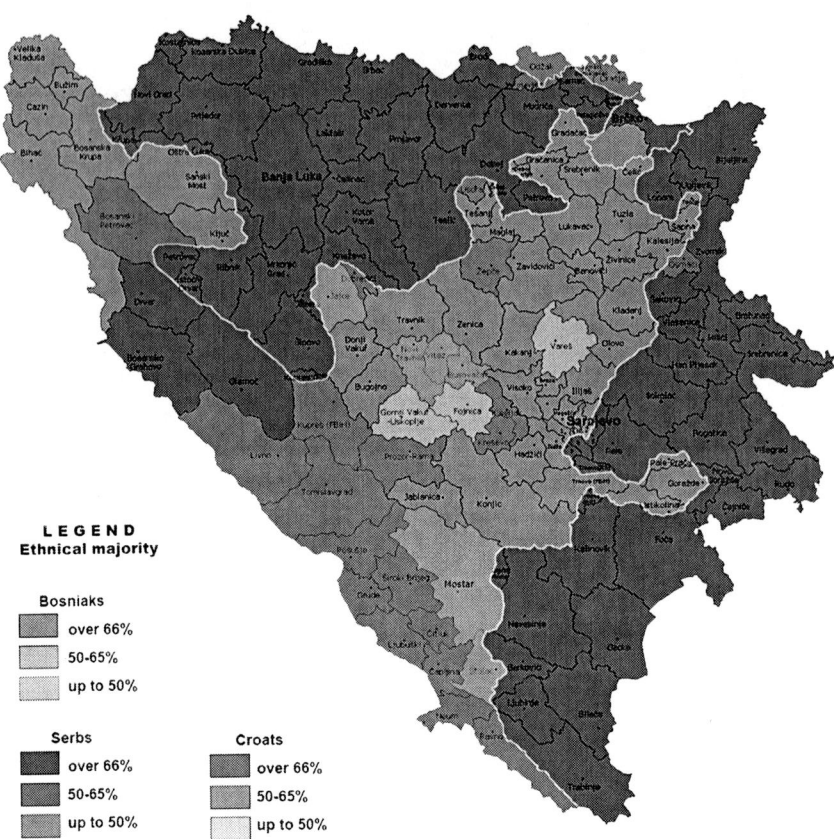

LEGEND
Ethnical majority

Bosniaks
over 66%
50-65%
up to 50%

Serbs
over 66%
50-65%
up to 50%

Croats
over 66%
50-65%
up to 50%

Figure 6.2 Bosnia and Herzegovina: Ethnic composition from 2006.

field of human rights. Systematic discrimination against refugees, displaced persons, and returnees continue to exist. The practice, both in municipality administrations and in courts, was discriminatory to such an extent that the *Human Rights Chamber*(CH/98/756-D&M, paragraph 80; CH/97/77-D&M, paragraph 58 and further) assumed that such practices were part of the nation's social structure (Steiner & Ademović, 2010, p. 450).[26] One typical case involved the returning to work of persons who, during the war, were not fired for "security" reasons, but as a result of their ethnic affiliation. The *Human Rights Chamber* determined that these individuals were denied the rights prescribed in *Articles 6* and *7* of the *International Covenant on Economic, Social and Cultural Rights*(CH/97/67-D&M; CH/99/2696-D&M), and were not corrected in the post-war period.

In case U 5/98, item 95 *In conclusion, Article 1* of the *Constitution of the RS* was proclaimed unconstitutional (U 5/98, item 98).The decision stated "that the discriminatory pattern, which is proved by this circumstantial evidence, can reasonably be linked to the institutional structures of the authorities in the Republic of Srpska" (U 5/98, art. 91). This is an important statement because it proclaims that ethnic discrimination stems from social structure; the patterned routine forms of behavior and social organization. Moreover, the *Constitutional Court* explicitly acknowledged that discrimination was reflected by a lack of other ethnic groups being represented in the executive and judicial branches of the Republic of Srpska (U 5/98, item 92-94). While this consociation ethnic model was de facto recognized as legitimate within the *Constitution of BH*, its political practice was disputed.

Post-Dayton Practice

Post-Dayton political practice was characterized by three factors:

- Attempts to Federalize the consociation ethno-territorial structure of the state
- To eliminate the ethnic component of representation
- Eliminating the Federal units, though such a goal has no basis in the *Constitution*, and the proposed Federal units would continue the practice of ethnic-based differentiation.

The latter issue was widely discussed. The key factors in these discussions were the constitutionality of *Article 7* of the *Constitution of the RS*, which defines the Serbian language as the official language of the Republic of Srpska, and the Cyrillic alphabet as the official script. Given that the interpretation of the constituent peoples was inclusive and not exclusive, the provision was proclaimed contrary to the *Constitution of Bosnia and Herzegovina*. The equality of the constituent peoples' languages is taken as transterritorial (U 5/98-IV).

Since *Annex 7* to the *Dayton Peace Agreement* stipulates accepting the return of refugees and displaced persons, segregation by ethnicity is considered anti-Dayton. On several occasions an argument was made that entity voting is not really ethnic voting, but such an argument is related to the failure of implementing *Annex 7*, which favors consociation.[27] The problem is that in this view of consociation, failing to protect Croatian people in the FBH will continue (Savanović, 2013).

In better understanding this problem a few facts should be noted. To begin with, the *Constitutional Court of BH* in its interpretation of appeal 5/98 used *Preamble 10* to derive certain normative and constitutional principles about the political and legal order in Bosnia and Herzegovina.[28] One such principle is that a multinational state and multi-ethnic society are not be threatened by the two-entity division of the state and the territorial division of the FBH. But there are conditions—these divisions will not continue the ethnic cleansing that began the war, and the ethnic-based homogenization of state institutions also will be negated (U 5/98, item 53-61) (Steiner & Ademović, 2010). Line 10 in the *Annex 7* of the *Constitutional Court* restored the multi-ethnic society as a goal of the *Dayton Peace Agreement* (U 5/98, item 73).

The *Dayton Peace Agreement* does not imply that identity should be based on territory and ethnicity, so the existing consensual mechanisms are not limited solely to identity (U 5/98, item 64-67). It is not clear how this interpretation can be compatible with the mechanisms of the constitution of the *House of Peoples of the Parliamentary Assembly*[29] (*Constitution of BH*, IV/1.1),[30] which directly establishes the contrasting principle of entity (territorial) and ethnicity.

Moreover, "the principle of collective equality prohibits privileges to any of the three constituent peoples" (U 5/98, item 60) (Steiner & Ademović, 2010). Although the *Constitutional Court of BH* accepts that the *Dayton Peace Agreement* as a consociational model of the *Constitution*, it does not accept the principle of collective equality which allows one of the constituent peoples the veto right (U 5/98, items 55 and 116) (Steiner & Ademović, 2010). Such an interpretation disputes the institution of *Vital National Interest*, and is of crucial importance to the constitutional order in BH.

Collective equality is a principle that protects the interests of ethnic groups. The Vital National Interests institution has the ability of raising questions in the *House of Peoples* about the protection of ethnic groups (*Constitution of BH*, 4/3, e). In the *Presidency of BH*, members are allowed to block any decision referring to the *Vital national interest*. If the issue of *Vital national interest* is raised by a member of the *Presidency of BH* from the Republic of Srpska, the decision is sent to the *National Assembly of the RS* that must confirm it by a two-thirds majority. If this happens, the decision of the *Presidency of BH* is null and void (*Constitution of BH*, 5/2, d). Although the *Constitutional Court of BH* generally accepts the *Dayton Peace Agreement* as a consociation *Constitution* (Steiner, 2010), it denies the implementation of basic mechanisms of consociation embedded in the *Constitution of BH*.

The *Constitutional Court of BH* promotes political practices that change the existing character of the BH Constitution. Such practices have led to serious political tensions. Representatives of the Republic of Srpska often raise the issue of the "pro-Bosnian" actions of the *Constitutional Court*. Their argument is supported by how members in the *Constitutional Court* are selected. According to the *Constitution of BH*, membership selection in the *Constitutional Court* has a specific process: two members selected by the *National Assembly of the RS*, four members selected by the *House of Representatives of the FBH*, and three members selected by the president of the *European Court of Human Rights* who must not be BH citizens (*Constitution of BH*, VI/1(a)).

According to *Article IV/1*, 1(a) of the *Constitution of BH*, judges are not representatives of the constituent peoples; in practice this means that each of the three constituent peoples are given two judges,[31] and the remaining three are the so-called "foreign judges." This enables one of the constituent peoples to have the majority when its representatives are coupled with "foreign judges." During the negotiations under the auspices of the *Contact Group* in Dayton, representatives of the Russian Federation expressed serious reservations regarding the existence of foreign judges at the *Constitutional Court of BH*, anticipating certain problems which would surface at a later date

The selection process for membership in the *Constitutional Court* has repeatedly served as a justification for challenging the legitimacy of its decisions. Another claim that has generated controversy is the provision in *Article IV/1*, 1(d) of the *Constitution of BH*—the selection process as stipulated in the *Dayton Peace Agreement* was to last five years. These challenges to the highest BH court have caused much political instability.

The basic argument against the *Constitutional Court of BH* is that it fails to protect collective rights, and that it is often opposed to the concept of human/individual rights. This point of view is strongly emphasized in debates about Article II of the *Constitution of BH*. By formulating the problem in this way, the *Constitutional Court* is seen as de facto challenging the consociation "spirit of Dayton" in favor of a civil model.

The consociation nature of the *Constitution of BH* has gradually moved to a majority model of governance. In interpreting appeal 5/98, the *Constitutional Court*, in addition to concluding that the *Constitution of BH* does approve the exclusivity of national entities, also drew a few unfounded conclusions. These conclusions clearly view democratic principles as majority-democratic principles. For example, item 55 states that being a constituent people must not be interpreted as the veto right of a minority group. Thus, the *Constitutional Court's* position was identical to the views held among Bosniak political representatives.[32]

The "tyranny of the majority" appears to be an important cause of conflict in BH. Vital national interest, as a *de-facto* veto institution, represents the decisive mechanism that prevents discrimination. The latest attempt at this type of intervention in the *Constitution* is the attempted implementation of the *Sejdić-Finci Verdict*. The verdict was aimed at the privileged position of the "constituent" peoples in relation to "Others," which is present in many articles of the Constitution. Thus, for example, the "constituent" peoples are given veto rights which are denied to "Others." Also, discriminatory provisions are promoted for the election of members of the *Presidency of Bosnia and Herzegovina*, which excludes the possibility of candidates from "Others" (*Constitution of BH*, article V, 1). The verdict mandates the elimination of all discriminatory provisions.

The solution proposed by the representatives of the Republic of Srpska is for *Article V.1* to be corrected—instead of "The Presidency of BH shall consist of three Members: one Bosniak and one Croat, each directly elected from the territory of the Federation, and one Serb directly elected from territory of the Republic of Srpska" in the part referring to the Republic of Srpska it states: "and one member directly elected from territory of the Republic of Srpska." Taking into account the ethnic composition of the RS, it is clear that this makes no *de facto* difference, but that it *de jure* involves the elimination of the discriminatory provision in the *Constitution*. The verdict is similar to a viewpoint put forward by the *Venice Commission* (2001, http://www.venice.coe.int/webforms/documents/?pdf=CDL-INF(2001)021-e), claiming that using territory and ethnicity as a basis for representation is discriminatory.

The problem of confounding territory and ethnicity stems from not implementing A*nnex 7*, and so the RS entity, "Serbian," is defined in terms of population. Consequently, the RS can insist on the ethno-territorial model of consociation protection, simply because the *Dayton Peace Agreement* has not been implemented, and if it had been implemented, the right to entity veto would not be the same as the right to ethnic veto. At first glance, this means that if *Annex 7* were implemented, if Serbs wished to preserve the mechanisms of protection of collective rights appearing in the *Constitution of BH*, they would have to accept the replacement of the ethno-territorial principle by an ethnic principle. Such a position is not sustainable. Serbs occupy the vast majority of the territory in the Republic of Srpska. Hence, due to the overlapping of entity borders with the ethnic map of the pre-war Bosnia and Herzegovina, the ethno-territorial principle and the trans-territorial principle are in fact equal solutions for Serbs. It is crucial to maintain a consociational model of the *Constitution*.

Still, such a solution is not applicable in the *Federation*—Bosniaks would always get to elect two representatives. Currently, Bosniaks may only select a Croat as a third member of the Presidency (Savanović, 2013). However, as a result of previous changes to the *Constitution* they would be allowed to select two Bosniak members. Hence, this solution would imply a change to the *Electoral Law*, which currently prevents such a possibility. Clearly a constitutional order based on the model of "three peoples in two entities" is discriminatory against Croats, and the "civil" model of elections in the *Federation* is less institutional oppressive.

CONCLUSION

Understanding history and culture is important in policy making. The transformation of the consociation nature of the *Constitution of BH* towards a majority model exhibits a profound lack of understanding of the historical emergence of BH as a state. A return to a "civil" model sends BH back to its status that caused the civil war.

Civil identity cannot be a realistic option in BH. Such a strategy for developing national identity would ignore consociation mechanisms that protect individual rights and guarantee equal representation among its competing ethnic groups. For example, given the demographic distributions in the three major nations in the Bosnia and Herzegovina region, it is possible that Bosniaks/Muslims constitute a simple majority. As the "majority" in a "civil" model of the *Constitution*, they would be allowed to impose their will on both Serbs and Croats. It is clear that such a scenario would lead to a crisis.

The problem with the consociational mechanisms embedded in the *Constitution of BH* is that they complicate and slow the decision-making process, and create the potential for misuse. Still, consociation mechanisms should not be abolished; it only means that more efficient models should sought. Taking into account the strength of national identifications in Bosnia and Herzegovina, consociation represents a model of constitutional order, which would confirm the spirit of the *Dayton Peace Agreement*.

NOTES

1. Institute for statistics of the Federation of Bosnia and Herzegovina, http://www.fzs.ba/Dem/Popis/NacPopE.htm, visited: 11/18/2013
2. Kecmanovic (2007), Savanovic (2011).
3. Amin Maalouf points out how one fabricates "butchers" because of the established ways of thinking and expression so deeply ingrained in all of us, especially because of the narrow-minded, strict, simplistic understanding which reduces the whole identity to a single affiliation, proclaimed with passion (Maalouf, 2003, p. 8).
4. By consociation we mean a political system formed by the cooperation of different, especially antagonistic, social groups on the basis of shared power.
5. Preliminary results of the 2013 Census of Population, Households, and Dwellings in Bosnia and Herzegovina, http://www.bhas.ba/obavjestenja/Prelimi-narni_rezultati_bos.pdf, visited: 11/08/2013
6. The Simpson Diversity Indices for both entities are displayed below.

Simpsons Indices	Federation of BH	Republic of Srpska
$D = (ni/N)^2$	.604	.680
$1 - D$	.396	.320
$1/D$	1.655	1.471

Where ni = number in a category, N = total population in an entity. D ranges from 0 to 1; 0 equals infinite diversity, 1 = no diversity. This is not clear, so the next index is more acceptable: 1 – D. This measure ranges from 0 to 1, where 0 is no diversity, and 1 is full diversity. Finally 1/D ranges from 1 to k, where k is the number of categories or group in the analysis. 1 means no diversity, and k is full diversity. In the Federation of BH, there are four groups being evaluated, and in the Republic of Srpska there are two groups. In both entities, there is little diversity, but especially in the Republic.

We wish to thank Richard R. Verdugo for providing the calculations.

7. Matt Prodger (2005). Evicted Serbs remember Storm, http://news.bbc.co.uk/2/hi/europe/4747379.stm, visited: 05/10/2013

8. Jan-Werner Müller. (2008). A general theory of constitutional patriotism, http://icon.oxfordjournals.org/content/6/1/72.full, visited: 06/11/2013

9. This is a series of studies carried out during 2010 and 2011: focus groups of students at universities in Sarajevo, Banja Luka, and Mostar, as well as surveys in several cities in the Republic of Srpska and Federation of BH, respondents were pupils in the final year of secondary school and students. More details in Majstorović & Turjačanin (2011). *U okrilju nacije (Etnički i državni identet kod mladih u BiH)* / In the shelter of the nation (Ethnic and state identity among young people in BH)/, Banja Luka: Centre for Culture and Social Improvement.

10. See: http://pressrs.ba/sr/vesti/vesti_dana/story/7121/BiH+%C4%87e+propasti,+a+NATO+i+EU+nisu+po%C5%BEeljni!.html and http://pressrs.ba/sr/vesti/vesti_dana/story/31612/Srpska+treba+da+se+otcepi+od+BiH!.html

11. For an interesting discussion and history of the area see Kaplan (1993).

12. From this it is clear that the war in BH was an ethnic "civil" war by its character. According to another two popular interpretations of the nature and character of the war in BH between 1992 and 1995, this was a "dissolution" war or "aggression" performed by Serbia and/or Croatia. The interpretation of "aggression" relies on the well-known (but disputable) meeting between Milošević and Tudman in Karadordevo, where they reportedly agreed on the division of BH and creation of the "Great Serbia" and "Great Croatia." However, regardless of this being true or not, our main diagnosis is that the key element of the BH crisis was the relationship between the national and civil, which is obvious from the constitutional solutions, and based on this the main characteristic of the war is "civil."

13. The *Referendum on Independence* was held between February 29th and March 1st 1992.

14. At the time, the "Bosniak" nation formally did not even exist; therefore, Bosniaks were declared as "Muslims" during the census.

15. Only when a community is consolidated and strengthened in terms of its institutions is it possible to begin a process of gradual, more or less intensive, movement toward the "civil."

16. In order to understand the situation in BH, it is important to note that consociation is not necessarily conditioned by the existence of ethnically homogeneous territories (in case of BH, three different homogenous ethnic entities), since it can also exist as trans-territorial (which was possible before war, because BH had ethnic structure shaped as a "leopard skin").

17. However, in the *Federation of BH* the Croatian people do not have such strong consociational mechanisms of protection, which produces permanent crisis within the *Federation*. (Savanović, 2013, p. 542).

18. According to one of the most important works dealing with consociation: (Lijphart, 1999) the relationship between the majority and consociational model

can be "measured" in the ten key points. The Constitution of BH has all ten of these points on the consociational side. See Savanović (2011).

19. A very lively debate ensued about the formal correctness of the appeal, given that the members of the National Assembly of the Republic of Srpska referred to the H. Kelsen's position stating that the preamble does not have a normative character and therefore cannot be a criterion. The Constitutional Court of BH eventually rejected this objection, citing the fact that the Dayton Peace Agreement was an international treaty, which is subject to the Vienna Convention, and that the Article 31.2 of that Convention clearly defined otherwise.

20. http://www.ccbh.ba/bos/odluke/index.php?src=2

21. "The Republic of Srpska . . . is a state of the Serbian People."

22. http://www.ccbh.ba/bos/odluke/index.php?src=2

23. The verdict of the *European Court of Human Rights* in the *Sejdić-Finci case* states that this criteria must be extended to the right to stand for election: the provision stating that a member of the *Presidency of BH* from the RS must be a Serb, and from the FBH members must be a Croat or a Bosniak, was declared discriminatory.

24. Obviously, the term "trans-territorialism" here is used within the existing state.

25. *The Human Rights Chamber* is a judicial body established under *Annex 6 to the Dayton Peace Agreement. The Chamber* had the mandate to consider alleged or apparent violations of human rights as provided in the *European Convention for the Protection of Human Rights and Fundamental Freedoms* and the *Protocols thereto,* and alleged or apparent discrimination arising in the enjoyment of the rights and freedoms provided in the *Convention* and 15 other international agreements listed in the *Appendix* to *Annex 6.* (http://www.hrc.ba/bosnian/home.htm).The mandate of the *Chamber* finished on December 31st, 2003.

26. Particularly widespread controversy was sparked by the debate about the changed "ethnicized" names of towns, in which attitudes of the *Human Rights Chamber* and *Constitutional Court* differed. In the appeal which referred to the renaming of the city Foča to Srbinje, the *Chamber* dismissed the appeal in strictly formal reasons, believing that it was not possible to sustain it, based on the strict text of the *European Convention for the Protection of Human Rights.* (CH/00/4244) Yet, the *Constitutional Court* had a dissenting opinion, basing its decision on the claim that such a renaming discouraged the return, while also being contradictory to the previously reasoned interpretation of "constitutionality" (C 44/01-1, item 54-55).

27. It is often stated that the realization of *Annex 7* would change the attitude of Serbs towards the *Dayton Agreement,* because it would prevent the Republic of Srpska from using the consociational-protection measures based on the ethno-territorial principle to ensure its rights.

28. See: Comment by Joseph Mark, PhD, judge rapporteur in case No.U5/98 (10 item).

29. See also: *Constitution of BH*, Article.IX/3.

30. *The Venice Commission* has indicated that provision IV/1.1 in several aspects represents a legally disputable solution. It denies all those who are not members of the constituent peoples the "stand-for-election" right, since they are

not allowed to be nominated for the *House of Peoples of the Parliamentary Assembly of BH* (CDL-AD (2005) 004).

31. This is a logical consequence of the fact that the procedure of selection of judges of the Constitutional Court is not within the competence of the state, but of the entities (Steiner & Ademović, 2010).

32. For example: (Silajdžić, 2000, p. 112).

REFERENCES

Ćorović, V. (2001). *Istorija srba.* Niš, RS: Zograf.

Dahl, R. (1956). *A preface to democratic theory.* Chicago, IL: University of Chicago Press.

Đurdev, B., Grafenauer, B., & Tadić, J. (1959). *Historija naroda jugoslavije II.* Zagreb, HR: Školska knjiga.

Golubović, Z. (2006). *Pouke i dileme minulog veka.* Belgrade, RS: FilipVišnjić.

Habermas, J. (1998). *Between facts and norms: Contribution to a discourse theory of lawand democracy.* Cambridge, MA: The MIT Press.

Halpert, D. Ž., & Kajdikel, D. (2002). *Susedi u ratu. Jugoslovenski etnicitet, kultira i istorija iz ugla antropologa.* Belgrade, RS: Semizdar B92.

Hantington, S. (2000). *Sukob civilizacija i preoblikovanje svjetskog poretka.* Podgorica, MNE: CID, Banja Luka, BiH: Romanov.

Heywood, A. (2005). *Političke ideologije - 3. izd.* Beograd, RS: Zavod za udžbenike i nastavna sredstva.

Kaplan, R. (1993). *Balkan ghosts: A journey through history.* New York, NY: St. Martin's Press.

Kasapović, M. (2005). *Bosna i hercegovina–podijeljeno drušvo i nestabilna država.* Zagreb, HR: Politička kultura.

Kecmanović, N. (2007). *Nemoguća država.* Banja Luka, BiH: Glas Srpske.

Lijphart, A. (1999). *Patterns of democracy: Government forms and performance in thirty-six countries.* New Haven, CT: Yale University Press.

Majstorović, D., & Turjačanin, V. (2011). *U okrilju nacije (Etnički i državni identitet kod mladih u BiH).* Banja Luka, BiH: Centre for Culture and Social Improvement.

Maalouf, A. (2003). *Ubilački identiteti.* Belgrade, RS: Paideia.

Milošević-Đordević, J. S. (2003). Jedan pokušaj klasifikacije teorijskih razmatranja nacionalnog identiteta. *Psihologija, 36*(2), 125–140.

Müller, J. W. (2008). A general theory of constitutional patriotism. *International Journal of Constitutional Law, 6*(1), 72–95. Retrieved from http://icon.oxford-journals.org/content/6/1/72.full

Nikolić, G. V. (2009). *Ethnic maps of BH 2009, of Brčko District 2009 and of changes in BH 1971–2011.* Retrieved from http://www.nspm.rs/sudbina-dejtonske-bih-i-republika-srpska/etnicke-mape-bih-2009-distrikta-brcko-2009-i-promena-u-bih-1971-2011.html?alphabet=1

Prodger, M. (2005). *Evicted Serbs remember Storm* (BBC News). Retrieved from http://news.bbc.co.uk/2/hi/europe/4747379.stm

Savanović, A. (2011). KonsocijacijskaprirodaAneksa 4 (Consociational nature of Annex 4). *Srpska Pravna Misao, 38*(45), 19–36, Banjaluka, BiH.

Savanović, A. (2013). Crises of Bosnia. *Mediterranean Journal of Social Sciences, 4*(9), 539–546. Rome, IT: MCSER.

Silajdžić, H. (2000). *On the road to a modern state.* Sarajevo, BiH: VKBI.

Steiner, C., & Ademović, N. (Ed.) (2010). *Constitution of Bosnia and Herzegovina – comment.* Sarajevo, BiH: Konrad Adenauer Stiftung.

Stojković, B. (2002). *Identitet i komunikacija.* Belgrade, RS: FPN, Čigoja štampa.

Stojković, B. (2008). *Evropski kulturni identitet.* Belgrade, RS: Official Gazette.

Tabeau, E., & Zwierzchowski, J. (2010, February). The 1992-1995 war in Bosnia and Herzegovina: Census-based multiple system estimation of causalities' undercount. *Conference paper for the international research workshop on 'The global costs of conflict' the households in conflict network (HiCN) and the German institute for economic research (DIW Berlin).* Retrieved from http://www.icty.org/x/file/About/OTP/War_Demographics/en/bih_casualty_undercount_conf_paper_100201.pdf

Vasović, M. (2007). *U predvorju politike.* Belgrade, RS: Official Gazette.

Verba, S. (1965). Comparative political culture. *Political culture and political development.* Princeton, NJ: Princeton University Press.

Venice Commission. (2001). *Opinion on the electoral law of Bosnia and Herzegovina.* Retrieved from http://www.venice.coe.int/webforms/documents/?pdf=CDL-INF(2001)021-e.

CHAPTER 7

THE MENTAL WALL

Identity in a United Germany

Dana Martin and Richard R. Verdugo

The concept of identity is both intricate and complex. Not only does national identity vary by individuals, but many factors affect a person's sense of belonging to a community. For example, immigration, out-migration, demographic shifts, wars, revolutions, and so on; all affect national identity. In this chapter we examine national identity in Germany by employing two concepts, which we refer to as *Terminus* and *Axial*. A *Terminus* concept refers to limits or boundaries in which national identity takes place. In this chapter, we use three *Terminus* elements in our analyses: thematic, chronological, and concentric.

A second concept we use refers to events that are pivotal for the emergence of national identity. As a group, we refer to these as *Axial* events (see Jaspers, 1953). Essentially, Axial events are events that change the course of history at any given level, though scholars have used the term on a global level (see Jaspers, 1953; Armstrong, 2006). We use two *Axial* elements in our analyses: political and social.

National Identity, pages 213–244
Copyright © 2016 by Information Age Publishing
All rights of reproduction in any form reserved.

THEORETICAL BACKGROUND

Theories of National Identity: Essentialists, Constructivists, and Civic Theories

Three views dominate national identity research. The earliest national identity theories were originally part of debates about ethnicity—Essentialist and Constructivist. In later years, a third national identity research has been added, though it has a long history in political thought—Civic identity. An extensive review of these theories is beyond the scope of our chapter, so we provide a brief summary. The categories are Essentialist/Primordialist, Constructivist/Postmodernist, and Civic Citizenship.

Essentialist/Primordialist

Essentialist scholars of national identity view national identity as fixed, based on ancestry, a common language, history, ethnicity,[1] and worldviews. Some noted scholars include Huntington (1996), Smith (1986, 1991), Geertz (1973), van den Berghe (1981), Armstrong (1982), and Connor (1994).

One Essentialist scholar, Anthony D. Smith (1991), proposes a middle of the range theory[2] about national identity. His view is marked by constructivism to essentialism—national identity is a hybrid of both "natural" continuity and conscious manipulation. Smith's position is interesting and, it seems to us, quite reasonable.

At its core, the Essentialist argument is based on culture and history. Other markers for the Essentialist framework are language, ancestry, and blood.

Constructivist/Postmodernist

Constructivism posits that dominant groups create, manipulate, and dismantle identities for their specific gains (Beaune, 1991; Berezin, 1997; Brubaker, 1992; Corse, 1996; Fine, 1996; Gillis, 1994; Griswold, 1992; Hobsbawm, 1992; Hobsbawm & Ranger, 1983; Kubik, 1994; Lane, 1981; Schudson, 1992; Schwartz, 1987, 1991; Spillman, 1997; Wagner-Pacifici & Schwartz, 1991; Zerubavel, 1995). Within this paradigm, there are two very interesting viewpoints, with the characteristics of paradigm shifts.[3]

The first viewpoint is embodied in the work of Anderson (1991) who posits that identity is an imagined construct. It is imagined because individuals in a given geopolitical entity do not and cannot interact with one another—there are simply too many people to allow for such activity. So symbols, rituals, and other ceremonials are used as means for bonding, and individuals thus *imagine* they have a community with other members of society. In Anderson's model, print Capitalism was crucial for building this imaginary identity. People in different parts of a nation were able to read the same documents in the same language that maximized sales and circulation. Readers began to understand one another and thus formed the basis for an imagined community. Anderson argues that the first European nation-states were founded around their national print languages.

The second viewpoint is advanced in the work by Hobsbawm and Ranger (1983)—national identity is invented for political reasons. Invented traditions are created in order to ensure continuity with the past. Indeed, a sure sign that there has been a break with the past or where existing modern norms and values are not effective in maintaining stability and order, is the utilization of traditions toward this end. Such instability may be brought on by rapid social change or other axial events, such as wars or economic crises.

Not all is well within the Constructivist camp. While Postmodernists support the Constructivist model, they have serious problems with its approach. To begin with, they argue that Constructivism seems to be a simple cataloguing of identity construction processes, devoid of content. Secondly, they argue that the paradigm underestimates the central role of power (Connell, 1987; Gilman, 1985), and that such an error leads them to incorrectly suggest that influence and agency are "multidirectional" (Calhoun, 1995, p. 199). Power for *Postmodernists* is the crucial concept.

At its core, Constructivism/Postmodernism is based on politics and the use of power by dominant groups in order to gain and maintain their privileged status in society.

Civic Identity

Civic identity is a form of identity where membership in a geopolitical entity is unfettered by ethnicity or culture. Instead, it is based on a set of shared values about rights and the legitimacy of State institutions to govern. The State's political legitimacy is derived from citizens' participation in many social institutions, such as politics, voluntary associations, unions, and so on. The notion of civic citizenship is closely aligned with Jean-Jacques Rousseau's (1762) *The Social Contract.*[4] Others who espouse a civic approach to national identity include Habermas (1994), Miller (1995), Tamir (1993), Greenfeld (1992), and Marshall (1964).

Theoretical Framework

In attempting to better understand the process of national identity formation, we have merged two broad concepts, which we call *Terminus* and *Axial* events.

Main Concepts: Terminus and Axial Events

Terminus events. By *Terminus* events we mean boundaries, either social or structural, that shape the process of national identity. Each of the three

Terminus elements embody this definition: thematic, chronological, and concentric.

Thematic events are the structures and institutions that affect national identity. In our case, we look at several domains that form German identity—economics, culture, history, politics, and social issues. A *chronological* approach, as used in this chapter, refers to two decisive periods in the second half of the 20th century: the post-war period (1945–1990) and post-reunification period from 1990. Finally, the *concentric* approach explores three levels at which identity can be analyzed: the nation, groups, and the individual.

Axial events. A second concept we employ we refer to as *Axial* events. By *Axial* events, we mean events that change the course of history or a social system, at any given level of analysis (Jaspers, 1953). These events include such things as the emergence of a new way of thinking, a new way of managing a social system, new norms and values, and more. We have two elements attached to *Axial* events: political and social. Our study focuses on the issue of Remembrance in German democratic and dictatorial regimes, especially in the Federal Republic of Germany (West Germany), and the German Democratic Republic (East Germany). The *political* identity in a unified Germany involves managing identity for the present and preparing it for the future. The most significant fractures of German national identity have been the transitions from national-socialist and communist dictatorships to a parliamentary democracy. The evolution of *social* identity is marked by discontinuity. In both Germanys, the transformation of lifestyles and attitudes was all the more profound and irreversible as it was both top-down and bottom-up.

A Theoretical Model

Figure 7.1 depicts our views about the relationships between *Axial* events, National Identity, and *Terminus* events.

The diagram makes the argument that the effects of *Axial* events on National Identity are mediated by *Terminus* events. For example, an *Axial* event, such as the Enlightenment change world history in the West, but its

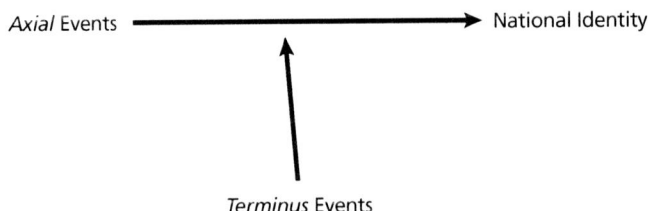

Figure 7.1

effects, and the time for such effects to take hold, depended on a nation's culture and history. In Germany, the effects of the national *Axial* events of separation and then reunification depended on the cultures and governance regimes of East and West Germany.

Research Hypotheses

We have three basic hypotheses based on the model depicted in Figure 7.1. The three hypotheses are driven by the *Axial* events of separation, reunification, and the process of integration, which are mediated by *Terminus* events.

> **H1:** *The separation, an Axial event of Germany divided into East and West, led to two different governance regimes. Democratic Germany was characterized by freedom, autonomy, and the rule of law. Communist Germany was based on a collective mentality, group norms, and a centralized, controlling governance regime. National identities, thus, were quite different: autonomous in the West, collective in the East.*

> **H2:** *Reunification led to some confusion and distrust among members from both social systems. However, it was East Germans who were more likely to feel anomie because they were moved into a Democratic system and culture of which they knew little about. National identity was a challenge, impossible in the early stages, and it was affected by Terminus factors.*

> **H3:** *Integration, that is, merging both Germanys, was a challenge to do with different cultures and experiences from different governance regimes. It would take several generations for both Germanys to be fully integrated and form one national identity. In fact, younger Germans are more likely to feel German than their parents or grandparents.*

ANALYSIS: NATIONAL IDENTITY IN GERMANY

Terminus Events

Thematic Issues

Studying identity requires giving equal importance to economics and culture. Both domains are fundamental pillars of modern, contemporary Germany. Germany is primarily a grouping of ethnic and linguistic communities, built on two foundations: its craft, industrial, and commercial expertise; and its artistic, intellectual, scientific, and cultural influence. In this section, we examine the potential effects of the economy, culture, and governance regime on German national identity. The latter is particularly important due to the separation of East and West, their development of their unique social structures, and then reunification.

Economy. German political unification created a major economic challenge. In West Germany, the economy was based on a market paradigm, while in the East, the paradigm was a planned economy. The two diametrically opposed systems in both theory and practice. In a market/Capitalist based economy, it is the supply and demand that drive the market in a free priced environment, with limited or non-existent government intervention, and the means of production are privately owned. Whereas in a planned/ command economy, the government or State organizes, plans, directs, and controls the economy; the management of the economy is centralized or decentralized (management is turned over to lower governing bodies). The State may also nationalize a company—assume ownership.

The "German model" is a West German creation. Whereas West Germany became a society of abundance and consumption, and its citizens became experienced, demanding consumers, East Germany operated under a Communist model. East Germans lived in an environment of shortages, they became expert in bartering and living on the margin. Thus, success by West Germany and failure in East Germany created an asymmetric power relationship: West Germans took the role of decision-makers, while East Germans, though having less power in this relationship, enjoyed the hitherto unobtainable benefits of living in a strong economy. For more than two decades rescuing the East was a national goal.

East German collective identity was formed around two contrasting poles: theory (that of a fair and efficient economic model), and reality (that of undersupply, which became endemic after the boom of the sixties). Other than some small operations, such as craftwork and fine catering, a private entrepreneurial sector did not exist. Heavily subsidized food staples were cheap and widely available, but other consumer goods were in short supply. In fact, these other goods were targeted for export, were very costly (such as appliances and furniture), or rarely available (such as building materials and cars, which had to be ordered more than ten years in advance). Life in East Germany was modest, but also "sustainable."

In West Germany, economic growth was swift and robust. The emergence of a consumer society led to much prosperity. Compared to East Germany and most other European nations, incomes in West Germany were higher, houses and cars more impressive, travel more exotic, food more sophisticated, and leisure more costly. The economic success in the West was a source of collective pride, but also of condescension towards the "poor cousins" of the East. After the reunification, the latter complained about being treated as second-class citizens—not without reason, though often aware that politically and economically they had no real alternative. Culturally, however, they have been more liable to criticize Western supremacy.[5]

Culture.   Over the Cold War period, East Germans and West Germans grew apart, not knowing much about one another. Overregulation and mismanagement characterized the daily lives of East Germans. The virtues of patience, flexibility, and humility were necessary responses to these daily contingencies. Planning was essential due to shortages of many consumer goods. Planning was supplemented by taking advantage of opportunities and by being creative. In a French blog, an East German remembers the daily shortages:

> If there was fresh milk in the morning it was gone by the afternoon. But meanwhile, potatoes, not to be found in the morning, had arrived. We could almost only get fruit and vegetables in season . . . which are sought after today for ecological reasons. . . . Everything depended on who you knew. Get me this and I'll get you that . . . Many goods were available, but in much too short supply. Many households had savings, but there was nothing to spend them on. . . . We learned to improvise and help each other. That's when do-it-yourself skills were indispensable. . . . One positive side to the shortage economy was that there was very little waste. Things were mended many times before they became really worn out.[6]

Daily survival skills and strategies varied by sector. In East Germany, the lack of resources led to stronger social ties and much individual initiative. Survival—in the sense of reaching out for the best possible quality of life—depended on mutual assistance, helping friends, and mobilizing knowledge. These were vital skills in a world of bartering and do-it-yourself mentality, which West Germans had no inkling about. In the West, customers could rely on the proficiency of political and economic agencies. Unlike their East German counterparts, West Germans enjoyed full employment and the social benefits that placed everyone on the same footing for education, health, and leisure, though they also had to deal with inequality and joblessness. Even so, the middle and working classes took full advantage of their improved quality of life. Two important cultural traits that emerged were an increasing self-confidence and positive outlook on life, and an increase in being more demanding, both of which were inconceivable among East Germans.

Culture is the lifestyle of a nation; a nation's values, views, norms, and traditions. In contrast to political, economic, and social history, cultural history is not constructed from events and cycles but formed by long processes and slow transitions (Braudel, 1949).

A widely used concept in intercultural research is "place of remembrance" or "realm of memory" (Nora, 1986/1992). It covers actual places and physical or abstract objects, events and persons, institutions or symbols. Its purpose is to explore references to identity in commemoration and taboo, self-image and image of others, social norms and values. Remembrance is the exclusion of events and things that do not fit preferred choices. Researchers must keep a critical distance from dogma, taboos, fashions, and ideals, which often prove fleeting and insubstantial (Rousso, 1987).

Governance regimes. In East Germany, the adoption of a Marxist-Leninist model created a socialist system closely linking ideology and social structure. The East German national identity was constructed and based on the propaganda of a single political party, the SED (*Sozialistische Einheitspartei Deutschlands; Socialist Unity Party of Germany*).

The spread of propaganda was intense. According to official doctrine, socialist countries were united in striving for greater international solidarity and understanding among solidarity of workers. Capitalist countries were degraded at school and at work (see McCauley, 1979; Gibbs, 2000; Grothe, 1958; Childs, 1983). All sciences and humanities were enlisted in the campaign against capitalist imperialism. The East German regime laid down an official line of thinking, from which it tolerated no deviation (Yèche, 2013). Only the predominantly Protestant Church, some dissenting circles, and some individuals managed to resist, provided they were discreet and did not draw attention. A Christian from East Germany comments on State atheism:

> The dictum of Karl Marx "Religion is the opium of the people" suffused the State system and the mental world of its leaders....An antireligious way of life was imposed by establishing a taboo on all contributions of religion to public life . . . The Church was soon forced to limit its activity strictly to the private sphere. Being a Christian in East Germany marginalised us. We could practice our religion only in the parish setting.... So I refused to participate in the *Jugendweihe*, which was compulsory for entrance to high school in East Germany.... I was able to qualify later by going to night school.... One result of this policy was to strengthen the common resolve of Christians in the face of hostility from the State. In that sense we had a common adversary and we were proud to offer what resistance we could, in the knowledge that we were courting trouble.[7]

The situation in West Germany was completely different. On the one hand, constitutionalism and the recognition of certain fundamental rights were secured. On the other hand, opinions and activities deemed anti-constitutional were not allowed. Even so, this young democracy did not tolerate extremism, whether left- or right-wing. The communist party was dissolved in 1956, and a 1972 law barred all anti-constitutional forces from public offices, such as extreme radicals.[8] The defense of constitutionalism, which forms the core of the West German political system, has been a foremost concern among all political leaders. All German citizens must abide by the rules of the democratic game.

Chronological Issues

"Historical identity" denotes two different but complementary meanings. First it refers to the evolution and nature of a collective entity, to the specific character of its members, and to a description of the processes and historical issues involved in the evolution of German identity. Secondly, historical identity includes the relation of a community to its past: its origins, its path, its positive or negative references, and changes over time. To distinguish between the two, the first will be called "historical," and the second "historiographic" (Mittler, 2012).

Germany after the war. From 1945 to 1990, German unity and national consciousness was not possible. The country's destruction, occupation, and division made it impossible to have such an identity. Under the management of the Soviet Union and the United States, two Germanys were created in 1949; the German Democratic Republic (GDR) and the Federal Republic of Germany (FRG) represented two attempts at nation-building. The East took as its model communism—or socialism, while the West adopted liberalism—or capitalism.

These hegemonic differences persisted throughout the Cold War. The example of "official memory" demonstrates how the two nations set out in opposite directions. For the East German leaders, there was no difference between fascism and capitalism. East German leaders, claiming to be the heirs of the communist resistance, refused to accept any responsibility for the war crimes and sided with the victims. The burden of the past lay more heavily on West Germany, where the indignation and political activity of the new generation moved the country toward "Remembrance" and began a process of catharsis.

After reunification, the idea of Remembrance underwent a semantic shift.[9] For national-socialists, the term "mastery of the past" or "coming to terms with the past" ("*Vergangenheitsbewältigung*"; coping with the past) still held. For Communism the past has been dealt with more neutrally and descriptively, through a process of facing up to the East German past ("*Aufarbeitung der DDR-Vergangenheit*"; reclamation of the East German past). This choice of terminology attests to a desire of separating the two systems and proceeding efficiently and fairly. In both cases, official Remembrance policy emphasizes the commemoration of the victims of totalitarianism. Concerning Nazism, numerous debates, such as that on the Berlin Holocaust Memorial, have focused on how best to honor the memory of all the persecuted groups, Jews but also non-Jews: political opponents, resistance fighters, homosexuals, Roma, and handicapped persons (Droit, 2007).[10] For the victims of the East German regime, discussions center on defining specific parameters, including the choice of appropriate criteria, and on the location and purpose of a commemoration.[11]

What about the roles of the leaders and their followers in the two successive dictatorships? This subject gives rise to fierce battles in the media. These are often sparked by a cultural event such as the publication of a book (*Hitler's Willing Executioners* by Daniel Goldhagen in 1997), or the organization of a touring exhibition (*War crimes of the Wehrmacht* by the Hamburg Institute for Social Research, 1995–2004).[12] In East Germany, the legal and moral condemnation of past crimes and human rights violations is a delicate topic because the facts are fairly recent and no clear judgment is possible. Thus, the Nuremberg trials (1945/46) and the trial of Adolf Eichmann in Jerusalem (1961) are not readily comparable to the legal action taken against former *Politbüro* members and border guards who fired on defectors. The broadest and most successful attempt to reconcile the interests of the two groups was the creation of the *Stasi* archives in 1990.[13]

During the post-war years, the identity and collective memory of the German people split into two strands. First, the German population was divided, East and West. Gradual differentiation and estrangement seemed inevitable, and yet a closer examination reveals numerous similarities. After the horrors of the Holocaust, shame, silence, and repression existed on both sides. Despite efforts to move away from Nazi ideology, former Nazi officials remained in place and some held key positions in institutions and firms in both Germanys.[14]

Over time, a feeling of moral duty led to the idea of examining the past and making amends. The Cold War spawned pacifist movements in the West. In the East, pacifist movements were small but highly symbolic. In the West, the focus was on drawing lessons from the past, by opposing West German re-armament: "No more war!" ("*Nie wieder Krieg!*"). In the East, a more forward-looking stance emerged in Christian circles, which, cautious by necessity, opted for biblical exhortations, turning "swords into ploughshares" ("*Schwerter zu Pflugscharen!*").

With reunification, the hope of building a better world and the fear of a third world war faded. Pursuing an agenda of Remembrance has remained a priority for some, while others demanded bringing closure to the past ("*Schlussstrichdebatte*"). Since the West German historians' quarrel in 1986/87, talk of closure and moving on has become highly sensitive. Likewise, the debate on the qualification of East Germany as a State "without the rule of law" ("*Unrechtsstaat*") has generated much divisiveness among former dissidents.[15] In a noteworthy contribution, the West German journalist Harald Martenstein derides those wishing to draw a line under the Nazi and communist past. He states that in his experience, this wish has been expressed mainly by those formerly in privileged positions, who wearily point to the supposed complexity of the system, yet very rarely by the disadvantaged, for whom the same system, with its pervading injustice, seems to have been perfectly intelligible.[16]

Individual identity. Individual identity is a complex issue. Several phases have to be distinguished: reconstructing a devastated country, the slow consolidation of the two States, and reunification. The memory of the Germans who lived through the early post-war years is marked by traumatic experiences: bombardments, expulsion or captivity, violence, spoliation, and deprivation. Although official historiographers accurately write about liberation, the complete collapse of Germany was widely experienced as a catastrophic defeat, painful, and humiliating—1945 was a descent into hell for most of the population, whose main concern focused on the barest necessities of life in order to survive and ensure basic security.[17] Having lived through such ordeals and yet called upon to shoulder the collective blame, they suffered a major psychological disjunction (Stark, 2011, p. 33).

Two founding myths enabled individuals to face up to the consequences of the Nazi past. The East considered itself the legitimate heir of "popular antifascist resistance," a creed that exonerated and absolved those not in the resistance, in other words almost everybody (Agethen, Eckhard, & Neubert, 2002). The West postulated an image that implied a fresh start and hopefully a peaceful and prosperous future.[18] Essayist Wolfgang Büscher has compared such a view to the two other turning points still to come, namely 1968 and 1989. Given that these two dates have very different meanings for the inhabitants of West Germany (student movement and inter-German encounter) and those of East Germany (Prague Spring and fall of the regime), this approach seems debatable (Büscher, 1998).

The two Germanys moved forward at different paces. In West Germany, identity moved in a straight line; in East Germany identity has been severely buffeted. The radical change of the political and socio-economic order produced a radical microscopic change in everyone's private and occupational lives. In the East, the merging of the two Germanys was perceived as an opportunity, liberation, and a promise, but also as an invasion, an annexation, and liquidation. The invasive character of Western supervision caused negative reactions. The best known manifestation of this negative feeling was nostalgia for the East (*"Ostalgie"*), a demonstrative attachment to products and practices of a country viewed as a paradise lost.[19]

But such a feeling was not held by all former East Germans. Indeed, a study of the *Bundeszentrale für politische Bildung* (Federal Agency for Civic Education) found two predominant motivations. First, idealization of a private life "had nothing to do with the political system." Secondly, there was an attempt at recalling the advantages and strengths of an alternative societal model that "also had its good points." A minority wanted to go back, but an appraisal of life in East Germany proved widely divergent in the old and new *Länder (regions)*. The West had a negative view, while the East voiced many divergent views. Another poll provides some good explanations. East Germans had to reconcile the improvement in their quality of life and the political system with a degraded social system that was, for many, a major source of disappointment. Tables 7.1 and 7.2 below confirm such a statement. When East and West Germans were asked their views about life in East Germany, there were differences in responses. Essentially, East Germans more than West Germans had more favorable views about life in East Germany. For example, if we sum the positive and somewhat positive views about East Germany, more than half (57%) of East Germans responded in this manner, while only 18% of West Germans did so.

In the same survey, respondents were asked to evaluate a selected number of domain related lives in East Germany. These data are displayed in Table 7.2. There are two important stories displayed in Table 7.2. First, only two domains were evaluated positively by a majority of respondents: standard of living and the political system. Second, in contrast to positive

TABLE 7.1 Appraisal of Life in East Germany			
Appraisal	All	West Germans	East Germans
Rather negative perception	22.00%	26.00%	8.00%
More negative than positive aspects	48.00%	52.00%	32.00%
More positive than negative aspects	20.00%	13.00%	49.00%
Rather positive perception	5.00%	5.00%	8.00%
Other	5.00%	4.00%	3.00%
Total	100.00%	100.00%	100.00%

Source: Survey by Bundeszentrale für politische Bildung (TNS Emnid, 2009), 2010, URL: http://www.bpb.de/geschichte/deutsche-einheit/lange-wege-der-deutschen-einheit/47560/unrechtsstaat?p=all (trans. Dana Martin/Richard Ryan, retrieved 03/01/14).

TABLE 7.2 Feeling of Better or Worse Situation in Different Domains in East Germany		
Domain	Improvement	Deterioration
Standard of living	65.00%	15.00%
Recognition of individual performance	27.00%	37.00%
Political system	55.00%	16.00%
Social justice	19.00%	60.00%
Social protection	19.00%	64.00%
Child minding and day care	8.00%	75.00%
Health system	25.00%	59.00%

Source: Survey of 1000 inhabitants of the Saxony-Anhalt region, Sachsen-Anhalt Monitor 2007 – Politische Einstellungen zwischen Gegenwart und Vergangenheit (Political opinions between past and present), Bundeszentrale für politische Bildung, 2010, URL: http://www.bpb.de/geschichte/deutsche-einheit/lange-wege-der-deutschen-einheit/47560/unrechtsstaat?p=all (trans. Dana Martin/Richard Ryan, retrieved 03/01/14).

evaluations, four domains were rated negatively by a majority of respondents: social justice, social protection, child care, and health care.

Concentric Issues

Views and feelings about identity vary by place. For a divided Germany, this is especially important because terms such as democracy, peace, progress, and humanity have different meanings.

German national identity.   Relations to authority say much about social structure. State power and Party authority expanded into the public sphere at the expense of the private sphere, and the two may have merged. East Germany presented itself as a "State of Peace," concerned with the defense of the homeland and other Socialist countries. Censuring the aggressive imperialism of West Germany served to justify the growing paramilitary discourse and activity in East Germany.[20]

In contrast, since the 1970s West Germany was becoming less authoritarian. The growing "alternative" movements, especially pacifist, ecologist, and feminist, ushered in a veritable democratization of social criticism. Feelings of belonging were less determined by social origin and their intergenerational transmission.[21] Increasing social mobility and the fragmentation of communities expanded the range of economic and social opportunities, and confirmed Granovetter's (1973) theory about the "strength of weak ties."[22] Interestingly, East Germans had no precise idea of life and social changes in West Germany.

For East Germans, reality set in with the "Fall of the Wall." It was only after the opening of the Iron Curtain that East Germans discovered their new reality: being confronted with new standards, codes, practices, and behavior patterns, both linguistic and cultural. East Germans had grown accustomed to respect existing hierarchies, in particular the older generations. The central figure in the East German system was a senior official, a veteran of the Communist resistance. A former exile or political prisoner, his mission was to set an example and guide the young in breaking from the past and build a better future. As in other Communist countries, seniority was a fundamental, unchallenged, status of authority.[23]

The Western model did not work this way. Although paternalism was part of social structure, authority was democratized. Persons with status, such as public officials, managers, teachers, and parents had ceased to present themselves as infallible and unassailable. Hence, everyone was encouraged to express their opinions. After Nazism, and facing communism, questioning authority became a norm.

In sum, the identities in the two societies were different. In West Germany, the importance of the individual outweighed the value of the collectivity. Individualism, as a societal goal, was actively sought, practiced, and valued. Individual fulfilment, the main reference of the post-war generation, was a cornerstone of West German modernity.

Group identity in Germany. Complementing the rigid and structured hierarchies in East Germany were two counterweights: the principles of gender equality, and institutionalized comradeship. Both were based on solidarity among peers but also on mutual surveillance (Giddens, 1994, pp. 125–126). Social relations in East Germany were ambiguous—conviction and compromise, protection and betrayal, truth and falsehood were interspersed and often hard to dissociate. East German citizens were able to makes sense of all this complexity.

West Germany tended to be hierarchical, anti-authoritarian, and preserving greater social distance between social strata, and between men and women.

Power was not equality distributed. In East Germany, the power gap, politically speaking, was based on political power, status, and prestige. Socio-economic inequalities were minimal. The upward social mobility and integration of the masses were fully attained objectives. Women were autonomous in every way: they had access to all occupations, and could enter spheres previously reserved for men. Gender equality was supported by a network of nurseries and childcare facilities, and the organization of leisure time and State aid. For example, the monthly day off for household tasks ("*Haushaltstag*") was a given since 1952 and applied to all married women.[24]

After 1990, a cultural clash ensued between West German traditionalism and the expectations of East German women, and led to much incomprehension and bitterness. West German women, who struggle to combine family and work, make a distinction between "career women" and "housewives," which are felt to be incompatible life choices. Working mothers are deprecated ("bad mothers"); a wife's mission being to support her husband and care for their children. For them, happiness in the home and successful upbringing of children depends largely on the mother-child relationship, which tends to be exclusive and overprotective. Sacrifice is encouraged for all generations and social groups, even by feminists.

There is no balance between work and life outside of work. Instead, there was freedom of choice (children or career), a separation of spheres (places reserved for women), integration measures (quotas for women, equality monitoring), and public awareness (feminization of the language). In West Germany, parental status is not taken into account. The testimony of the West German feminist Christina Thürmer-Rohr is pertinent:

> We failed to communicate with a neighbouring society where the words feminism and patriarchy seemed only to be terms of abuse used to sneer at the decadence of Western capitalism.... We had the impression that our oppositional role was devalued, and by those who were supposed to become our

allies.... In Universities, the detachment and disinterest shown by female students from East Germany when feminist issues were addressed was quickly palpable.... Of course, we could not pretend that our relation in its political dimension was balanced or symmetrical.[25]

West Germans enjoyed much freedom. The principle of freedom of conscience and choice were the guiding principles of a new set of ethics. Moreover, despite diverging political opinions, there was much consensus in West Germany. Buoyed by this newly acquired freedom and its protection, political and social protest emerged. Citizen initiatives, demonstrations, petitions, and sit-ins were prevalent.

East German protest movements were different. Protests were much less virulent, influential, and visible, especially before 1989. Still, in their own way they were ethically and morally demanding. The German sociologist Detlef Pollack identifies four protest movements accompanying the decline of East Germany: "human rights supporters, communist reformers, participants in mass demonstrations, and those opting for defection to West Germany."[26] The protagonists formed alliances and counter-alliances with aims that were sometimes compatible, sometimes conflicting, and at times unrelated. Initially these protests were led by a minority of militants, but soon they became more radical and more opportunistic than the protests of first generation dissidents.

Axial Events

Political Events

The forty-year division of Germany had significant consequences for a German national identity. The post-war years saw the emergence of two Germanys; one a dictatorship, the other a social democracy. It was an odd set of events. To begin with, both Germanys were under the supervision of allies that ensured authority and protection. Reunification seemed remote, yet it was defended by West German leaders, who referred to the "reunification clause" ("*Wiedervereinigungsgebot*") in the preamble to the Basic Law ("*Grundgesetz*"), the Constitution of the Federal Republic. However, the refusal of neutrality in favor of Western integration stalled progress towards unity. East German leaders, eager for international recognition, determinedly ruled out any national reconstitution (Höfele, 2006; Reichel, 2005). West Germany's membership in NATO and East Germany's inclusion in the Warsaw Pact (1955), together with the belated admission of both German States as members of the United Nations Organization (1973), helped to secure the division.[27] Despite declarations of intent on both sides, in reality the destiny of the two Germanys depended on the intentions and ambitions of the two superpowers, the USA and Russia.

Reunification became possible by the reforms launched by USSR leader Mikhail Gorbachev.[28] The terms "glasnost" (openness) and "perestroika" (economic restructuring) soon became watchwords synonymous with transparency and freedom. For the first time since the Second World War, movements of protestation and opposition were not brutally quashed. The international community witnessed the disintegration, then the absorption, of East Germany. From a strictly territorial point of view, Germany in 1990 no longer had its pre-war borders. The partisans of a new Germany advanced the principle of trust among partners;[29] whereas opponents emphasized the risk of a relapse into excess and a desire for hegemony.[30]

Collective identity has been largely shaped by regimes and how citizens participate in the political process. Thus, the division of Germany brought about two antagonistic modes of political regimes: Federalism in West Germany and Centralism in East Germany (Felbick, 2002). Whereas Bonn remained a provincial capital and the seat of a provisional government (1949), East Berlin was made part of East Germany and permanently severed from its western part by the Berlin Wall (1961).[31] Thereafter, the East Germans lived in a country mapped out into 15 new districts (*Bezirke*).[32]

New governance systems affected Germans in each sector. In the East, the transition to Socialism reflected a new reality: compliance with the dictates of Moscow, which would not tolerate any form of dissidence. West Germans lived with three occupying forces, which accepted a constitution that granted a large degree of autonomy to the 11 regions (*Länder*) (Zippelius, 2006). In the West, the historical diversity of the region was preserved, along with certain traditions and attitudes, in particular Christianity and paternalism. The importation of a parliamentary democracy was both an opportunity and an unprecedented challenge. The outcome was far from certain, as it meant starting from scratch with no precedents.

Social Events

The post-reunification years were a time of mixed feelings: high expectations, bitter disappointments, hope, disillusionment, recognition, and reproach. This was not only the case among West and East Germans, but also within the old and new *Länder*. The most obvious and largely publicized conflicts were those between the self-righteous "*Besserwessis*" (arrogant West Germans) and the insecure "*Jammerossis*" (whining East Germans). The French sociologist Marie Hoquet explains the reasons for such derogatory stereotyping:

> These accusations, fuelled by the daily incursions of the opposite group gave rise to a rhetoric of mutual rancour, where the West Germans were blamed for

their selfishness, conquering attitude and superficiality, while the East Germans were decried for being uncivil, sluggish and prone to self-pity.... Gradually a moral judgment crept into inter-German relations: West Germans pointed accusatory fingers at the biographies of their East German compatriots, while the latter reproached the former for their haughtiness and condescension.[33]

In a report covering the last 20 years, Poppe (2010) confirms two important factors: the lack of interest by the West for the East, and the feeling harbored by the former inhabitants of East Germany that they are treated like second-class citizens. However, these observed differences seem to be diminishing.[34]

Being for or against governance varied by the East/West sector. In East Germany, political opinions or personal convictions were a marker of identity and a factor of sociability. A minority of East Germans, those opposed to the regime, were wary of the State and its institutions and representatives; for the others, life in East Germany left some room for freedom. Employees could openly criticize managers or discretely disobey orders without fear of losing their jobs. Despite latent discontent, most of the population identified with or took for granted their socialist homeland, which was predictable and provided for the future. Everyday security and comfort (such as housing, employment, health and education) was a benefit and a source of pride: East Germany had no unemployment and no poverty.

The situation in West Germany was different. Indeed, views about government affected participation, social relations, and trust. Moreover, significant inequalities continued.[35] Interestingly, West Germans, who were confident in their country and in themselves, were not fully aware of such disparities. For them, East Germany remained ill-defined and abstract, grey, and boring. They knew little about and were not interested in their neighbors. The emergence of the half-humorous, half-pejorative term "*Dunkeldeutschland*" ("Dark Germany") is currently the subject of much debate in online forums.[36]

"We wanted justice and we got the rule of law."[37] The fall of the Wall was clearly not viewed as liberation by the whole East German population. The State shaped perceptions of the event: an optimistic view for those mistrustful of the State ("*staatsfern*"), pessimistic for those who remained loyal ("*staatstreu*"). The bitter comment made by the painter Bärbel Bohley attests to this. The readjustments and reappraisals made after the opening of the Berlin Wall ("*Nachwendezeit*") elicited either enthusiasm or disenchantment according to individual experiences and expectancies. In reality, the situation was not positive for all: unemployment and divorce rates increased, while the number of marriages and births dropped.[38] East Germans had to take a stance about a new Germany. The 2010 social report of the Berlin-Brandenburg centre for sociological research reviews the evolution of the last twenty years. (See Tables 7.3 and 7.4)

Data in Table 7.3 suggest that East Germans do not feel part of the Federal Republic, and yet would not go back to East Germany. In contrast, West Germans tend to be non-committal to the new Germany. Table 7.4 presents data on views about Democracy. Generally, Westerners have better views than Easterners about Democracy as a governance system. They are more satisfied and believe that their futures will improve. In contrast, East Germans are less satisfied with democracy, and are not as likely to see improvement in their futures.

Continuity and success varied by sector. East Germans experienced discontinuity and collective failure, West Germans continuity and collective success. Hence East Germans, collectively, have had negative experiences: suspicious of the unknown and feeling left behind, bewildered, or helpless. However, for East Germans, confronting the West was compulsory and inescapable, whereas West Germans had little reason to feel self-doubt or any need for re-examination. Identifying with a united Germany and its Democratic regime was more likely among the educated and those with a better standard of living, and who enjoy stability in social relations.

TABLE 7.3   Identification with Germany 20 Years after Unity

As an East German...		As a West German...	
After 20 years, I now feel a full citizen of the Federal Republic	25%	Only since reunification do I feel like a full German	6%
I wouldn't like to go back to East Germany, but I don't yet feel at ease in the Federal Republic	59%	I feel better since the reunification	20%
I would like to go back and live in East Germany	9%	I don't feel any different since the reunification	44%
Don't know/no reply	7%	I don't feel at ease any more in today's Federal Republic	10%
		I would like to go back to the time of the Wall	11%
		Don't know/No reply	9%
Totals	100%		100%

Source: Sozialreport 2010. Die deutsche Vereinigung—1990 bis 2010—Positionen der Bürgerinnen und Bürger. Im Auftrag der Volkssolidarität (2010)—Bundesverband e.V., erarbeitet vom Sozialwissenschaftlichen Forschungszentrum Berlin-Brandenburg e.V., p. 28/30/31. URL: http://www.sfz-ev.de/zeitnahe%20veroeffentlichungen.htm; http://www.sfz-ev.de/index_htm_files/1_Sozialreport_2010.pdf (annual report based on a survey of 2090 East and West German citizens in 2010, translation Dana Martin / Richard Ryan, retrieved 22/04/16).

TABLE 7.4 Evaluation of Democracy*			
	Germany	Old Länder	New Länder
Democracy as a Value			
Very important	79%	82%	69%
Moderately important	14%	13%	20%
Not important/not at all important	4%	3%	8%
Don't Know/No reply	3%	3%	3%
Totals	100%	100%	100%
Satisfaction With Democracy			
Very satisfied / satisfied	24%	26%	16%
Partly satisfied	40%	41%	33%
Dissatisfied/very dissatisfied	31%	28%	45%
Don't Know/No reply	5%	5%	6%
Totals	100%	100%	100%
N	Insert sample size	2.090 citizens	Insert sample size
Expected Trends in Democracy			
Improvement	10%	11%	7%
No change	52%	53%	46%
Deterioration	31%	29%	38%
Don't Know/No reply	7%	7%	8%
Totals	100%	100%	100%
N	Insert sample size	2.090 citizens	Insert sample size

Source: Sozialreport 2010. Die deutsche Vereinigung—1990 bis 2010—Positionen der Bürgerinnen und Bürger. Im Auftrag der Volkssolidarität–Bundesverband e.V., erarbeitet vom Sozialwissenschaftlichen Forschungszentrum Berlin-Brandenburg e.V., p. 31 URL: http://www.volkssolidaritaet.de/cms/sozialreport_2010_deutsche_einheit.html; www.volkssolidaritaet.de/cms/vs_media/.../100831SR2010langDF.pdf (annual report based on a survey of 2090 East and West German citizens in 2010, translation DM / RR, retrieved 03/01/14).

CONCLUSION

To conclude, it is useful to bear in mind the degree to which the switch from division to unity was accompanied by hope, especially in Germany, and fear, especially outside Germany. The quip ascribed to François Mauriac—"We love Germany so much that we're glad there are two..."—speaks volumes about the scepticism of Germany's neighbors.[40] The famous speech of Willy Brandt, made after the fall of the Berlin Wall, reflects the German point of view: "The war and the division of the victors divided Europe, Germany and Berlin. Those meet now who are to join as one. We live to see, and I thank God I am able to be there, the different parts of Europe come together."[41]

The fall of the Wall changed the rules and the stakes, and created a fresh situation. East Germans witnessed one of the fastest transformations in history: they saw their world collapse as if stricken by an earthquake or a tidal wave. Whether it is experienced as an opportunity, a dramatic upheaval or both together, any sudden metamorphosis comes as a shock. However, the impact of this great event and its aftermath were in no way shared by the West Germans, whose stable existence continued unstirred. It is important to bear in mind that This difference is a fundamental one, and the ultimate effects of which must not be underestimated. The split will mend with time, but will never close completely. The question then arises of whether unity will have caused a bringing together of one nation or on the contrary an estrangement between East and West Germans.

Is the famous "Wall in our heads," a concept largely popularised in the German media and elsewhere, a myth or a reality? Opinions diverge, and in all likelihood will continue to do so for a long time.[42] The mere question is just as revealing as the balance of opposing opinions, which can be variously interpreted. Whether the phenomenon is deemed or not to exist tells us nothing about how it is judged. The term "Wall" implies painful division and problematic severance, especially for the generations who have lived in its shadow, but when it is replaced by "difference," especially by the younger generations, it loses its sternness. If we take into account the fact that in Germany, differences are traditionally perceived as self-evident and a source of enrichment, we may hope that the days of the mental Wall will soon be over. It will fold into collective memory.

APPENDIX A
A Methodological Note

The construction and transformation of identity forms a rich, broad field of study that is also shifting and controversial. A sound methodological strategy is approaching the topic from three levels of analysis, macro (national identity), meso (collective identity) and micro (individual identity), and marking a division between thematic units and historical periods. The aim of such a methodology is to proceed in an interdisciplinary and intercultural manner. The starting point is a corpus of both primary sources (testimony and analysis by citizens and observers), and secondary sources (surveys and research). Such an approach is supported by the work of researchers in different areas of expertise, of different nationalities, and with different affiliations, in order to condense knowledge and different perspectives.

The present text was first drafted in French and then translated to English (by Richard Ryan). The utmost caution was needed in the choice of terminology, as French and both East and West German usage had to be reconciled, while at the same time catering to an English-speaking audience. Any vagueness or confusion arising from these linguistic, intercultural and scientific acrobatics is entirely our responsibility.[39] Painting a portrait of a country's identity and that of its people is a difficult task: a transversal synthesis was therefore chosen to gain a simple overview of its current configuration.

NOTES

1. Note that ethnicity has different definitions: in America, ethnicity is associated with a minority group, or some other ethnic group. In Europe, especially in Eastern Europe, ethnicity refers to a people or peoplehood. It has greater community or group connotations.

2. Though we identify Smith's strategy middle of the range, it is not to be confused with Merton's (1957) definition of middle-of-the-range theories, which contrast Talcott Parson's Grand Theorizing or Minor theories. Merton defines middle-of-the-range theory as "... theories that lie between the minor but necessary working hypotheses that evolve in abundance during the day-to-day research and the all-inclusive systematic efforts to develop a unified theory of social behavior, social organization, and social change" (Merton, 1957, p. 39).

3. Paradigm shifts are associated with T.S. Kuhn's masterwork, *The Structure of Scientific Revolutions*. The shift refers to a revolutionary change in how scientific problems are viewed and framed. Kuhn's work was heavily influenced by the earlier work of Ludwik Fleck (1935[1979]). Fleck argued that scientific truth was situational to a specific scientific community, and that truths and falsehoods could never truly be established. Fleck's notion of a scientific community predated Kuhn, and is an especially important concept that led to the emergence of the Sociology of Science discipline, in which scientists are studied much like other communities.

4. Rousseau's vision of identity is in contrast to J. G. Fichte's, which is based on ethnicity, blood and social traits such as language. See Fichte (1807/08). Reden an die deutsche Nation. The German version may be downloaded from www.gutenberg.org, or in English from www.ghi-dc.org.

5. Cf. Thierse, Wolfgang (2013). Künste im geteilten Deutschland. Eine Erinnerung. Talk presented at the meeting 'Autonomie und Lenkung. Die Künste im doppelten Deutschland' Sächsische Akademie der Wissenschaften zu Leipzig / Zeitgeschichtliches Forum Leipzig, 04/04/2013. URL: http://www.dradiowissen.de/ddr-geschichte-die-normale-und-die-besondere-kunst.88.de.html?dram:article_id=257748 (retrieved 15/01/14).

6. *Source:* Christof (graduate engineer), Vivre en RDA, 10 November 2009, URL: http://verel.typepad.fr/verel/2009/11/vivre-en-rda.html (retrieved 30/07/13).

7. Source: Steffi (teacher), Être chrétien en RDA, 08 November 2009, URL: http://verel.typepad.fr/verel/2009/11/etre-chr%C3%A9tien-en-rda.html (retrieved 30/07/13).

8. For more information on occupational bans ("Berufsverbote") see the internet site of a collective assistance initiative that exists since 2011, URL: http://www.berufsverbote.de/ (retrieved 30/07/13).

9. In French, the term "duty to remember" ("Erinnerungspflicht") is used: this term is not very common in German.

10. The triple Berlin memorial (to the memory of the Jews of Europe, homosexuals and European Roma) was unveiled in 2005, after nearly 20 years of debate. For more information: Stiftung Denkmal für die ermordeten Juden

Europas, Denkmal für die im Nationalsozialismus verfolgten Homosexuellen, Denkmal für die im Nationalsozialismus ermordeten Sinti und Roma Europas, URL: http://www.stiftung-denkmal.de/ (retrieved 04/01/14).

11. Concerning the victims of East German communism see also URL: http://www.berliner-zeitung.de/berlin/zentraler-gedenkort-die-neue-wache-als-denkmal-fuer-ddr-opfer-,10809148,22092170.html; URL: http://www.bundesstiftung-aufarbeitung.de/wettbewerbe-1440.html (retrieved 03/01/14).

12. Cf. Hamburger Institut für Sozialforschung, http://www.his-online.de/en/; Bartov, Brink, Hirschfeld, Kahlenberg, Friedrich, et al. (2000) Bericht der Kommission zur Überprüfung der Ausstellung "Vernichtungskrieg. Verbrechen der Wehrmacht 1941 bis 1944." November 2000, 103 p. URL: http://www.his-online.de/index.php?eID=trackdown&uid=1096&cHash=8aa08019b061be813698cf820c93e8b0 (retrieved 03/01/14).

13. Cf. Behörde des Bundesbeauftragten für die Unterlagen des Staatssicherheitsdienstes der ehemaligen Deutschen Demokratischen Republik, http://www.bstu.bund.de (retrieved 03/01/14). The directors of this now emblematic institute were Joachim Gauck (1990–2000), Marianne Birthler (2000–11), Roland Jahn (since 2011).

14. For West Germany: German History in Documents and Images (GHDI), Images–Denazification and War Crimes Trials under the Allies, Denazification Questionnaire (1946), http://germanhistorydocs.ghi-dc.org/sub_image.cfm?image_id=1012 (retrieved 04/01/14). For East Germany: Foitzik, Jan (ed.) (2012). Sowjetische Interessenpolitik in Deutschland 1944–1954: Dokumente. München / Berlin, Institut für Zeitgeschichte. 629 p.

15. For example: Claer, Thomas (2010), www.justament.de/archives/1420; Herzog, Roman (1996), www.bundespraesident.de/SharedDocs/Reden/DE/Roman-Herzog/Reden/1996/03/19960326_Rede.html; Holtmann, Everhard (2010), www.bpb.de/themen/YIC2C0.html; Regner, Freihart / Rink, Johannes (2012), www.inter-homines.org/unrechtsstaat_ddr_lstu11.pdf; Rolleke, Gerd (2009), http://www.faz.net/aktuell/feuilleton/debatten/zeitgeschichte-war-die-ddr-ein-unrechtsstaat-1813196.html; Schwan, Gesine (2009), www.zeit.de/2009/27/Oped-Schwan#commen (retrieved 30/07/13).

16. *Source:* Martenstein, Harald (2009). Muss auch mal Schluss sein? Unser Kolumnist fragt sich, ob er in der DDR bei der Stasi gewesen wäre. In: Die Zeit, 06/2009, URL: http://www.zeit.de/2009/06/Martenstein-06 (retrieved 30/07/13).

17. Among a great number of publications, see for example the diary of a woman of Berlin who describes the spring of 1945. Anonyma (2003). Eine Frau in Berlin: Tagebuchaufzeichnungen vom 20. April bis 22. Juni 1945. Rheda-Wiedenbrück / Gütersloh, RM-Buch-und-Medien-Vertrieb. 291 p. A film with the same name was made by Max Färberböck in 2008.

18. Cf. Hein-Kircher, Heidi (2013). "Deutsche Mythen" und ihre Wirkung. In: Aus Politik und Zeitgeschichte, (APuZ 13-14/2013), URL: http://www.bpb.de/apuz/156772/deutsche-mythen-und-ihre-wirkung?p=0; Hein-Kircher, Heidi (2007). Politische Mythen. In: Aus Politik und Zeitgeschichte (APuZ 11/2007), URL: http://www.bpb.de/apuz/30604/politische-mythen?p=0 (retrieved 04/01/14).

19. On the subject of "Ostalgie" see also URL: http://www.handelsblatt.com/un-ternehmen/industrie/20-jahre-wirtschaftsunion-welche-ddr-marken-heute-noch-stark-sind/3478302.html (retrieved 30/07/13).

20. On militarism in East Germany: Sachse, Christian (2004). "Genosse Direktor, ich melde ...". Zur Militarisierung der Volksbildung in der DDR. In: Horch und Guck, Zeitschrift zur kritischen Aufarbeitung der SED-Dikatur, Heft 47/2004 | ddr – schulkonflikte, p. 39-47, URL: http://www.horch-und-guck.info/hug/archiv/2004-2007/heft-47/04708/ (retrieved 28/07/13).

21. In essence, in the new West Germany, merit based on intelligence, hard work, and talent were seen as the prime movers of attainment. However, such a system also engenders much inequaliy.

22. In Granovetter's seminal paper, he theorized that isolated communities fail to realize economic gains unless they expand outward to the larger community. One factor in being isolated is a strong sense of community that keeps its inhabitants within their community and its value system.

23. See the novel by Eugen Ruge, awarded the Deutscher Buchpreis in 2011 (*In Zeiten des abnehmenden Lichts*, 2011). For further information: http://www.drb.ie/essays/fathers-and-sons (retrieved 03/01/14).

24. Cf. GMD (Geschichte Mitteldeutschlands) - Das Magazin, MDR Fernsehen: Der Haushaltstag: Einer für alle? (20.12.2011), interview with Carola Sachse, Professor of contemporary history at the University of Vienna URL: http://www.mdr.de/geschichte-mitteldeutschlands/magazin/haushalt124.html (retrieved 04/01/2014); Labrousse, Agnès (2003). L'évolution de l'activité féminine en Allemagne orientale. Une analyse institutionnelle comparée. Working paper 03-2 CEMI (EHESS), February 2003, 38 p.

25. *Source:* Thürmer-Rohr, Christina (2010). Dossier 1989—und danach? Denkbewegungen vor und nach 1989 (Part 2), URL: http://www.forumcivique.org/de/artikel/dossier1989-und-danach-denkbewegungen-vor-und-nach-1989-2-teil; Additional document (Part 1): http://www.forumcivique.org/de/artikel/dossier-1989-%E2%80%93-und-danach-denkbewegungen-vor; curriculum vitae: http://home.snafu.de/thuermer-rohr/ (retrieved 06/01/14).

26. *Source:* http://www.marianne.net/Personne-n-a-rien-compris-a-la-chute-du-Mur_a182697.html (retrieved 05/01/14).

27. Cf. http://www.hdg.de/lemo/html/DasGeteilteDeutschland/index.html

28. See the chapter in this volume on Russian National Identity by Oxana Karnaukhova and Richard R. Verdugo.

29. For example, see the publications of Jacques-Pierre Gougeon, 2009 URL: http://www.ac-strasbourg.fr/academie/espace-presse/communique/article/jacques-pierre-gougeon-nouveau-recteur-de-lacademie-de-strasbourg-1/, or Henri de Bresson, URL: http://www.parisberlinmag.com/qui-sommes-nous/ (retrieved 07/01/14).

30. For example, see the publications of Michel Meyer (*Histoire secrète de la chute du mur de Berlin*, 2009 / *Le Roman de l'Allemagne*, 2013), URL: http://www.editionsdurocher.fr/Le-Roman-de-l-Allemagne_oeuvre_11012.html, http://www.rfi.fr/emission/20130921-allemagne-histoire-michel-meyer-roman-renaissance-edition-rocher (audio file, 4 min.), or Édouard Husson, http://www.edouardhusson.com/CV-francais_a211.html (retrieved 07/01/14).

31. On the German capitals: http://www.documentArchiv.de/in/1945/besat-zungszonen-deutschlands_fst.html; http://einestages.spiegel.de/static/topi-calbumbackground/3634/kampf_der_moechtegern_metropolen.html (re-trieved 28/07/13).

32. There were initially 14 Bezirkes, but East Berlin was added in 1961. The 15 were: East Berlin, Leipzig, Dresden, Karl-Marx-Stadt, Magdeburg, Rostock, Halle, Erfurt, Potsdam, Gera, Schwerin, Cottbus, Zwickau, Jena, and Dessau.

33. *Source:* Hocquet, Marie (2011). Mémoire, oubli et imaginaires urbains. Étude de deux hauts-lieux de la mémoire communiste à Berlin-Est : le Palais de la République et le Musée de la Stasi. Doctoral thesis in sociology, supervised by Michel Rautenberg (University of Saint-Etienne), p. 444/445; URL: tel.archives-ouvertes.fr/docs/00/69/08/60/PDF/These_-_Hocquet.pdf (re-trieved 08/01/2014).

34. Cf. Poppe, Ulrike (2010). "Wessis" und "Ossis"—Wirklichkeit oder Stereotyp? In: Reiner Marcowitz (ed.), Ein 'neues' Deutschland? Eine deutsch-franzö-sische Bilanz 20 Jahre nach der Vereinigung / Une 'nouvelle' Allemagne? Un bilan franco-allemand 20 ans après l'unification. Ateliers des Deutschen Historischen Instituts Paris, vol. 7. Oldenbourg Verlag, 187 p, p. 120-131.

35. Capitalism and social inequality are highly correlated, and some degree of inequality will exist in Capitalist driven economies.

36. For example, several online forum discussions: http://mundmische.de/bedeutung/6081-Dunkeldeutschland; http://www.forum-3dcenter.org/vbulletin/archive/index.php/t-368808.html; http://de.answers.yahoo.com/question/index?qid=20100906114456AA2PVJw (retrieved 08/01/2014). In the past, the best known terms were "Zone" ("Soviet occupation zone") and just after reunification, "Neufünfland" ("Five Newfoundländer"). However, the word "Nullhoffnungszone" ("no hope zone"), discussed by French Ger-manists, is much less representative Cf. Herbet, Dominique (2009): «Dun-keldeutschland, Nullhoffnungszone»: quelle image la presse allemande véhicule-t-elle à la veille des vingt ans de la chute du mur? In: Allemagne d'aujourd'hui, 189/2009, p. 217–228.

37. *Source:* http://www.baerbelbohley.de/zitate.php (retrieved 02/01/2014).

38. Cf. Blum, Buscher, Gabrisch, Günther, Heimpold, et al. (2010). Ostdeutsch-lands Transformation seit 1990 im Spiegel wirtschaftlicher und sozialer Indi-katoren. 2nd edition, Halle/Saale, URL: http://www.iwh-halle.de/d/publik/sh/ dkompendium.pdf; http://www.berlin-institut.org/online-handbuchde-mografie/bevoelkerungsdynamik/regionale-dynamik/ostdeutschland.html (retrieved 02/01/2014).

39. For example, the Federal Republic of Germany is denoted BRD in German, an abbreviation that was, however, more often used in the East than in the West, where "Deutschland" (Germany) or "Bundesrepublik" (Federal Repub-lic) were preferred terms. This highly significant linguistic and political detail is not necessarily familiar to non-Germans. Similarly, the terms "communism / socialism / social-democracy" or "capitalism vs. social market economy" have different meanings in France and in Germany.

40. Cf. dossier "1949–1961: de la partition de l'Allemagne à la construction du mur de Berlin," URL: http://www.sciencespo.fr/bibliotheque/pratique/collections/dossiers-presse/1949-1961 (retrieved 10/01/14).
41. Translation Dana Martin/Richard Ryan. The citation in German: "Aus dem Krieg und aus der Veruneinigung der Siegermächte erwuchs die Spaltung Europas, Deutschlands und Berlins. Jetzt wächst zusammen, was zusammengehört. Jetzt erleben wir, und ich bin dem Herrgott dankbar dafür, daß ich dies miterleben darf: die Teile Europas wachsen zusammen." Source: http://www.cvce.eu/obj/discours_de_willy_brandt_a_l_occasion_de_la_chute_du_mur_de_berlin_berlin_10_novembre_1989-fr-0f8f11b6-6a7f-4d6d-b925-7c6f71a454cb.html (retrieved 12/01/14).
42. Cf. http://www.welt.de/politik/article3775359/Ost-und-Westdeutsche-entfernen-sich-voneinander.html; http://www.bpb.de/geschichte/deutsche-einheit/lange-wege-der-deutschen-einheit/47423/wohlbefinden?p=all (retrieved 07/01/14).

REFERENCES

Agethen, M., Eckhard, J., & Neubert, E. (2002). Der missbrauchte Antifaschismus. *DDR-Staatsdoktrin und Lebenslüge der deutschen Linken*. Breisgau, DE: Herder, Freiburg.

Anderson, B. (1991). *Imagined communities*. London, UK: Verso.

Anonyma. (2003). *Eine Frau in Berlin: Tagebuchaufzeichnungen vom 20. April bis 22. Juni 1945*. Munich, DE: btb Verlag.

Armstrong, J. (1982). *Nations before nationalism*. Chapel Hill, NC: University of North Carolina Press.

Armstrong, K. (2006). *The great transformation: The beginning of our religious traditions*. New York, NY: Knopf.

Bartov, O., Brink, C., Hirschfeld, G., Kahlenberg, F. P., Messerschmidt, M., Rürup, R., Streit, C., & Thamer, H-U. (2000). *Bericht der Kommission zur Überprüfung der Ausstellung Vernichtungskrieg. Verbrechen der Wehrmacht 1941 bis 1944*. (p. 103). Retrieved from http://www.his-online.de/index.php?eID=trackdown&uid=1096&cHash=8aa08019b061be813698cf820c93c8b0

Beaune, C. (1991). *The birth of an identity: Myths and symbols of nation in late medieval France*. S. R. Huston (Trans.). Berkeley, CA: University of California Press.

Berezin, M. (1997). *Community of feelings: Culture, politics, and identity in fascist Italy*. Ithaca, NY: Cornell University Press.

Blum, U., Buscher, H. S., Gabrisch, H., Günther, J., Heimpold, G., Lang, C., Ludwig, U., Rosenfeld, M. T. W., & Schneider, L. (2010). *Ostdeutschlands transformation seit 1990 im Spiegel wirtschaftlicher und sozialer Indikatoren*. (2nd ed.). Retrieved from http://www.berlin-institut.org/online-handbuchdemografie/bevoelkerungsdynamik/regionale-dynamik/ostdeutschland.html

Braudel, F. (1949). *La Méditerranée et le monde méditerranéen à l'époque de Philippe II*. (9th ed.). Paris, FR: Armand Colin.

Brubaker, R. (1992). *Citizenship and nationhood in France and Germany*. New York, NY: Cambridge University Press.

Bundeszentrale für politische Bildung. (2010). Survey of inhabitants of the Saxony-Anhalt region, Sachsen-Anhalt Monitor 2007 – Politische Einstellungen zwischen Gegenwart und Vergangenheit (Political opinions between past and present). *Bundeszentrale für politische Bildung*. Retrieved from http://www.bpb. de/geschichte/deutsche-einheit/lange-wege-der-deutschen-einheit/47560/ unrechtsstaat?p=all

Büscher, W. (1998). Drei Stunden Null. *Deutsche Abenteuer*. Berlin, DE: Fest.

Büscher, W. (2005). *Deutschland, eine Reise*. Berlin, DE: Rowohlt Verlag.

Calhoun, C. (1995). *Critical social theory: Culture, history, and the challenge of difference*. Oxford, UK: Blackwell.

Childs, D. (1983) *The GDR: Moscow's German ally*. London, UK: George Allen and Unwin Publishers Ltd.

Connell, R. W. (1987). *Gender and power: Society, the person, and gender politics*. Cambridge, UK: Polity Press.

Connor, W. (1994). *Ethno-nationalism: The quest for understanding*. Princeton, NJ: Princeton University Press.

Corse, S. (1996). *Nationalism and literature: The politics of culture in Canada and the United States*. New York, NY: Cambridge University Press.

Droit, E. (2007). Le goulag contre la shoah. Mémoires officielles et cultures mémorielles dans l'Europe élargie. *Vingtième Siècle, 94*, 101–120. Retrieved from www.cairn.info/revue-vingtieme-siecle-revue-d-histoire-2007-2-page-101.htm (retrieved 14/01/2014).

Felbick, D. (2002). *Schlagwörter der Nachkriegszeit 1945–1949*. Berlin, DE: Walter de Gruyter.

Fine, G. A. (1996). Reputational entrepreneurs and the memory of incompetence: Melting supporters, partisan warriors, and images of President Harding. *American Journal of Sociology, 101*(5), 1159–1193.

Foitzik, J. (ed.). (2012). *Sowjetische Interessenpolitik in Deutschland 1944–1954: Dokumente*. München, DE: Institut für Zeitgeschichte.

Geertz, C. (1973). *The interpretation of cultures*. London, UK: Fontana.

Gibbs, M. (2000). *Propaganda in der DDR, 1949–1989*. Erfurt, DE: Landeszentrale für Politische Bildung Thüringen.

Giddens, A. (1994). *Les consequences de la modernité*. Paris, FR: Harmattan.

Gillis, J. (1994). *Commemorations: The politics of national identity*. Princeton, NJ: Princeton University Press.

Gilman, S. L. (1985). *Difference and pathology: Stereotypes of sexuality, race, and sexuality*. Ithaca, NY: Cornell University Press.

Goldhagen, D. J. (1997). *Hitler's willing executioners: Ordinary Germans and the Holocaust*. London, UK: Abacus.

Gougeon, J-P. (2009). *L'Allemagne du XXIe siècle – Une nouvelle nation ?* Paris, FR: Armand Colin.

Granovetter, M. S. (1973). The strength of weak ties. *American Journal of Sociology, 78*(6): 1360–1380.

Greenfeld, L. (1992). *Nationalism: Five roads to modernity*. Cambridge, MA: Harvard University Press.

Griswold, W. (1992). The writing on the mud wall: Nigerian novels and the imaging village. *American Sociological Review, 57*(5), 709–724.

Grothe, P. (1958). *To win the minds of men—Communist propaganda war in East Germany.* Palo Alto, CA: Pacific Books.

Habermas, J. (1994). Struggles for recognition in the democratic constitutional state. In A. Gutmann (Ed.), *Multiculturalism* (pp. 106–184). Princeton, NJ: Princeton University Press.

Hein-Kircher, H. (2013). "Deutsche Mythen" und ihre Wirkung. *Aus Politik und Zeitgeschichte.* Retrieved from http://www.bpb.de/apuz/156772/deutsche -mythen-und-ihre-wirkung?p=0

Hein-Kircher, H. (2007). Politische Mythen. *Aus Politik und Zeitgeschichte.* Retrieved from http://www.bpb.de/apuz/30604/politische-mythen?p=0

Hobsbawm, E. (1992). *Nations and nationalism since 1780: Programme, myths, and reality.* New York, NY: Cambridge University Press.

Hobsbawm, E., & Ranger, T. (1983). *The invention of tradition.* Cambridge, UK: Cambridge University Press.

Hocquet, M. (2011). *Mémoire, oubli et imaginaires urbains, Étude de deux hauts-lieux de la mémoire communiste à Berlin-Est: Le palais de la république et le musée de la stasi.* (Doctoral thesis in sociology). University of Saint-Etienne, FR. Retrieved from tel.archives-ouvertes.fr/docs/00/69/08/60/PDF/These_-_Hocquet.pdf

Höfele, B. F. (2006). *Deutsche Nationalhymnen: Geschichte – Melodien – Texte.* Norderstedt, DE: Books on Demand GmbH.

Huntington, S. (1996). *The clash of civilizations and the remaking of the world order.* New York, NY: Simon and Schuster.

Jaspers, K. (1953). *The origin and goal of history.* New Haven, CT: Yale University Press.

Kubik, J. (1994). *The power of symbols against the symbols of power: The rise of solidarity and the fall of state socialism in Poland.* University Park, PA: Penn State University Press.

Labrousse, A. (2003). *L'évolution de l'activité féminine en Allemagne orientale. Une analyse institutionnelle comparée.* Working paper 03-2 CEMI (EHESS).

Lane, C. (1981). *The rites of rulers.* Cambridge, UK: Cambridge University Press.

Marshall, T. H. (1964). *Class, Citizenship, and Social Development.* Westport, CT: Greenwood Press.

Mc Cauley, M. (1979). *Marxism-leninism in the German democratic republic: The socialist unity party.* New York, NY: Harper and Row.

Meyer, M. (2009). *Histoire secrète de la chute du mur de Berlin.* Paris, FR: Odile Jacob.

Meyer, M. (2013). *Le Roman de l'allemagne ou l'histoire secrete d'une renaissance.* Paris, FR: Éditions du Rocher.

Miller, D. (1995). *On nationality.* Oxford, UK: Clarendon Press.

Mittler, G. R. (2012). *Geschichte im Schatten der Mauer. Die bundesdeutsche Geschichtswissenschaft und die deutsche Frage 1961–1989.* Zürich, DE: Schöningh.

Nora, P. (Ed.). (1986/1992). *Les lieux de mémoire.* Paris, FR: Gallimard.

Poppe, U. (2010). "Wessis" und "Ossis"—Wirklichkeit oder Stereotyp? In R. Marcowitz (Ed.), *Ein 'neues' Deutschland? Eine deutsch-französische Bilanz 20 Jahre nach der Vereinigung / Une 'nouvelle' Allemagne? Un bilan franco-allemand 20 ans après l'unification. Ateliers des Deutschen Historischen Instituts Paris, vol. 7.* München, DE: Oldenbourg Wissenschaftsverlag.

Reichel, P. (2005). Schwarz – rot – gold. *Kleine Geschichte deutscher Nationalsymbole nach 1945.* Bonn, DE: Bundeszentrale für Politische Bildung Schriftenreihe Band 492.

Rousseau, J. J. (1762). *The social contract or principles of political right.* (G. D. H. Cole, Trans.), Retrieved from www.ucc.ie

Rousso, H. (1987). Vingtième siècle. *Revue d'Histoire, 15,* 151–154, Retrieved from http://www.persee.fr/web/revues/home/prescript/article/xxs_0294-1759 _1987_num_15_1_1913_t1_0151_0000_3

Ruge, E. (2011). *In Zeiten des abnehmenden Lichts.* Hamburg, DE: Rowohlt.

Sachse, C. (2004). "Genosse Direktor, ich melde…" – Zur Militarisierung der Volksbildung in der DDR. Horch und Guck, Zeitschrift der Gedenkstätte Museum in der „Runden Ecke" Leipzig, (pp. 39–47). Retrieved from http://www.horch-und-guck.info/hug/archiv/2004-2007/heft-47/04708/

Schudson, M. (1992). Watergate in American memory. *How we remember, forget, and reconstruct the past.* New York, NY: Basic Books.

Schwartz, B. (1987). *George Washington; The making of an American symbol.* Ithaca, NY: Cornell University Press.

Schwartz, B. (1991). Mourning and the making of a sacred symbol: Durkheim and the Lincoln assassination. *Social Forces, 30*(2), 343–364.

Smith, A. D. (1986). *The ethnic origins of nations.* Oxford, UK: Blackwell.

Smith, A. D. (1991). *National identity.* Reno, NV: University of Nevada Press.

Spillman, L. (1997). *Nation and commemoration: Creating national identities the United States and Australia.* New York, NY: Cambridge University Press.

Stark, H. (2011). *La politique internationale de l'Allemagne. Une puissance malgré elle.* Villeneuve d'Asq, FR: Presses universitaires du Septentrion.

Tamir, Y. (1993). *Liberal nationalism.* Princeton, NJ: Princeton University Press.

Thierse, W. (2013). Künste im geteilten Deutschland. *Eine Erinnerung.* Talk presented at the meeting "Autonomie und Lenkung. Die Künste im doppelten Deutschland" Sächsische Akademie der Wissenschaften zu Leipzig / Zeitgeschichtliches Forum Leipzig, 04/04/2013. Retrieved from http://www.dradiowissen.de/ddr-geschichte-die-normale-und-die-besondere-kunst.88.de.html?dram:article_id=257748

Thürmer-Rohr, C. (2010). Dossier 1989 – und danach? Denkbewegungen vor und nach 1989 (Part 2). Retrieved from http://www.forumcivique.org/de/artikel/dossier1989-und-danach-denkbewegungen-vor-und-nach-1989-2-teil Additional document (Part 1): http://www.forumcivique.org/de/artikel/dossier-1989-%E2%80%93-und-danach-denkbewegungen-vor

Van Den Berghe, P. (1981). *The ethnic phenomenon.* New York, NY: Elsevier.

Volkssolidarität. (2010). Die deutsche Vereinigung—1990 bis 2010—Positionen der Bürgerinnen und Bürger. Im Auftrag der Volkssolidarität–Bundesverband e.V., erarbeitet vom Sozialwissenschaftlichen Forschungszentrum Berlin-Brandenburg e.V., (p. 10). Retrieved from http://www.volkssolidaritaet.de/cms/sozialreport_2010_deutsche_einheit.html; www.volkssolidaritaet.de/cms/vs_media/.../100831SR2010langDF.pdf

Wagner-Pacifici, R. & Schwartz, B. (1991). The Vietnam veterans memorial: Commemorating a difficult past. *American Journal of Sociology, 97*(2), 376–420.

Yèche, H. (2013). Image et instrumentalisation de la culture sorabe dans l'ancienne RDA. *Revue du centre Européen d'etudes slaves–Représentations culturelles et historiques slaves.* Retrieved from http://etudesslaves.edel.univ-poitiers.fr/index.php?id=182

Zerubavel, Y. (1995). *Recovered roots: Collective memory and the remaking of Israeli national tradition.* Chicago, IL: University of Chicago Press.

Zippelius, R. (2006). *Kleine deutsche Verfassungsgeschichte: Vom frühen Mittelalter bis zur Gegenwart.* München, DE: C. H. Beck, Beck'sche Reihe 1041.

LINKS

http://bibliobs.nouvelobs.com/romans/20120203.OBS0514/la-rda-etait-un-projet-utopique.html (retrieved 30/07/13).

http://blog.theeuropean.de/2012/03/homo-digitalis-%E2%80%93-universelle-datenverfugbarkeit-erleichtert-den-alltag-doch-was-bedeutet-das-fur-meine-digitale-identitat/ (retrieved 15/01/14).

http://de.answers.yahoo.com/question/index?qid=20100906114456AA2PVJw (retrieved 08/01/2014).

http://de.statista.com/statistik/daten/studie/180267/umfrage/besonders-wichtig-fuer-die-nationale-identitaet/ (retrieved 15/01/14).

http://einestages.spiegel.de/static/authoralbumbackground/1813/_wir_schaemen_uns_nicht_fuer_unsere_liebesgeschichte.html (retrieved 30/07/13).

http://einestages.spiegel.de/static/topicalbumbackground/3634/kampf_der_moechtegern_metropolen.html (retrieved 28/07/13).

http://germanhistorydocs.ghi-dc.org/sub_image.cfm?image_id=1012 (retrieved 04/01/14).

http://ksta.stadtmenschen.de/blogs/mod_blogs_eintrag/blog/kstablog/thema/Politik_koeln/eintrag/Deutsch_sein_Deutschland_Heimat/ocs_ausgabe/ksta_blogs/index.html (retrieved 15/01/14).

http://mundmische.de/bedeutung/6081-Dunkeldeutschland (retrieved 08/01/2014).

http://verel.typepad.fr/verel/2009/11/etre-chr%C3%A9tien-en-rda.html (retrieved 30/07/13).

http://verel.typepad.fr/verel/2009/11/vivre-en-rda.html (retrieved 30/07/13).

http://www.ac-strasbourg.fr/academie/espace-presse/communique/article/jacques-pierre-gougeon-nouveau-recteur-de-lacademie-de-strasbourg-1/ (retrieved 07/01/14).

http://www.baerbelbohley.de/zitate.php (retrieved 02/01/2014).

http://www.berliner-zeitung.de/berlin/zentraler-gedenkort-die-neue-wache-als-denkmal-fuer-ddr-opfer-,10809148,22092170.html (retrieved 03/01/14).

http://www.berufsverbote.de/ (retrieved 30/07/13).

http://www.bpb.de/apuz/27249/vernetzte-welten-identitaeten-im-internet (retrieved 15/01/14).

http://www.bpb.de/geschichte/deutsche-einheit/lange-wege-der-deutschen-einheit/47423/wohlbefinden?p=all (retrieved 07/01/14).

http://www.bpb.de/politik/hintergrund-aktuell/68778/bundesfreiwilligendi-enst-01-07-2011 (retrieved 05/01/2014).

http://www.bpb.de/veranstaltungen/netzwerke/teamglobal/67376/identitaet-und-kultur-in-einer-globalisierten-welt (retrieved 15/01/14).

http://www.bstu.bund.de (retrieved 03/01/14).

http://www.bundesstiftung-aufarbeitung.de/wettbewerbe-1440.html (retrieved 03/01/14).

http://www.cvce.eu/obj/discours_de_willy_brandt_a_l_occasion_de_la_chute_du_mur_de_berlin_berlin_10_novembre_1989-fr-0f8f11b6-6a7f-4d6d-b925-7c6f71a454cb.html (retrieved 12/01/14).

http://www.dhm.de/ausstellungen/4november1989/cwolf.html (retrieved 02/01/2014).

http://www.documentArchiv.de/in/1945/besatzungszonen-deutschlands_fst.html (retrieved 28/07/13).

http://www.editionsdurocher.fr/Le-Roman-de-l-Allemagne_oeuvre_11012.html (retrieved 07/01/14).

http://www.edouardhusson.com/CV-francais_a211.html (retrieved 07/01/14).

http://www.electru.de/2010-08-02/deutsche-identitaet-von-bratwurst-sprache-und-kultur/ (retrieved 15/01/14).

http://www.eltern.de/foren/2009-plauderforum-neu/1112192-denkt-ihr-ueber-sekundaertugenden.html (retrieved 28/07/13).

http://www.europaforum.public.lu/fr/actualites/2009/01/ipw-expo-chute-du-mur/index.html (retrieved 12/01/14).

http://www.faz.net/aktuell/feuilleton/debatten/zeitgeschichte-war-die-ddr-ein-unrechtsstaat-1813196.html (retrieved 30/07/13).

http://www.forum-3dcenter.org/vbulletin/archive/index.php/t-368808.html (retrieved 08/01/2014). http://www.goethe.de/ges/spa/sui/de2039211.htm (retrieved 15/01/14).

http://www.handelsblatt.com/unternehmen/industrie/20-jahre-wirtschafts-union-welche-ddr-marken-heute-noch-stark-sind/3478302.html (retrieved 30/07/13).

http://www.hdg.de/lemo/html/DasGeteilteDeutschland/index.html (source consultée le 09/10/13).

http://www.his-online.de/en/ (retrieved 03/01/14).

http://www.marianne.net/Personne-n-a-rien-compris-a-la-chute-du-Mur_a182697.html (retrieved 05/01/14).

http://www.mdr.de/geschichte-mitteldeutschlands/magazin/haushalt124.html (retrieved 03/01/14).

http://www.parisberlinmag.com/qui-sommes-nous/ (retrieved 07/01/14).

http://www.rfi.fr/emission/20130921-allemagne-histoire-michel-meyer-roman-re-naissance-edition-rocher (retrieved 07/01/14).

http://www.sciencespo.fr/bibliotheque/pratique/collections/dossiers-pres-se/1949-1961 (retrieved 10/01/2014).

http://www.sinus-institut.de/en/solutions/sinus-milieus.html (retrieved 14/01/14).

http://www.stiftung-denkmal.de/ (retrieved 04/01/14).

http://www.spiegel.de/kultur/gesellschaft/ard-stasi-drama-geliebtes-schnueffel-schwein-a-547539.html (retrieved 30/07/13).

http://www.tagesspiegel.de/kultur/martensteins-holumne-sag-mir-wo-du-stehst/1525580.html (retrieved 30/07/13).

http://www.tagesspiegel.de/meinung/identitaet-wo-bleibt-der-deutsche-traum/3944454.html (retrieved 15/01/14).

http://www.welt.de/fernsehen/article1900356/Stasi-Drama-12-wird-heftig-kritsiert.html (retrieved 30/07/13).

http://www.welt.de/politik/article3649214/Die-Deutschen-lieben-ihr-Land-irgendwie.html (retrieved 15/01/14).

http://www.welt.de/politik/article3775359/Ost-und-Westdeutsche-entfernen-sich-voneinander.html (retrieved 07/01/14).

http://www.zeit.de/2009/06/Martenstein-06 (retrieved 30/07/13).

http://www.zeit.de/online/2009/18/identitaet-deutsche (retrieved 15/01/14).

https://www.dialog-ueber-deutschland.de/DE/20-Vorschlaege/10-Wie-Leben/Einzelansicht/vorschlaege_einzelansicht_node.html?cms_idIdea=205 (retrieved 15/01/14).

www.b4p.de/.../2_3-Menschen-Die-Sinus-Milieus-b4p.pdf (retrieved 14/01/14).

www.bpb.de/themen/YIC2C0.html (retrieved 30/07/13).

www.bundespraesident.de/SharedDocs/Reden/DE/Roman-Herzog/Reden/1996/03/19960326_Rede.html (retrieved 30/07/13).

www.consilium.europa.eu/uedocs/cms.../118813.pdf (retrieved 12/01/14).

www.inter-homines.org/unrechtsstaat_ddr_lstu11.pdf (retrieved 30/07/13).

www.justament.de/archives/1420 (retrieved 30/07/13).

www.sinus-institut.de/ (retrieved 14/01/14).

www.zeit.de/2009/27/Oped-Schwan#commen (retrieved 30/07/13).

CHAPTER 8

NATIONAL IDENTITY IN FRANCE

Immigration and the Validity of Civil Tests

Andrew Milne

In the 1980s, sociologists and politicians in France asked whether it was possible to assimilate immigrants, erasing all traces of their previous cultural background, and thus increasing cohesion in France. Some thirty years later, the question is still being asked, though in a different manner.

Currently, 35% of the French population are immigrants or descendants of immigrants.[1] According to the 2006 French census, 16.9% of people living in France are immigrants (born outside of France to non-French nationals). Approximately 18% of the French population is made up of people born on French soil, but with at least one parent not of French nationality.[2] Immigration and immigrants are important topics in France and at the center of much current debate.

The current question, as opposed to the one asked many years ago, is not about how to assimilate immigrants, but about protecting France from

National Identity, pages 245–270

being substantially changed by the presence of its immigrant populations, and thus about French national identity, which has become a topic of much debate in France. Since 2007, the question of national identity has been brought to the forefront of all debates in France—namely, how best, if at all, to preserve and maintain diversity and at the same time maintain a unique French culture? This question raises many others. Will immigrants be able to maintain their culture in the face of a dominant French culture, which presses them to identify as French? Is it possible to promote not just one but many cultures and at the same time maintain the cultural heritage of France? Is France flexible enough to adapt and take into account the recognition needs of its immigrant populations? By national identity I mean the constructed set of values, symbols, and beliefs that come to be viewed subjectively by a group of people as being ancestrally related and originating in the long-forgotten past that pre-dates even the nation. Nancy Morris calls it "an individual's sense of belonging to a collectivity that calls itself a nation" (Morris, 1995, p. 14).

The values, the symbols, and the beliefs, as well as the mindset, language, traditions, and even religion have become those elements that are to be claimed by a community as common amongst them. Community members might even state that they have a common destiny. Their past, present, and future are controlled for all intents and purposes by a national identity that is considered to be real. Often, national identity is applied to a community grouped together into a nation, and on rare occasions subgroups, such as the Breton community in Brittany, France, or the Corsicans, might state that they too possess a national identity different from the dominant French identity. However, national identity relies upon the subjective belief of a community that is transformed into a state of being. The community believes that they have the common elements that founded their group. National identity is a crucial factor in integrating individuals into a nation. Milton Esman defines national identity as the "set of meanings that individuals impute to their membership in an ethnic community, including those attributes that bind them to that collectivity and that distinguish it from others in their relevant environment. A psychological construct that can evoke powerful emotional responses, ethnic identity normally conveys strong elements of continuity" (Esman, 1994, p. 27).

With this in mind, in recent years integration in France has meant passing a national test (at first in written format and then orally which is administered at the time that an immigrant applies for French nationality). Despite the fact that there was no official law requiring a test to be taken by applicants to nationality, it was systematically carried out. The test attempts to tap into immigrants' knowledge of French culture, and by implication, their desire to be French citizens. But, how valid are these tests at tapping into a respondent's' knowledge of French culture and history, let alone their desire in identifying as French? There is an underlying assumption being made that French citizens are knowledgeable about French culture simply by being born and living in France. If this is so, then French nationals should perform well on these civic exams. The assumption lends itself nicely to an empirical examination. The purpose of my chapter is to test such an assumption. I examine results from tests administered to two populations: a sample of the general French population and a sample of university students. My results seriously call into question the validity of such tests if they assume that French nationals would perform well simply by being born and raised in France. Another validity concern is whether these exams actually measure national identity, but examining such a question is beyond the scope of this chapter.

Before starting my analyses, I provide a brief overview and discussion of the national identity research, how the research is reflected in debates in France, and where France stands in relation to these theories. I am particularly interested in the relationship between France's civic tests and their relationship to the major theories of national identity.

BACKGROUND

Theories of National Identity

Essentialist and Constructivist Theories of National Identity

Essentialists. Essentialist theories regarding national identity espouse the belief that there are innate attributes that are essential to the founding and the functioning of a national identity of a particular nation. The essence of national identity is unalterable, unchanging, and eternal. National identity is fixed and based on ethnicity, a common language, common values, birth, and blood.

Not only does essentialist theory entail the listing of essential elements, but it also allows the condemnation of those that either do not possess these elements, or those that possess different national identities. National identities, as seen through the eyes of essentialists, limit movements and halt changes "to impose a single, drastically simplified group identity, which denies the complexity of people's lives, the multiplicity of their identifications and the cross-pulls of their various affiliations" (Fraser, 2001, p. 24). Culture becomes the property of the dominant group and can only be possessed by that group. All others are forbidden from either participating in or benefiting from the community until they have shown themselves to be worthy: "it risks reifying cultures as separate entities by over-emphasizing the internal homogeneity of cultures in terms that potentially legitimise repressive demands for cultural conformity" (Benhabib, 2002, p. 68).

Essentialist discourse places the value upon bloodlines, ethnicity, and national homogeneity that are unbending and cannot be criticized; it is a fixed and tightly wound viewpoint: "ever more tightly into precisely the same national logic of purity, authenticity and fixity" (Cowan, 2001, p. 171).

Essentialism reduces national identity to elements that are both historicized and yet, at the same time, de-historicized. National identities are built out of a fictitious history that comes to be taken as national tradition, become unchanging and can never be modified. Social and cultural change becomes impossible. All attempts to change national identity are simply returned to the ancestral beginnings of the community, and is so far in the past that it has become unquestionable.

Constructivists. The constructivist approach describes national identity as a socially constructed concept. According to this theoretical paradigm, French national identity is socially constructed, and emerges through the interaction of individuals. National identity is used by politicians to maintain their power by manipulating the population. Politicians, via state institutions, are given the authority of carrying out structural changes, such as domestic and international affairs, and other processes that influence national identity and alter society (Wendt, 1992). Social structures, the patterned and routine ways of behavior and social organization, are controlled by the state.

Individuals or groups that are viewed as speaking "the truth" (Burr, 1995) or those with power (politicians) gain control over identities. They become powerful forces in manipulating a nation's population. The constructivist approach views national identity as continuously and dynamically constructing itself:

> Community exists in the minds of its members, and should not be confused with geographic or socio-graphic assertions of "fact." By extension, the distinctiveness of communities and, thus the reality of their boundaries, similarly lies in the mid, in the meanings which people attach to them, not in their structural forms. (Cohen, 1985, p. 98)

The discourse of national identity in constructivism tends to views immigrants as part of the "Other," rather than the "In" group that adheres to national identity:

> Immigrants are 'Others' within the own national territory, who trigger the explicit or implicit reproduction of categories and characteristics of national identity.... Confronted with or challenged by immigration, nations tend to redefine or reinforce what they believe to be the basic characteristics binding together the members of their particular 'in group.' (Kleiner-Liebau, 2009, p. 34)

Immigrants are seen as a possible source of distorting national identity since they represent different cultures and views of society. Following a constructivist approach, national identities are a collective identity constructed by the belief and the feeling that a community belongs together due to their language, culture, religion, common history, or civic elements (such as secularism in France and the belief that they are "equal" in society). As social roles change in society, so does national identity.

Critique

Identities serve group interests and they are believed to be the essence of a nation, and yet are used for political gain. Huntington believed that one reason why civilizations clashed was due to cultural differences that are immutable, stating that "cultural differences promote cleavages and conflicts" (Huntington, 1996, p. 128). Essentialists believe that identity is ahistorical, coherent, integrated, and fixed. Constructivists believe that national identity can be changed and that politicians use national identity as a means of influencing people. Can we not also consider the development of the *metissage* of society to counteract the Essentialist arguments? There is some danger from political discourse claiming that we must not allow national identity to be altered, and that we must preserve national ideals and myths. For example, does France really treat all its citizens equally despite equality being a significant factor in its national identity motto? Until 2015, France has as its most recent gender-equality law dating back to 1975. The 1975 law and the 2015 laws both promote equality between men and women in the workplace, and yet women continue to earn about 16% less than men for the same job. When did France, upholding the precepts of democracy, have a good rating on the Democracy Index, where it is currently listed as being a "flawed democracy," ranking 27th position (2014) in the world?

Looking back into the past to one's roots may be important to a community; however, one's roots are just a minor part of identity. The problem with national identities is that they tend to be constructed upon myths and lies. They are given a disproportionate place in the nation by the State, as a way of controlling its population. Searching for one's identity is part of growing into something different and it is part of what makes us who we are. However, I would argue that our national identities are not unalterably fixed. Viewing national identity as fixed ultimately places a nation in the past, not the present. Using a civic test to determine one's integration in society is superficial because it fails to tap into a feeling of belonging, nor will it measure the same feelings citizens have of their own country.

When the State only recognizes citizens, it becomes a closed system and blurs the balance between citizenship and nationality, which gave birth to the nation-state:

> The tragedy of the nation-state was that the people's rising national consciousness interfered with these functions. In the name of the will of the people the

state was forced to recognize only "nationals" as citizens, to grant full civil and political rights only to those who belonged to the national community by right of origin and fact of birth. This meant that the state was partly transformed from an instrument of law into an instrument of the nation. (Arendt, 1998, p. 110)

Separating nationality from citizenship would allow Republicans political power (Arendt, 1968). To be sure, citizens would actively participate in public affairs, but national identity would wane. Cultural unity based upon nationality is dangerous, and enforced national identity fragments society. Active citizenship is influenced by making allowance for multiple identities rather than just one national identity.

Essentialists, Constructivists, and National Identity in France

In 2007, the Ministry of Immigration, Integration, National Identity, and Co-development[3] was created by the President at the time, Nicolas Sarkozy, and brought the topics of immigration and national identity to the forefront of national debate. The creation of the Ministry was not merely symbolic, it reflected a real national concern about French national identity and growing fears among some segments of the French population about immigrants and how they were changing French society.

National identity is assumed to create group cohesion through a sense of belonging to a community (Meyran, 2009; Resch, 2001). Creating a feeling of belonging to a country is based on similarity among a national population. Globalization, democratization, and travel all increased contact with other cultures and heightened knowledge of differences among cultures (Huntington, 1997). These factors also led to fears that unique national identities will be lost unless they are protected. In this section, I attempt to place recent debates in France about national identity within the national identity research. That is, I organize the French national identity debates within one of the two major identity models: Essentialist/Primordial versus Constructivist/Postmodernist. I then attempt to identify where France's strategy of testing immigrants' knowledge of French culture falls within this framework.

The Essentialist/Primordial Argument and Practices in France

France's national identity is largely based on cultural elements from the Roman Empire and Antiquity (Resch, 2001). Cultural elements were chosen that are synonymous with the French Republic (the olive branch in the right hand of Marianne, the Fasces of Lictor,[4] etc.), but when they were constructed in the 19th century, they had little to do with France. In creating their national identities, many countries emulated the Roman Republic and aspired to become recognized for their greatness. Mythology is a defining factor in a nation's history, though France presents this mythology as historical fact, thus giving it some legitimacy.

The construction of French identity was clearly planned. In the moments that followed the French Revolution, the revolutionary decision-makers had the belief that there should be complete liberty to speak the language that one should wish in the regions of France. Monarchs in France had done very little historically to stop subjects speaking anything other than their local vernacular. The Ordinance of Villers-Cotterêts (1539) only made French the language of legal documents and the written laws, but it did not impose French as the official language of the nation. However, when the old provinces of the monarchy and the Revolution reinforced the unification of the country and the centralization of the administrative power in France, it became increasingly necessary to construct French identity through the notion of one language and one nation. Allowing the peasants to speak their regional languages would mean that they would remain in obscurantism. French would enable enlightenment and unification. Henri Grégoire wrote the "*Rapport sur la nécessité et les moyens d'anéantir les patois et d'universaliser l'usage de la langue françoise*"[5] in 1794 and presented it to the French state. It showed that at that time only one in five French people actually spoke French. The lack of linguistic uniformity would bring about antidemocratic feelings if the people of the country were unable to understand and participate in debates that were going on in the opinion of the decision-makers. Thus, the objective was to annihilate local minority languages by forbidding them and imposing French as the language of instruction and daily use everywhere. French revolutionaries constructed that unity through language.

Rituals, symbols, and cultural practices are important for national identity. A nation needs shared values in order to be operational (Schnapper, 2007). However, no culture can exist on its own without interaction with other cultures. If it chooses to remain isolated, it will become stagnant in terms of its development (Lévi-Strauss, 1952). We can only be French, by opposition to the British, the Germans, or the Dutch. We can only find identity where we recognize our differences with those that are outside the group. But opposition from within the group is also important for further development. France has faced many external and internal tensions challenging its identity (Lagrange, 2010; Rivera, 2010). Consequently, national identity has emerged as an important topic, especially in the promotion of specific French values and symbols.

However, in promoting national identity, immigrants are portrayed as the Other, not really part of the Republic. The external pressures placed upon France may be due to a feeling of humiliation, defined as "the enforced lowering of a person or group, a process of subjugation that damages or strips away their pride, honour or dignity" (Lindner, 2000). The Old World has been in decline since the late 19th century, and France is one of formerly great old world empires that has been in decline. The French Empire has lost its once-immense power, declining from a world leader to a middle power that attempts to save its lost power by attempting to maintain influence around the world (Wolton, 2004, p. 13). France has endeavored to maintain that influence by threatening other world powers that it will act alone on major global issues, such as when President De Gaulle withdrew from NATO in 1966 due to the lack of fair balance of power between the United States and other members, or with regard to President Bush's invasion of Iraq, and France's threat to use its veto at the United Nations Security Council. France's lost world status has driven it to make superficial and feeble stances on many important global issues.

The invasion of France in June 1940 by Nazi Germany and the occupation of the country, followed by the loss of colonies in Asia and Africa in the 1950s and the 1960s, signaled its historic downfall. The defeat and occupation of France has had a profound effect on the perception of national identity. The historical discourse in the post-war years by De Gaulle strongly promoted the need to present history in other terms, so that the French people might have "dreams that elevate them instead of truths that degrade them" (De Gaulle, 2000).

Other events have also conspired to humiliate France. The recent killings at the satirical newspaper *Charlie Hebdo* in Paris and the subsequent hostage taking at the kosher supermarket by three radical Islamic-fundamentalist terrorists have brought into question the validity of certain policies in France, such as the banning of the wearing of the full veil (September 14th 2010: *Loi interdisant la dissimulation du visage dans l'espace public,* "Act prohibiting concealment of the face in public space") or the real or perceived integration of Muslims in France.

Implemented or proposed policies reflecting the Essentialist paradigm. In the wake of the terrorist attacks in Paris in January 2015 perpetrated against the satirical newspaper *Charlie Hebdo,* political discourse became radically Essentialist. The suburbs, the seat of the apparent social problem in France, according to politicians, is due (in their words) to the violence that categorizes those places. The inhabitants of such places are no longer seen as the result of the social dysfunction of certain zones in the country, but as a sub-population considered to be dangerous for France.

Rather than addressing the problem of inequalities in the suburbs, there have been comments about the need to increase and tighten control of these areas. Essentializing and racializing the immigrant suburbs raises questions about ethnic origins and exacerbates the Essentialist view of national identity. Valérie Pécresse (former spokeswomen of the Sarkozy government between 2011 and 2012 as well as Minister of the Budget at the same date) immediately spoke of the "need for a U.S.-style Patriot Act."

The French government, headed by Prime Minister Valls, had already adopted measures to fight terrorism in September 2014, and in the process eroded civil liberties. These measures included travel restrictions, controlling the freedom of movement via bans on leaving the country, or administrative blocking of certain internet websites. But, in the wake of the terrorist attack in January 2015, Prime Minister Valls proposed individualized prison cells for terrorists' prisoners in an effort of removing the spread of radical and dangerous ideologies into the French suburbs that are perceived to be a threat to France's Essentialist national identity. In 2007, Nicolas Sarkozy's government proposed screening immigration applicants for DNA to prove their genetic bloodlines when applying to join family members; it was refused by the Constitutional Council of France. French decision makers and politicians continue to deny the real source of the problem: social isolation, exclusion, and severe economic inequalities. As Albert Einstein once said, "You cannot solve a problem with the same mindset that created it."

The Constructivist/Postmodernist Argument and Practices in France

Constructivism in France. National identity is based on the invented or imagined history of a nation's past. National identity is a myth, constructed in the present and based on the past (Meyran, 2009; Anderson, 1996; Hobsbawm & Ranger, 1983). A common history is based on ambiguous points of time in the past, handed down from generation to generation, deformed and changed and that becomes a myth. National myths are part of national identity. The origins and beginnings of a nation are either imagined or so far in the past that they are barely recognized by a nations' citizenry, who simply acquiesce and accept these invented/imagined myths.

The French state has addressed its concern about national identity by testing its immigrant populations. The test was the creation of the Ministry. The Ministry was intended to promote national identity in France. Indeed, its main goals may be deduced from its official title: The Ministry of Immigration, Integration, National Identity, and Co-development. Its name embodies a specific ideological view about immigrants and yet is destined to fail in its goal because it negatively emphasizes differences about immigrants; it basically sends a message to the nation that immigrants are the "Other." National identity has been reduced to a list of elements that French citizens should possess as proof of their *Frenchness*.

When the Ministry was created it had four main objectives, which were to:

1. Control immigration in France
2. Create a program of integration for immigrants
3. Conserve and maintain French national identity

4. Provide for the possibility of co-development in the country of origin of immigrants.

There is a current fear of foreigners in France. In times of crisis (economic, social, and political) there is an introverted assertion of one's identity (Ramet & Adamovic, 1995, pp. 102–103).

Globalization has brought about the fear of losing one's national identity in an ever-increasing crisscrossing of geographical and relational boundaries. Technology and other factors have led to growing tensions and fears that national identities will lose or are losing their hold on a nation's population. Identities should be in constant evolution, but the mythological part, a major component of national identity, forbids such flexibility and progress. Identities of nations were chosen and constructed; they are different from the identities of other nations.

Implemented or proposed policies reflecting the Constructivist paradigm. The *Charlie Hebdo* killings drove the state into action. The state debated whether satirical newspapers printing caricatures of Mohammed were tantamount to blasphemy. France, as a secular country, was fearful that there would be misunderstandings about the freedom of speech and the principle of freedom of the press. The state and political leaders used the killings as a means of reiterating the importance of separating Church and State, and thus upholding a long established law: blasphemy has not been considered a crime since 1789 (although they failed to point out that in the region of Alsace-Moselle, the same is not true[6]). The State proposed a superficial ritual.

The State recommended that students take a minute's silence in memory of those killed. Over 200 complaints were lodged because some students refused to participate in the State's recommended ritual. In response, it was suggested that civic education become compulsory and that students be asked to sing the *Marseillaise*, the French national anthem, in class either regularly or every day to ensure that they understand the patriotism that is necessary to live in France. Granted, the singing of a song in unison may arouse sentiments of togetherness and belonging, but a feeling of belonging has to exist in the first place. Politicians in France continue to design and implement strategies driven by a view that national identity is immutable and mythological; it is an illogical and misguided viewpoint.

Critique of the Literature

The problem with the idea of national identity is that it is based on the power of emotional attachment, on inflexibility, and has a negative focus on differences of those who are not in the inner circle (de Buron-Brun, 2010). But, the question remains as to how to create that emotion in immigrant populations. Therein lays the difficulty.

We live in an era of unprecedented melding of cultures. Perhaps we might benefit from actually recognizing positive differences that exist between immigrants and nationals. If we were to peel away these differences, and if we were to concentrate upon the positive aspects, then it might lead to greater understanding and improve the likelihood of integration.

Durkheim advanced the conjecture that humans have two selves. First, there is the individual, composed of unique character traits, personal history, background, and origins. The second self is our social being, made up of the sum of habits, standards, values, ideas, thoughts, and emotions. The sum of our individual and social beings is our personal identity. Durkheim stated,

> There exist two beings, while inseparable except by abstraction, remain distinct. One is made up of all the mental states which apply to ourselves and the events of our personal lives. This is what might be called the individual being. The other is a system of ideas, sentiments and tendencies which express in us, not our personality, but the group of different groups of which we are part; these religious beliefs, moral beliefs and practices, national or professional traditions [. . .]. (Durkheim, 1956, p. 29)

Sarup believes that there are "two models of identity. The traditional view is that all dynamics (such as class, gender, and 'race') operate simultaneously to produce a coherent, unified, fixed identity. The more recent view is that identity is fabricated, constructed, in process, and that we have to consider both psychological and sociological factors" (Sarup, 1996, p. 14). But, if the sum of our individual and social beings is our personal identity, then what is national identity?

It is possible that as society becomes too diverse with too many personal identities that do not resemble each other, it tends to fragment society, but it is also possible that if social unity is too great, society may suffer from a form of sclerosis as noted by Levi-Strauss (1952, p. 41) who pointed out that "... if a culture were left to its own resources, it could never hope to be 'superior' ... and it is for this reason that mankind has remained stationary for nine-tenths or even more of its history." There must be a balance between diversity and unity for a social system to progress.

National identity defines who and what we are in relation to the "Other." Through the construction of national identity we create boundaries; boundaries between things that are and those that are not. The values and symbols chosen are within that boundary, protected against infiltration, and change regardless of whether a group member crosses over a geographical border.

Theory and Research Questions

My basic argument is that national identity is a changing and developing element of the nation, influenced by culture and the mindset of those making up the community. The issue is postmodernist and constructivist, since a test given to applicants for residency confirms the notion that French national identity is not something that is handed down from generation to generation through blood ties, but something that the State believes may be acquired or learned. This raises two questions:

1. Are the present civil tests able to determine immigrants' "Frenchness"?
2. If these tests were valid, how would French nationals perform on these exams?

Both questions lead to the following research hypothesis:

Hypothesis: *French nationals are expected to perform well on these civic exams since they are persons who were born and raised in France and have acquired knowledge and experiences about being French.*

It is with this in mind that I decided to undertake research regarding French nationals and their ability to correctly answer the questions that are asked of applicants for nationality.

METHODOLOGY

The Integration Test

Since the enactment of the July 24, 2006 law (in effect from January 1, 2007) it is a legal obligation for all immigrants who wish to set up residence in France to sign a *"Contrat d'acceuil et d'intégration"* (Welcome and Integration Contract). The contract is usually signed after attending a half-day information class. Before obtaining residency (temporary for the first two years), the immigrant must pass various tests, including a French Language Test. I now discuss other tests.

Integration Test

Immigrants are asked eight questions. At the present time there is a suggested list of questions and no set type of question. In theory, the immigrant may be asked to answer a question on anything related to France, French life and French society. Currently, there are no plans to either publish a full list of questions or to bring out a book that all immigrants should learn in order to pass the test. The French administration refuses to do either of these things since it does not wish immigrants to actually just learn the answers off by heart or to respond without real proof of their form of integration.

Areas of testing. There are two areas which should play an important role in that test: The symbols of the Republic and the values of French society. There are 9 official symbols of the French Republic:

1. Face: Marianne
2. National Anthem: *Marseillaise*
3. Emblem: *Tricolore* flag
4. Motto: *Liberté, Égalité, Fraternité* (Liberty, Equality, and Brotherhood)
5. National holiday: July 14th
6. Founding charter: The Declaration of the Rights of Man and of the Citizen
7. Animal: Rooster
8. Authority: Seal of the Republic
9. One nation: Fasces of Lictor

Values being tested and testing procedures. Five values are officially representative of the French Republic:

1. Rights
2. Equality
3. Fraternity
4. Secularism
5. Protection

After arrival, migrants will be evaluated five times if they request naturalization. First, there will be an interview upon arrival and a request for a visa. It should be noted that this process only pertains to migrants from outside the Europe Union.

Secondly, there will be another test and information gathering during the half-day. The third test will be administered after the first year of French residency. The immigrant will be evaluated a fourth time when applying for a residency permit. The permit can only be applied for after one year and will allow the immigrant to live in France for five years. The permit is renewable. Finally, the immigrant will be evaluated upon filing a request to become a naturalized French citizen.

The questions related to the symbols and the values of the French Republic could be in any format (multiple-choice, open, or closed questions). It is up to the person (prefect or the mayor depending on the size of the town) administering the questions to determine what and how they wish to evaluate an immigrant.

The Questions. The French administration uses eight questions to evaluate immigrants' French cultural knowledge. These items are based on suggested areas to be dealt with by the *Haut conseil à l'intégration* (The High Council for Integration). The questions are:

1. The 14th of July is a national holiday in France. But, what year does it commemorate?
2. What is the name of the text that separated the Church from the State in France?
3. Children that are born outside of wedlock have:
   a. More rights than those born in wedlock?
   b. Fewer rights than those born in wedlock?
   c. The same rights as those born in wedlock?
4. What do the following elements symbolize?

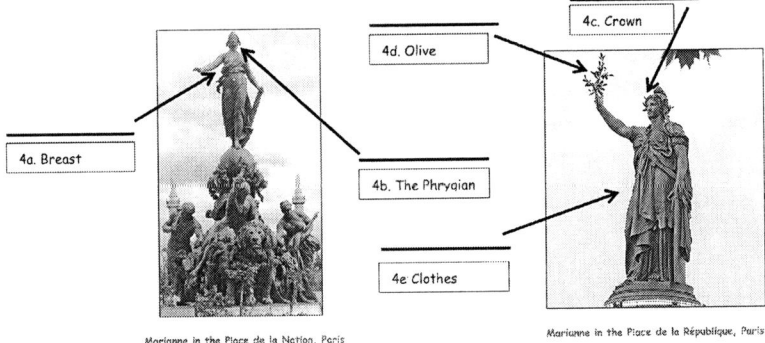

Marianne in the Place de la Nation, Paris   Marianne in the Place de la République, Paris

5. What year did the symbol of Marianne first appear in France?

The first question relates to the foundations of the French Republic and finds its roots in the historical background of the country. The answer that we should be looking for in this instance is, in actual fact, 1790. The French Republic in creating a national holiday on July 14th decided to ignore the date of July 14th 1789 (the Storming of the Bastille) since it was a bloody reminder of the loss of lives in the early hours of the Republic. Instead it was decided that July 14th should commemorate the year 1790 (when there was the *Fête de la Fédération*, or the Federation Festival, on the Champ de Mars in Paris), when French citizens united and celebrated the newly founded Republic in unity.

The second question concerns the central value of France: secularism. The founding text was the law of 1905, the year in which the Church and the State became separate entities. From this date onward, France ceased to have an official religion. Schools became secular institutions and in the name of equality, religion was banished from public life and relegated to the private sphere.

The third question concerns the notion of equality in the Republic. All children, whether born in or out of wedlock, have exactly the same rights as citizens. The question is supposed to test one's knowledge of equality of people in French society.

The images shown of the allegorical figure of Marianne point to central values of the Republic. Marianne is often represented in paintings or statues with a naked breast since she represents the nurturing mother (or wet nurse) of France. The Phrygian cap that she wears is a piece of clothing that dates back to the Roman Empire when freed slaves were given the right to wear it as a means of recognition that they were free. The cap represents French citizens now being free from the slavery of monarchy. The crown represents power of the people. The olive branch is a promise of national peace in response to the bloodshed of the Revolution. Lastly, Marianne wears the clothes of the Roman Empire, because the French Republic will be as strong and as widespread as the Roman Empire once was.

Lastly, with reference to question five, 1792 is the date when the allegorical figure of Marianne first appeared in France.

Clearly, the questions put to immigrants are based on founding symbols and the values of French society, values that one would expect every French-born citizen to know.

Research Samples

I use students as the starting point for the research on the civil tests. Students should be in the best position to answer such questions because they have recently been exposed to French culture and its symbols. I decided to interview the students in their 1st year and 5th year of higher education at university level. The cohort was chosen as a starting point since the Institut d'Études Politiques (Institutes of Political Studies, IEP) is a prestigious establishment in France and part of the Sciences-Po network.

Students enrolled in the IEP are selected for entry through an entrance examination. Traditionally those students with the highest grades after the French Baccalaureate (High-School leaving diploma) are taken after successfully passing the entrance examination. Part of that examination involves French history and general culture of France. Once admitted, students follow set courses in History and Law about France.

It also seemed interesting to interview 5th year students since it would determine whether or not the central values and symbols to the Republic remained engrained 4 years later. So for all intents and purposes we should expect a good score on the civil tests from the two groups of students.[7] The cohort was divided into 2 distinct parts (1st year and 5th year) in order to determine if there was a discrepancy in the answers provided.

In the 1st year cohort the age range of respondents was from 16 to 21 years of age. There were more females than males (61.18% for females and 38.82% for males). This is a demographic factor is exhibited in every year at Sciences-Po. There are a total of 170 students in this cohort. In the 5th year cohort the average age was 23 years old and the ages ranged from 21 to 23 years of age. The ratio of females to males was almost identical as for the 1st year (62.5% for females and 37.5% for males). There were 88 people in this cohort, making a total of 258 people that were interviewed over a period of 4 days at the IEP of Toulouse, France.

With regard to nationality, 162 people out of 170 for the 1st year cohort were French nationals. There were 8 people in this cohort that had dual nationality, French being one nationality. However, it should be stressed that all were born French and not naturalized. The other nationalities were Algerian, Belgian, Congolese, German, Irish, Italian, Swiss, and Turkish.

In the 5th year cohort, 92.05% of the people interviewed were French by birth. There were six people who were dual French nationals (Algerian, Cameroonian, Moroccan, Portuguese, and Swiss). One person was not French, but a Chinese national resident in France for 5 years.

RESULTS

Question One: Commemoration of July 14th

The correct answer to the first question about the commemoration of July 14th should be 1790. For the 5th-year cohort, 5.68% of those questioned provided the correct answer. Some 94.32% provided an incorrect answer. Perhaps this is not surprising since the date of 1789 (and the storming of the Bastille) is so very much a part of French culture and has superseded the date of the Federation Festival of 1790. It is surprising however that one of the questions that is recommended as being a founding element of the French Republic is answered incorrectly by those people that might be the most apt at answering it. Interestingly, one immigrant student also gave the 1789 answer and exhibited his integration in French society, but the French authorities would consider his answer incorrect. There are only five correct answers from the 5th year cohort out of a total of 88 people interviewed.

The 1st year cohort, composed of 170 students, provided the same sort of answers. There is a slight improvement over the score that was provided by the 5th year cohort. Two people interviewed decide not to answer the question. This may be attributed to the fact that students in the 1st year are younger and perhaps not as sure about their responses. There were 37 correct answers and 130 incorrect answers. In percentages this means 1.18% did not provide an answer, 77.06% provided an incorrect answer, and 21.76% provided the correct answer.

Question Two: Separation of Church and State

The second question concerned the separation of Church and State that occurred in 1905. Given the debates that have been occurring all over Europe about religion, especially about the wearing of the Muslim veil, the removal of all ostentatious religious signs in schools,[8] in the civil service or in public places, and the prohibition of the wearing of the Burqa or the Niqab in public places,[9] it would seem that the separation of Church and State in 1905 would be well known by French citizens.

Among the 5th year cohort, 89.77% (79 people) provided the correct answer. Those that did not provide any answer to the question amounted to 6.82% (6 people), while an incorrect answer was provided by 3.41% (3 people). Consequently, almost 90% of the students in the 5th-year cohort replied correctly to the question. It would seem that the secularism of France is well known by this cohort.

The 1st year cohort was more likely than the 5th year cohort to answer incorrectly. However, only 50% (49.41%) provided the correct answer, 20% (20%) did not respond at all, and 30.59% provided an incorrect answer.

If we combine both groups of students, we see a general tendency: 63.18% replied correctly by citing the Law of 1905, 21.32% provide the incorrect answer, and 15.5% leave the answer blank.

Question Three: The Rights of Children Born out of Wedlock in France

The third question concerned the rights of children born out of wedlock in France. The correct answer was: Children born out of wedlock have the same rights as those who are born in wedlock in the name of the Republic's value of equality.

For the 5th year cohort, 88.64% answered correctly, 9.09% incorrectly, and 2.27% failed to provide any answer. It would seem surprising today in French law to imagine that children who are born outside of marriage have fewer rights than those that are legitimate children from the marriage. However, up until 2001 this was not the case.

The 1st year cohort provided 159 correct answers (93.3%), 11 incorrect answers (6.47%), and no questions were left unanswered. The fact that no students left the answer blank suggests that the answer was most likely considered easy by students. How many actually know that it was only introduced legally in the constitution in 2001 is a different matter and perhaps this might be taken further.

Among both samples, a total of 258 people interviewed, 91.86% responded correctly, 7.36% answered incorrectly, and 0.78% left the question blank.

Perhaps the reason behind these excellent scores is that students at the IEP have extensive legal training during their 1st year.

Question Four: French Symbols

Question 4a: The Symbolic Meaning of the Naked Breast of Marianne

Among the 5th year cohort, only 15.9% answered correctly, 67.06% answered incorrectly, and 17.05% left the question blank. Of the 59 incorrect answers, 27 people provided the same incorrect answer of "Liberty." Only 14 people provided the correct answer of the symbolic meaning for a "nurturing foster mother"; the Republic that looks after and protects the citizens of the newly formed State.

The 1st year cohort did a bit worse. Indeed, 13.53% provided a correct answer, 41.18% answered incorrectly, and 13.53% left the question blank.

Overall, 14.34% of the total sample provided a correct answer, despite the fact that the allegorical figure has been part of French symbolism since 1792. It would seem that the deep symbolic meaning is indeed unknown by over half of my sample.

Question 4b: Wearing of the Phrygian Cap

The cap has its origins in Greece (Trojans such as Paris is depicted as wearing one,[10] also Castor and Pollux wear a similar one in mythology), and in the late Roman Republic, symbolizing freedom from tyranny since slavery. The descendants of slaves wore the cap to show that they were emancipated and citizens of the Empire. In France, the origins of the Phrygian cap date back to 1790 in the town of Troyes where it was first seen on a statue representing the nation. It became associated with the idea of freedom and a rallying point to the cause of revolutionaries, during the Great Terror (1793–1794). It also became associated with the figure of Marianne.

For the 5th year cohort there were 9 correct answers (10.23%) and 75 incorrect answers (85.23%), along with 4 answers left blank (4.54%). The vast majority of respondents answered the 'Revolution' (32 people, 42.67%) or the "Republic" (28 people, 31.82%). The original meaning of freedom from slavery and enfranchisement seems to be completely unknown among this cohort.

The 1st-year cohort performed better, with 49 providing correct answers (28.82%), 97 incorrect answers (57.06%), and 24 answers that were left blank (14.12%). There were almost three times more correct answers in this cohort than in the 5th year cohort. There were also more answers that were left blank. There was also a reduction in terms of incorrect answers provided for this question in the 1st year cohort.

Among both cohorts, 66.67% provided incorrect answers to this question, 10.85% left the question blank, and 22.48% answered correctly. One of the important founding symbols of the French Republic is recognized but its symbolic meaning is unknown.

Question 4c: Crown Worn by Marianne

The crown symbolizes the power of the people and the Republic. The 5th year cohort provided 10 correct answers (11.36%), 51 incorrect answers (57.95%), and there were 27 answers left blank (30.68%). The overriding incorrect answer (provided by 22 people) was that of "sovereignty." Eight people replied that the symbolic meaning was "monarchy."

For the 1st year cohort there was a greater number of those not replying to this question (60.59% or 103 people). There was a dramatic decrease in the number of correct answers (3.53% or 6 respondents), and a decrease in the number of incorrect answers (35.88% or 61 people). The two responses that stood out in the list of incorrect answers were "victory" (17 people) and "sovereignty" (16 people).

For both cohorts, 50.39% left it blank. Only 6.20% provided a correct answer, and 43.41% answered incorrectly.

Question 4d: The Olive Branch Held by Marianne

It is meant to symbolize peace after the bloody Revolution.[11] The 5th year cohort provided 63 correct answers (71.59%), 16 incorrect answers (18.18%), and left 9 answers blank (10.23%).

The 1st-year cohort did not perform as well as the 5th year cohort. Sixty-eight people (40%) answered the question correctly. There were 39 people who answered incorrectly (22.94%), and 63 1st year cohort respondents left the answer blank (37.06%). Overall, there were a total of 131 correct answers (50.78%), 21.32% provided an incorrect answer and 27.91% left the answer blank.

Question 4e: Clothes Worn by Marianne

The Roman toga was traditionally worn by Roman citizens only and was not allowed to be worn by slaves nor by workers. One had to be free and a Roman citizen to be able to wear this piece of clothing. The fact that Marianne represents the foster mother of the French people, coupled with the fact that she is sometimes depicted wearing the toga means that the French people benefit from the fundamental rights of the Roman Republic (the right to vote (*jus suffragii*), the right to property (*jus census*), and the right to bequeath one's goods to one's heirs, amongst others.

The question was somewhat difficult to answer correctly among the 5th year cohort. There were no correct answers at all, 39 incorrect answers (44.32%), and 49 answers left blank (55.68%). There were many proposals for the symbolic meaning of the clothes worn by Marianne: 18 different incorrect answers were provided, of which a few stood out (democracy, republic, and Latin heritage).

The 1st year cohort provided answers along the same lines as the 5th year cohort. One person gave the correct answer (0.59%). There were 74 incorrect answers (43.53%) and 95 respondents left the question blank (55.88%). There were 14 different incorrect answers provided by this cohort including once again answers such as "democracy" or "Latin heritage."

Question Five: The Origin Date of Marianne

The 5th and final question of the questionnaire concerned the date when Marianne first appeared. The correct answer is 1792. Marianne was officially adopted by the National Convention of September 25th, 1792 and has been used as the iconic symbol on the Republic's official seals ever since. The figure disappeared under Napoleon (on November 9th, 1799) but resurfaced under the 3rd Republic (1870–1940). In terms of Marianne's origins, it is unclear. Marianne could be based upon the revolutionary Occitan song entitled *Garisou de Marianno* or she could be the contraction of two names Marie and Anne (the aristocracy would have used a hyphen ("Marie-Anne"), whereas the one-word name 'Marianne' would have been considered less aristocratic and more connected with the common people[12]).

The 5th year cohort provided 4 correct answers (4.55%), 50 incorrect answers (56.82%), and 34 respondents left the question blank (38.64%). Amongst the incorrect answers there were 27 different responses were offered by this cohort. Dates range from 1789 to 1974. The overriding answer is the year 1848 (the start of the 2nd Republic in France).

The 1st year cohort provided 5 correct answers (2.94%), 95 incorrect answers (55.88%), and 70 left the question blank (41.18%). The percentages remain very similar between the two cohorts.

Overall, for both cohorts, 3.49% provided the correct answer, 56.2% provided the incorrect date, and 40.31% left it blank.

Given the poor performance on these questions by IEP students, it would seem interesting to widen the scope of the research by examining responses among the general public. My research hypothesis did not receive confirmation from these findings. I did not find that native born students performed well on these questions. More importantly, it tends to cast doubt on the ability of such a test to evaluate the "Frenchness" of natives, much less immigrants. Table 8.1 provides data for the above study.

As a control, I decided to compare these results with those from the general French public.[13] Please refer to Table 8.2.

Overall, the general publics' responses exhibited a strong association with the IEP student responses. I will only focus on those answering correctly. Among the general public, the question with the greatest correct responses was Question 3: equality. For this question, nearly 84% of the public

TABLE 8.1 Overall Numbers and Percentages From Both Cohorts of IEP Students

		Numbers			Percentages		
		Blank	Correct	Incorrect	Blank	Correct	Incorrect
Q1	July 14th	2	42	**214**	0.78	16.28	**82.95**
Q2	Secularism	40	**163**	55	15.50	**63.18**	21.32
Q3	Equality	2	**237**	19	0.78	**91.86**	7.36
Q4a	Foster Mother	85	37	**136**	32.95	14.34	**52.71**
Q4b	Freedom	28	58	**172**	10.85	22.48	**66.67**
Q4c	Peace	**130**	16	112	**50.39**	6.20	43.41
Q4d	Power	72	**131**	55	27.91	**50.78**	21.32
Q4e	Roman Republic	**144**	1	113	**55.81**	0.39	43.80
Q5	1792	104	9	**145**	40.31	3.49	**56.20**

Note: Bolded numbers indicate answers with highest score.

TABLE 8.2 Overall Numbers and Percentages for the General Public

		Numbers			Percentages		
		Blank	Correct	Incorrect	Blank	Correct	Incorrect
Q1	July 14th	33	50	**474**	5.92	8.98	**85.10**
Q2	Secularism	**230**	159	168	**41.29**	28.55	30.16
Q3	Equality	2	**467**	88	0.36	**83.84**	15.80
Q4a	Foster Mother	**214**	151	192	**38.42**	27.11	34.47
Q4b	Freedom	171	69	**317**	30.71	12.39	**56.91**
Q4c	Peace	205	**226**	126	36.80	**40.57**	22.62
Q4d	Power	**276**	35	246	**49.55**	6.28	44.17
Q4e							
Q5	1792	225	56	**276**	40.39	10.05	**49.55**

Note: Bolded numbers indicate answers with highest score.

provided the correct answer. In contrast, question 4d, power, received the lowest correct response rate: only 6% answered correctly

The overall trend of both cohorts combined provided us with the following percentages in Table 8.3. Both samples did not perform well on the test. Of the eight questions that were common between the two cohorts, four exhibited a significant number of incorrect answers (the national holiday, the foster mother of France, freedom and 1792), two had a large number of blanks (peace and power), and questions had a majority of correct responses (secularism and equity). The question regarding equality in the Republic is the only one where a majority of respondents answered correctly (nearly 90% of people answered it correctly).

TABLE 8.3 Responses From Combined IEP and Public				
		Percentages		
		Blank	Correct	Incorrect
Q1	July 14th	3.35	12.63	84.02
Q2	Secularism	28.40	45.86	25.74
Q3	Equality	0.57	87.85	11.58
Q4a	Foster Mother	35.69	20.72	43.59
Q4b	Freedom	20.78	17.43	61.79
Q4c	Peace	43.60	23.39	33.01
Q4d	Power	38.75	28.53	32.74
Q4e				
Q5	1792	40.35	6.77	52.88

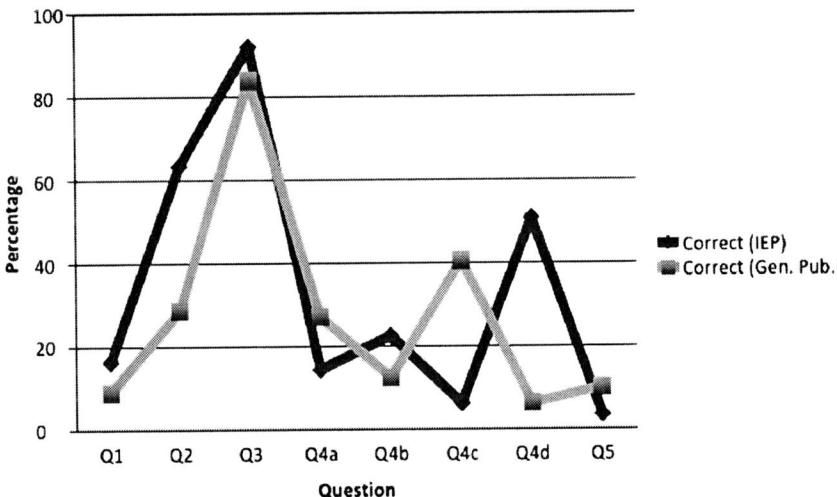

Figure 8.1 Correct answers between IEP cohorts and the general public.

Figure 8.1 displays the relationship between the percentage of correct answers among the IEP cohorts and the general public. Seven of the answers provided by the general public cohort were below 50% (in comparison to five of the IEP cohort).

There is a clear association between the correct responses between both samples. Unfortunately, the overriding conclusion is that both groups would have failed the exam, and failed to qualify for residency in France.

CONCLUSIONS

France, in its attempt at integrating immigrants, has used a strategy of testing their knowledge of French culture and history. The assumption being made by those advocating for the use of the test is that French nationals would perform well on the test simply because they are French. This is an assumption that has received little, if any, empirical examination. The purpose of my chapter was to examine the validity of such an assumption by administering the test to two samples of French citizens: a group of IEP students and the general public.

The findings from my study show that the majority of French nationals have little knowledge of the cultural elements that make up their national identity. While such results do not make them any less French, it does raise serious questions about the validity of the civics test and whether there is a discrepancy between the official French administration and the reality of French society. Will answering these questions ensure that one is more French or that one is more likely to integrate (or is capable of integrating) into French society? Another question that my research raises is: Does it make sense to demand something from immigrants which the general public is unable to provide as well? The civics test is clearly inadequate for its intended purpose.

Integration takes time. Research has consistently found that over time, the children of immigrants and their own children will be well integrated into their host society (Abramson, 1981; Child, 1943; Glazer, 1993; Gleason, 1981; Warner & Srole, 1945; Whyte, 1955). But this research also finds that integration takes many paths, depending on several factors, such the reception context, the socio-economic status of the co-ethnic community, and the degree of hostility/discrimination (Portes & Zhou 1993; Zhou 1997). The linear path that French officials seem to prefer would require developing positive contexts for immigrants, such as economic opportunities for immigrants that would provide economic stability; good, safe school; and the reduction of hostility and discrimination against immigrants.

NOTES

1. Retrieved from http://www.iau-idf.fr/detail-dune-etude/etude/les-descendants-dimmigres-vivant-en-ile-de-france.html on February 23rd 2015.
2. Between September 2008 and February 2009, there was a study carried out ('Trajectoroires et origines'—transalated as Trajectories and Origins) to determine this figure, along with the existing statistics provided by the 'Institut national de la statistique et des etudes économiques' (French National Office of Statistics, INSEE).

3. This ministry became known from 18th March 2008 as the Ministry of Immigration, Integration, National Identity and Joint Development.

4. *Fasces lictoriae* symbolize power in ancient Rome. The lictors were a group of subordinate officials that carried fasces (a bundle of birch rods with an axe blade emerging from the side) and accompanied magistrates. It came to represent both unity (the birch rods were bound together and formed one) and power and jurisdiction. It came to be associated with the unity of France and the supremacy of power and justice in post-revolutionary France.

5. "Report on the Necessity and Means to Annihilate the Patois and to Universalize the Use of the French Language."

6. In 1905, the Concordat of 1801 was abrogated in France, except in the area of Alsace-Moselle. Due to Alsace-Moselle being under German rule at the time, the Concordat still held, meaning that four religions were recognized: the Jewish religion, Catholicism, the Lutheran religion and the Reformed church. Religious education is therefore compulsory there both in primary and secondary schooling (unless the parents opt out of that, with a secular equivalent). It is also true that blasphemy laws must still be abided by (except, naturally, for Islam, since this religion was never recognized as an official religion in 1801 in the original law). So, in theory, it would be acceptable to commit blasphemy against Islam, but not against Catholicism or the other three religions.

7. The interviews took place on November 3 and 4, 2010 (1st year) and November 25 and 26, 2010 (5th year) on the premises of the IEP in Toulouse.

8. This has not been allowed in schools since 2004. As from July 2010 the French national Assembly approved a bill that banned the wearing of full veils on public transport and in public services. In September 2010 this law was extended to cover all public places in France (effective as from April 2011).

9. Despite the fact that the Ministère de l'Intérieur (Home Office) stated in July 2009 that there were only 367 women in France who wore a full veil.

10. A *pileus* or *pileum* was a traditional cap often in felt.

11. The olive branch is often associated with the Roman goddess *Pax* or can find its roots in the olive branch that was carried by the dove as a sign from God to Noah after the Great Flood.

12. There is also the added reference here to the name of Mary, mother of Jesus and her own mother, Anne. Thus, the result is that we have a religious element that is the founding symbol of a secular country today. This seems to point to the fact that France has only been secular since 1905. However, the religious aspect in the reading of the symbol of Marianne seems to have been lost today by French citizens. Secularism is so part and parcel of their make-up in society today that they could hardly conceive of there being any time presecularism.

13. A study was carried out via a questionnaire on internet made available to the general public between January 26th and January 31st 2011. This cohort will be referred to as the 'general public cohort' and was made up of 557 people. Ages ranged from 18 to 46 years old, but the vast majority (447) was aged between 19 and 25 years old. This was important since the ages corresponded to the ages that we had already interviewed at the IEP and meant that a cor-

relation would be significant. The general public cohort was made up of predominantly French nationals (537 people or 96.41%).

REFERENCES

Abramson, H. J. (1981). Assimilation and pluralism. In S. Thernstrom (Ed.), *Harvard encyclopedia of American ethnic groups* (pp. 150–160). Cambridge, MA: Harvard University Press.

Anderson, B. (1996). *L'Imaginaire national: Réflexions sur l'origine et l'essor du nationalisme.* Paris, France: La Découverte & Syros.

Arendt, H. (1958/1998). *The human condition.* Chicago, IL: University of Chicago Press.

Bak, J. (2007). *La société mosaïque.* Paris, France: Dunod.

Burr, V. (1995). *An introduction to social constructionism.* London, England: Routledge

Benhabib, S. (2002). *The claims of culture: Equality and diversity in the global era.* Princeton, NJ: Princeton University Press.

Calhoun, C. (1994). *Social theory and the politics of identity.* Cambridge, MA: Blackwell Publishers.

Cohen, A. (1985). *The symbolic construction of community.* London, England: Routledge.

Cowan, J. (ed.). (2001). *Culture and rights: Anthropological perspectives.* Cambridge, MA: Cambridge University Press.

Child, I. L. (1943). *Italian or American? The second generation in conflict.* New Haven, CT: Yale University Press.

Daniel, J. (2008). Comment peut-on être français? *Entretien sonore: Fadela amara.* Vincennes, France: Frémeaux & associés.

De Buron-Brun, B. (2010). *Altérité-identité-interculturalit: Perceptions et représentations de l'Étranger en Europe et dans l'arc Atlantique.* Paris, France: L'Harmattan.

De Gaulle, C. (2000). *Mémoires.* Paris, France: Gallimard.

Dessajan, S., Hossard, N., Ramos, E. (2009). *Immigration et identité nationale: Une altérité revisitée.* Paris, France: L'Harmattan.

Dubar, C. (2000). *La crise des identités.* Paris, France: Presses Universitaires de France.

Durkheim, E. (1956). *Education and sociology.* New York, NY: Free Press.

Esman, M. (1994). *Ethnic politics.* Ithaca, NY: Cornell University Press.

Fraser, N. (2001). Recognition without ethics. *Theory, Culture and Society, 18*(2), 21–42.

Finkielraut, A. (2007). *Qu'est-ce que la France?* Paris, France: Éditions Stock.

Glazer, N. (1993). Is assimilation dead? *The Annals of the American Academy of Political and Social Science, 530,* 122–136.

Gleason, P. (1981). American identity and americanization. In S. Thernstrom (ed.) *Harvard encyclopedia of American ethnic groups* (pp. 31–58). Cambridge, MA: Harvard University Press.

Heran, F. (2007). *Le temps des immigrés: Essai sur le destin de la population française.* Paris, France: Seuil.

Hobsbawm, E., & Ranger, T. (1983). *The invention of tradition.* Cambridge, England: Cambridge University Press.

Huntington, S. P. (1996). *The clash of civilizations and the remaking of world order.* New York, NY: Simon & Schuster.

Huntington, S. P. (1997). *Le choc des civilisations.* Paris, France: Éditions Odile Jacob.

Kastoryano, R. (2005). *Les codes de la différence.* Paris, France: Presses de la Fondation nationale des sciences politiques.

Kleiner-Liebau, D. (2009). *Migration and the construction of national identity in Spain.* Madrid, ES: Iberoamericana Editorial Vervuert S. L.

Kozakaï, T. (2000). *L'étranger, l'identité: Essai sur l'intégration culturelle.* Paris, France: Payot et Rivages.

Lagrange, H. (2010). *Le déni des cultures.* Paris, France: Seuil.

Lassalle, D. (2009). *L'intégration au royaume-uni: Réussites et limites du multiculturalisme.* Paris, France: Éditions Ophrys.

Lévi-Strauss, C. (1952). *Race and history.* Paris, FR: UNESCO.

Lévi-Strauss, C. (2001). *Race et histoire /Race et culture.* Paris, France: Albin Michel.

Lindner, E. (2000). What every negotiator ought to know: Understanding humiliation. *Oslo and coalition for global solidarity and social development.* Peace and Conflicts. Retrieved from http://www.humiliationstudies.org/documents/evelin/Negotiator.pdf

Meyran, R. (2009). *Le mythe de l'identité nationale.* Paris, France: Berg International.

Morris, N. (1995). *Puerto Rico: Culture, politics, and identity.* Westport, CT: Praeger.

Pelissier, M., Paecht, A. (2004). *Les modèles de l'intégration en question – Enjeux et perspectives.* Paris, France: IRIS.

Portes, A., & Zhou, M. (1993). The new second generation: Segmented assimilation and its variants. *The annals of the academy of political and social science, 530,* 74–96.

Resch, Y. (2001). *Définir l'intégration? Perspectives nationales et représentations symboliques.* Montreal, CA: XYZ Editeur.

Ramet, S., & Adamovic, L. (1995). *Beyond Yugoslavia: Politics, economics, and culture in a shattered community, Eastern Europe after communism.* Boulder, CO: Westview Press.

Rivera, A. (2010). *Les dérives de l'universalisme: Ethnocentrisme et islamophobie en France et en Italie.* Paris, France: La Découverte.

Sarup, M. (1996). *Identity, culture and the postmodern world.* Athens, GA: University of Georgia Press.

Schnapper, D. (2007). *Qu'est-ce que l'intégration?* Paris, France: Gallimard.

Warner, W. L., & Srole, L. (1945). *The social systems of American ethnic groups.* New Haven, CT: Yale University Press.

Wendt, A. (1992). Anarchy is what states make of it: The social construction of power politics. *International Organization, 46,* 391–425.

Whyte, W. F. (1955). *Street corner society.* Chicago, IL: University of Chicago Press.

Wolton, T. (2004). *Brève psychanalyse de la France.* Paris, France: Plon.

Zhou, M. (1997). Growing up American: The challenge confronting immigrant children and children of immigrants. *Annual Review of Sociology, 23,* 63–95.

PART III

NATIONAL IDENTITY: THE IMMIGRANT EXPERIENCE

"HOW CAN I FEEL BELGIAN IF BELGIANS DON'T ACCEPT ME?"

Ethnic Boundary Perception and National Identity Among Turkish Belgians

Klaartje Van Kerckem

This chapter presents an empirical study about perceptions of exclusion by the mainstream among Turkish Belgians, and how these perceptions shape their national and ethnic self-identifications. Being Europe's largest immigrant and Muslim population, Turkish Europeans have been the target of many anti-immigrant and Islamophobic sentiments and practices. Different studies demonstrate that stereotypes and anti-immigrant sentiments are stronger towards Muslims, compared to other immigrant groups (Allen & Nielsen, 2002; Strabac & Listhaug, 2008).

In many European countries, the strained relationship between the mainstream population on the one hand, and several Muslim populations on the other hand, can best be described as "bright ethnic boundaries"

National Identity, pages 273–309
Copyright © 2016 by Information Age Publishing

(Alba, 2005). Muslim immigrants and their descendants not only experience general anti-immigrant sentiments, but are also seen as the quintessential Other that is difficult to integrate (Betz & Meret, 2009; Field, 2007; Kunst, Tajamal, Sam, & Ulleberg, 2012). In both everyday and public discourse, Muslims are depicted as *"the outsider within"*: a group that is different from "Europeans" in terms of culture and religion, and therefore non-belonging.

In addition to such discursive practices of *Othering* (Jensen, 2011; Schneider, 2001), there is also the de-facto exclusion of members of Muslim groups, through everyday and institutional discrimination in the labor market, in housing, in education, and in social relations (De Rycke, Swyngedouw, & Phalet, 1999; Granato & Kalter, 2001; Silberman, Alba, & Fournier, 2006; Skrobanek & Jobst, 2010; Stevens, 2008; Vandezande, Fleischmann, Baysu, Swyngedouw, & Phalet, 2009; Van der Bracht & Van de Putte, 2013). Muslims are an excluded group.

I have two objectives in this study. First, I wish to explore how exclusionary practices are experienced by members of the Turkish population in Belgium. A large number of studies focus on various ways in which individuals and institutions from the mainstream culture draw and enforce ethnic boundaries, but little is known about how members of the targeted group experience and interpret these exclusionary behaviors and practices in their daily lives. This is an important issue in studying the impact of exclusion on subjective perceptions of *belonging*, and *ethnic* and *national self-identification*.

I argue that in exploring how exclusionary practices are experienced, it is important to pay attention to both *behavioral* and *symbolic* practices. Most studies that focus on how an exclusionary context shapes national or ethnic self-identification take *perceived discrimination* as their independent variable. However, ethnic boundaries have both a symbolic and a behavioral dimension (Wimmer, 2013), and it is therefore important to not only focus on perceived *behavioral* discrimination, but also to study how ethnic boundaries are constructed through discourse and other forms of *symbolic* representation and how this is perceived by members of minority groups.

A second objective of this study is to examine how exclusionary discourses and behaviors shape Turkish Belgians' ethnic and national self-identification. Acts of categorization and exclusion can have a far-reaching impact on ethnic minorities' self-identification (Jenkins, 2008; Rumbaut, 2005; Waters, 1990), and the discursive context in which the second generation grows up directly affects feelings of belonging (Crul & Schneider, 2010). Surprisingly, European scholarship has devoted very little attention to how anti-immigrant and Islamophobic sentiments and discourses shape the self-identification of Muslim immigrants and their descendants. A limited number of studies have investigated how *perceived discrimination* affects self-identification, ethnically and nationally (Martinovic & Verkuyten, 2012; Maxwell, 2009; Skrobanek, 2009). Yet, much less research has been conducted on how *discursive boundary drawing*—for instance through practices of Othering, categorization, or subtle "everyday racism" (Essed, 1991)—shapes national and ethnic identification. In this study, I address both.

The structure of this chapter is as follows. After a brief introduction to the Turkish population in Belgium, I introduce the theoretical model that will guide the data analysis. I start with a discussion of mechanisms of ethnic boundary construction, focusing on both its behavioral and symbolic dimensions. This section subsequently reviews theories of ethnic and national identification, paying particular attention to the importance of the internal-external dialectic of identification. In the final part of the theoretical section, I put the two together to build a theoretical model that can help to analyze how symbolic and behavioral exclusion shapes ethnic and national identification.

After an overview of the data and methods used, I present the findings to the two main research questions. I start by analyzing the participants' *narratives of exclusion*, discussing the different ways in which Turkish-Belgian research participants experience exclusion in their everyday lives. In the second part of the analysis, I analyze the participants' *identity narratives,* and link them to their narratives of exclusion. I distinguish five different narratives, based on how Turkish Belgian research participants position themselves in terms of national and ethnic identity, and draw attention to the *internal-external dialectic of identification*—how self-identity is shaped by both internal assertions and external categorizations (Jenkins, 1994). As such, I set out to demonstrate that both context (exclusion and Othering) and self-understandings interact in the formation of a stable identity, and that people are active agents in constructing their own identities by reclaiming, reaffirming, or rejecting those identities that they are denied from the outside.

THEORETICAL BACKGROUND

Turks in Belgium: A Brief History

Turkish migration to Belgium offers a classic example of the labor migration typical in Western Europe during the 1960s and early 1970s (Reniers, 1999). Immigrants originated mainly from rural areas in Turkey and had little or no formal education (Phalet & Heath, 2011). In 1961, 320 Turkish nationals resided in Belgium, but by 1970 the number increased to 20,000 (Schoonvaere, 2013). In 1974, the Belgian government stopped granting visas to low-skilled workers in 1974, but migration from Turkey continued, via family reunification and family formation. The Turkish population is now the fifth largest foreign population in Belgium behind the Moroccan, Italian, Dutch, and French populations.

Over fifty years after the first Turkish migrants arrived in Belgium, ethnic boundaries between the established population and Turkish Belgians are still *bright*, both in social and symbolic terms. The social aspect of the boundary is reflected in high inequality and an ethnic patterning of social relations. Turks occupy one of the lowest rungs on the socioeconomic ladder and are "at the bottom of the ethnic hierarchy" (Phalet & Heath, 2011, p. 162). Turkish immigrants and their offspring are among the most disadvantaged members in Belgian society in terms of educational attainment (Timmerman, Vanderwaeren, & Crul, 2003). Although the second generation does significantly better than their parents in terms of educational attainment, the "ethnic disadvantage" (Phalet & Heath, 2011) persists into the second generation. A significant number of Turkish children are funneled into lower-ranked vocational tracks, have drop-out rates four times greater than Belgian students, and the number of Turkish Belgians who attend university is low (Duquet, Glorieux, Laurijssen, & Van Dorsselaer, 2005; Lacante et al., 2007; Phalet, Deboosere, & Bastiaenssen, 2007). Additionally, the unemployment rates for Turkish Belgians are much greater than for the Belgian population. Moreover, Turkish Belgians are less likely to enter professional, administrative, and managerial careers (Phalet & Heath, 2011; VDAB, 2012; Vertommen & Martens, 2005).

Social boundaries may also be measured by intermarriage rates. In 1991, 7% of all married Turkish men and 3.8% of Turkish women had a Western-European spouse (Lievens, 1999). A recent study documents an increase in intermarriage rates between Turks and Western Europeans over the past two decades, but numbers still remain relatively low: 14.3% of the Turkish men who got married in 2008—but only 8.2% of the women—married an EU-citizen (Van Kerckem, Van der Bracht, Stevens, & Van de Putte, 2013).

Belgium is one of Europe's "leading" countries regarding racist and anti-immigrant sentiments and right-wing opinions (Quillian, 1995; Zick, Pettigrew, & Wagner, 2008). In addition, such sentiments are consistently stronger when it concerns Muslims. For instance, in 2000, Belgium ranked second compared to 29 other European countries in terms of ethnic prejudice towards Muslims, with 22.7% of the respondents objecting to a Muslim neighbor (Strabac & Listhaug, 2008). These findings have been corroborated by Billiet and Swyngedouw (2009), who report that in Flanders, 48% of the voters have "an extremely negative opinion on Islam and Muslims," 42% consider Islamic culture more violent than other cultures, and a stunning 81% believe that Muslim men are "too domineering" towards their women. In Flanders, these Islamophobic and anti-immigrant sentiments are reflected in high political racism, expressed as a vote for Vlaams Belang, an extreme-right wing party with anti-immigrant views (Billiet & De Witte, 2008). Undoubtedly, the violence committed by a few Muslim extremists, and the January 2015 and June 2015 attacks in France, are fueling and exacerbating Islamophobia and anti-Muslim sentiments. Given these attitudes, it should not surprise that Turkish Belgians—being Muslim—experience much discrimination, especially in the labor market and in housing (De Rycke et al., 1999; Stevens, 2008; Van der Bracht & Van de Putte, 2013).

Boundary Construction by the Mainstream

The above described forms of exclusion and Othering can all be regarded as ways in which the mainstream contributes to the construction of the ethnic boundary between the established population and people of Turkish descent. According to Barth (1969), ethnic boundaries between groups do not persist because of continuing cultural differences, but because of the continuous construction of these boundaries by groups on both side of the boundary. Processes of ethnic boundary construction can be subdivided into two separate, but equally important mechanisms: (a) marking the boundary—the symbolic dimension of ethnic boundary construction; and (b) creating barriers that structure intergroup relations and access to resources—the behavioral component of ethnic boundary construction. Both dominant and subordinate groups actively take part in the construction of ethnic difference and boundaries. For the purpose of this study, however, I limit the following discussion to the different ways in which the *established population* draws boundaries (for an example of how subordinate groups draw boundaries, see Van Kerckem, Van de Putte, & Stevens, 2013).

Symbolic Dimension of Boundary Construction

A first step towards the construction and maintenance of a boundary is the continuous dichotomization and marking of a symbolic boundary between insiders and outsiders (Barth, 1969; Lamont & Molnar, 2002; Wimmer, 2013). This process of boundary marking consists of the categorization of others as members of another group, as well as the identification of particular contrasting cultural diacritica—a careful selection of those cultural differences that help to define one's group identity in opposition to that of the other group. It is through these carefully chosen contrasting diacritica that dichotomous notions of "us" versus "them" are created, lumping individuals together in "objectively" differentiated groups.

Symbolic boundaries are essentially cognitive, but they tend to manifest themselves through discourse—language in use, both in spoken and written form. On a micro-level, examples of discursive boundary drawing include practices of social categorization and Othering. The practice of

Othering serves to mark and name those thought to be different from one-self, and magnifies and enforces the idea that "the other" is essentially different (Weis, 1995). In essence, Othering is a type of discursive *everyday racism*—a term coined by Essed (1991) to refer to "practices that infiltrate everyday life and become part of what is seen as 'normal' by the dominant group." In societies where most citizens express commitment to democratic principles of justice, equality, and fairness, the notion of *everyday racism* is important to understand how ethnic and racial inequalities and boundaries are perpetuated (Beagan, 2003).

Taken individually, the effect of each utterance might seem trivial, but the cumulative impact is far less so: "Each racist joke, each racist assumption, occurs in the context of a personal and collective history of such trivial incidents, in the context of one's own past experiences of racism and the experiences of friends and loved ones" (Beagan, 2003, p. 853).

Boundary construction is not necessarily restricted to the micro-level: symbolic boundaries can also be marked on a meso- or macro-level, outside of direct interaction. Examples include political pamphlets of anti-immigrant parties, policy documents that focus on integration of immigrants/ethnic minorities, or representations of Muslims in print media. Considering that public discourse is typically transmitted through the media, media play a very important role in shaping and reproducing interethnic relations, ethnic boundaries, and identities. Consequently, the media have to be a major target in the analysis of identity politics and boundary work (Schneider, 2001).

Behavioral Dimensions of Boundary Construction

The symbolic dimension of ethnic boundary construction can be coupled with a behavioral dimension, in which case people behave in a particular way vis-à-vis in-group and out-group members. Behavioral dimensions of ethnic boundary construction include processes related to social closure—the creation of barriers that make valued resources within the group unavailable to outsiders—as well as processes that aim to strengthen in-group cohesion. Social closure typically occurs through discrimination of members of the other group, hence denying them access to resources within one's own group. Wimmer (2013) distinguishes three modes of discrimination, depending on the degree of formalization. *Legalized discrimination* is formal and involves the institutionalization of ethnic boundaries by differentiating between the rights of members of different ethnic categories. Extreme examples include South Africa's Apartheid regime in the mid-1900s and American Jim Crow Laws of the late 19th and early 20th century. *Institutional discrimination* refers to discrimination that is part of the day-to-day workings of the state administration that lacks a legal basis. Wimmer (2013) gives the example of preference and quota policies as a soft form of institutionalized ethnic discrimination. *Everyday discrimination,* finally, happens in interactions outside the domains of state control. Examples here include discrimination by employers in the labor market or by property owners in the housing market.

Symbolic and Behavioral Exclusion of Turkish Belgians

To what extent now are Turkish Belgians the targets of symbolic and behavioral exclusion? Given that most people of Turkish descent are Muslim, and increasingly perceived as such by the established population, symbolic and behavioral exclusion of Turkish Belgians should be considered against the backdrop of the country's attitude towards Islam and Muslims.

In European immigration debates and public discourse, Islam is the focus of attention, because European identity, despite national variations, remains deeply embedded in Christian tradition in which Muslim immigrants constitute a visible "other" (Zolberg & Woon, 1999). In Europe, religious boundaries function in the same way as racial boundaries in the United States (Bail, 2008; Foner & Alba, 2008): it is religion—more specifically Islam—that marks the boundary between "us" and "them," between those who belong to the mainstream and those who are considered outsiders. The boundary is "bright" (Alba, 2005) because there is no ambiguity over who belongs where: Islam and the culture of Muslims are presented as essentially different from Western values, and more often than not they are essentialized and represented as monolithic, unchangeable, and incompatible with European identity. Given that most Turks in Europe are Muslim, Turkish Europeans are—together with those of Moroccan descent—considered as prototypical foreigners and essential others (for Belgium, see Spruyt & Elchardus, 2012).

The contemporary perception of Islam can be seen as an example of neo-orientalist thinking (Saeed, 2007) in the sense that it homogenizes and essentializes the Muslim population, and represents so-called Muslim culture and religion as essentially different from Western identity. Muslim societies and culture are represented as overly patriarchal, and characterized by tribal or feudal values and a culture of honor in which the status of women is low. In contrast, the prototypical European is conceived of as modern, tolerant, equality-minded, and individualist (Razack, 2004). The image of the Muslim today strongly resembles Mosse's description of "the Wandering Jew" decades ago: "The eternal foreigner in our midst who clings to his backwardness and who could never learn to speak the national language properly or strike roots in the soil" (Mosse, 1985, p. 115).

When it comes to behavioral boundary drawing, several studies point out that in Europe (and Belgium is no exception), discrimination versus Muslims is pervasive in many countries and different domains of life. Everyday discrimination of Turkish Belgians has been documented in the labor market, housing market, in public space, and in contact with authorities (Kalter & Kogan, 2006; Van der Bracht & Van de Putte, 2013; Vandezande et al, 2009).

In addition, Muslims are also prone to legalized and institutional discrimination. A typical example of institutional discrimination is the prohibition of headscarves in all GO! schools—the public school system in Flanders. On September 11, 2009, the Board of GO! Introduced a general ban prohibiting the display of religious and philosophical symbols, a ban that applied to pupils, teachers, and anyone else charged with pedagogical tasks. According to Amnesty International, such a ban "has a disproportionate impact on Muslim girls who wish to wear headscarves and discriminates against them in the exercise of their rights to freedom of religion or belief and to freedom of expression." (Amnesty International, 2012, pp. 64–65). Institutional discrimination also occurs because certain institutions are not (yet) adapted to increasing linguistic and religious diversity in society, resulting in discrimination against members of particular immigrant populations. Examples of such indirect discrimination include observance of Catholic national holidays, but not Islamic ones, and the lack of attention paid to dietary restrictions of particular religious groups in private or public institutions.

Legalized discrimination, finally, can be found in the nation-wide prohibition against wearing a full veil that covers the face in public. According to Human Rights Watch, this prohibition "violates the fundamental right to freedom of religion, thought, and conscience as well as the right to personal autonomy." The law prohibits "the wearing of clothing that conceals the face partially or entirely in public places in a way that makes identification impossible." As such, one could say it is formulated neutrally, but, in fact, it is clearly targeted towards Muslim women wearing a niqab or burka (it is commonly referred to as "the burka ban") as it disproportionately targets them. A second example of indirect legalized discrimination is the tightening of the regulation of marriage migration. Even though the law applies to all Belgian citizens, it mainly targets Turkish and Moroccan Belgians, as they are the ones who more commonly marry transnationally. In response to a similar law passed in the Netherlands, Human Rights Watch has warned that the law "disproportionately impacts two of the largest migrant communities in the Netherlands—Moroccans and Turks—who wish to bring family members to the Netherlands." Consequently, it might give people of these origins the feeling they are being discriminated against, even by the state they are born in, which potentially reinforces their sense of exclusion.

To the best of my knowledge, apart from a number of quantitative studies on discrimination, very little research has been carried out on how Muslims—in this case Turkish Belgians—experience the above described

mechanism of boundary construction. A first objective of this study, therefore, is to examine in what ways Turkish Belgians experience boundary
construction in their daily lives. By analyzing their narratives of exclusion,
I hope to get a better insight into different mechanisms of boundary construction—both symbolic and behavioral—and Turkish Belgians' subjective
experiences of exclusion.

By most indicators, Turks in Belgium are considered Outsiders, and this
has affected socioeconomic status as well as the degree to which they identify as Turkish, as Belgians, or as both Turks and Belgians. In the next section
I review the research on ethnic and national identity and use it in formulating my thoughts about how boundary mechanisms shape the national and
ethnic identity of the Turkish population in Belgium.

Theories of Ethnic and National Identity

Theories of ethnic and national identity can be broadly subdivided in two
strands, namely essentialism, which sees groups and identities as stable and
rooted in nature, and constructivism, which regards groups and identities as
social constructions, and therefore multiple, fluid and context-dependent.

Essentialist and Primordialist Visions of Ethnic and National Identity

Essentialism can be defined as "the attribution of behavior or thinking to the intrinsic, fundamental nature of a person, collectivity, or state."
(Suny, 2001). Essentialist visions of identity accept identity as stable, singular, bounded, internally harmonious, and rooted in nature. Within an essentialist view, ethnic and national communities and identities are seen as
having grown organically out of preexisting cultural communities (Eriksen,
2001). Such a view aligns with a Herderian social ontology that sees each
people as defined by three characteristics: the formation of a community
held together by strong ties among its members, a shared group identity
based on a sense of shared historical destiny, and a common culture and
language.

Essentialist approaches to nationalism stress that national and ethnic
identity are inextricably linked, in the sense that nations represent (dominant) ethnic groups, and that, therefore, ethnic and national identities are
essentially the same. Smith (1991), for example, stresses the importance of
preexisting ethnic groups for the development of nationalism. Such a view
leaves little room for hybrid and multiple identities, as one's ethnic identity
is seen as defining one's national identity. As such, immigrants or ethnic
minorities are easily considered as outsiders, who have pre-existing ethnic
or national attachments, and can therefore not identify with the (new) nation. Such a view has its roots in *primordialism*—which stands for "the idea

that ethnic and racial identities are fixed, fundamental, and rooted in the unchangeable circumstances at birth" (Cornell & Hartmann, 2007).

In academia, this view has been criticized extensively (See for instance Cornell & Hartmann, 2007; McKay, 1982), and for many social scientists, essentialism and primordialism now "appear as dated as pre-darwinian biology" (Eriksen, 2001, p. 45). In European public and political discourse however, primordialism and essentialism still hold sway. As I have demonstrated above, certain ethnic and religious groups—in this case Turkish Muslims—are regarded as the essential other that will never be able to adapt to European society, as their values and identities are incompatible and essentially different.

However, some scholars still see merits in the primordialist approach (Bayar, 2009; Roosens, 1994). Those who do, do not see ethnicity as anchored in blood ties, given by birth, fixed and unchanging, but draw attention to the idea of *constructed primordialities*. This refers to the idea that ethnicity is often felt or constructed as being something primordial:

> Whatever [the] actual origins, [ethnicity is] experienced by many people as touching something deeper and more profound than labels or interests or contingency. This felt power...seems to be rooted in intimately shared experiences and interactions, in the sense of connection to the past, and in the quasi-mystical significance often attributed to blood ties. (Cornell & Hartmann, 2007, p. 93)

The power of these so-called *primordial attachments* (Geertz, 1963) lies in the human need to belong to communities of interaction and meaning, based on something more meaningful than mere rational or utilitarian interests (Shils, 1957). Even in increasingly individualized industrial and postindustrial societies, individuals need relationships that give them a feeling of deep and lasting connectedness, and ethnic and racial ties often satisfy this need (Cornell & Hartmann, 2007, p. 58).

Constructivist Approaches to Ethnic and National Identity

Nowadays, most social scientists agree that ethnic and national identities are not fixed and unchangeable but rather fluid, dynamic, constructed, and situational (For national identity see Anderson, 2006; Gellner, 1997; for ethnic and racial identity see Hall, 1992; Jenkins, 2008; Nagel, 1994; Waters 1990). Moreover, constructivists do not see identities as singular and internally harmonious, but rather as hybrid, complex, and multidimensional. Following McBeth (1989), Nagel (1994) talks about the "layering of ethnic identity," arguing that every individual carries a portfolio of identities that are more or less salient in various situations and vis-à-vis various audiences. For instance, Padilla (2006) and Espiritu (1993) find that individuals choose from an array of pan-ethnic and nationality-based identities, "depending on the perceived strategic utility and symbolic appropriateness of the identities in different settings and audiences" (Nagel, 1994, p. 155).

For constructivists, national communities and identities do not organically grow out of preexisting, culturally bounded communities, but are rather the result of conscious nation-building efforts. According to Gellner (1997), nations are entirely modern creations which "more or less fraudulently invent their past to gain a semblance of antiquity and deep roots" (Eriksen, 2001, p. 45). Also, Anderson's idea of *imagined communities* fits with a constructivist approach to national identity. For Anderson (2006), a nation is an imagined community that invents cultural traditions and asserts commonness. It is imagined, because members of even the smallest nation will never know most of their fellow members; it is a community because "it is always conceived as a deep, horizontal comradeship," despite actual inequality and exploitation within the imagined community.

The constructivist approach to *ethnicity* similarly stresses the fluid, hybrid, constructed, and contextual nature of ethnic groups and identities. The constructivist approach is rooted in Weber's definition of ethnicity (1968, p. 389), in which ethnic groups are "human groups that entertain a subjective belief in their common descent because of similarities of physical type or of customs or both, or because of memories of colonization and migration." What matters in this view of ethnicity is not a set of common cultural practices or blood ties, but rather a subjective belief or social construction of common descent, either by in-group or out-group members.

At the core of the constructivist approach is that ethnic identification is context-dependent. One of the most important factors in this respect are processes of *external ascription* and *social categorization* (Jenkins, 1994), because these create boundaries which designate which categories are available for individual identification (Nagel, 1994). Waters (1990) for instance claims that the "ethnic options" available to individuals are limited to socially and politically defined ethnic categories, and she hence attributes the difference in identification between Blacks and Whites in the United States to the limits of individual choice. Applying the same rationale to Turks in Belgium, it seems likely that—given the high degree of othering by the established population—identity options are limited to "Muslim" and "Turkish," with no room for a national "Belgian" identification.

Considering the impact of mere categorization on identification, a strong impact of behavioral exclusion through discrimination should not surprise. Discrimination and divisive political campaigns sharpen ethno-racial identity boundaries and increase the salience of the category on the basis of which people experience unfair treatment (Rumbaut, 2005, p. 146). In the face of these perceived threats, descendants of immigrants can develop a so-called *reactive ethnic identity* (Portes & Rumbaut, 1990; Rumbaut, 1994). Research on this matter among immigrants in Europe has yielded mixed results. Studies among Turks in the Netherlands and Germany have found a direct positive effect of perceived discrimination on (re-)ethnicization (Skrobanek, 2009), as well as a negative relationship between perceived discrimination and national identification (Kunst et al., 2012; Martinovic & Verkuyten, 2012). In contrast, among Pakistanis in Norway, national identification was not influenced by perceived Islamophobia or religious discrimination (Kunst et al., 2012).

Given the bright symbolic boundary and the realities of everyday, institutional and legalized discrimination towards Turkish Belgians and Muslims in general, this study aims to contribute to the debate by linking people's narratives of exclusion to their identity narratives. As such, I set out to explore how people's experiences with symbolic exclusion, and how everyday institutional and legalized discrimination shape their identification in ethnic and national terms. In doing so, I pay particular attention to how people construct a positive identity in a context where certain identity options are made unavailable from the outside. It is for that reason that I now turn to theories that focus on the internal-external dialectic of identification.

The Constructionist Vision: Focus on the Internal/External Dialectic of Identification

Combining elements of both the primordialist and the constructivist approaches, Cornell and Hartmann's constructionist approach focuses on the fluidity of ethnicity as well as on the power of primordial attachments. In their vision, both self-ascription and ascription by others are critical in the making of ethnic groups and identities. Ethnicity and race, they argue, are not simply labels forced upon people; they are also identities that people accept, resist, choose, specify, invent, redefine, reject, actively defend, and so forth. They involve not only circumstances, but also active responses to circumstances by individuals and groups, guided by their own preconceptions, dispositions, and agendas.

This approach matches well with what Jenkins (1994) has termed "the internal-external dialectic of identification," which refers to the observation that identity construction is the result of a dialectic between external ascription and internal assertion. In the field of ethnicity, Rumbaut stressed that ethnic self-identities "emerge from the interplay of racial and ethnic labels imposed by the external society" on the one hand, and "the original identification and ancestral attachments asserted by the newcomers" on the other hand (Rumbaut, 2005, p. 3).

Theoretical Model

In order to explore how symbolic and behavioral exclusion shapes Turkish Belgian's identification in national and ethnic terms, one needs to focus on two separate but interrelated aspects. A first step in the analysis is to explore Turkish Belgians' perception of exclusion by the established population. Following theories of ethnic boundary construction, I argue that in exploring subjective feelings of exclusion, it is important to pay attention to both behavioral exclusion through discrimination, and to symbolic exclusion through—for example—othering. This will be done by analyzing people's "narratives of exclusion," which are treated as representing people's subjective experiences of exclusion. Second, I analyze research participants' identity narratives, paying particular attention to the internal-external dialectic of identification. Given that both internal and external factors shape identification, a thorough analysis of these narratives should pay attention to both the role of circumstances (in this case symbolic and behavioral exclusion), but also on how people actively respond to circumstances, guided by their cultural practices, history, and pre-existing identities.

DATA AND METHOD

My results are based on a qualitative study carried out among 63 second and third generation Turkish Belgians. The main research method was in-depth interviews in order to flesh out the complexities of the identification processes. I restricted my sample to the cohorts who were born in Belgium in the 1980s and 1990s, and living in Flanders. Flanders is a region with a high degree of anti-immigrant sentiments and political racism. Thus, our respondents were raised in a time when anti-immigrant feelings took center stage in public and political discourse.

The sample includes both second and third generation Turkish Belgians. Following Lievens (1999), I define the *second generation* as those who were socialized primarily in Belgium (born in Belgium or moved there before the age of 6). The *third generation* includes individuals who have at least one second generation parent. The sample is heterogeneous with regard to gender, age, and educational attainment.

All participants in the study were told about the purpose of the research and promised confidentiality and privacy. Each was given the opportunity to choose the interview location and his or her own pseudonym. All interviews were carried out in Dutch, since all respondents were born and raised in Belgium. Most respondents were interviewed only once; interviews lasted from 36 minutes to 2 hours 45 minutes, and were transcribed verbatim.

Before the start of the interview, respondents were asked to complete the Twenty Statement Test[1] (Kuhn & McPartland, 1954) in order to determine how much importance they attached to the different social identities that would be discussed during the interview. Subsequently, respondents were given a series of labeled cards, each of which had a particular social identity written on it (such as "Turk," "Turkish Belgian," "Muslim," "Husband/wife," "student") and were asked to choose those that they considered applicable to themselves. I deliberately focused on more than just ethnicity or nationality-related identifications in order to obtain a broad view of the respondent's self-identification, and to contextualize their ethnic and national identification. The entire interview was built around several issues: these labels, a discussion why some had been chosen and others not, a discussion about constructing and explaining the hierarchy and salience of their responses, and a discussion about the meaning respondents gave to the labels.

The research is based on a Grounded Theory approach to data-analysis, using a combination of *open-ended* and *axial* coding. *Open coding* is "the part of the analysis that pertains specifically to the naming and categorizing of phenomena through close examination of data" (Strauss & Corbin, 1990, p. 62), making it essentially about *data management. Axial coding* refers to "a set of procedures whereby data are put back together in new ways after open coding, by making connections between categories" (Strauss & Corbin, 1990, p. 96), and is hence all about the *generation of findings.*

In a first phase, I read through the first interviews and identified interesting themes (including, for instance, *perception of exclusion* and *self-identification*), and applied them to the data, systematically indexing (coding) the data using computer software package NVIVO. Once the first interviews were organized in this manner, I read through the raw data again and used an iterative approach in creating a refined and inductively generated tree structure. The initial theme *self-identification,* for instance, was broken up into second-level codes *ethnic identity, national identity, gender identity, local identity,* and so on.

I used several of the Grounded Theory techniques grouping the different codes in a meaningful way. One such technique was to use basic questions that denote a type of relationship (who, when, where, what, how, why?) in grouping different codes into one category. For instance, I grouped all the ways (how?) in which ethnic boundaries manifested themselves to the researchers, which resulted in second-level codes *ethnic jokes, othering, discrimination,* as subtypes of the first-level code *ethnic boundary perception.*

After this first phase of data management, I began looking closely at the different codes and established links between the different categories, using principles of axial coding. This included a close reading and narrative analysis of the coded data, and identifying explicitly mentioned links between different codes (e.g., when respondent him/herself links a self-identification to exclusion). Finally, I looked at differences in ethnic-boundary perception and self-identification and tried to account for them by linking them with socio-demographic and other relevant characteristics.

RESULTS

Perceived Ethnic Boundaries: Body Language, Discourse, and Discrimination

In line with the distinction between symbolic and behavioral exclusion, we can discern at least three sets of mechanisms that give people the feeling that they are excluded. First of all, we can distinguish between discursive manifestations (reflecting the symbolic) and behavioral manifestations. In addition, our analyses show that it is also important to consider body language as a way of inferring boundaries.

Body Language

Body language is one way in which respondents felt categorized. Male informants in particular mentioned people looking at them in a fearful or negative way, which they interpreted as a sign of prejudice or anti-immigrant behavior.

> [Q: Do you often get the evil eye?] Seriously. Yes, always, yes, yes. I can see it on people's faces (imitates it). They walk away, their eyes like this. You just see it.... They only have to pass a mosque, even then. Instead of just saying hello.... You often get the evil eye and if you pay attention to it, it destroys you, but most Turks do not pay attention to it anymore. They say: it is just a Belgian. (Ömer, 21M)

> They look at you with a different eye, some people. They look like ... yeah, a foreigner or something. Or "what is he doing in our country?" And then you have a hard time because, you know, you are born here, you cannot do anything about it. We know the language, our nationality is Belgian, but we continue to be seen as Turks. (Seyid, 16M)

Both quotes are very powerful examples of how exclusionary it feels to be looked at as if one is dangerous or not welcome. By saying that he feels that people are looking at him as if he is "a foreigner," Seyid signals his perception of being categorized, and implicitly rejects the label of "foreigner." The fact that he is looked at as someone who does not belong in Belgium makes him feel bad ("you have a hard time") because of his powerlessness due to this categorization: he is Belgian by nationality and he knows the language, but still people see him as Turkish.

Discourse

Our respondents' identity narratives reflect the many ways in which members of the established population construct ethnic boundaries in discourse, ranging from subtle everyday racism (Essed, 1991) to blatant forms of discursive racism.

A first manifestation of everyday racism that is mentioned by our respondents is the widespread use of the word *allochtoon* (meaning both *allochtonous* and *allochton*—the noun derived from the adjective). In the 1990s, the word became common in Flanders and the Netherlands as a term to refer to migrants and their descendants. Although semantically, *allochtoon* refers to "someone who comes from elsewhere," it is most commonly used in policy practice and public discourse to refer to members of non-Western (read: Muslim) ethnic groups considered disadvantaged or less integrated into Belgian/Dutch society.

There is a shared understanding among the respondents that the term is denigrating and exclusionary. People describe the word as "horrible" (*afschuwelijk*), "humiliating" (*vernederend*), "third division player" (*derdeklasser*), and the practice as unacceptable and narrow-minded.

> I even think it is not acceptable, considering the whole migration history. I can understand that our ancestors were seen as migrants. But that in the case of the present generation, that you [Belgians] still feel the need to stick the label *allochtoon*, I find this . . . you know, I think that is in fact the narrow-mindedness of the people who live here [in Belgium]. (Aleyna, 27F)

According to Aleyna, it is unjustified to make a difference between established Belgians and those with foreign roots. By saying "considering the whole migration history," she means that Turks have been present in Belgium since the 1960s, and that by now, their descendants should no longer be considered as foreigners. Yet, the word *allochtoon* continues to be used and she attributes this to "the narrow-mindedness" of the Belgians.

Our respondents view the term negatively. The word not only signals an ethnic boundary between those with foreign ancestry and ethnic Belgians, but it also has a negative ring to it because it is applied to those who are considered problematic. To put it in the words of one of our informants: "If the media says 'a couple of allochtonous youngsters'—if you put *youngsters* behind it, then the fences are down—then you know what is going to follow: 'have caused a riot,' 'have demolished,' there is no other way." The word "*allochtonen*" tends to be used in negative contexts only. *Allochtonen* are never just "people from elsewhere" but treated as "second class citizens, never quite the norm, as a problem, lagging behind" (Essed & Trienekens, 2008, p. 58).

A second way in which everyday racism manifests itself to our informants is through so-called *ethnic jokes* (Davies, 1982). Those who utter them consider them "just a harmless joke," but the narratives of our respondents illustrate their power as an exclusionary mechanism:

> I am like conditioned to think that all Belgians see me as *allochtoon*. I don't know how come, but that is how I feel. And . . . sometimes it happens that it

is ostentatiously manifested. For example in the train last time, children of eight years old were laughing amongst each other, they were joking and then one tells a joke and he says "And it was a Turk!" And then they all started laughing [she laughs] and you know, it really was like extremely funny. But it felt like—so I am *the other*, the different one so to say. Yes, I think Belgians see me as *allochtoon*, I do think so. I do not think that I will ever fit one hundred per cent in the group as Belgian. (Dilek, 27F)

Dilek perceives the joke as a sign of categorization and exclusion. In the beginning of her narrative, she says that she assumes that all Belgians see her as *allochtoon*, and uses the story about the joke to support this impression. Although she thought the joke was funny, it gave her the feeling of being an outsider. Based on her joke narrative, she concludes that she will never fit a hundred per cent in the group as Belgian. The observation that jokes about ethnic minorities are part and parcel of ethnic boundaries has been discussed extensively by Davies (1982, 1990). She argues that ethnic jokes delineate both social and moral boundaries of a nation or ethnic group and that "by mocking peripheral and ambiguous groups, they reduce ambiguity and clarify boundaries or at least make ambiguity less frightening" (Davies, 1982, p. 400).

Third, many informants feel categorized and excluded through cases of *Othering*, and a repeated focus on ethnicity in everyday interethnic encounters:

It is like people do not feel at ease when you arrive in a certain group and . . . they seem to feel the need to make a remark about your cultural background. Like about talking Dutch, or our weddings, or you know our kebab places. Those are the things you always hear. (. . .) It is like if I would move to Paris, and I would tell to every Parisian I meet "wow your Eiffel tower!" You get what I mean? Come on, it is . . . I think it is not useful and I think . . . instead of just seeing me as a person . . . Like who am I and who is [Aleyna]? They just automatically put it in the cultural context. (Aleyna, 27F)

By referring to her ethnicity, people give Aleyna the feeling that she is reduced to her Turkish roots. Instead, she would like to be seen in her entirety, as a person. Aleyna's frustration is exemplary for the difficulties many members of ethnic minority groups have in conveying "the humanity that encompasses [their] total identity" (Lyman & Douglass, 1973, p. 353). According to Schneider and Crul (2013, p. 33), the dominant discursive context in most European countries presents a serious challenge for belonging, because "it overemphasizes ethnic background as the main signifier in all societal contexts." Indeed, in another part of the interview, Aleyna explains that she perceives this categorization as very exclusionary: "A couple of times, [my classmates] gave me subtle remarks like 'Oh, I thought that in your culture it was not like that.' So they kind of exclude you automatically." By referring to how things are done differently "in [her] culture," her classmates give Aleyna the feeling that she is an outsider to their group. Aleyna considers this subtle boundary as even worse than overt racism or discrimination, because these are people she trusts, which makes it all the more painful to realize that they too see her as an outsider.

Another example of everyday racism is subtle expressions of *prejudice* and cases of *group homogenization*. Utterances that signal ethnic prejudice are irritating and frustrating, even when they are positive or neutral about Turkish-Belgians. Many respondents were especially irritated by comments such as "Wow, your Dutch is really good!" which they not only consider ridiculous because they are born in Belgium, but also irritating because it signals a prejudice that all Turkish people in Flanders speak bad Dutch. Another example is the expectation that all Turkish girls have only limited freedom and are expected to stay at home rather than going out:

> There are question marks immediately—always, in all sorts of ways. Also at work: "[Emine], we are going out to party, will you be able [signifying *allowed*] to come?" And I HATE that. I tell them "Why not? Why not?" It is just like, everybody sees it as different. And that is a pity. (Emine, 26F)

The tendency to *Essentialize*[2] and see the Turkish population as a homogeneous cultural entity also manifests itself in the utterance "but you are different":

> Sometimes people say—and I hate that utterance—"But you are not a real Turk, you are different... I really hate that little sentence "You are not a real Turk." Why am I not a real Turk? Are all Turks like THAT? I mean, just go to Turkey, just not to those regions where people here originate from, and you will notice that they are much more modern than people here. That is really something I hate. (Emine, 26F)

People like Emine, who do not fit the stereotypical idea of what Turkish people are like, are often labeled as "different from other Turks" and therefore "not a real Turk." In doing so, ethnic Belgians homogenize the Turkish population and reaffirm existing stereotypes. Labeling people who do not fit the stereotype as "not real Turks" signals that they consider particular cultural practices—in this case limited freedom for young women—as essential for defining Turkish identity, hence conveying the idea that all Turks are the same.

In addition to cases of everyday racism, some informants have also been confronted with blatantly racist or anti-immigrant comments, either directed at themselves or others. Sometimes these comments are even uttered by those occupying a formal position, such as teachers:

She really hated that teacher, my daughter. She had bad grades with that teacher. It was a teacher who looked through the window (...) and said "Look, the little criminals of the future." I swear. I swear. "Little criminals of the future." About two little Moroccans. It didn't matter [that they were Moroccan], [my daughter] is Turkish, but it does not matter, this is something you don't say. Just the fact that this teacher utters these words to the children, that hurts. [My daughter thought] "If they say it behind their back, they will probably do the same about me." (Pinar, 49F)

Pinar continues her narrative by saying that such cases of racism play an important role in her children's identity formation, particularly because they happen in her children's most formative years and in a context in which they should feel safe, rather than be exposed to identity threats. The idea that age matters is also implicit in the following quote:

I might write down [that I am] "Belgian" but I experienced a lot of negative things, cases of racism, as a soccer player. As young soccer player, I was in a rather good team (...) and there were a lot of *allochtonen* in the team. (...) It was a good team and it was met with frustration by the parents of the opponents. With comments such as "brown monkey" and this and that. Shouting at twelve year old boys (...) and in a way, that has shaped the idea in my head "Look [Achmed], you are no Belgian dude, that is not how they treat." So no, you are not looked at as Belgian. (Achmed, 27M)

In this narrative, Achmed shows how racist comments made him realize that ethnic Belgians do not accept him as a true Belgian. In the opening sentence, he implicitly rejects a self-identification as Belgian, because of these experiences. He goes on with an example to illustrate and justify his claim, and concludes by making the link between his self-identification ("you are no Belgian dude") and his sense of not being considered Belgian.

Discrimination

Most of our respondents explicitly said that they encountered very few cases of discrimination. Given that many discriminatory practices are related to particular life-course events, such as finding a job or a house, this limited experience with discrimination might be related to the informants' age: at the time of the interview, the majority were in their early or mid-twenties and many were still studying and living with their parents. Consequently, chances are low that they had already encountered discrimination in the labor or housing market, simply because they have not been looking for jobs or housing yet.

The examples of discrimination that *were* mentioned were exclusively cases of what Wimmer (2013) labels *everyday discrimination*—discrimination by individual people during everyday interactions outside the domains of state control. Several of our male interviewees for instance experienced discrimination when they tried to enter nightclubs:

> I was often denied entrance in nightclubs and stuff. Especially in Belgium. In the Netherlands it is not that bad, but in Belgium we were often rejected. One time we were going to Zillion, we were four guys, and we had found (sic) three girls in the parking lot. Probably Pakistani, or Indian. They looked a bit like us (laughs). You behave decently, friendly and ask them to maybe try and get in together. Four guys, three girls, maybe that is a good group. They [the girls] did not reject us, so I would be really grateful if I would see them again. We arrived at the door, we were happy, they let us in and we get a piece of paper, a form, and we move on and it turns out to be a horror tunnel, like the fairground attraction: we enter one door and exit just like that through another one. Accompanied. And we could not go anywhere because the bouncer was in our way. (laughing) He accompanied us to the other door and that was the exit. So we were back outside, the entire group. We were looking at each other and realized we had been rejected. (Armageddon, 32M)

> Sometimes I think maybe [the bouncers at clubs] heard a lot about fights or God knows what. I do not blame them, but I am not saying that everyone is the same. They say: "Yes you are a Turk, we have heard so much about you," you know, that is what you always hear. "Fights and the like, so you cannot enter [the club]." But not everyone is the same. (. . .) You are denied access, but I think people should get a chance. I mean the Turks who have not done anything. (Sedat, 25M)

Like Armageddon and Sedat, many men talked about how they were often denied access to a nightclub, just because they were Turkish. Sedat's narrative shows that he understands that he is denied entrance based the prejudice that "Turks cause trouble," and to a certain extent, he even partly accepts this discriminatory practice as legitimate. At the same time however, he considers the generalization that the prejudice entails as unfair, because "not everyone is the same," and "people should get a chance."

The narrative of Armageddon shows that men develop strategies in order to enhance the chance of being granted access. It is not uncommon for Turkish men to try and find a couple of women who are willing to show up at the door of a nightclub with them, as if they are a group of friends that wants to enter together. In doing so, men show they are aware of the stereotypes that exist about them: by arriving at the door with young women, they signal to the bouncers that they are not there to harass women or cause trouble—two prejudices that many ethnic Belgians have about young Muslim men.

Several informants, both male and female, also referred to discriminatory practices when they were looking for a job or a place to live. In most cases, they felt the discrimination was based on prejudices, as is illustrated in the following narratives:

> I went to the job office and that lady said "Oh good morning, I have not had time yet to look at your file, but I will do so right away." And then she looks at it and says "(surprised tone) Higher education?" It sounded like "Good gracious! Higher education . . . you?!" (. . .) And that lady, really, she was constantly trying to undermine my self-confidence. After I went to see her for the second time, I really thought I would never find a decent job. She always gave me the lousy jobs. I mean, lousy, like social sector and stuff, and I thought "how are those good for me?" I mean seriously, what am I going to do in the social sector? Nothing. (Damla, 27F)

> [Finding an apartment] was completely traumatizing. I never imagined it would be that bad. I always thought "We speak Dutch, we do not wear a headscarf and I am already a bit blonde." So I did not think it would be problematic. But finding a place to stay really was a trauma. We were refused everywhere. And in the job market it is even more difficult to check. You are rejected, ok, but you do not know who the other candidates were and which qualities or skills they possess that I don't have. I notice that all *allochtonen* who graduated, and who have a job, are doing a job that is related to *allochtonen*, and I think it is really unfair. I feel like, if I graduate from university I have the same qualities as my co-students. We should be equal on the job market. I want to be in competition with them in the private job market. Why do I have to do a job that involves *allochtonen* and be dealing with those problems and matters. I might as well do my thing in the [regular] economy. (Dilek, 27F)

Both women have experienced difficulties in the job market and both explicitly or implicitly convey the message that this is due to the prejudice that Turkish Belgians do not do well in school. Due to the generally low educational attainment among second and even third generation Turks, ethnic Belgians seem to have the prejudice that all Turkish Belgians do poorly in terms of education. Both women, who have both done very well in relation to many of their co-ethnics, experience frustration because they are not treated equally compared to ethnic Belgians with the same educational level. As Dilek argues, it is difficult to prove differential treatment, because one never knows anything about the skills and qualities of other job applicants. However, several highly publicized cases of ethnic discrimination in the job market[3] signal that their gut feeling about not getting a fair chance is probably right.

The Importance of Gender and Education

There are socio-demographic differences in perceptions of ethnic boundaries. First, as with previous research (De Rycke et al., 1999), I found that there are gender differences: compared to women, men report more blatant forms of exclusion, such as explicit racism and discrimination, and they have more concrete examples of personal everyday discrimination. Women on the other hand discuss subtle and discursive ethnic boundaries, and many state that they personally have not experienced blatant racism or discrimination. The observation that men experience more discrimination compared to women is probably partly related to the fact that they spend a larger amount of their time in public spaces. In addition, it might also be related to the stereotypical image of Muslim men as "dangerous" and "threatening," which stands in sharp contrast with the stereotype of the Muslim woman as a victim.

Secondly, there seem to be differences in ethnic-boundary perception according to educational level: the better educated more frequently report being excluded, compared to those who only have a high school education. One possible explanation is that more-educated people are more politicized in their behavior and attitudes, and therefore more sensible to discrimination or *Othering* practices. Another hypothesis is that the better educated are also more likely to be confronted with ethnic boundaries because they have more contact with prejudiced ethnic Belgians. Turkish Belgians who do not move on to tertiary education have generally been in a vocational track at secondary school. Because this track is especially popular among ethnic-minority pupils, these pupils might have a lower perception of being different, both because there are many co-ethnics, and because the ethnic Belgian pupils and teachers are used to ethnic diversity. Those people who go to schools that are specialized in the higher-ranked general track—schools which often have a low proportion of ethnic minority pupils—seem to experience more categorization and exclusion. When people move on to tertiary education, chances are high that they experience even more categorization as a result of increased contact with people who are not used to ethnic diversity and are hence more prejudiced. Thus, the context surrounding ethnic-boundaries is important.

Exclusion by Turkish Turks

Before I move on to the discussion of different identity narratives, it is important to point out that many informants not only feel excluded and *Othered* by members of the established population in Belgium, but that they equally have a feeling of being outsiders during their trips to Turkey:

> People do not see me as Turkish either you know. Because the moment you are on holiday abroad or in Turkey, you are the one who comes from Europe, you are European. You are the German in fact. If I were to say "I pack my belongings and move to Turkey," I would not be one of the guys. Maybe I would be after a while, but I will always be considered as the European. (Achmed, 27M)

Because ethnic Belgians do not consider them as true Belgians, and Turks do not consider them as Turkish, several interviewees reported a feeling of not belonging anywhere and some even said they were confused about their identity. Such a feeling may be related to what Durkheim referred to as *Anomie* (Durkheim, 1951); that is a breakdown in the bonds between an individual and the community.

But a feeling of being an outsider does not necessarily lead to identity crises. In what follows, I demonstrate how identification is to a large extent shaped by processes of Othering and exclusion, while simultaneously highlighting that people are active agents in constructing a positive identity.

From a Sense of Exclusion to an Inclusive Identity: Five Identity Narratives

Based on how people position themselves *vis-à-vis* the labels "Turkish" and "Belgian," I identify five different identity narratives. In discussing each of these narratives, I zoom in on the meaning people give to the labels "Belgian" and "Turkish," as well as on how they link their self-identification to perceptions of exclusion and *Othering*, hence uncovering the internal/external dialectic of identification. We treat these identity narratives as expressions of the different ways in which people make sense of their multidimensional identity and as the internal/external dialectic of identification in action, and not as an reified, exhaustive list of all possible "identification types."

Narrative One: Belgian on Paper, Turkish by Heart
The first identity narrative is one in which people combine a strong feeling of being Turkish with recognition that they are Belgian by birth:

> I feel like . . . I am Turkish but I am born here in Belgium so I am actually also a Belgian. And that is the thing, you feel very Turkish . . . but actually you are Belgian. . . . So if you ask me, yes I am Belgian, but I am a Belgian from Turkey. Most people say "I am just Turkish," no, if you are born here, you are Belgian. (Emine, 26F)

For people who identify as Belgian on paper and Turkish by heart, the two identities each have a different meaning, as Emine's narrative illustrates. When she talks about the label "Belgian," she uses the verb *to be*, whereas she uses *to feel* in the context of her Turkish identification. Hence, what it means to be Belgian is defined in terms of nationality, whereas *being Turkish* is defined in emotional terms. In many cases, people smile or touch their heart while talking about being Turkish, signaling a strong emotional attachment. They talk about how they feel closer to the Turkish culture than to the Belgian one, and about how they feel better around Turkish people.

This distinction between an emotional identification on the one hand and a civic, national one on the other hand, mirrors Verkuyten and De-Wolf's (2002) distinction between *being, feeling,* and *doing.* Just like the Chinese in their study, many of our respondents make an unconscious distinction between what could be labeled as an emotional identification (*feeling*) and a categorical one (*being*); the latter referring to a category they merely belong to, without necessarily feeling closely attached to it.

In many cases, the lack of emotional identification with the label *Belgian* is explicitly or implicitly linked to the perception of being excluded or considered different by ethnic Belgians.

> "Do you feel Belgian?" [my teacher] asked me. I replied: "The moment that you are going to see me walk in the streets as a Belgian, I mean, when you walk in the street and you think 'Hey, look, that Belgian kid there,' then I will feel Belgian," I said. "I promise." (Achmed, 27M)

> Yes, I am a ... Turkish Belgian. Or Belgian Turk. You can maybe look at it from both sides. One who actually ... who feels more Turkish here in Belgium. And who still has these feelings that you are seen by some people as, you know, let's say "the brown one," you know. (Ayhan, 31M)

In the first narrative, Achmed signals that he is conscious of the fact that his teacher categorizes him as Turkish, and links this categorization to his emotional self-identification: he promises that once the teacher starts to *see him* as Belgian, he himself will in turn *feel* Belgian. What he is saying more implicitly is that as long as people categorize him as Turkish, he will never feel Belgian. Also, Ayhan links his emotional identification to external categorization: he feels more Turkish (compared to Belgian) and immediately links this to the fact that he is racially categorized by some people as "the brown one." Both narratives demonstrate the power of symbolic exclusion and everyday racism, the "mere" categorization as foreign or different, even in the absence of behavioral exclusion, gives people a strong sense of being otherized, which has an impact on how they emotionally identify.

But the limited emotional identification with the label *Belgian* does not imply that people *reject* a Belgian identity. In fact, many informants stress their Belgian identity as a way of reclaiming an identity that is denied to them from the outside. They object to the limited "identity options" (Waters, 1990) available, and narratively assert their Belgian identity by stressing that they are good Belgian citizens, and that Belgium is the country where they are born and have spent all of their lives.

> It is not because I have other habits, another culture, that we do not belong here. Because we go ... we also follow the same rules as the Belgians. We also have to do our paperwork, we also have to do payments. ... In terms of life

in Belgium, everything is the same. We also do our payments for instance. When we go shopping, we also wait in line for our turn like the Belgians do. (Serpil, 27F)

As a result of exclusion and categorization, Serpil does not *feel* very Belgian, but this quote shows that she does identify as such in terms of citizenship. Based on her Belgian citizenship and the fact that she fulfills her duties as a Belgian citizen, she demands equal treatment: she observes the rules just like ethnic Belgians do, so she should be treated equally and be seen as belonging in Belgium.

In sum, this narrative combines a strong emotional identification as Turkish and a more categorical national or civic identification as Belgian, which serves to reclaim an identity that is denied from the outside. The limited emotional identification as Belgian is often explicitly linked to perception that they are not considered "true Belgians" by ethnic Belgians. Such a distinction again shows that discursive manifestations of ethnic boundaries are potentially as important as actual or perceived discrimination.

Second Narratives: Belgian With Turkish Roots

The second identity narrative is built around a strong emotional identification as Belgian and recognition of one's Turkish roots. Here again, people make a distinction between how they *feel* (i.e., Belgian) and what they recognize they *are* (i.e., Turkish):

We are born in Belgium but you cannot just ignore your roots. You cannot say "my parents are Belgian," because that is not the case. We are Turks, we are Turks by roots. And I see myself as a Belgian Turk. I cannot say that I am hundred per cent Turk, no. I am born here [in Belgium], I live here, I speak the language, I work between these people, I have always lived here. I do feel Belgian. (Otoman, 32M)

The difference between the previous identity narrative and this one is that people in this category feel Belgian and recognize their Turkishness, whereas in the former pattern it was reversed. What it means to be Belgian is in this case not only defined in terms of citizenship, but the identification is also emotionally felt. This narrative is most typically found among those who have frequent, close contacts with ethnic Belgians and have lost much of their sense of being Turkish. They seem to have a stronger sense of being integrated into Belgian society.

Most respondents who identify this way have experienced cases of *Othering* or exclusion just like anyone else, but these experiences do not take up a prominent role in their identity narratives. Rather, their negative experiences are minimized, or presented as something they actively try to prevent:

It is the way it is, you don't have to complain about it. My name is not Jan, or Peter. You know? You don't get to choose your parents, nor your origins. But you have to assert yourself. That is how I function. Someone else would say "(lamenting tone) Uuuu, we are not accepted and blahblahblah." No, you have to make yourself accepted (Ferhat, 28M).

According to Ferhat, Turkish people have to accept that they are treated differently because of their ethnic origin, but that does not mean they have to be passive about not being accepted. Rather, his stance is that people are active agents who need to assert themselves and make themselves accepted. Rather than focusing on potential threats to his Belgian identification, Ferhat chooses to not give too much importance to exclusionary discourses or practices, but to actively make himself accepted. As such, he eliminates potential threats to his Belgian identity, hence making such identification possible.

The idea that Turkish Belgians have to work especially hard "to prove themselves" *vis-à-vis* ethnic Belgians also surfaced in other identity narratives. Those espousing such views saw this as being "exhausting" and "unfair." Within this identity narrative, however, respondents accepted it as legitimate, and as something one "just has to do" in order to become accepted.

Narrative Three: The Essential Turk and Rejecting Belgian Identity

In this third identity narrative, people stress and are proud of their Turkish identity and reject a Belgian one:

In fact, I do not feel Belgian at all. I have Belgian friends and stuff. But...I know of myself that I have Turkish blood and that I am not a Belgian in fact, that I would rather have been born in Turkey; or would rather live there than here. (Seyid, 16M)

In the *Essential-Turk narrative*, Turkish and Belgian identities are reified and presented as mutually exclusive. *Turkishness* is described as an essential part of who they are and as something that is incompatible with Belgian identity. The rejection of Belgian identity is usually accounted for by referring to a sense of being essentially different from Belgians, and a strong sense of belonging in Turkey. People who identify as such describe Turkey as "their country" and long to be reunited with "their people." Such a way of self-identifying is a clear example of what Cornell and Hartman have termed "constructed primordialities" (2007, p. 93).

What is remarkable in the identity narratives of *the essential Turk* is that they do not explicitly link their identification with a sense of exclusion. They are proud of being Turkish and link their identification up with *Essentializing* narratives in which they refer to blood ties and roots, rather than narratives of exclusion. However, all of them talk about a strong sense of exclusion and cases of discrimination at some point in the interview. It seems they have constructed a reactive ethnicity (based on their already present ancestral attachments) and attached a positive meaning to it.

Narrative Four: The In-Between Narrative

The most dominant narrative among our respondents is that of being *in-between*. This sense of being in-between is usually described as *feeling both* Turkish and Belgian, but as *considered neither* of the two:

> I am a Turk and I am also a Belgian, because I am born here, I have the Belgian nationality, I went to school here, I studied here, I work here. I feel both. But I personally think that we are in-between. Like when we go on holiday to Turkey, they say like . . . "look, there's a Belgian." They do not accept us as Turks (. . .) [And here in Belgium], they will definitely say "that is a migrant," "that is a stranger." And in Turkey it is exactly the same. We are not accepted there, nor here . . . We are in-between. (Azra, 34F)

The sense of being in-between results from the combination of a self-identification as both Turkish and Belgian, and the awareness of being considered an outsider in both Turkey and Belgium. Depending on which feeling dominates, a distinction can be made between *attached* and *unattached* in-between narratives. In *attached in-between narratives*, people highlight the positive aspects of being in-between in cultural terms, referring to a *creolization* process in which they combine the positive of both worlds. Also, they do not seem to favor one of the two identities (i.e., Belgian and Turkish). They stress that they can feel both, usually depending on the circumstances. In the *unattached in-between narratives*, people interpret their in-between position negatively in terms of *belonging nowhere*—a state which is characterized by the absence of a positive social identification as Turkish and/or Belgian, and labeled and felt as an *identity crisis*. Considering the fluidity of identification however, it is likely that as time passes, this identity crisis fades away, as people find an alternative source of identity, which is not ethnic or national but, for instance, local, religious, or supra-national.

Narrative Five: The World Citizen/Human Being

A final identity narrative is one in which people stress their identity as a *world citizen* or *human being*, either because these all-embracing categories provide an alternative identity in the absence of other positive options, or because they simply refuse to identify in ethnic or national terms. The case of Dilek is illustrative for the first of these motivations. Dilek has a strong sense of exclusion, and during the interview she explicitly rejected Belgian identity. While talking about how she lives her life however, she started to consider her own narrative as very contradictory:

Actually, maybe I do have an identity crisis. Because I am very contradictory.
I say that I am Turkish, but in fact I have a hundred reasons (laughs) [why
I am not Turkish]....You know, maybe...Isn't it possible that because I am
not Belgian, or I do not want to call myself Belgian, and because I do not fit
in with being Turkish, that I comfort myself with the idea that I am a world
citizen. So that is maybe how I identify.... Because I do not fit into those two
things, I see myself as a world citizen. And it is so broad, that I cannot but fit
in (laughs). That is a category that suits me. Yes, world citizen! (Dilek, 27F)

This quotation reflects Dilek's pathway to the construction of an all-embracing identity: in reaction to a high sense of exclusion by Belgian society,
she has constructed a strong Turkish identity, but during her narrative she
starts to realize that she "does not fit in with being Turkish" either. Because
she now feels she can neither identify as Belgian, nor as Turkish, she chooses the label *world citizen* as an alternative inclusive identity.

In Dilek's case, the identification as a world citizen grew out of a lack
of other group identities, but for others it can also grow out of a refusal to
think in terms of, ethnic boundaries:

[I put *world citizen* at the top of the hierarchy] because I am a human being.
What is most important for me is a human being. We are all built with the
same raw material. You, me, Jan, Ahmet, Mustafa or Abdel of Jean. We are
all human beings. That is [what] world citizen [means to me]. (Armageddon, 32M)

Armageddon first and foremost wants to identify as a human being,
and chooses this label because it is all-inclusive and uniting. It focuses on
what links people together, rather than on the differences and boundaries. By identifying as a world citizen, they represent the change they want
to see.

In socio-demographic terms, this identity narrative is especially common among the better educated, who in most cases have a strong sense
of exclusion. Because of their better education, they have more contact
with ethnic Belgians, which has led to a cultural creolization process in
which they have mixed Turkish and Belgian cultural practices and attitudes into a new hybrid culture. To a certain extent, they feel similar to
ethnic Belgians in terms of lifestyle; but the experienced or perceived
exclusion—both in Belgium and in Turkey—results in a strong sense of
exclusion. Although some of the informants were at the time of the interview still struggling with the resulting identity crises, many have found a
way out by identifying with an all-embracing category such as world citizen
or human being.

CONCLUSION

Summary and Discussion

Research has demonstrated that Belgium is one of Europe's "leading" countries with regard to ethnic prejudice and anti-immigrant sentiments, and that these negative feelings are even stronger towards the Muslim population (Quillian, 1995; Strabac & Listhaug, 2008). Being the largest Muslim population in Europe and the second largest in Belgium (the largest being the Moroccan population), Turks are exposed to an array of orientalist prejudices, discursive *Othering* practices and institutional and everyday discrimination. Considering the importance of exclusion and categorization for self-identification, this study focuses on how these discourses, the practices of exclusion, and *Othering* shape Turkish Belgians' national and ethnic self-identification. Drawing on in-depth interviews with second and third generation Turkish Belgians, I explore how Turkish Belgians themselves experience ethnic boundary construction in their everyday lives and how their narratives of exclusion and *Othering* act out in their identity narratives.

I find that Turkish Belgians are confronted with ethnic boundaries through a variety of practices: ethnic Belgians' body language, discourse, and discriminatory practices. The observation that boundaries manifest themselves in both discourse and practice echoes Wimmer's (2013) claim that boundaries always consist of a categorical (or symbolic) and a behavioral dimension. The categorical dimension is acted out by ethnic Belgians through a myriad of discursive practices, including both subtle everyday racism (Essed, 1991) and blatantly racist utterances. The behavioral dimension translates itself in everyday discrimination in the housing and labor market and within certain social settings, most particularly nightlife—in short, the behavioral component is part of Belgian social structure or the routine, organized way of life in Belgium. Compared to cases of discursive exclusion and everyday racism, cases of discrimination are much less frequently voiced, and mentioned almost exclusively by male respondents.

Our analysis shows that even in the absence of explicit racism or personal discrimination, many of our respondents have the feeling of being considered different and excluded, as a result of subtle ethno-religious boundaries implicit in discourse and behavior among ethnic Belgians. In fact, many more respondents based their sense of exclusion and being different on practices of categorization and subtle everyday racism than on factual discrimination. One hypothesis for this strong impact of everyday racism and discursive exclusion is that it is much more socially acceptable and therefore more widespread than actual discrimination. Moreover, the fact that it not only occurs in hostile contexts but also in friendly interactions with friends and in supposedly safe settings such as a therapy session or the school context, makes it all the more painful and maybe an even bigger identity threat for those who experience it.

In line with previous research (Cornell & Hartmann, 2007; Jenkins, 2008), the analysis demonstrates that identification of Turkish Belgians is the result of a dialectic between external processes of ascription and exclusion on the one hand, and internal assertion on the other hand. I have identified five different identity narratives, based on how people position themselves vis-à-vis the labels *Turkish* and *Belgian*, and on how they link their self-identification to their experiences of exclusion and *Othering*. Although I observed that narratives of *Othering* and exclusion often take center stage within the identity narratives, I also found that perceived symbolic exclusion or discrimination do not necessarily result in a rejection of a Belgian identity or in the adoption of a reactive, Turkish identity.

Results suggest that a sense of exclusion does not determine identity construction in an inescapable manner, but that people are active agents who can reject categorization and assert certain identities. In the absence of an emotional identification with Belgians, people do seem to need another identity that provides them with a sense of belonging. For some people, this sense of belonging is provided by their membership in the Turkish community. Those identifying as *Turkish by heart, Belgian on paper* and as *the essential Turk*, compensate their sense of exclusion with the positive feelings attached to being Turkish. When the sense of belonging in the Turkish community is not strong, people nevertheless are able to construct a positive, inclusive identity by identifying with the all-embracing categories of *world citizen* or *human being*. In case of no alternative identification, people can perceive an identity crisis, but given the fluidity of identification, this is most likely to be a temporary phase which will eventually end as people find alternative forms of identification.

The different identity narratives not only represent different constellations of ethnic, national, and supra-national identities, but also different ways of negotiating ethnic boundaries and responding to discourses and practices of exclusion: those who identify as *Belgian on paper, Turkish by heart* report that it is hard to *feel* Belgian, but nevertheless reclaim the Belgian identity that is denied to them from the outside, by stressing their Belgian citizenship. The few who identify as being *Belgian with Turkish roots* refuse to see themselves as victims of exclusion and actively try to be accepted and hence eliminate a possible threat to their Belgian identity. *Essential Turks* have constructed a narrative that presents their ethnic identity as reified, primordial and incompatible with Belgian identity, hence making external categorization seem inconsequential. In the *in-between narrative,* the double sense of exclusion is counterbalanced with the positive feelings associated with having "the best of both worlds." In the final narrative—that of the *world citizen* or *human being*—people react to ethnic boundaries and exclusion by rejecting the idea of boundaries and stressing what unites people, hence "being the change they want to see."

This study confirms Jenkins' findings that externally-located processes of social categorization are very influential in the production of social identities. To a certain extent, it also confirms the finding that categorization and exclusion can limit the availability of ethnic options (Waters, 1990). In particular, when it comes to emotional identification, those who have a sense of being excluded by ethnic Belgians do not feel any emotional attachment to Belgium, but this does not mean that they do not identify as such.

Our most remarkable finding is that people not only find alternative ways of identification when certain options are unavailable, but that they also actively reclaim those identities that have been denied to them.

Overall, reactive identifications such as the essential Turk are rather uncommon, given the observation that a sense of exclusion or *Othering* is widespread among our respondents. This finding puts into perspective the quantitative studies on the link between perceived discrimination and reactive ethnicity (Maxwell, 2009; Skrobanek, 2009). Although there is certainly a relationship to be found between the two, our analysis shows that it should not be assumed that perceived discrimination or exclusion necessarily leads to a reactive ethnic identity. Some people choose to ignore that exclusion, or re-claim the identity that is denied to them by others, referring to their nationality, birth, or good-citizenship practices.

Our analysis also suggests that much remains to be done. First, I have demonstrated that both subtle and blatant forms of ethnic-boundary drawing shape self-identification, but quantitative research is necessary to study the exact impact of both. Based on the presented findings, I hypothesize that practices of everyday racism—such as ethnic jokes, a repeated focus on one's ethnicity, generalizations and categorizing labels such as *allochtoon*—are experienced as at least equally exclusionary as actual discrimination. Such forms of discrimination are more widespread and they tend to occur in supposedly safe and familiar contexts. Consequently, I hypothesize that identification is shaped at least as much by the subtle discursive experiences of ethnic boundaries as by practices of discrimination.

Secondly, I have hinted at the role of temporal and life course factors have for understanding the exposure to and impact of exclusion. Nevertheless, more research is needed to understand whether the impact of *Othering* and exclusion differ according to age or between particular stages in the life course. For instance, does it make a difference if one experiences exclusion and discrimination early on in the life-course—during one's most formative years? What happens when people start being confronted with discrimination after having grown up in a context with little or no experiences of exclusion?

Finally, the study also does not allow for an in-depth exploration of how patterns of identification shape perceptions of exclusion or *Othering*, nor does it enable us to answer how *perceived* exclusion relates to actual *experiences* of personal discrimination. All of these are interesting research questions in their own right and I hope that our study will be an incentive for other researchers to take up the challenge to tackle them.

In conclusion, I want to draw attention to three of the most remarkable findings of this study. First, symbolic boundary construction is by many respondents experienced as equally, if not even more, exclusionary than behavioral exclusion. One possible explanation for this observation is that symbolic boundary drawing through, for example, othering and other forms of daily racism are more socially acceptable, and therefore more omnipresent. Second, despite a high sense of symbolic exclusion and, consequently, restricted identity options, people manage to construct a positive identity. Even if people feel like outsiders or excluded, many are still active agents that invent strategies to avoid negative consequences of exclusion: they reclaim a Belgian identity, minimize negative experiences, and stress their own responsibility in avoiding them; find strength in primordial attachments or a reactive ethnicity; reframe being in-between in positive terms; or—in case they do not have a sense of primordial attachment—identify with a broad, all-inclusive category. Third, people seem to make a distinction between what could be labeled as a categorical identification (being) and an emotional identification (feeling), and boundary drawing seems to impact both differently. Whereas symbolic and behavioral exclusion seems to limit "ethnic options" for emotional identification, this is much less the case for categorical identification. On the contrary, exclusion might even strengthen the need to reaffirm and hence reclaim one's national identity.

NOTES

1. The Twenty Statements Test (TST) is a socio-psychological test designed by Kuhn and McPartland to "measure" people's self-concept. The test is a survey in which people are asked to give 20 different answers to the open-ended question "Who am I?." According to Kuhn, answers can be grouped into 5 categories, including "social groups and classifications," "ideological beliefs," "interests," "ambitions" and "self-evaluations." In our own study, we asked the informants to complete the test before the start of the interview, and did so for two reasons. First, it gave us an idea of the total self-concept of the informant in question, which helped us to contextualize how important their ethnic, national and religious identities were. Second, it helped in establishing rapport and contributed to the flow of the interview because it identified those aspects which were most central to the informants' self-concept and which, consequently, they could and liked to talk about at length.

2. By essentializing I mean giving specific traits to a group, which is a factor in categorizing a group.

3. In 2008, gate manufacturer Feryn was convicted for discrimination because the director publicly declared that he refused to hire mechanics of foreign origin. He argued that he did not want to hire "Moroccans" because his customers preferred someone of Belgian origin and would not appreciate a mechanic with foreign roots (CGKB, 2008). In 2001, ex-employees of the job agency Adecco disclosed that their former employer kept track of "ethnic preferences" of their customers (i.e., corporations or employers that hired their help to find candidates for job openings). During the investigation, over a hundred files were found that thad the code "BBB" (which stands for "Bleu Blanc Belge," a well-known Belgian cow race), in addition to 34 other files that mentioned "no foreigners," "no Blacks," "no Arabs."

REFERENCES

Alba, R. (2005). Bright vs. blurred boundaries: Second-generation assimilation and exclusion in France, Germany, and the United States. *Ethnic and Racial Studies, 28*(1), 20–49.

Allen, C., & Nielsen, J. S. (2002). *Islamophobia in the EU after 11 September 2001: Summary report.* Vienna, AT: European Monitoring Centre on Racism and Xenophobia.

Amnesty International. (2012). Choice and prejudice. *Discrimination against Muslims in Europe.* London, UK: Amnesty International.

Anderson, B. (2006). *Imagined communities: Reflections on the origin and spread of nationalism* (New Edition). London, UK: Verso.

Bail, C. A. (2008). The configuration of symbolic boundaries against immigrants in Europe. *American Sociological Review, 73*(1), 37–59.

Barth, F. (1969). Ethnic groups and boundaries. *The social organization of culture difference.* Boston, MA: Little, Brown.

Bayar, M. (2009). Reconsidering primordialism: An alternative approach to the study of ethnicity. *Ethnic and Racial Studies, 32*(9), 1639–1657.

Beagan, B. L. (2003). Is this worth getting into a big fuss over? Everyday racism in medical school. *Medical education, 37*(10), 852–860.

Betz, H. G., & Meret, S. (2009). Revisiting Lepanto: The political mobilization against Islam in contemporary Western Europe. *Patterns of Prejudice, 43*(3–4), 313–334.

Billiet, J., & De Witte, H. (2008). Everyday racism as predictor of political racism in Flemish Belgium. *Journal of Social Issues, 64*(2), 253–267.

Billiet, J., & Swyngedouw, M. (2009). Etnische minderheden en de Vlaamse kiezers. *Een analyse op basis van de postelectorale verkiezingsonderzoeken.* Leuven, BE: ISPO-KULeuven.

Cornell, S., & Hartmann, D. (2007). *Ethnicity and race: Making identities in a changing world.* Thousand Oaks, CA: Pine Forge Press.

Crul, M., & Schneider, J. (2010). Comparative integration context theory: Participation and belonging in new diverse European cities. *Ethnic and Racial Studies,* *33*(7), 1249–1268. doi: 10.1080/01419871003624068

Davies, C. (1982). Ethnic jokes, moral values and social boundaries. *British Journal of Sociology, 33*(3), 383–403.

Davies, C. (1990). *Ethnic humor around the world: A comparative analysis.* Bloomington, IN: Indiana University Press.

De Rycke, L., Swyngedouw, M., & Phalet, K. (1999). De subjectieve ervaring van discriminatie: Een comparatieve Studie bij Turken, Marokkanen en laagopgeleide Belgen in Brussel. In M. Swyngedouw, K. Phalet, & K. Deschouwer (Eds.), *Minderheden in Brussel. Sociopolitieke houdingen en gedragingen* (pp. 109–148). Brussels, BE: VUBPress.

Duquet, N., Glorieux, I., Laurijssen, I., & Van Dorsselaer, Y. (2005). Problematische schoolloopbanen: Zittenblijven, waterval en ongekwalificeerde uitstroom in het secundair onderwijs. Brussels, BE: TOR Research Group.

Durkheim, E. (1951). *Suicide: A study in sociology* (J. A. Spaulding & G. Simpson, trans.). Glencoe, IL: The Free Press.

Eriksen, T. (2001). Ethnic identity, national identity and intergroup conflict. The significance of personal experiences. In R. D. Ashmore, L. Jussim, & D. Wilder (Eds.), *Social identity, intergroup conflict and conflict reduction* (pp. 42–68). Oxford, UK: Oxford University Press.

Espiritu, Y. L. (1993). *Asian American panethnicity: Bridging institutions and identities.* Philadelphia, PA: Temple University Press.

Essed, P. (1991). *Understanding everyday racism: An interdisciplinary theory* (Vol. 2). Thousand Oaks, CA: Sage.

Essed, P., & Trienekens, S. (2008). 'Who wants to feel white?' Race, Dutch culture and contested identities. *Ethnic and Racial Studies, 31*(1), 52–72.

Field, C. D. (2007). Islamophobia in contemporary Britain: The evidence of the opinion polls, 1988–2006. *Islam and Christian Muslim Relations, 18*(4), 447–477.

Foner, N., & Alba, R. (2008). Immigrant religion in the U.S. and Western Europe: Bridge or barrier to inclusion? *International Migration Review, 42*(2), 360–392.

Geertz, C. (1963): *Old societies and new states: The quest for modernity in Asia and Africa.* New York, NY: The Free Press of Glencoe

Gellner, E. (1997). *Nationalism.* London, UK: Weidenfeld & Nicholson

Granato, N., & Kalter, F. (2001). The persistence of ethnic inequality in the German labor market: Discrimination or under-investment in human capital? *Kolner Zeitschrift fur Soziologie und Sozialpsychologie, 53*(3), 497–520.

Hall, S. (1992). New ethnicities. In J. Donald & A. Rattansi (Eds.), *Race, culture and difference* (pp. 252–259). London, UK: Sage.

Jenkins, R. (1994). Rethinking ethnicity: Identity, categorization and power. *Ethnic and Racial Studies, 17*(2), 197–223.

Jenkins, R. (2008). *Social identity.* New York, NY: Routledge.

Jensen, S. Q. (2011). Othering, identity formation and agency. *Qualitative Studies, 2*(2), 63–78.

Kalter, F., & Kogan, I. (2006). Ethnic inequalities at the transition from school to work in Belgium and Spain: Discrimination or Self-exclusion? *Research in Social Stratification and Mobility, 24*(3), 259–274.

Kuhn, M. H., & McPartland, T. S. (1954). An empirical investigation of self-atti-tudes. *American Sociological Review, 19*(1), 68–76.

Kunst, J. R., Tajamal, H., Sam, D. L., & Ulleberg, P. (2012). Coping with Islamopho-bia: The effects of religious stigma on Muslim minorities' identity formation. *International Journal of Intercultural Relations, 36*(4), 518–532.

Lacante, M., Almaci, M., Van Esbroeck, R., Lens, W., De Metsenaere, M., De Schryver, M., Depreeuw, B., et al. (2007). Allochtonen in het hoger onder-wijs: Onderzoek naar factoren van studiekeuze en studiesucces bij allochtone eerstejaarsstudenten in het hoger onderwijs. *Brussel–Leuven: Vrije Universiteit Brussel–Katholieke Universiteit Leuven.*

Lamont, M., & Molnar, V. (2002). The study of boundaries in the social sciences. *Annual Review of Sociology, 28*, 167–195.

Lievens, J. (1999). Family-forming migration from Turkey and Morocco to Belgium: The demand for marriage partners from the countries of origin. *International Migration Review, 33*(3), 717–744.

Lyman, S. M., & Douglass, W. A. (1973). Ethnicity: Strategies of collective and indi-vidual impression management. *Social Research, 40*(2), 344–365.

Martinovic, B., & Verkuyten, M. (2012). Host national and religious identification among Turkish Muslims in Western Europe: The role of ingroup norms, per-ceived discrimination and value incompatibility. *European Journal of Social Psy-chology, 42*(7), 893–903.

Maxwell, R. (2009). Caribbean and South Asian identification with British society: The importance of perceived discrimination. *Ethnic and Racial Studies, 32*(8), 1449–1469.

McBeth, S. (1983, November). *Layered identity systems in Western Oklahoma Indian communities.* Paper presented at the Annual Meeting of the American Anthro-pological Association, Washington, DC.

McKay, J. (1982). An exploratory synthesis of primordial and mobilizationist ap-proaches to ethnic phenomena. *Ethnic and Racial Studies, 5*(4), 395–420.

Mosse, G. L. (1985). *Toward the final solution: A history of European racism.* Madison, WI: University of Wisconsin Press.

Nagel, J. (1994). Constructing ethnicity: Creating and recreating ethnic identity and culture. *Social Problems, 41*(1), 152–176.

Padilla, A. M. (2006). Bicultural social development. *Hispanic Journal of Behavioral Sciences, 28*(4), 467–497.

Phalet, K., Deboosere, P., & Bastiaenssen, V. (2007). Old and new inequalities in educational attainment: Ethnic minorities in the Belgian Census 1991–2001. *Ethnicities, 7*(3), 390–415.

Phalet, K., & Heath, A. (2011). Ethnic community, urban economy, and second-generation attainment: Turkish disadvantage in Belgium. In R. D. Alba & M. C. Waters (Eds.), *The next generation. Immigrant youth in a comparative perspective* (pp. 135–165). New York, NY: New York University Press.

Portes, A., & Rumbaut, R. G. (1990). *Immigrant America: A portrait.* Berkeley, CA: University of California Press.

Quillian, L. (1995). Prejudice as a response to perceived group threat: Population composition and anti-immigrant and racial prejudice in Europe. *American So-ciological Review, 60*(4), 586-611.

Razack, S. H. (2004). Imperilled Muslim women, dangerous Muslim men and civilised Europeans: Legal and social responses to forced marriages. *Feminist Legal Studies, 12*(2), 129–174.

Reniers, G. (1999). On the history and selectivity of Turkish and Moroccan migration to Belgium. *International Migration, 37*(4), 679–713.

Roosens, E. (1994). The primordial nature of origins in migrant ethnicity. In H. Vermeulen & C. Govers (Eds.), *The anthropology of ethnicity: Beyond "ethnic groups and boundaries"* (pp. 81–104). Amsterdam, NL: Het Spinhuis.

Rumbaut, R. G. (1994). The crucible within: Ethnic identity, self-esteem, and segmented assimilation among children of immigrants. *International Migration Review, 28*(4), 748–794.

Rumbaut, R. G. (2005). Sites of belonging: Acculturation, discrimination, and ethnic identity among children of immigrants. In T. S. Weiner (Ed.), *Discovering successful pathways in children's development: Mixed methods in the study of childhood and family life* (pp. 111–163). Chicago, IL: University of Chicago Press.

Saeed, A. (2007). Media, racism and Islamophobia: The representation of Islam and Muslims in the media. *Sociology Compass, 1*(2), 443–462.

Schneider, J. (2001). Talking German: Othering strategies in public and everyday discourses. *International Communication Gazette, 63*(4), 351–363.

Schneider, J., & Crul, M. (2013). Comparative integration context theory: Participation and belonging in diverse European cities. In M. Crul, J. Schneider, & F. Lelie (Eds.), *The European second generation compared: Does the integration context matter?* Amsterdam, NL: Amsterdam University Press.

Schoonvaere, Q. (2013). Demografische studie over de populatie van Turkse herkomst in België. Brussels, BE: Centrum voor Gelijkheid van Kansen en voor Racismebestrijding.

Shils, E. (1957). Primordial, personal, sacred and civil ties: Some particular observations on the relationships of sociological research and theory. *The British Journal of Sociology, 8*(2), 130–145.

Silberman, R., Alba, R., & Fournier, I. (2006). Segmented assimilation in France? Discrimination in the labour market against the second generation. *Ethnic and Racial Studies, 30*(1), 1–27.

Skrobanek, J. (2009). Perceived discrimination, ethnic identity and the (re-) ethnicisation of youth with a Turkish ethnic background in Germany. *Journal of Ethnic and Migration Studies, 35*(4), 535–554.

Skrobanek, J., & Jobst, S. (2010). Cultural differentiation or self-exclusion on young Turks and repatriates dealing with experiences of discrimination in Germany. *Current Sociology, 58*(3), 463–488.

Smith, A. (1991) *National identity.* Harmondsworth, UK: Penguin.

Spruyt, B., & Elchardus, M. (2012). Are anti-Muslim feelings more widespread than anti-foreigner feelings? Evidence from two split-sample experiments. *Ethnicities, 12*(6), 800–820.

Stevens, P. A. J. (2008). Exploring pupils' perceptions of teacher racism in their context: A case study of Turkish and Belgian vocational education pupils in a Belgian school. *British Journal of Sociology of Education, 29*(2), 175–187.

Strabac, Z., & Listhaug, O. (2008). Anti-Muslim prejudice in Europe: A multilevel analysis of survey data from 30 countries. *Social Science Research, 37*(1), 268–286.

Strauss, A. L., & Corbin, J. M. (1990). *Basics of qualitative research. Grounded theory: Procedures and techniques.* Newbury Park, CA: Sage.

Suny, R. G. (2001). Constructing primordialism: Old histories for new nations. *The Journal of Modern History, 73*(4), 862–896.

Timmerman, C., Vanderwaeren, E., & Crul, M. (2003). The second generation in Belgium. *International Migration Review, 37*(4), 1065–1090.

Vandezande, V., Fleischmann, F., Baysu, G., Swyngedouw, M., & Phalet, K. (2009). Ongelijke kansen en ervaren discriminatie in de Turkse en Marokkaanse tweede generatie. Onderzoeksverslag CeSO/ISPO, 11.

Van der Bracht, K., & Van de Putte, B. (2013). *Het not-in-my-property-syndroom (NIMPY): Etnische discriminatie op de huisvestingsmarkt.* Gent, BE: Universiteit Gent.

Van Kerckem, K., Van der Bracht, K., Stevens, P. A. J., & Van de Putte, B. (2013). Transnational marriages on the decline: Explaining changing trends in partner choice among Turkish Belgians. *International Migration Review, 47*(4), 1006–1038.

Van Kerckem, K., Van de Putte, B., & Stevens, P. A. J. (2013). On becoming 'too Belgian': A comparative study of ethnic conformity pressure through the city as context approach. *City & Community, 12*(4), 335–360.

VDAB. (2012). Kansengroepen in kaart. *Allochtonen op de Vlaamse arbeidsmarkt.* (2nd ed.). Brussels, BE: VDAB Studiedienst.

Verkuyten, M., & DeWolf, A. (2002). Being, feeling and doing: Discourses and ethnic self-definitions among minority group members. *Culture & Psychology, 8*(4), 371–399.

Vertommen, S., & Martens, A. (2005). Allochtone werknemers op lokale arbeidsmarkten [Migrant employees on local labor markets]. *Over-Werk, 2*(3), 73–78.

Waters, M. C. (1990). *Ethnic options: Choosing identities in America.* Berkeley, CA: University of California Press.

Weber, M. (1968). *Economy and society: An outline of interpretive sociology.* New York, NY: Bedminster Press.

Weis, L. (1995). Identity formation and the processes of "othering": Unraveling sexual threads. *Educational Foundations, 9*(1), 17–33.

Wimmer, A. (2013). *Ethnic boundary making: Institutions, power, networks.* Oxford, UK: Oxford University Press.

Zick, A., Pettigrew, T. F., & Wagner, U. (2008). Ethnic prejudice and discrimination in Europe. *Journal of Social Issues, 64*(2), 233–251.

Zolberg, A. R., & Woon, L. L. (1999). Why Islam is like Spanish: Cultural incorporation in Europe and the United States. *Politics & Society, 27*(1), 5–38.

CHAPTER 10

BRITISH MUSLIMS' DISCOURSES OF NATIONAL IDENTITY

Saliha Anjum, Andrew McKinlay,
and Chris McVittie

The terrorist attacks on the World Trade Center in New York in 2001 has kept Islam and Muslims at the forefront of international debates. There have been extensive discussions about terrorism, Islamophobia, and the resulting discrimination against Muslims. This has also led to demands that Muslims show their loyalties to their country of residence. While there is much research on Muslims' identity, there is still much to learn about how Muslims in the United Kingdom make sense of their identities. This chapter seeks to build on earlier research about national identity by examining the different ways British Muslims construct identity across generations.

National Identity, pages 311–337

THEORETICAL BACKGROUND

Muslims in the United Kingdom: A Brief History

Brief Demographic Profile of Muslims in Great Britain

Islam is the second largest religion in the United Kingdom according to data from the 2011 UK Census. In 2011, there were an estimated 2,786,635 Muslims in the UK and Wales, or about 4.4% of the total population.

Table 10.1 presents some additional demographic data on the Muslim population in England and Wales from 1961 to 2011.

The Muslim population has grown significantly since 1961, and the effects on the demography of England and Wales are important. Indeed, from 1961 to 2011, the percent change in the total Muslim population has been over 5,000%. In turn, the percent of the Muslim population of the total population in England and Wales increased from less than 1% in 1961 to nearly 5% in 2011 (4.83%). Moreover, as the Muslim population increased so have the number of Mosques in the nation, from 7 in 1961 to approximately 1,500 in 2011.

Being Muslim is a religion, not an ethnicity or race. Table 10.2 displays the race and ethnicity of the Muslim population in England. The three largest Muslim race/ethnic groups, self-identified, in 2011 were British Asians (1,830,560), White (210,260), and Arab (178,195).

Muslims tend to be concentrated in certain areas in England. Figure 10.1 displays this concentration. The darker the color, the greater percentage of the Muslim population in that area of England. However, they do not appear to be isolated and lacking in interaction with Christians. The isolation index for 2011 is 14.16, and the interaction index is 49.98.[1]

TABLE 10.1   Muslims in England and Wales, 1961–2011

Year	Muslim Population	Percent of Population in England and Wales	Registered Mosques
1961	50,000	0.11	7
1971	226,000	0.46	30
1981	553,000	1.11	149
1991	950,000	1.86	443
2001	1,600,000	3.07	614
2011	2,706,000	4.83	1,500
Percent change: 1961 to 2011	5,312%	4,290%	21,329%

Source: www.brin.ac.uk/figures

TABLE 10.2 Race and Ethnic Composition of the Muslim Population in England, 2011	
Race/Ethnicity	Population
White	210,260
Mixed	102,582
British Asian	1,830,560
Black/Black British	272,015
Arab	178,195
Other	112,094
Total	2,706,066

Source: www.brin.ac.uk/figures

Figure 10.1 Distribution of Muslims in England. *Source:* http://en.wikipedia.org.

Religious and British Identities

Available research on the religious and national identities of British Muslims shows mixed results.[2] In some studies, religious identity dominates the life of Muslims, while in other research belonging is more important. According to the Labour Force Survey (2003–2004), about 65% of Muslims describe themselves in terms of their national identity as British, English, Scottish, or Welsh rather than in terms of their ethnic identity, and 93% of UK-born Muslims also considered their national identity to be British. Furthermore, more than half of the Muslim adults living in England and Wales reported their religion to be very important for their self-identity (Attwood, 2003).

A larger percentage of second generation Muslims compared to first-generation Muslims consider themselves British. Din (2006) found that second generation youth prefer being British than Asian or Pakistani. Hyphenated identities are often used, such as Asian-British, Scottish-Asian, and Pakistani-Scot. An interesting feature is that young people perceived their parents as more Pakistani rather than more British. Young people express more attachment and adjustment to Britain through language skills, employment, and length of stay, in contrast to identifying with their ethnic group. Research suggests that few young people describe themselves as "Asians" and most present themselves as culturally "British," which is reflected in their appearance, forms of socializing, and choice of entertainment (Modood, Berthoud, Lakey, Nazroo, Smith, Virdee, & Beishon, 1997; Stopes-Roe & Cochrane, 1990; Ghuman, 1999).

Geography within Britain has a role in national identity. Hopkins (2007) examined national and religious identity among Scottish-Muslims, and focused on two themes: being Scottish and being Muslim. Hopkins found that though there were some ties in ethnicity, these Muslims preferred their Scottish identity over other identities. This is attributed to the fact that they were born and brought up in Scotland, received their education there, and had Scottish accents.

The research shows that British Muslims identify as British. Yet, other research argues that British Muslims give more importance to their religious identity than to other cultural identities. Jacobson (1997) conducted research on the dual identities among British-Pakistani Muslims. Her young respondents gave more importance to their religious identity than to their ethnic identity. Moreover, because nationalism is forbidden in Islam, they expressed their belongingness to a more global Muslim Umma (brotherhood). They draw very clear boundaries between what is right and wrong in their religion and think that their ethnic identity is not well defined, so they prefer their religious identity (Jacobson, 1997).

Thus we can see that the identities of British Muslims are mixed and not conclusive. There is no general agreement on whether British Muslims give more importance to their religious identity or to their national identity. According to another study, in order to show the two aspects of their culture and nationality, second generation Muslims make use of hybrid identities like British-Pakistani (Modood et al., 1997). A similar idea has been very skilfully discussed in the following words of Ansari (2002):

> Among young British Muslims, there is much heart searching about where they belong—in Britain, or in an "Islamic" community? They are developing their perceptions of national, ethnic and religious belonging, and negotiating new ways of being Muslim in Britain, in which the British element of their identity form important part of the equation.

This indicates that being British and being Muslim are the part of same equation, as seen in hyphenated identities. But how these two identities function together is another question that is beyond the scope of our research. In this chapter, we focus on how acceptance or rejection by the host society affects national identity.

Acculturation and Being Muslim

Non-acceptance by White peers is a major stressor experienced by some Muslim immigrants. Moreover, well settled, high profile British Muslims view British multiculturalism as a superficial strategy: it fails to accept the individual, focuses on certain aspects of the individual, and does not welcome different faiths (Modood & Ahmad, 2007).

Assimilation[3] is a complaint among some Muslims as are the negative attitudes toward Muslims held by some of the White British population. Both factors may be a barrier for Muslims from identifying as "British" (Modood et al., 1997). Jacobson (1997) reported that Muslim respondents believed that their being accepted as British is linked to assimilation: an unreasonable demand for them to leave their culture. The negative perceptions of the White British population may not be speculative. Khan (2000) found that British citizens consider Islamic values and culture to be backward and out-dated. Acceptance, then, is a major challenge in the way of Muslims fully integrating into British society.

Another factor challenging Muslim integration is language. Vedder (2005) found that national language proficiency contributes to high self-esteem among Muslim immigrant students in Netherlands, whereas ethnic language proficiency and ethnic identity leads to negative adaptation to the host country (Vedder, 2005). Based on this and similar findings, we may hypothesize that Muslims in Britain may also face similar challenges to Muslims in the Netherlands.

It is clear that there is much research on the national identity among British Muslims, but little on the collection and analyses of discursive information. A discursive design allows us to look at their everyday lives, how they perceive how others perceive and interact with them, and how these factors lead to the construction of identity. In this chapter, we look at two themes of national identity construction: (a) positive construction of national identity, and (b) negative construction of national identity. Moreover, we also examine and discuss dilemmas associated with the construction of national identity, including how British Muslims make sense of their British national identity.

Theories of Nations and National Identity

Essentialists and Primordialists

Previous research has offered highly contrasting ways of studying and understanding national identities. One version proposes that nations are rooted in primordial elements of human experience, such as kinship ties or genetic similarities (e.g., Van Den Berghe, 1990). For them national identity is a matter of fixed, unchanging factors. In another form of this argument, language is presented as marking an essential feature of the nation and of national identity. In these terms, language is seen as an intrinsic part of establishing a nation, with language use denoting identification with the nation (Fishman, 1972; Wright, 2000). For other scholars, nations have less to do with the manifestation of primordial or essential elements than they do with the embodiment of political and social forces.

Modernists point to the construction of nations as part of the formation of social units that were required for the effective implementation of certain forms of production (Hobsbawm & Ranger, 1983). On this argument, national identities, instead of being indicators of inherent factors that link the individual to the community, are outcomes of historically and politically situated forms of social organisation. All such approaches to understanding nations, then, have somewhat different implications for studying national identities: they can be seen either as ostensibly natural and inherent entities, or as historical and political products. Smith (1986; 1991; 1999) has argued that these differences can be reconciled, with nations encompassing a range of features taken up by its populations. What approaches share is the central tenet that nations exist beyond individuals' grasp, and that national identities incorporate essential, pre-existing features.

Postmodernists and Constructivists

Other theories of national identities, by contrast, adopt a different perspective about national identities. Postmodern theorists such as Anderson (1991) and Bhabha (1990), for example, have argued that nations should be understood as a collection of cultural artifacts that are in effect linguistic or imagined constructions. In a similar vein, discursive writers (Billig, 1995; Condor, 2000) have pointed out that nations do not "exist" beyond individuals per se, but are imagined. Billig (1995), for example, points to the ways in which nations are routinely presented to us in unnoticed "banal" ways that do not reflect external realities but, instead, construct specific versions of reality. Similarly, Condor

(2000) points to how descriptions of a world made up of nation states permeate many of the ways in which people make sense of themselves and of others, and are reworked to the requirements of local contexts. National identities are constructions that are designed to accomplish more specific objectives.

It is this latter understanding of national identities that forms the basis for our research. We look to extend previous understandings of how British Muslims negotiate and construct their identities, British or Muslim. As will be seen below, individuals, in constructing their identities, refer to specific elements of a nation, such as language, that they use as links with others. Our focus is on the actions that respondents take, via their descriptive accounts, and the contextual nature of how national identities are constructed.

Theoretical Framework: Identities and Discourse Analysis

In order to examine how British Muslims construct their identities, we draw upon the theoretical approach of discourse analysis (McKinlay & McVittie, 2008). Discourse analysts treat discourse as a topic in its own right and not just the expression of one's inner thoughts. Discourse has certain properties that people recognize and use to accomplish certain goals.

Another feature of discourse is social construction of identities in a particular interactional context. So identities do not occur in vacuum, but require a social setting where two or more people are involved in a social action (McKinlay & McVittie, 2011).

The discourse analytic perspective has particular implications for understanding identity. McKinlay and McVittie (2011) have summarized the important features of identities: Identities are the discursive characterizations about self or others that are not condensable to objective facts about that person, such characterizations develop an identity that is either unique or common with others, these characterizations are action oriented and bound up with social actions, and these categorizations are situational. Based on this approach, identities are constructed, fluid in nature, subject to change, negotiated, resistant, and acceptable.

Applying this perspective to the study of national identity offers an understanding that is markedly different from that found elsewhere. In this regard, the map of nations as they appear in the world atlas with rigid boundaries is considered to be misleading in many ways. For example, according to Giroux (1995), processes like globalization and development of supra-national political bodies such as the European Union are some of the major threats to the status of the nation state. Rather than treating national identities as (mere) indicators of geographical affiliation, therefore, discourse analysis turns attention to the issue of what people are actively doing when they claim, resist or rework descriptions of identity. For example,

De Cillia, Reisigl and Wodak (1999) suggested that people draw their national identity on cultural similarities and national boundaries while focusing on common national myths, symbols, memories and rituals of everyday life. According to them, these symbolic processes of national identity are not static but instead are constructed dynamically in discourse. In this regard, Reicher and Hopkins (2001) point towards the importance of understanding the way in which people are constructed as belonging to one's own nation. They further suggested that analysts should be aware of the wide variety of resources like economic development and cultural histories that are available to the individual to draw from, in a particular context of discourse, to construct his national identity. This suggests that there should be some particular forms of discourse that could be attributed to nationalism. For example, Billig (1995) used the term "banal nationalism" to refer to the practices of nationalism that is, nationalist talk and expressions like "we" and "us." He further argues that these are the expressions that are used by individuals to reproduce their relationship with their nations. The research in the field of discourse of national identity indicates that national identities are characterizations of oneself and others through the use of 'identification' with a nation. Moreover, such characterizations also attribute common features of a nation to oneself and others. Below, we will see how British Muslims draw upon and use characterizations such as these.

METHODS

Data: The Semi-Structured Interviews

For this study, data were collected using semi-structured interviews and focus groups conducted with first and second generation British Muslims residing in Edinburgh and Glasgow (both in Scotland, UK). The data come from 40 semi-structured interviews and four focus groups, conducted between June 2011 and December 2012. This study has used the term British instead of Scottish because many of the respondents moved to Scotland from England, so they consider their identity as British and not specifically Scottish. The interview questions were constructed as open-ended in order to resemble naturalistic conversation.

Participants' age range was from 17 to 70 years. Both first and second generations of Muslims were included in the study to provide diverse observations of the subject under study. First generation Muslims included participants who migrated to Britain from their home countries as an adult or as a teenager and were conscious of their migration from home country to Britain. Second generation Muslims were those participants who were either born in Britain or came to Britain at a very young age (up to 8 years) along with their parents. Both of these generations were included in the study in order to explore the differences of their experiences in relation to Britain. Similarly, participants belonged to both genders, which allowed us to have a cross-gender understanding of their lives in Britain. This is important because Muslim males and females have different roles in life based on their religious beliefs. Therefore, men and women were expected to display somewhat different aspects of experiences. Current study has not related its findings with participants' other demographic information such as education or employment status; therefore, it is not mentioned here. Considering the fact that the majority of first generation Muslims in Britain are from South Asia, especially from Pakistan, interview and focus group schedules were translated into Urdu. In order to validate the translated version of interview schedule it was reviewed by two multilingual professionals. In providing English translations of Urdu interviews and focus groups, every attempt was made to ensure that translated data were as close as possible to the wordings used by the participants themselves. As a reliability measure, the final extracts for data analysis were reviewed by a multilingual researcher to establish the closeness of translation to the actual data.

All discussions were audio-recorded with the consent of the participants and later transcribed using an abbreviated version of Jeffersonian transcription notation (Jefferson, 2004). This form of transcription notation is used to transcribe not just the words used by participants but also features of how talk is delivered, including speakers' use of speech particles, pauses, emphasis, overlapping talk, and so on. For present purposes, transcriptions of the extracts presented below include the following features:

(2.0)   numbers between parentheses indicate a pause between utterances measured in seconds;
  (.)   a dot within parentheses indicates a brief (untimed) pause between utterances;
 a::   colons indicate that the immediately preceding sound has been prolonged;
(name)   words in parentheses indicate descriptions of material that has been rendered anonymous by the transcriber;
that-   hyphen indicates broken off speech;
   I   is abbreviation for Interviewer;
  FM   initials of the respondent.

These extracts therefore should not be seen as free from grammatical errors as they are designed to reproduce both what the participants said and how it was said.

Data were analysed for major themes, then all the extracts were selected if national identity was mentioned. These extracts were then micro-analyzed for identifying the discursive strategies and patterns used by the respondents. Finally, nine extracts that exemplified the participants' uses of positive and negative constructions of national identity were selected for analysis and use in this chapter.

FINDINGS

Our analyses cover both positive and negative construction of British identity. We examine results from a series of semi-structured interviews in putting together a portrait of what each type of identity entails and the reasons behind such identities.

Positive Constructions of British Identity

This section covers the positive constructions of national identities among first and second generation British Muslims. The first two extracts are from second generation participants, and the last three from first generation Muslims. We explore how the two generations make different claims about their identity while using positive references from their daily lives.

Second Generation Respondents

The first extract is taken from an interview with a second generation female. We will see her construct multiple identities and how they facilitate one another.

Extract 1: FM

1	I	While living in UK how would you define your religious identity as a British
2		Muslim?
3	FM	Umm yes I am an (sect name) Muslim in Britain and but as an (sect) Muslim I
4		can be Insha'Allah on God willing I will be (sect) Muslim wherever I lived
5		umm and the fact that (.) God so fitted me to be born in this country that must
6		be a good- it's a good thing I am very fortunate because when I- because in this
7		country I am allowed to practice my faith I don't have any restrictions upon me
8		you know saying *aslamoalaikum* (.) greeting people you know with the you
9		know with a little prayer for them and (0.5) you know I can practice my faith
10		as I like to (.) some people might think it strange (.) some people sometimes
11		people can abuse you for it but they can't there is not actually a law to say that
12		what they are doing is right so the law is actually saying that you can practice
13		your faith so I think that's why this is a:: this is a wonderful country to live in.

FM is responding to the question about her religious identity. She began by introducing herself as belonging to a particular sect of Muslims in Britain, and added an additional dimension to her British Muslim identity by introducing the sect along with her Muslim identity. She then claims that she will remain a Muslim of that sect regardless of where she might live. Her loyalty to her sect is clear based on her saying that no matter where she lives she will maintain her Muslim identity. Further, by using the expression of "God willing" in Line 4, she presents her identity in terms of her religion; she is relying on the belief that whatever happens, happens by God's Will.

In Line 5, FM attributes her birth "in this country" as a good event, and associates the event with God. Mentioning God as a divine who allowed her to be born in this particular country is constructing her identity around her strong belief in God. There is also the notion of attributing "goodness" to being born "in this country"—Britain. FM is building her identity based on *place*, which is an important factor in constructing identity (Dixon & Durrheim, 2000).

FM merges two identities in her responses. In the first two lines of her response, FM merges her religious identity as a Muslim belonging to a specific sect with her British identity. Further, *Goodness* is important to FM. In Line 6, FM used the word good twice, and strengthens her claim about *Goodness*. The reason for such a clam is that she is allowed to practice her faith in Britain. Britain is a place where she is free to practice her religion. She supports her claim with the example of greeting people with a small prayer, and thus provides a vivid example of her freedom in Britain.

Although she enjoys the freedom of practising her religion in Britain, she introduces the possibility that some people might not be so receptive. However, she immediately claims that people cannot prohibit or abuse her right to practice her religion as it is her legal right to do so. This has also been put forth as the reason for this country being "wonderful." So Britain is presented as a wonderful country in which to live because it gives her freedom to practise her religion and legal security for her religious beliefs.

In this extract, FM has constructed three forms of identity i.e., sectarian, Muslim, and British. The confluence of these three identities suggests the possibility of hyphenated identities that incorporate multiple aspects of an individual's experiences. In FM's case, being British is a facilitating factor because it allows her to practice her religion freely.

Our second extract is from a second generation female respondent. In this extract, MS describes how her parents helped her understand her culture and religion and its differences from British culture.

Extract 2: MS

1 I   As you said earlier that British culture is different from Islamic culture so how
2   you manage to adapt here?

3 MS I think because like I said before my parents gave me a very good grounding

4   (0.8) in terms of my values- my moral values that they gave me at home (0.8)

5   so I was able to become an own person (.) I didn't have to be like my friends

6   (0.5) my friends actually accepted me for the way that I was (1.0) because they

7   had so much respect for the fact that I respected my values that I have been

8   given at home by my family (1.0) in terms of my (1.0) umm religious

9   obligations (.) I use to wear the hijab when I was at school and the university

10   (0.8.) I use to umm (1.5) pray (.) if I had to pray (0.5) I go and pray in school

11   or university and all those things were accepted by my friends (.) and I think

12   that is an aspect of British society (.) which allows us to be Muslims here (0.5)

13   even now that you are a British Muslim (0.5) I think it's the way that the

14   British (2.0) the British culture is very adaptable to other people's

15   circumstances (0.8) and in fact I find that they are (1.5) I think that the British

16   people are actually more willing and much more accommodating for your

17   needs than even our own culture is (.) if you go to Pakistan and you need to do

18   something in terms of observing a certain thing (.) regardless of whether you

19   are a Muslim or Christian (0.8) they don't have the same umm understanding

20   and the same willingness to cooperate with you (0.8) as the British society does

21   and that's an amazing quality that the Brits have (0.8) that they would go out of

22   their way to allow you to live your life the way you want to live it (1.0) and I

23   think that's very important (.) I think that's been a great I have had (1.0) I am

24   very lucky I have had very good experiences in my life where I haven't felt like

25   (2.0) I have to accommodate myself in any other way (1.0) I can be myself

26   (0.5) and I think I have been able to do that throughout my life and it's been (.)

27   I have been happy to live my life as the British Muslim (0.8) I am a British

28   person (0.8) I have my Muslim values (.) I have Pakistani values as well that

29   my family has given me (0.5) but (0.5) I am own person.

In this extract, MS was asked about her being Muslim and her adjustment to British society. MS responded by referring to how her parents had given her sound moral values. According to MS, this grounding has helped her become "an own person"; the basis of her individual identity are the moral values instilled in her by her parents. MS is constructing her identity as a unique person, different from her friends, who may be British, but who still accept her. Her friends are very accepting and respect her religious values. In Lines 9 and 10, MS gives examples of the religious obligations that she used to follow, including wearing hijab and offering prayers and "all those things." According to MS, these religious obligations were accepted by her British friends, and are an indication about the acceptance of her values by British society.

In Line 12, she states that this acceptance by British society actually "allows her to be Muslim here." She expands this argument by giving details that British society is "adaptable to other people's circumstances." This is similar to what FM mentioned in the previous extract—being British facilitates her identity as a Muslim. MS makes the same claim but in greater detail. MS's view about the acceptance by British society is further supported by comparing British society with Pakistani society in Line 16.

MS continues to claim that British society is very accommodating by noting that it is more accommodating than her Pakistani culture. This use of the expression "out of the way" indicates the intensity of the efforts made by Britons to accommodate people from different religious backgrounds. In Lines 23–24, MS uses the expression, "I am very lucky." She is content with her life in Britain as a British Muslim.

Second generation Muslims tend to have multiple parallel identities. In the last three lines of her responses, MS summarizes her responses by constructing her identity as a hyphenated British-Muslim-Pakistani. This extract is a good example of second generation Muslims' construction of multiple identities. Like FM, MS has also constructed being a British citizen as something facilitating her Muslim identity. FM attributed this to the religious freedom in Britain, and MS attributed it to the acceptance found in British society. In both the extracts, there is no mention of any identity conflict between these multiple identities—as described by the respondents, these hyphenated identities seem to facilitate one another. Moreover, it is clear that MS feels happy and fortunate to be a British citizen.

Our results suggest that second generation Muslims construct a positive British identity because they view British society as accepting of their Muslim backgrounds. Being born in Britain appears to be a primary reason for such a positive construction of one's identity among these two second generation Muslims. This raises an interesting question about place of birth and national identity. In the next extract we examine the views of first generation Muslims.

First Generation Muslims and Identity

The following extract is by a first generation male, who has been living in UK for the past 40 years. In this extract he is discussing his culture and identity.

Extract 3: SMR

1	I	What different things of both cultures do you follow?
2	SMR	I don't think so that it is aa::: if you ask this question from my children then I
3		think they can give you a better answer than this, but although we are British
4		but our culture is still Pakistani, culture of our children is possibly different but
5		we are still Pakistani, we have Pakistani culture, meaning we follow
6		everything.

This extract is from a first generation British Muslim male. He was asked to discuss some aspects of his home and host culture. Interestingly, he did not begin the interview by talking about his culture but began with the use of "I don't think so," and then advised the interviewer that she should address this question to his children in order to get a better answer. By saying this, SMR is positioning himself as someone not suitable to answer this question, and minimizing the possibility of later accountabilities.

After establishing his inability to provide a "better answer," he returns to the actual question and goes on to develop at greater length, his national identity as "British." He used the words "we are British," which indicates the addition of some unspecified people in his response. The question was directed towards SMR individually, but he has used "we," which may indicate that he might be constructing this response on behalf of people of his generation and nationality and not about himself. This use of "we" may be seen as an example of "banal nationalism" as was briefly discussed in the introduction.

Although SMR initially claimed to be British, he added a cultural condition to this identity construction. SMR is British but his culture is Pakistani. Multiple identities are being raised, but SMR is constructing his national identity as British but his cultural identity as Pakistani. He is forming the hyphenated identity of a British-Pakistani. This construction of multiple identities is very similar to what we have seen in earlier extracts from FM and MS, but without the Muslim attachment.

SMR views his culture as different from his children's. He does so in Line 4. SMR has positioned himself so that his culture is different from his children's. In Line 5, he lists three things in asserting his Pakistani identity by saying that he is "still Pakistani," has Pakistani culture, and follows everything in that culture. The use of the phrases such as "still Pakistani" is pointing towards the continuation of his Pakistani identity (Lines 4 & 5).

Although he claimed earlier that he is British, soon afterwards he claims that he is "still Pakistani." Both identities seem to work together smoothly, and this may indicate that he is claiming to have both simultaneously. Then, after giving some examples about his culture, he introduces his religious identity into this equation of hyphenated identities. Let us see how he further constructs his identity in the following extract.

Extract 4: SMR

1	SMR	. . . we are a:: proud to be Muslims we are proud as well as to be British as well
2		as but obviously we live here and we are hundred percent dedicated to this
3		country aa we going to die here, we going to be buried here and our children
4		are here now, our roots are, we are leaving our roots in this country in UK so
5		obviously we are British and we are also loyal to this country but if there is
6		anything happen in Pakistan which is now a days are I feel very pain . . .

In the first line of this extract, he is claiming to have Muslim identity as well as British identity. Moreover, he give them equal status. He then expands on his British identity by giving a detailed list of examples of why such an identity is important to him. First, he argues that he is 100% dedicated to the country. As a first generation immigrant this claim is significant because his discussion about his other identities may have put into question his loyalty to Britain. He has made it clear that he is fully dedicated to Britain.

SMR then claims that he will be buried in Britain, and further highlights his loyalty to his British identity. This could be seen in the context of many first generation immigrant Muslims wishing to be buried in their homelands. Some people might want to be buried in their country of origin, but SMR is expressing his desire to be buried in Britain. SMR goes further by arguing that since his children are here, his roots are in Britain. So not only is SMR claiming a wish to be buried in Britain, but he is also creating a lasting relationship with the country by leaving his roots here in the form of his children.

In Line 5, after claiming to be British he then discusses his home country and constructs a relationship with it by stating that anything negative happens in his home country, "I feel very pain." So now he is working up his relationship with his home country. This may be an effort at avoiding any accountability for not being loyal to his home country. So though he claimed loyalty to Britain, he also claims that he feels pain if anything happens in Pakistan. There is no way for us to know exactly the meaning behind these statements. For him, then, identity is not a straightforward matter of aligning either with Britain or with Pakistan but involves elements of both.

Similarly to FM and MS, SMR worked up his identity using three different identities as British-Muslim-Pakistani. Also, SMR saw no conflict between these identities—they exist parallel to one another. Interestingly, SMR also represented his British national identity by using a positive discourse, but unlike FM and MS, SMR used different examples to support such an identity. FM and MS argued that acceptance by British society is a major factor of their British identity, whereas SMR focused on his children and being buried in Britain. SMR did not mention the acceptance or rejection of British society as factors in his British identity. Moreover, he also fluctuated between his cultural, religious, and national identity throughout his discourse. SMR's comments offer one or more interpretations. First, his comments may express a desire not to be held accountable from any society. Second, SMR may have very tactfully presented all three identities as of equal importance to him. Finally, his comments may indicate that national identity is a complex and at times confusing process.

In some cases, national identity is also constructed as a source of personal benefits. The following extract is an example of this kind of identity construction produced by a first generation male who has been living in the UK for over 40 years.

Extract 5: GA

1	I	Describe about your attachments to these countries?
2	GA	The point is this that the difference between Pakistan and Britain (1.0) life style
3		and:: (2.0) in practical life like the problems a person face so because in this
4		country (1.0) this is a developed country so comparatively there are more
5		opportunities and therefore we feel more comfortable here and therefore we
6		have also kept our nationality British because we have ease in it but our country
7		is our so as far as we are concerned (1.0) we remember our country (0.5) but
8		because of the circumstances there we don't go there sometimes (1.0) or go
9		reluctantly so it is a separate thing but the love of your country is still there (.)
10		we were born there and we got education from there also (.) Masters I did from
11		Government college Lahore MA Economics (.) so my all education is from
12		there (.) after coming here I haven't taken any further education but as compare
13		to this what I have noted in my kids (1.0) that the kids doesn't feel that what we
14		feel about Pakistan (.) for them this is (pointing downwards) more important (.)
15		and they in fact- as we live in Scotland so they call themselves Scottish (0.5)
16		my one daughter who is married and living in Luton (.) she also feel good in
17		calling herself Scottish (.) so the next generation is of this condition (0.5) they
18		have more with this country (.) with Pakistan:: because their parents- father is
19		from there they have some attachment but not more than this.

GA was asked about his attachments to his native and host countries. GA begins by constructing life style differences between Pakistan and Britain, though he was not asked about differences. GA then expands the comparison by using the example of problems in practical life, and claims that Britain has more opportunities because it is a developed nation. First, GA concludes that Britain is better in terms of opportunities and uses this conclusion as a reason for his comfort in Britain and for maintaining his British nationality. So GA is claiming to have British identity because of the benefits to be realized in Britain that are not available in Pakistan.

In Line 7, GA reminisces about Pakistan. If he introduces himself as a British national with no regards to his home country, he may be held accountable for being forgetful or disloyal to his home country, especially since earlier he had stated his preference for his British identity over a Pakistani identity. He attends to this dilemma by claiming that he still remembers his country and also claims to love it in later lines.

He addresses the issue of not going to Pakistan or going there reluctantly because it is, to him, a separate matter. He is not going to discuss the issue. Regardless of the circumstances he still loves his native country where he was born and educated, and uses the name of his college alma mater to reaffirm his statement. "Place identity" is at work here as GA is relating to his place of birth.

Generational differences exist between GA and his children regarding Pakistan. GA states that whatever he feels for Pakistan, his children do not feel the same, and they feel proud in calling themselves Scottish. Because his children live in Scotland, they identify with Scotland rather than with Pakistan. GA uses his daughter as an example, which is interesting because it suggests a division of two national identities within Britain. According to GA, his daughter lives in Luton, which is in England, but she prefers to call herself Scottish. Thus, in spite being part of Great Britain, his daughter specifies her identity as Scottish. His children have little attachment to Pakistan because it is not the country in which they were born. This seems to be a consistent finding between first and second generation immigrants: first generation Muslims relate more to their home country because it is their birth place, while second generation Muslims relate more to their Scottish or British identity *because it is their country of origin.*

In this extract, we have seen two forms of national identities. First, GA's construction of his identity as British and then later his construction of his children's identity as Scottish. Both the constructions use positive evaluations. First GA associates his British identity with comfort and ease and secondly, he then reports that his daughter feels "good" about her Scottish identity. Also, GA discusses concerns about his native country, balancing his attachment to both Great Britain and Pakistan. This has also been seen in the extracts of SMR in that he constructed his British and Pakistani identity together to create a balance. Moreover, like SMR, GA has constructed his whole response with the use of "we" instead of "I," thus using some form of expression that indicates something about nationalist inclusion.

Negative Constructions of British Identity

This section deals with somewhat negative constructions of national identity and identity dilemmas. We examine, in detail, how first and second generation British Muslims differ in making use of negative social cues in constructing their national identities. The first two extracts are from first generation respondents, and the last two are from second generation British Muslims. The following extract is taken from an interview with a first generation Muslim female discussing the negative cues she receives due to her ethnicity.

Extract 6: MA

1   I   So how that impacts you?

2   MA   Yes I feel dishearten a lot (.) I feel a lot of pain that what is the reason (.)

3	although we are now British nationals (.) after coming home if I tell my
4	husband sometimes about this he says to me that the way she spoke to you, you
5	also speak with her in the same manner, what is lacking in you, you have the
6	same passport as she has, he says this to me that talk in the same manner as she
7	does, why don't you talk to her similarly, you have got the same passport as
8	hers (.) but:: I can't be like that I mean I don't feel myself on their level or (.) I
9	mean or I also have language problem that I cannot talk like that (.) but my
10	husband tells me that you are same like they are nationals here we are also
11	nationals here, there is nothing like that (.) if somebody talk to you equally
12	reply them back (1.0) whatever rights they have got, you also have same rights
13	as a British national (1.0) if there is any problem (.) if they can go to court, we
14	can also go so (1.0) there is no such problem.

MA begins with an emotional response. The use of words like "feel," "dishearten," and "pain" indicates the construction of emotions as a result of being treated poorly by others. MA is not only explaining that she "felt dishearten" but also enhancing its intensity by using the expression "a lot." In the next line, she does the same while using the expression of "pain." An extreme level of emotional discomfort has been constructed here as a response to the attitude of local people. MA paints herself as a victim. Agency is located here in the local people, who are the agents of creating such intense feelings in MA as a result of their rejecting of her; to them she is not British.

Later, she changes this emotional discourse into a search for reasons why she is being rejected. She constructs her identity as a British national and looks for the reason(s) for her mistreatment in spite of being British. The implication also indicates that being British is a status which should protect her from such behavior or attitudes. If she is not British then such attitudes are justified, but if she is a British national these attitudes are not justified— she is an equal to local people.

Having British nationality is or should be associated with a certain status in society. In the following line, she reports her husband's response to this issue. First, in Line 4, the use of "sometimes" refers to the frequency of her reporting these events to her husband, which indicates that these events happen on a number of occasions and she reports only a few to her husband. So when she tells this to her husband he advises her to speak with the locals in the same manner. According to MA, her husband asks "what is lacking in you?" and then answered the question himself by referring to the fact that that "you have got the same passport." Having a British passport is seen as having the licence to speak with local people as equals. The use of "what is lacking in you?" makes it clear that she needs to stand up for herself and assert that she be treated as a British citizen.

Later, MA repeats her husband's response and constructs its significance. Later she does admit her inability to view herself as at the "same level" as locals (Line 8). MA is struggling with her status, and has trouble placing herself on equal footing as locals, which she attributes to her inability to speak English. If MA does not speak English adequately, then she cannot respond to the local people even if she wishes to do so. Thus, language is an important factor in British identity. In MA's case, her difficulties with language are a problem in being accepted as a British national by the local community.

In this extract, national identity is constructed through equal status between locals and immigrants, language, and the entitlement of civic rights as citizens. MA constructs her identity as being a British citizen even though her construction of a British identity is not recognised or accepted by locals, and as a result she does not "feel [her]self on their level." MA has attributed all the discourse about equality with locals to her husband and that she "actively voices" (Wooffitt, 1992) his responses in her descriptions of her problems.

By attributing to her husband the potential for challenging other people's actions, MA is able to develop her claims to identity in two ways. First, the active voicing of her husband's words provides apparent corroboration of her claims to identity and suggests that these are not simply based on her own words and actions. Second, she distances herself from making these challenges against others. Should these challenges be unsuccessful, any further querying of identity is likely to be directed at the nominated source of the challenge, that is MA's husband, rather than at MA herself. MA is thus able to offer a defence of her claims to be British while also protecting that defence from non-acceptance that would further undermine the identity that she is claiming. All of this discursive work points to the sensitive and potentially problematic description of identity that MA proposes for herself.

Extract 7: SAL

1	I	Like how you feel about "rude attitudes" that you mentioned earlier?
2	SAL	I feel pain from this sometimes that when I this thing when I went to Pakistan
3		two years back then I noted this thing a lot (.) in fact I felt pain from this thing
4		(1.0) that I mean when we are here then they say us overseas (1.0) or I mean
5		they say us refugees (1.0) right but when we go to our country then they say
6		they have come from abroad (1.5) they live there (.) so when I came back I
7		said I mean from this point of view we don't have an identity (.) these people
8		say us that we are, mean we are no matter we have got British nationality (.)
9		anything happens (.) we are still called Pakistani (1.0) right (1.0) we are from
10		here mean no matter how much we say that we are rooted here I don't think so
11		(.) from this perspective I don't think this so (.) no matter if we live here years
12		after years (.) no matter how long we have been here but no.

This discourse is from a first generation female from Pakistan (SAL). The discussion began with the interviewer's question about her earlier mention of the rude attitudes of British people and its impact on her happiness. Like MA in Extract 6, SAL is hurt by the bad attitudes displayed by British people. She expands her response by adding other experiences affecting her emotional pain. She mentions her visit to Pakistan two years previously and associates "a thing" with it, which she first mentions as "noticed" but then says "in fact I felt pain from this thing" (Line 4). She unfolds that "thing" as a sort of dilemma that she is called a *refugee* in her host country and an *overseas citizen* in her home country. After explaining this situation she claims that, based on this, "we don't have an identity."

There is a general strategy of avoiding personalizing problems. SAL uses "we" instead of "I" and has generalized her problems to all Pakistani immigrants like her. This is indeed a very painful construction of her identity dilemma of being an immigrant, because she has presented herself as having a home and not having an identity of her own. She has constructed a complaint about British society as non-accepting of refugees, and also a non-acceptance by her native society because of the fact that they no longer live in Pakistan. So she presents the situation as one in which her home country has accepted her permanent immigration to the host country, and the host country is resisting accepting her as a legitimate member. This is an ideological dilemma facing many immigrants (Billig, Condor, Edwards, Gane, Middleton, & Radley, 1988).

SAL states that even if she is a British national she will be referred to as Pakistani by natives. She expands her comment by saying "anything happens (.) we are still called Pakistani." She thus constructs an identity dilemma—having no identity—and then claims that there is no way of resolving this dilemma. Though she is rooted and has a strong connection to Britain, it does not help her from being viewed as a refugee. Regardless of what happens, she is going to have that dilemma throughout her life. She has constructed a pessimistic future by saying that this situation will remain the same even if "we live here years after years."

SAL's extract exhibits how non-acceptance by the host society can lead to the formation of identity dilemmas among some immigrants. The responses of local people play a crucial role in building an immigrant's sense of his or her national identity.

Such identity dilemmas are not limited to first generation Muslims; in fact, they are also prevalent in the second generation of British Muslims who have not known any other national identity than being British. The following extract is taken from a second generation female, who has spent most of her life in Britain and visited her parent's home country just once. Let us see how she constructs such events in her discourse and her reaction to that.

Extract 8: FMA

1	FMA	....another thing that my grandfather told me when I was very younger umm
2		(1.0) because when I was younger another thing that I use to do to show
3		attitude or something (0.5) was that I didn't use to speak Urdu (.) and I say I
4		just don't want to speak it (.) I said this isn't my language you know this is not
5		m- I am British I speak English I don't speak that language you know and (.)
6		my grandfather used to just you know he just used to be very mildly poking
7		fun at me says that look (.) anybody would look at your face they would not
8		say that you are British and I say no I am British it doesn't matter it doesn't
9		matter by that I am British I am British and (0.5) unfortunately umm I have
10		(1.0) come across many experiences with my grandfather what he said to me
11		was proved right because many people don't (.) don't unfortunately consider
12		me British (.) when I open my mouth they so oh (.) good English you speak
13		(laugh) you know terrible things like that you know (.) so but it's that's not
14		umm that's not it's not a terrible thing

This particular extract is taken from the middle of the interview, and it is the continuation of her (FMA) response to a question about her future hopes of living in the UK. Just before this point FMA was discussing her children's identity as not being confined to just one country and saying that they are the citizens of world. She then changed the topic and began discussing an event from her childhood. She says that at a young age she used to show "attitude" and refused to speak Urdu. She is associating the refusal to speak Urdu with a sort of arrogance as she used the word "attitude." Her reason for her not speaking Urdu and rejecting Urdu as her language was due to her being British and speaking English. Being British is constructed as a matter of pride. Thus having a British identity and speaking English is associated with something honorable in comparison to speaking Urdu. It is similar to the higher status associated to being British by MA (extract 6). Moreover, language is constructed here as a crucial component of one's national identity.

In Line 6, FMA returns to what she was saying in the beginning about what her grandfather used to tell her. However, before reporting her grandfather's speech FMA tries to minimize the seriousness of what is coming by saying that he used to say that while "poking fun" at her. After this, she states that he said that anybody looking at her face will not identify her as being British. In this way, FMA says that her grandfather was pointing out one visible aspect of her identity: her somatic appearance. Somatic similarities (Van Den Berghe, 1990) with people of a nation are important in one's national identity, and in this case it would appear to put in doubt FMA's claim to be British. FMA thereafter attends to this possibility in Lines 8 and 9 by discounting this suggestion by stating that "it doesn't matter, it doesn't matter by that" and by restating her description of herself as British. Thus, FMA rejects the suggestion that appearance is an essential part of national identity, in her case of an identity other than being British, and instead returns to her description of herself as being British on the basis of her own feelings and preferences.

Later she moves to her current life experiences and constructs its relation to her grandfather's earlier comments about her identity. She continues by explaining how her grandfather's joke has become the reality of her life. FMA has used "unfortunately" twice in this sentence, which indicates the negative emotions associated with her grandfather's comments. In Line 11, she said "many people" do not consider her British, which is pointing out the non-acceptance by these people who are perhaps local people. This is similar to the earlier extracts in which speakers argued that everything boils down to the acceptance or rejection of one's British identity by local people. In this extract, this rejection of British identity has been constructed as something "unfortunate." FMA gives an example of people's reaction to her language skills in order to support her claim. As people do not consider her British, sometimes when she speaks English they offer her a compliment (Line 12). Although she reproduced this example while laughing, at the same time she has used words like "terrible" for such incidences. She might be using laughter to position herself as not bothering about such events, but her use of "terrible" indicates that she evaluates them negatively. Later in her responses she changes her claim saying that it's not a "terrible thing." Like the use of laughter, this can also be seen as an effort to reduce the significance of such events in her life. Initially, she claimed that such rejection of her British identity by local people was a terrible event and also requested an approval from the interviewer by using "you know" twice. However, at a later point she has tried to minimize the intensity by claiming that it is not that terrible, reducing the significance of such events.

Here, FMA is struggling to show the minimal impact of those rejecting her British identity. This can be seen throughout the extract—her grandfather's speech, using humor, but then she used "unfortunate" for the negative experiences of being not seen as British. Later she narrated an example while laughing, but then again used the word "terrible" for such events, and then, yet again, denied their being terrible. Local people apparently play a role in judging whether FMA is British.

FMA's responses also show English speaking ability as an important component of one's British identity by both locals and immigrants. FMA connects her British identity with the English language and refused to speak Urdu. Similarly, the local populace seem to be surprised by FMA's English language skills because, in their view, she does not look British.

In Extract 9, MS1 described the opportunities she has as a result of being a British citizen, and how she is constructing threats to her national identity by the local populace.

Extract 9: MS1

1	MS1	. . . I just felt I was treated as a British individual but I do feel NOW that in
2		society for example like I was talking about when I went to (0.5) when I came
3		to this area I was treated as if I didn't know how to speak English (0.5) THAT
4		was a bit of shock to my system because I have never experienced that before
5		umm (1.0) and I don't know whether that's the result of just this particular area
6		(1.0) umm and you know the move from London to Scotland and you know
7		there isn't that much diversity in this part of Edinburgh (.) and maybe that's the
8		reason for it

The extract is part of MS1's response to a question about her future expectations about living in Britain. In the beginning, she claims that she was treated as a British person; she then moves to her current status. This use of temporal discourse is made along with her noting that she has moved to a different area. The move is to an area where she is treated as a person with limited English speaking ability. MS1 is highlighting the importance of language in her British identity. Afterwards, MS1 notes that it was a "bit of shock to my system" (Lines 3–4). The shock results from questions about her ability to speak English for the first time. Later, she rationalizes these events by noting that she moved from London to Scotland. She associates the non-accepting behavior to her British identity with a geographical area and its lack of cultural diversity.

DISCUSSION AND CONCLUSIONS

In this chapter, we examined the positive and negative constructions of national identity by first and second generation British Muslims. There is little research in the realm of discursive psychology on the national identity among this group of immigrants. Our research hopes to fill this void.

British national identity among our second-generation Muslims in Britain is a dilemma free process of merging three identities: British, Muslim, and the homeland origin of their parents. Specifically, the second generation seems to have successfully merged their hyphenated identities from religion, nationality, culture, and sectarian. Such use of hyphenated identities by second-generation British Muslims has been discussed in previous research (Din, 2006; Hopkins. 2007; Jacobson, 1997). However, our results exhibit an interesting role taken by British identity—it acts as a facilitator for other identities rather than conflicting with them. Such positive constructions about British national identity were also related to acceptance by British society. The British were depicted as welcoming and accepting, and it is because of this that second generation British Muslims articulate feelings of happiness and being fortunate.

First generation British Muslims have different perceptions. First generation respondents successfully construct their national identities as British-Pakistani-Muslims in a balanced way. While they claim to have British national identity, they also have strong attachments to Pakistan. They may have a British identity and an attachment to Pakistan in order to avoid being criticized by their community for being disloyal to their country. Thus, in order to avoid such accountability, they make mention of their home country while claiming to be British at the same time.

First generation respondents also associated their British national identity with positive words like "comfort," "ease," "dedication," and "loyalty." The use of such positive language suggests the high value they place on their British identity. In a way, this is similar to the earlier extracts where British identity is constructed as having a somewhat higher status. However, unlike other respondents, first generation respondents made no reference to acceptance or rejection by British society in relation to their national identity. Clearly, this group does not care what others might say or think of them. Instead, they have built their identity based on their own views; it is internally constructed, as opposed to externally driven.

There are also negative constructions that are associated with British national identity. The main element in such a construction is one's status as an immigrant and their treatment by members of the host society. Our research indicates that among immigrants, British identity has higher status than an identity from the country of origin. Such a higher status is associated with being born in Britain, and two other traits associated with being accepted by members of the host society: physical appearance and English language speaking ability. So here we can see again how local people's treatment of immigrants plays a crucial role in how immigrants construct their national identity. Modood and Ahmad (2007) argued that such rejection by local community acts as a stressor for even high profile British Muslims. According to Modood and colleagues (1997), such negative treatment by the host society works as a barrier towards one's national identity as a British person.

Moreover, the construction of British identity may become a dilemma. When one is rejected by both the host society and one's country of origin, it leads to the dilemma of having no identity. So these immigrants are looked upon as overseas citizens in their home countries and as refugees in the host country, meaning that they question whether or not they have an identity at all. The acceptance or rejection of the host society plays a vital role in the life of an immigrant and his or her well-being. Previous research by Phinney, Horenczyk, Liebkind, and Vedder (2001) proposed an interactional perspective of immigration, wellbeing, and ethnic and national identity, where immigrant adaptation involves the interaction between the attitudes and characteristics of the immigrant and the responses of the receiving society. We reach a similar conclusion in our study in acceptance: Acceptance by British society leads to positive accounts of one's British identity, whereas rejection results in negative accounts of British national identity.

Such dilemmas are not limited to the first generation immigrants, but are also visible among the second generation. Although the second generation people are born and bred in Britain and have a positive sense of being British, they also report events where their identity as British nationals has been put into question. They are treated negatively by some locals based on their somatic appearance and are accused of having limited English language ability. If the local population sees that they speak English well, they are given compliments by locals because of the perceived discrepancy between their appearance and their command of the English language. Researchers have also highlighted the significance of host-language proficiency and concluded that lack of such proficiency often results in immigrants having low self-esteem and lesser satisfaction with their lives (Vedder, 2005; Liebkind & Jasinskaja-Lahti, 2000).

We have drawn several conclusions from our analyses. First, the construction of national identity is not invariant. Many factors play a role; the most important may be whether one is a first, second, or later generation immigrant. The negotiation of national identity is no straightforward matter.

Second, we found that having a positive British national identity works to facilitate other forms of identity. In fact, a hyphenated form of identity: British-Muslim-Pakistani. This facilitating role of national identity needs more research. In our view, the most important questions are (a) why does national identity act as a facilitator for other forms of identity, and (b) is a hyphenated identity among a segment of the population a positive or negative for the country. For a multiculturalist it may be, but for others it may not. Further research may provide some important answers.

Finally, we find that the behavior of the local population has an important effect on how and if immigrants develop positive or negative views of national identity. A local population bases its views and kinds of interactions it has with immigrants on immigrants' physical appearance and their ability to speak the host society's native language. The effects are not straightforward, though. They appear to depend on immigrants' generation status and level of self-confidence. Of particular importance is the individual trait of self-confidence. The greater an immigrant's self-confidence, the more they rely on internal dispositions in developing national identity. In contrast, the less the self-confidence, the more an immigrant will rely on external factors, such as the behavior and views of the local populace, in constructing their national identity.

NOTES

1. Both Indices were computed by Richard R. Verdugo from the 2011 UK Census.
2. Some 38% of England's Muslims live in London, where 1,012,823 identified as Muslim in 2011 (12.4% of London's population).
3. Assimilation is the complete or near complete absorption of a group in the larger community. In contrast, acculturation is associated with adaptation to a larger community, but still maintaining important elements of one's culture.

REFERENCES

Anderson, B. (1991). *Imagined communities: Reflections on the origins and spread of nationalism* (2nd ed.). London, England: Verso.

Ansari, H. (2002). *Muslims in Britain.* London, England: Minority Rights Group International.

Attwood, C. (2003). *2001 home office citizenship survey: People, families and communities.* Retrieved from 217.35.77.12/CB/England/research/ pdfs/2003/hors270.pdf

Bhabha, H. (Ed.) (1990). *Nation and narration,* London, England: Routledge.

Billig, M. (1995). *Banal nationalism.* London, England: Sage.

Billig, M., Condor, S., Edwards, D., Gane, M., Middleton, D., & Radley, A. (1988). *Ideological dilemmas: A social psychology of everyday thinking.* Thousand Oaks, CA: Sage Publications, Inc.

Condor, S. (2000). Pride and prejudice: Identity management in English people's talk about "this country." *Discourse & Society, 11,* 175–205.

De Cillia, R., Reisigl, M., & Wodak, R. (1999). The discursive construction of national identity. *Discourse Studies, 10,* 149–173.

Din, I. (2006). *The new British: The impact of culture and community on young Pakistanis.* Hampshire, England: Ashgate Publishing Limited.

Dixon, J., & Durrheim, K. (2000). Displacing place-identity: A discursive approach to locating self and other. *British Journal of Social Psychology, 39,* 27–44.

Fishman, J. A. (1972). *Language in sociocultural change.* Stanford, CA: Stanford University Press.

Ghuman, S. (1999). *Asian adolescents in the West.* Leicester, England: The British Psychological Society.

Giroux, H. A. (1995). National identity and the politics of multiculturalism. *College Literature, 22,* 42–57.

Hobsbawm, E., & Ranger, T. (1983). *The invention of tradition,* Cambridge, England: Cambridge University Press.

Hopkins, P. (2007). Blue squares, proper Muslims and transnational networks: Narratives of national and religious identities amongst young Muslim men living in Scotland. *Ethnicities, 7*(1), 61–81.

Jacobson, J. (1997). Religion and ethnicity: Dual and alternative sources of identity among young British Pakistanis. *Ethnic and Racial Studies, 20*(2), 238–256.

Jefferson, G. (2004). Glossary of transcript symbols with an introduction. In G. H. Lerner (Ed.), *Conversation analysis: Studies from the first generation* (pp. 13–31). Amsterdam, NL: John Benjamin.

Khan, Z. (2000). Muslim presence in Europe: The British dimension–identity, integration and community activism. *Current Sociology, 48*(4), 29–43.

Liebkind, K., & Jasinskaja-Lahti, I. (2000). Acculturation and psychological wellbeing among immigrant adolescents in Finland: A comparative study of adolescents from different cultural backgrounds. *Journal of Adolescent Research, 15*(4), 446–469.

McKinlay, A., & McVittie, C. (2008). *Social psychology and discourse.* Oxford, England: Wiley-Blackwell.

McKinlay, A., & McVittie, C. (2011). *Identities in context: Individuals and discourse in action.* Oxford, England: Wiley-Blackwell.

Modood, T., & Ahmad, F. (2007). British Muslim perspectives on multiculturalism. *Theory Culture Society, 24*(2), 187–213.

Modood, T., Berthoud, R., Lakey, J., Nazroo, J., Smith, P., Virdee, S., & Beishon, S. (1997). *Ethnic minorities in Britain: Diversity and disadvantage.* London, England: Policy Studies Institute.

Phinney, J. S., Horenczyk, G., Liebkind, K., & Vedder, P. (2001). Ethnic identity, immigration, and wellbeing: An interactional perspective. *Journal of Social Issues, 57*(3), 493–510.

Reicher, S., & Hopkins, N. (2001). *Self and nation: Categorization, contestation and mobilization.* London, England: Sage.

Smith, A. D. (1986). *The ethnic origins of nationalism,* Oxford, England: Blackwell

Smith, A. D. (1991). *National identity.* London, England: Penguin.

Smith, A. D. (1999). *Myths and memories of the nation.* Oxford, England: Oxford University Press.

Stopes-Roe, M., & Cochrane, R. (1990). *Citizens of this country: The Asian-British.* Bristol, England: The Multilingual Matters Ltd.

Van Den Berghe, P. (1990). *State violence and ethnicity.* Niwot, CO: University of Colorado Press.

Vedder, P. (2005). Language, ethnic identity and the adaptation of immigrant youth in the Netherlands. *Journal of Adolescent Research, 20*(3), 396–416.

Wooffitt, R. (1992). *Telling tales of the unexpected: The organization of factual discourse.* London, England: Harvester Wheatsheaf.

Wright, S. (2000). *Community and communication: The role of language in nation state building and European Integration.* Clevedon, England: Multilingual Matters.

CPSIA information can be obtained
at www.ICGtesting.com
Printed in the USA
FFOW01n1311231116
29745FF

9 781681 235233